Notorious in the Neighborhood

SEX AND FAMILIES ACROSS THE

COLOR LINE IN VIRGINIA, 1787–1861

Joshua D. Rothman

The University of North Carolina Press   *Chapel Hill & London*

Notorious in the Neighborhood

VIRGINIAN LUXURIES.

© 2003 The University of North Carolina Press
All rights reserved
Set in New Baskerville and Snell Roundhand
by Keystone Typesetting, Inc.
Manufactured in the United States of America
The paper in this book meets the guidelines for
permanence and durability of the Committee on
Production Guidelines for Book Longevity of the
Council on Library Resources.

Library of Congress Cataloging-in-Publication Data
Rothman, Joshua D.
Notorious in the neighborhood : sex and families across the color line in Virginia,
1787–1861 / by Joshua D. Rothman.
p. cm.
Includes bibliographical references and index.
ISBN 0-8078-2768-1 (cloth: alk. paper)
ISBN 0-8078-5440-9 (pbk.: alk. paper)
1. Interracial marriage — Virginia — History. 2. Miscegenation — Social aspects —
Virginia — History. 3. Racially mixed people — Virginia — History. 4. Miscegenation —
Law and legislation — Virginia — History. 5. Virginia — Race relations — History. I. Title.
HQ1031 .R695 2003
306.84′6′09755 — dc21
2002007568

Portions of this work have appeared previously, in somewhat different form,
as "James Callender and Social Knowledge of Interracial Sex in Antebellum Virginia," in
Sally Hemings and Thomas Jefferson: History, Memory, and Civic Culture, ed. Jan Lewis and Peter
S. Onuf, 87–113 (Charlottesville: University Press of Virginia, 1999); " 'Notorious in the
Neighborhood': An Interracial Family in Early National and Antebellum Virginia," *Journal
of Southern History* 67, no. 1 (February 2001): 73–114; and " 'to be freed from thate curs
and let at liberty': Interracial Adultery and Divorce in Antebellum Virginia," *Virginia
Magazine of History and Biography* 106, no. 4 (Autumn 1998): 443–81. They are reprinted
here with permission.

cloth 07 06 05 04 03   5 4 3 2 1
paper 07 06 05 04 03   5 4 3 2 1

FRONTISPIECE
Virginian Luxuries (artist unknown), ca. 1815 (Abby Aldrich Rockefeller Folk Art Museum,
Colonial Williamsburg Foundation, Williamsburg, Va.)

FOR MY PARENTS,

whose love of knowledge is an inspiration

Contents

Illustrations

Acknowledgments

Every historian ought to recognize the inestimable value of helpful and knowledgeable archivists and librarians. I have been blessed on this project to have found many such people. Much thanks to those at the Library of Virginia, the Valentine Museum, and the University of Virginia Library's Department of Special Collections. Particular debts are owed to Teresa Roane at the Valentine, who put me onto sources that I might never otherwise have found, and to Brent Tarter, Gregg Kimball, and John Kneebone at the LOV, with whom I shared enriching discussions at many a lunch.

Thomas Jefferson would surely be proud of the intellectual community cultivated at and near his beloved Monticello. I am grateful to the Thomas Jefferson Foundation for providing me both with a year-long dissertation fellowship and with a space to work at Kenwood, the home of the International Center for Jefferson Studies and surely one of the most aesthetically pleasant environments in the United States for reading, writing, and contemplation. James Horn, the Saunders Director of the ICJS, is both a fine scholar and a primary reason for the collegiality evident at Kenwood. I am also extremely grateful to Cinder Stanton, Shannon Senior Research Historian of the ICJS, and to Dianne Swann-Wright, the center's Director of African-American and Special Programs, both of whom I am fortunate to have as friends and whose work has added immeasurably to my understanding of the Hemings family specifically and of slavery at Monticello generally. Both also read and commented on parts of the manuscript on which this book is based.

One of the smartest choices I have ever made was attending graduate school at the University of Virginia. The Corcoran Department of History, the Center for Children, Family, and the Law, and the Carter G. Woodson Institute for Afro-American and African Studies all provided much needed financial support. Studying at Virginia also brought me into contact with friends, mentors, advisers, and colleagues who played large roles in making this book possible. Thanks especially to Reginald

Butler, Jeffrey Hantman, Phyllis Leffler, Turk McCleskey, Fraser Neiman, Bob Vernon, Henry Weincek, Camille Wells, and other participants in what was then known as the Central Virginia Social History Project for their comments, criticism, and guidance. Eric Lott helped shape how I think about history and race, and also served as an outside reader on my dissertation committee. I am unashamed to say that the three members of Virginia's history faculty who served on my committee are my professional heroes. Both individually and collectively, Ed Ayers, Joe Miller, and Peter Onuf taught me how to think, how to write, and how to teach. Each has earned a lifetime of gratitude, and I hope this book makes them proud to be associated with it.

I also learned a great deal from my fellow graduate students, many of whom graciously gave me their intellectual insights and their friendship, the latter of which was especially critical to surviving what can sometimes be the disheartening experience of getting a doctoral degree. Andy Morris, Amy Murrell, Steve Norris, Scott Taylor, Andy Trees, and I shared many therapeutic dinner conversations and many equally therapeutic bottles of Red Stripe beer at Monday evening meetings of our "dissertation support group" at the Blue Moon Diner. Thanks also to Watson Jennison and John Riedl, with whom I spent what was probably an inordinate amount of time. I doubt I ever became anything more than a mediocre basketball player by playing with them, and I know I never learned anything from the hours we spent late at night watching Jerry Springer. But I am certain that I am a better person and a better scholar for knowing them. Others who deserve to be acknowledged include Amy Feely, Scot French, Juliette Landphair, Matt Lassiter, Andy Lewis, Jeff McClurken, Anne Rubin, Philip Troutman, and Kirt von Daacke. Special thanks are due to Woody Holton for alerting me to the existence of the image that appears on the cover.

Jim Baumgardner, Mary Frances Berry, Jane Dailey, Paul Gilje, Graham Hodges, Linda Sturtz, and Elizabeth Varon commented on various conference papers that grew out of the research for this book. I presented the earliest version of Chapter 1 in March 1999 at a conference in Charlottesville dedicated to discussing the meaning and significance of the Jefferson-Hemings DNA study, and benefited greatly from the comments of all my fellow presenters, especially Annette Gordon-Reed and Philip Morgan. Paul Apostolidis, Nelson Langford, Jan Lewis, Scott Marler, Elizabeth Shown Mills, and Juliet Williams guided articles and essays through the process of publication. Martha Hodes, George Rable,

Diane Sommerville, Peter Wallenstein, and an anonymous reader from the University of North Carolina Press read the manuscript in its entirety. Kari Frederickson helped with drafts of the introduction. Tom Buckley offered valuable suggestions on several versions of Chapter 5 and was also generous enough to share with me some of his own research on the history of divorce in Virginia. At UNC Press, Chuck Grench and Amanda McMillan saw this book through the process of acquisition and Ron Maner served as project editor. All of these individuals saved me from analytical mishaps, factual errors, and bungled prose along the way, and I thank them for it. Whatever screw-ups remain are due to my own stubbornness and are entirely my own fault.

Anyone who has ever written a book understands the loneliness inherent to the process. I must thank Calvin for making the solitude easier. He doesn't speak much, and he can't read this, but it should be noted for the record that his feline contributions are greatly appreciated.

In February 1998, I went to a party in Charlottesville hosted by a friend of a friend, who turned out to be one of the strangest people I have ever met. She was also one of the most charming, outgoing, funny, talented, and beautiful people I have ever met. So I married her. I always assumed there were things in life more important than this book, but until I met Rebecca I wasn't entirely sure what they were. Now I know. God bless the goose.

I dedicate this book to my parents, Bonita and Jeffrey Rothman. Their commitment to the education of their children is boundless, their moral and financial support have never flagged even for a moment, and their intellectual curiosity and engagement with the world make them role models for living the well-examined life. Thanking them adequately is impossible.

Tuscaloosa, Alabama
March 2002

Notorious in the Neighborhood

Introduction

Late on the night of September 3, 1792, in Henrico County, Virginia, two white men named Peter Franklin and Jesse Carpenter took captive a runaway slave boy they found in the home of a free woman of color named Angela Barnett. Questioning the boy led the two men to believe that Barnett harbored other runaways, and they returned to the house the next night. After forcing their way inside, they and Barnett engaged in a verbal and physical confrontation, during which Franklin advanced toward Barnett with a weapon in his hand. But before Franklin could reach her, Barnett grabbed an adze from behind a trunk and drove its blade six inches deep into Franklin's skull, fatally wounding him. Barnett was arrested and sent to jail to await trial. In April 1793 a jury found her guilty of murder and sentenced her to hang.[1]

Angela Barnett lived just outside the city limits of Richmond, but she had worked in the city proper for many years and had powerful friends among the white elite of Virginia's capital. Dozens of Barnett's supporters pleaded with Governor Henry Lee not to hang her, and they assured him that she was not normally a violent woman. William Richardson, with whose family Barnett had lived around 1780, wrote that she had always "conducted herself in a very decent & orderly manner." Major William Duval, one of Richmond's most prominent citizens, sent a note to the governor indicating that Barnett had lived with his family for an entire year, during which time "she conducted herself as a faithful servant, and had the care of my children, which Trust she discharged with Integrity & Fidelity." Thirty-eight other Richmonders—most of whom were white women from the city's wealthiest neighborhood—cosigned a petition recommending mercy for Barnett. The support of Barnett's influential white friends, however, appears to have had no impact on the governor, who ignored their petitions. Barnett's execution remained on schedule.[2]

On May 9, 1793, just eight days before her sentence was to be carried out, Barnett took matters into her own hands. She wrote to the governor herself and informed him that during her incarceration she had entered into a sexual relationship with and become pregnant by a fellow inmate. She identified her partner as one Jacob Valentine, a white man who served time on two separate occasions during Barnett's imprisonment for failure to pay debts. Hoping that "the Guiltless infant" she carried would "not be murdered by her execution," Barnett asked Governor Lee for a pardon. At the very least, she requested a stay of execution until she gave birth.[3]

This new set of circumstances prompted the governor to give Barnett a temporary reprieve. In the interim before the birth of her child, Barnett's supporters in the white community sent several additional petitions to the governor. They now made the case that in killing Peter Franklin, Barnett had acted only in self-defense. Moreover, they alluded in their pleas to the "peculiar distress" she now suffered because of her pregnancy. They believed the burdens of carrying a child "must have added to the miseries of imprisonment" and felt that such an "unfortunate situation" ought to provide additional grounds for mercy. This time, their entreaties worked. In September 1793 Governor Lee pardoned Angela Barnett. She continued to live near Richmond until her death in 1810.[4]

It hardly seems unusual that under slavery a woman of color — treated inequitably by Virginia's judicial system — would be placed in proximity to a white man such that her control over her own sexuality was significantly compromised. But a closer investigation of the strange and remarkable story of Angela Barnett and Jacob Valentine shows the need to rethink many of the usual generalizations and assumptions about sex across the color line in the South before the Civil War. Given the circumstances under which it developed, it would be difficult to maintain that Angela Barnett engaged in an entirely consensual sexual affair with Jacob Valentine. Indeed, in her letter to the governor, Barnett indicated that Valentine "persuaded" her to have sexual relations and that she "yielded to [his] desires."[5]

Yet it seems possible that Barnett's involvement with Valentine was a conscious choice and part of a larger plan to save herself from the hangman, her language in addressing the governor carefully chosen so that she might appear more sympathetic. Even before her trial, Barnett likely well understood that while she might be acquitted, her chances with a white jury on the charge of murdering a white man were dicey at best. She also probably knew that the kind words of her white supporters might have little influence with the governor. She may have seen pregnancy as her only realistic chance for survival, and she took it. Elements of both coercion and consent attended to Angela Barnett's sexual behavior, but that she could use her own body—frequently the site of greatest vulnerability for black women—as the source of her salvation demonstrates how sex across the color line might serve purposes of liberation for some women of color even as it signified the depths of enslavement for so many others.[6]

Following the path of Jacob Valentine beyond his stints in jail with Angela Barnett bolsters the notion that Barnett's pregnancy was a strategy for saving her own life. We might easily construe Valentine's interactions with Barnett simply as a white man opportunistically exploiting a woman of color's vulnerability for the sake of his own sexual gratification. But he may have used sexual intercourse purposefully because it enabled him to help a woman who suffered for her willingness to fight against slavery. Four years after Angela Barnett's release from prison, Jacob Valentine was arrested yet again. This time, the issue was far more serious than debt, as Valentine was charged with "inciting and encouraging an Insurrection among the Slaves of the City of Richmond."[7] The papers confiscated from Valentine's home by the Richmond authorities and used as evidence against him are an extraordinarily odd and cryptic collection, consisting mostly of scrawls on loose scraps of paper. They leave no clear indication of whether Valentine actually intended to start a slave uprising, although he was convicted and spent seven months in jail.

Valentine's papers do strongly suggest, however, that his sympathies for the enslaved ran deep, and it appears that at the very least he fantasized about playing some role in making black Americans free. One paper, for example, read in part, "the strong works of Gibralter must be stormed. Let me see whether the thing can be done. If all things are fairly and consciously done Valentine's the fellow." Another announced: "I will set all your Blacks free and still you shall be the Greatest men of the Nation." In a letter to the mayor of Richmond, meanwhile, Valentine admitted to musing in public that "the Blacks were a hardy race of People and if emancipated they would defend this Country with every exertion and activity that they are masters of against every Enemy."[8]

Given his attitudes toward slavery, Valentine may well have seen his sexual relationship with Angela Barnett as an expression of his own imagined heroism and as his own direct contribution to black liberation.

It is impossible to determine whether Valentine's ideas about freedom for America's slaves predated his encounter with Angela Barnett or grew out of it, but surely they were related in some way. Political and sexual fantasy merged in the Richmond jail in the late eighteenth century. Sex across the color line so often reinforced racial hierarchy under slavery, but here it can be read as a deeply political statement of another sort, part of an antislavery agenda Barnett and Valentine each pursued in his or her own way. Angela Barnett was only in jail to begin with because of her active participation in helping the enslaved escape their bondage, a role she was willing to defend with her life if need be. For Jacob Valentine, interracial sex served as the enactment of his emancipatory political dream.

The ambiguities swirling around the relationship between Angela Barnett and Jacob Valentine suggest that understanding sex across the color line in the South before the Civil War necessitates a capacious scope, one that takes full account of the complexities and contradictions of a social order where power was predicated fundamentally on racial domination yet where individuals demonstrated the unavoidably intimate interracial contact characteristic of American slavery. This book explores the phenomenon of interracial sex in Virginia from 1787, when Sally Hemings left Monticello for France (where she would join her owner and eventual sexual partner Thomas Jefferson), to 1861, when the Civil War began that would destroy slavery and consequently change the racial regime of Virginia in fundamental ways.

Laws against fornication and interracial marriage militated against sex across the color line in Virginia before the Civil War. Politicians and ministers condemned the practice as an "abomination" that degraded white participants and that blurred idealized racial boundaries and the line between free and slave. Yet interracial sex was ubiquitous in urban, town, and plantation communities throughout the state. Moreover, as Angela Barnett's supporters demonstrated, knowledge of precisely who participated in it was widely shared. Virginians, however, only rarely took legal or extralegal action to try to eliminate sexual criminality in their midst. White Virginians rightfully believed that racial distinctions were cornerstones of their society, but they also recognized that both forced and consensual sexual connections between blacks and whites were constituent of familial and communal life in that society. Even if they never approved of it, white Virginians, like white southerners elsewhere, tolerated and accommodated a wide array of sexual activity across the color line, ranging from viable and supportive interracial families that bound extended networks of free and enslaved blacks and whites together across space and time to family-shattering rapes that exposed the routine abuse, violence, and ruthless power of racial slavery with which we are all too familiar.[9]

Reconstructing some of the economic and social networks of particular communities reveals the internal workings of diverse kinds of interracial sexual relationships, the responses of other blacks and whites to those relationships, and the spectrum of human emotions — from love, ardor, and desire to hatred, jealousy, and rage — they provoked among every person whose life they touched. In most circumstances white community members clucked their tongues behind closed doors more than they complained to legal authorities. But there were moments when they did publicly discuss what they knew about such matters. Tracing the series of events that brought about public exposure, harassment, or prosecution of people who violated laws or cultural mores against illicit sex suggests that the timing and motivation underlying such instances had little to do directly with a sense of outrage at the crossing of racial boundaries. Instead, public grievances were grounded in a wider constellation of economic competition or personal discord between two or more, usually white, individuals. With varying degrees of success, antagonists wielded accusations of engagement in interracial sex as weapons to humiliate, infuriate, or badger alleged participants. Sometimes accusers simply wanted to lash out at an enemy. Sometimes they had more specific goals of personal advantage in mind.

When interracial sex played a role in legal matters that could not be handled within local jurisdictions, resolution lay at the capital in Richmond, where Virginia's governors, state legislators, and judges sometimes chose to respond in less-than-obvious ways to very obvious violations of the laws governing sexual and racial behavior. Rather than acting rigidly or uniformly to punish sexual criminals, perhaps thereby sending a message not only to the guilty but also to local communities that the behavior they tolerated was in fact intolerable and dangerous, state officials determined their courses of action mostly on a case-by-case basis. Receiving information from petitions, court papers, and other documents in which white neighborhood residents familiar with the nuances of local contexts offered their own understandings of events, state authorities sometimes acted as white communities wished in the belief that their members knew best how to manage their own affairs. Communal consensus, however, was far from universal. Moreover, a judge, a legislator, or a state executive considered a series of interrelated social, economic, and cultural factors broader than the concerns and circumstances of any particular community. Depending on the nature of the case, a state official might have to evaluate the ramifications of his decision upon the racial order, slavery, gender roles, class hierarchies, property rights, criminal justice, and the white family. Interracial sex provoked disputes that touched on nearly every significant component of Virginia society. Maintaining social stability, rather than enforcing draconian implementation of the law, dictated the strategy of governing officials when they confronted such potentially explosive matters.

In the past twenty years, social historians have documented in numerous case studies how racial and sexual relations in the early national and antebellum South were far more intricate than we had previously imagined and that power among blacks and whites, slaves and free people, and men and women flowed in extraordinarily complicated and contradictory ways. Books by Michael Johnson and James Roark, Melton McLaurin, Kent Anderson Leslie, Adele Logan Alexander, and T. O. Madden Jr., for example, all demonstrate the gaps between the ideals white southerners often projected about themselves and their world and the substance of life on the ground in their society. Collectively, these scholars suggest that understanding the rules of race, sex, gender, and class in the antebellum South requires looking at the exceptions to those rules and at how both whites and blacks reacted to unusual situations as they arose.[10] Other historians have formed case studies into larger narratives, demonstrating that instances of sex across the color line — particularly those involving white women — were not only less exceptional than previously thought but in fact were regular enough to have social rules of their own. These rules in turn fit into larger regional frameworks of authority and dominance.[11]

No single study, however, encompasses the gamut of interracial sexual connections and holds them together with and against one another. Only in juxtaposition can we see how these relationships both supported and undermined racism and slavery in the early national and antebellum South, with all the accompanying implications that had for the rest of the socioeconomic order. Using a single state as the unit of examination, this book capitalizes on the best features of case studies, recognizing the central importance of local contexts in different settings for appreciating the astonishing degree of flexibility and fluidity Virginians built into their seemingly rigid system of race and interracial relations. Simultaneously, the framework of a state study enables a systematic look at the interactions between those local settings and the decisions made by men at the highest levels of state government. Cutting through multiple layers of the social, legal, and political worlds of early national and antebellum Virginia — from personal associations between individuals to lawsuits and criminal trials in county courts to petitions, letters, and appeals to state officials — allows for generalization without diluting the significance of the local environment. In addition, such an approach demonstrates the frequency with which the customary toleration for sex across the color line by local communities came into direct collision with the law and revealed its fissures, loopholes, and blind spots. Consequently, the relationship between law and custom regarding racial intermixture was always shifting, which in turn forced Virginians throughout the early national and antebellum periods into constant negotiation and renegotiation of the meaning and significance of racial boundaries, racial hierarchy, and ultimately race itself. All instances of interracial sex had political implications, not only those as dramatic as the involvement of Angela Barnett and Jacob Valentine.

Arguing for any state's "typicality" or "representativeness" is always a dubious enterprise, but understanding Virginia is undeniably central to understanding the larger phenomenon of sex across the color line in the South before the Civil War. Virginia was the first colony in mainland British North America to define race in law, and its legal system and judicial decisions served as models for much of the South throughout the early national and antebellum periods. In addition, even as more people of African descent lived in Virginia than anywhere else in the United States before 1861, white Virginians and their slaves also left their native state by the thousands in the decades of southern expansion between the American Revolution and the Civil War. They filled newer parts of the South, bringing with them the cultural standards regarding race and sex they had learned in Virginia. Surely the circumstances surrounding interracial sex varied state by state and were adjusted everywhere to meet local conditions. But in establishing and perpetuating a society torn between its policies and its passions, Virginia was a leader no less than in so many other areas of American life.

This book begins with an examination of the most famous interracial sexual affair in American history: that between Thomas Jefferson and Sally Hemings. Chapter 1 assesses the factors that shaped their relationship but also looks at the larger context of public knowledge of the couple's liaison before 1802 and at the reasons why journalist James Callender chose to expose their sexual association in print. Direct evidence as to the nature of the Jefferson-Hemings relationship is sketchy, yet the hazy picture that does emerge exemplifies some of the central contradictions of sex across the color line under slavery—the public objection and distaste; the private intimacy and emotion; the unequal power relationships between masters and slaves; the significance of skin color, race, and racial identity; the complicated dynamics engendered when a powerful white man had two families simultaneously; and, from the perspective of a historian, the ambiguity of available evidence. Remaining in Albemarle County, but moving from the plantation world of Monticello to the nearby town of Charlottesville where the extended Hemings family was embedded in a larger interracial community on Main Street, Chapter 2 focuses on one interracial family's struggle for economic stability. For years, a free woman of color and a white Jewish man cautiously built a family together in Charlottesville without interference. Ultimately, though, they and their family lived trouble-free only with the assent of a white community that constantly watched them, and some of whose members eventually tried to take advantage of the family's vulnerability for personal financial gain.

The sexually charged interracialism of Virginia's cities presented special challenges for law enforcement. Chapter 3 explores the urban environment of Richmond, Virginia's capital and one of the first cities in the United States to have a regular nighttime police force. Studying Richmond also reveals how attitudes toward sex across the color line changed over time in Virginia, as local, regional, and national economic, demographic, and political shifts in the 1840s and 1850s yielded markedly decreased forbearance for social and especially sexual interaction among whites, free people of color, and slaves. Finally, as the state capital Richmond was the gathering place for legislators, the site of the governor's home, and the location of Virginia's General Court. In Richmond, political leaders cumulatively tried to foster a legal environment that would contain interracial sexual relationships, even as the very creation of such legislation implicitly acknowledged that such sexual connections were common and troublesome enough to establish the need for policy in the first place.

The persistence of sex across the color line brought about the need for state-level legal intervention in innumerable ways. The systematic sexual abuse of enslaved women by white men, for example, normally went untouched by the law or the community in Virginia. Slaves were property, and slave owners could treat their property how they wished, making legal recognition of the rape of a slave nonexistent and interference from fellow slave owners very rare. Occasionally, though, enslaved men and women fought back against the sexual brutality perpetrated on themselves and their families. Chapter 4 closely examines two such instances, which not only forced communal involvement in the criminal trials for the rebellious slaves but which also found their way to the desk of the governor, who reviewed all cases where slaves received the death sentence for a crime. Turning from the power relationships between masters and slaves to those between married white men and women, Chapter 5 focuses on divorce cases in which at least part of the filer's complaint revolved around the adulterous behavior of his or her spouse with one or more African Americans. Before 1851, nearly all pleas for divorce on the grounds of adultery had to be submitted in the form of a petition to the state legislature, which in turn meant that lawmakers repeatedly confronted the choice of taking a stand against racial intermixture and the violation of proper gender roles within marriage or upholding the integrity of the white family at all costs.

Even more than sex across the color line itself, mixed-race children produced by interracial sexual intercourse posed a formidable conundrum for the social order in Virginia before the Civil War. Especially when they were not enslaved, people who could trace their ancestry both to Europe and to Africa (and sometimes to North America as well) threatened the abilities of whites to draw clearly the distinctions and set the boundaries between free and unfree that were necessary for defining status in a society rooted in racial slavery.[12] For all intents and purposes laws and social practice equated dark skin with inferior status, and whites generally treated people of any visually discernible African descent accordingly. But appearances could be deceiving. By some point in the late eighteenth or early nineteenth century, Europeans and Africans had become so genetically intertwined that the visual cues white Virginians depended on to distinguish people believed to be "negro" or "mulatto" from "white" occasionally failed them. The documentary record is strewn with references to people described as "white negroes" or "mixed bloods," or to individuals of some African descent considered by their white neighbors to be "socially white." A concluding chapter discusses the challenges such liminal individuals posed for both local communities and the legal order. Virginia defined the color line in law for the first time in 1705 and redefined it in 1785, but the law never unambiguously established a racial status for everyone in Virginia. By the 1850s, some white Virginians began clamoring for the rigidity in racial definitions that we usually associate with the "one-drop" rule of the postbellum period. Significant changes in the racial mind-set of white Virginians that would shape their society for more than a hundred years after the Civil War were already well under way before the first shot was fired at Fort Sumter.

Evidence for hundreds of sexual acts that crossed the color line appears in this study. Testimony to thousands of others lies buried in the archives, in county and state records, and, more rarely, in private diaries. Even when in the public record, however, such affairs frequently remain elliptical and ambiguous at best. When a white man freed an enslaved woman and her children in his will, for example, did that mean he found her lifelong service worth the reward of emancipation, or did the act of manumission conceal a more intimate relationship? In most cases, we cannot know. The "mulatto" population of Virginia, which might be taken as an indicator of the extent of interracial sex, probably grew throughout the early national and antebellum periods. But since individuals considered "mulattoes" could be and often were born to parents also considered mulattoes, this demographic fact says little about sex between those considered white and those considered black. In addition, the extent of a person's blackness or whiteness was absurdly indeterminate, and frequently in the eyes of the white beholders who kept public records. Any effort to compile statistical evidence on the prevalence of interracial sex is destined to give only the illusion of conclusiveness or comprehensiveness, and an incalculable number of individual cases can never be recovered at all. Evidence of them died with their participants, and they are lost to us forever.[13]

"On questions of color and sexuality," historian Catherine Clinton once perceptively noted, "attitudes rather than numbers elucidate the subject."[14] What follows is very much designed in that spirit, in the belief that trying to peel away the social and cultural layers of a paradoxical Virginia based on notions of white supremacy yet firmly grounded in biracialism may yield insight to some of the relevant contradictions of our own time. That Sally Hemings left Virginia for France in the same year that the delegates to the Philadelphia Convention signed the United States Constitution is nothing more than a historical coincidence, but it is an appropriate one. The significance of both their legacies is crucially linked and eludes us still.

Interlude Stories Told about Monticello

In 1868 Henry Randall, one of Thomas Jefferson's earliest biographers, penned a letter to James Parton, who was at the time also working on a biography of the deceased president. Randall explained to Parton that although the story about Jefferson's alleged sexual relationship with an enslaved woman named Sally Hemings had at one point in time been "extensively believed by respectable men," it was in fact entirely false. As proof, Randall offered a conversation he had once had with Jefferson's grandson, Thomas Jefferson Randolph. Randolph, he explained, told him that Peter Carr, one of the president's nephews, had actually fathered Hemings's children. Moreover, Randolph claimed to have witnessed Peter and his brother Samuel tearfully confessing to bringing "disgrace" on their uncle. Jefferson himself, Randolph believed, not only had never had sexual relations with any of his female slaves but was also generally as "immaculate a man as God ever created."[1]

Anticipating that Parton might ask him why none of Jefferson's supporters ever revealed the true paternity of Sally Hemings's children when Richmond newspaper editor James Callender first printed the rumor of her relationship with Jefferson in the *Richmond Recorder* in 1802, Randall claimed that hardly anyone knew the real story. "Nobody could have furnished a hint of explanation outside of the family," Randall explained, because "the secrets of an old Virginia manor house were like the secrets of an Old Norman Castle." Even those living near Jefferson who might have been curious about enslaved children who looked suspiciously like their owner would never have thought of attributing paternity to Jefferson. "An awe and veneration was felt for Mr. Jefferson among his neighbors," Randall wrote, "which in their view rendered it shameful to even talk about his name in such a connexion."[2]

In 1853, fifteen years before Randall offered Parton his observations on the matter of Thomas Jefferson and Sally Hemings, John Hartwell Cocke commented in his journal about the prevalence of sex across the color line in his native Virginia. Particularly addressing the practice of white men having children with enslaved women, Cocke noted that ardent defenders of slavery would argue that such instances were aberrations. But he knew better. "[I]t is too well proved," Cocke wrote, "they are not few, nor far between. I can enumerate a score of such cases in our beloved Ant. Dominion that have come in my way thro' life, without seeking for them. Were they enumerated with the statistics of the State they would be found by hundreds. Nor is it to be wondered at, when Mr. Jeffersons notorious example is considered."[3]

John Hartwell Cocke owned a large plantation, was an original member of the University of Virginia's Board of Visitors, and during Thomas Jefferson's lifetime was a close friend who had repeatedly visited Jefferson's Monticello home. Cocke was in a far better position than Henry Randall ever could have been to assess whether Thomas Jefferson had been sexually involved with Sally Hemings, whether people knew about it, and whether people talked about it. Apparently, Cocke was among those "respectable men" who believed the story. And indeed, the preponderance of combined historical and genetic evidence indicates that, contrary to his grandson's assertions, Thomas Jefferson almost certainly did father at least one and probably all of Sally Hemings's children and that Peter Carr, with even greater certainty, did not.[4] Henry Randall, trapped by his own awe and veneration for his subject, wholly accepted the Jefferson family story. In so doing, Randall helped perpetuate a mythical understanding not only of Thomas Jefferson but also of the networks of information flowing through early national and antebellum Virginia society. Virginia plantations were not fortresses. Slave owners were not kings and lords. Local communities, free and slave, were not imaginary medieval fiefdoms where peasants spoke only in hushed and reverent tones about their superiors. Quite the opposite. Before the Civil War, Virginians — black and white and of all genders and classes — paid close attention to the lives of their friends, neighbors, families, and owners and shared all sorts of information about them. The exchange of knowledge that took place wherever and whenever people gathered to gossip included — and given its prurience, probably especially included — information about the illicit interracial sexual activities they knew went on all around them. Thomas Jefferson's involvement with Sally Hemings was no exception.

1 Thomas Jefferson, Sally Hemings, James Callender, and Sex across the Color Line under Slavery

The sexual relationship between Thomas Jefferson and Sally Hemings was not an isolated or even an unusual case in Virginia before the Civil War. Sexual contact between masters and slaves specifically and whites and blacks generally was commonplace in Virginia and in all slaveholding states. Because few professional historians have believed the Jefferson-Hemings story until recently or admitted publicly that they did, however, the relationship has never been thoroughly assessed in terms of its larger social context. James Callender, for example, was an angry, bitter, and cynical man who made a career out of invective and character assassination. He ruthlessly, viciously, and often crudely ravaged anyone unfortunate enough to be caught in his journalistic sights, and contemporaries and historians alike have found him an easy target for attacks on both his personal and professional practices. Consequently, amid their zeal to defend Jefferson, scholars typically have dismissed Callender's reports as categorically unreliable. Instead of undertaking any serious effort to assess Callender's claims and their origins, they have brushed them aside as the libelous rants of a scandal-mongering, drunken, and disgruntled office seeker. Historian John Chester Miller, for example, wrote that "Callender made his charges against Jefferson without fear and without research. . . . [H]e never made the slightest effort to verify the 'facts' he so stridently proclaimed. It was 'journalism' at its most reckless, wildly irresponsible, and scurrilous. Callender was not an investigative journalist; he never bothered to investigate anything."[1]

Similarly, instead of reading Jefferson's sexuality in the context of interracial sex in his place and time, historians have primarily written about the "Sage of Monticello" in this regard only in context of himself. Most notably, scholars have relied heavily on the "character defense" to refute the story of Jefferson's relationship with Hemings. By this rationale, Jefferson was by turns too much a racist, too much a gentleman, too much a master of his own passions, or too devoted to his white family to have engaged in sexual intercourse with a female slave. Such a rhetorical posture has always consisted more of assertion than evidence, and scholars who convinced themselves that they "knew" Jefferson by extensively studying him have frequently and stubbornly discounted alternative readings of available historical evidence that conflicted with their position. Take, for example, the response of some of the most prominent Jefferson historians to Fawn Brodie's brave if sometimes hypersentimental and overpsychologized presentation of evidence for the Jefferson-Hemings relationship in her 1974 biography, *Thomas Jefferson: An Intimate History*. Dumas Malone referred to Brodie's work as a "mishmash of fact and fiction . . . not history as I understand the term," and insisted that to him "the man she describes in her more titillating passages is unrecognizable." Merrill Peterson, meanwhile, hardly deigned to admit that Brodie had evidence for her case at all, writing that he saw "no need to charge off in defense of Jefferson's integrity when we have no solid grounds for doubting it."[2]

To reach a more realistic understanding of Jefferson and Hemings's relationship, it must be understood in terms of the larger patterns of master-slave sexual associations in Virginia. Such relationships ranged from acknowledged affairs that lasted for a lifetime, produced many children, and were familial in every sense but a legally recognized one to brutal acts of rape and sexual assault where slave owners showed the inhumanity for which slavery was notorious among its opponents. The available historical evidence on the relationship between Jefferson and Hemings indicates that it fell along, rather than at either end of, this spectrum. Their association was rooted in a complicated, evolving, and sometimes contradictory set of power relationships — a concatenation of calculation and trust, practicality and affection, coercion and consent. As the couple's children together grew older, Jefferson neither embraced nor rejected his enslaved family. Instead, he adhered to the conventions of propriety those of his class and time were expected to follow.

James Callender's publication of the Jefferson-Hemings connection and his motivations also deserve reassessment, for two reasons. First, Callender's avowed campaign of hostility toward Jefferson illustrates perfectly why and when knowledge of sexual affairs across the color line went from being common knowledge in particular communities to public knowledge available to anyone. For much of the five years before Callender printed his allegations about Jefferson's sexual life in the newspaper, the journalist championed Jefferson and believed in turn that the president supported his career. Only when their relationship soured did Callender look into rumors about Jefferson's involvement with Sally Hemings, publishing them as a vindictive act of revenge for perceived wrongs. Callender used the partisan newspaper as his sword, but the thrust against Jefferson was purely personal. Second, on rereading Callender's articles it becomes clear that his reportage was remarkably accurate and well researched, if purposefully sensationalistic. Even examining the few inaccuracies in Callender's articles points to the extent of social knowledge about Jefferson and Hemings in Albemarle County and among the Virginia gentry long before anything about the couple appeared in the press. James Callender was a lot of things, but he was not usually a liar. When he ran the Jefferson-Hemings story in 1802, he believed it to be the most damaging information he had on the president, and he hoped it would ruin Jefferson's political career. He knew Jefferson's supporters would deny it, but he wanted to be certain they could not refute it, and he repeatedly dared them to do so. They never did.

In short, the relationship between Thomas Jefferson and Sally Hemings and how and why it became news must be historicized. To do so requires awareness not only of the particular parties involved but of the social and cultural environments in which the two made decisions about their sexual affairs. The Jefferson-Hemings story has remained in the minds of Americans for two hundred years, serving — as is often the case when Thomas Jefferson is involved — as a metaphor for contemporary attitudes toward race, slavery, the origins of the republic, and the nation's "Founding Fathers." Currently, the story fascinates because it encapsulates growing public awareness of a multiracial nation and a shared cultural heritage, significant factors under consideration in the popular effort to predict the sociological course of the next century. Surely something weighted with such meaning deserves more than stereotypes about forbidden love or monstrous exploitation.[3]

Sally Hemings was thirteen or fourteen years old when she boarded a ship with eight-year-old Mary (Maria) Jefferson in May 1787.

Eventually arriving in Paris, the girls joined Thomas Jefferson and his eldest daughter Martha (Patsy). Jefferson, then serving as America's minister to France, had sent for Mary after his youngest daughter, Lucy, died of whooping cough in Virginia. Hemings had been selected by Francis Eppes, Jefferson's relative and Mary's caretaker in her father's absence, despite Jefferson's request that an older slave accompany Mary, one who had already been exposed to smallpox.[4] Hemings was inoculated and she stayed in France as Mary Jefferson's personal attendant, but the European trip also served as the occasion of Hemings's reunion with her older brother James, who was already living with Jefferson while training to be a chef. According to Madison Hemings's recollection of his mother's story, by the time Thomas Jefferson returned to Monticello in December 1789 with his daughters and the two Hemingses, Sally Hemings was already pregnant with her owner's child.[5]

Sally Hemings did not have to return to Virginia with Jefferson at all. Slavery would not be formally abolished in French law until 1794, but consistently from at least the sixteenth century almost any slave brought into France by a French colonist or a foreign visitor could acquire his or her freedom by petitioning a French admiralty court. Hemings (and her brother, for that matter) would have had to procure a lawyer to represent her, but as historian Sue Peabody notes, there were numerous eighteenth-century French lawyers, especially in Paris, who either sought out freedom causes or took them on without pay. Between 1755 and 1790, every single slave, 154 in total, who brought a cause for freedom to the Admiralty Court of France eventually won his or her case. Sally Hemings could not simply assert her freedom and become free in France, but she surely could have gained emancipation with a small amount of effort.[6]

If she needed any incentive beyond freedom itself to convince her to remain in France, Hemings's experiences abroad certainly provided it. She traveled, she began to learn a foreign language and seamstressing skills, she wore elegant clothing when accompanying Mary Jefferson in society, and sometimes she earned a monthly salary. During her twenty-six-month stay overseas, Sally Hemings received greater exposure to the possibilities of life as a free person than almost any plantation slave in Virginia would get in a lifetime.[7] Hemings, in fact, seems to have seriously considered remaining in France. At first, she refused to go back to Monticello, but before leaving France she and Jefferson made an arrangement. As her son Madison recounted, in exchange for her return

Jefferson offered Sally Hemings "extraordinary privileges, and made a solemn pledge that her children should be freed at the age of twenty-one years. In consequence of his promise, on which she implicitly relied, she returned with him to Virginia."[8]

Thomas Jefferson wrote his *Notes on the State of Virginia* just a few years before he and Sally Hemings began having a sexual relationship. In the *Notes*, Jefferson expressed horror when considering the possibility of free African Americans and whites living together in the same nation, a theme he returned to repeatedly over the course of his adult life. Afraid simultaneously of blacks taking violent revenge for slavery and of white "blood" becoming somehow tainted by sexual intermixture with what he believed to be a significantly inferior race of people, Jefferson concluded that if slaves were to go free, blacks and whites would have to remain "as distinct as nature has formed them." Jefferson professed to believe in the immorality of slavery and the need for emancipation but felt that ideally, freed slaves would be sent to their own separate country at some unspecified future date, "colonized to such place as the circumstances of the time should render most proper."[9] How Jefferson may have tried to reconcile his stated philosophy with his sexual practices is considered further below. First, however, it is necessary to examine how and why Jefferson even entered into an interracial sexual relationship and the conditions under which that relationship was designed to continue on returning to the United States.

In 1789 Jefferson was a widower, his wife Martha having died in 1782 after complications from childbirth. According to Edmund Bacon, Jefferson's overseer between 1806 and 1822, the slaves present when Martha Jefferson died used to tell Bacon's wife that Mrs. Jefferson said "she could not die happy" if she knew her children might someday have a stepmother. Thomas Jefferson took her hand and "promised her solemnly that he would never marry again."[10] Israel Jefferson, who had been enslaved at Monticello, confirmed in his 1873 recollection that "it was a general statement among the older servants at Monticello, that Mr. Jefferson promised his wife, on her death bed, that he would not again marry."[11] Jefferson never did remarry, but seven years after his wife's death he was still only forty-six years old. He must have begun to consider the possibility that he would want to have sexual relations again. It was not uncommon for bachelor and widowed Virginia slave owners in particular to have sexual relationships with female slaves. Though surely he knew of other comparable cases, Jefferson needed only to look to his father-in-law John Wayles for an example. The thrice-widowed Wayles was, after all, also Sally Hemings's father, having been sexually involved for at least a dozen years with Betty Hemings, one of his own slaves, until his death in 1773.[12] As an enslaved woman whom he knew would be impossible to marry, who was said to be beautiful, and who may have resembled Jefferson's deceased wife given that she was her half sister, Sally Hemings was a perfect match for Jefferson's needs.[13]

The reality that the Jefferson-Hemings relationship was in part rooted in sexual gratification calls for a discussion of the possibility that Sally Hemings was coerced into her relationship with Jefferson. In the early national and antebellum South, many if not most incidents of interracial sexual intercourse can only be described as rapes. Perpetrators of these abuses expressed power and contempt rather than sexuality or affection, and a perusal of both contemporary and twentieth-century slave narratives amply demonstrates that enslaved women lived in a state of constant anxiety that they could be victimized by the sexual predations of white men.[14] Southern state laws dictating that children of African Americans followed the servile status of their mothers, an economic system encouraging profiteering from bartering in human property, gendered double standards demanding the protection of white female chastity even while winking at male sexual conquest, and racial stereotypes pointing to black female sexual salacity all helped produce an environment in which white men could violate slave women and suffer few if any consequences. White anxieties and insecurities about maintaining absolute domination over their slave population coexisted with these economic, legal, and cultural factors, making sexual violence as basic and integral a tool of the American slave regime as the whip, one productive of both physical damage and psychological devastation.[15]

No evidence exists to indicate that Thomas Jefferson ever physically forced himself on Sally Hemings. That the couple continued to have sexual relations over at least an eighteen-year span (Hemings gave birth to her last child in 1808) after coming back to the United States discourages such a suggestion, but even if their relationship was not founded on sexual assault, that hardly discounts the possibility that Jefferson coerced Hemings in other ways. When Jefferson and Hemings negotiated her return from France, complicated considerations were at play, all of which point to the reality that when it came to sexual relationships between masters and slaves, even if rape in its conventional understanding was not an issue, the line between coercion and consent could often be a blurry one.

Sally Hemings had some leverage when she and Jefferson discussed the terms under which she would return to Monticello. Because Hemings could have likely freed herself in France she knew that even without any sexual entanglements, Jefferson had to make her some sort of offer if he wanted her back in Virginia. That the couple had — or even if they had not yet but wished to — become sexually involved only enhanced Hemings's negotiating power. It meant that if Jefferson wanted to continue their affair after leaving France, he wanted Hemings to return with him for much more than performing the usual domestic tasks of a slave. At what point Jefferson and Hemings established the terms of their relationship is unknown. If their discussion postdated the discovery of Hemings's pregnancy, then she also carried Jefferson's child who, depending on his ideas about the couple's future, would be seen by Jefferson as either a familial or a financial addition, or both. Whatever the case, Sally Hemings was in the unusual position of being an enslaved woman with some legally supportable claim to ownership of her own body, giving her a number of chits to work with when bargaining with Jefferson.

It is even possible that Hemings conceived the terms of the arrangement herself and proposed them to Jefferson. We will never know who initiated their sexual relationship, but once Hemings and Jefferson had become involved she might have been able to see what the future had in store for her. Both her mother and her grandmother had had children with white men.[16] While Betty Hemings and her family had achieved positions of great privilege in the Wayles and Jefferson households partially as a consequence of the Hemings-Wayles relationship, John Wayles never freed either Betty Hemings or any of their children together. Sally Hemings knew that she might become the sexual partner of her master, but by being in France she also knew she had the opportunity to demand some promises from Jefferson. Numerous examples from slave narratives suggest that enslaved women in Virginia sometimes exchanged their participation in sexual relationships for favored treatment in their owner's household. Alice Marshall, who had been a slave in Nottoway County, for example, recalled in the 1930s that her mother "was de house maid an' de seamstress on de place. She ain' never got beat; she kinda favorite wid de white folks. . . . My father? Well, I reckon I oughter to tell dat, but it ain' my shame. 'Twas ole massa Jack Nightengale, mistiss' husband."[17] Ex-slave James Smith, meanwhile, told of his family's life on the Guttridge plantation in Lancaster County, where an enslaved woman named Cella worked as head of the plantation household, a position secured in part by her involvement in a long-term sexual relationship with Thaddeus Guttridge, the plantation owner.[18] Sally Hemings, it seems, had the chance to get more than "extraordinary privileges." By enabling her children to live as free adults, she could surpass the efforts of anyone before her to end the enslavement of the Hemings family.

For his part, Jefferson might hope that Hemings would not claim her freedom, but he had to know there was little he could do to force her to return to Virginia as his slave if she tried to remain free in France. As he wrote in 1786 concerning a young enslaved boy brought overseas by Paul Bentalou, "the laws of France give him freedom if he claims it, and . . . it will be difficult, if not impossible, to interrupt the course of the law." Jefferson advised Bentalou to say nothing about the boy to anyone. It was only a small risk that the French would act without solicitation to free him, and Jefferson argued that the boy was too young to demand freedom for himself.[19] Sally Hemings turned sixteen in 1789. Perhaps Jefferson thought he could expect such naiveté from her as well. If he did, he was wrong. Either Sally or her twenty-four-year-old brother James apparently understood that French courts did not care for slavery in the kingdom and that Sally could use that fact to her advantage.

Ultimately, though, Thomas Jefferson still had vastly more bargaining power than Sally Hemings could ever have. Whatever she chose to do entailed insecurity. There was a small free black community in Paris, but unless her brother James remained abroad with her, Sally would essentially be on her own. It seems likely that by the time Jefferson and Sally Hemings discussed their arrangement, James Hemings had already cut his own deal with Jefferson, agreeing to return with him in exchange for being paid for his work and for eventual emancipation. If this were the case — and at the very least, Sally and James surely discussed their options together and she understood in which direction he leaned — Sally Hemings's foreseeable future in France was uncertain at best. She would be unprotected in a foreign country whose language she spoke haltingly, with only her skills as a domestic servant and a seamstress to help her make her way. She might never return to the United States or see any members of her family again.[20]

Alternatively, if Sally Hemings returned to Virginia with Jefferson under prearranged conditions, she was still inherently vulnerable because she had no choice but to trust Jefferson to keep his word. Their arrangement was contractual in a way, but it was a contract without even the remotest legally binding authority to support it. Thomas Jefferson's promise was not only the supreme authority but also the sole one. Once back in the United States, Hemings would lose much of the bargaining position she had in France. She could refuse to continue having sex with Jefferson if she felt he violated the terms of their agreement, but even if the child she carried back from France lived to the age of twenty-one, the crucial portion of the agreement relating to her children's freedom would not take effect until 1811. By then, Hemings would be thirty-eight years old and Jefferson would be sixty-eight. Who knew if he would even want to continue having an intimate relationship at such a late date? Thomas Jefferson could easily nullify their arrangement simply by ignoring its terms. And what if Jefferson died before freeing her children? There was no way to be sure that whoever assumed control of the estate would hold up Jefferson's end of the bargain. Cella, the enslaved woman from Lancaster County, for example, found that when Thaddeus Guttridge died, his brother Bill inherited the plantation. Bill Guttridge immediately installed a different woman as the chief household slave. Cella, furious and desperate, tried to poison the woman and her entire family. Bill Guttridge responded to this action by severely beating Cella, whereupon she ran away. She was caught shortly thereafter and sold in Norfolk, along with her child by Thaddeus Guttridge.[21] Hemings women had lived in the Wayles and Jefferson families for many years by 1789, and Sally Hemings probably thought she knew and could trust Thomas Jefferson. But given the limited track record of the Wayles and Jefferson families for emancipating slaves, and given human fragility, she also knew she took a huge risk.

Thomas Jefferson also took a risk entering into a sexual relationship with Sally Hemings. He probably did not choose to become involved with Hemings simply because she was an attractive woman with whom he could have sex and never had to marry. No matter how many white men in Virginia had sexual relations with their slaves and how many people knew the truth about such things, appearances mattered most for retaining public respectability. Gossip was unpleasant and threatened one's reputation, but it was scandalous to flaunt an interracial sexual affair. If Jefferson were going to involve himself sexually with an enslaved woman, he would have been sure she was someone he thought he could rely upon absolutely to be discreet, careful at all times and especially in front of others about how she spoke to him, acted around him, and even looked at him. Jefferson would have wanted to be reasonably certain that, in his grandson Thomas Jefferson Randolph's words, not "a motion, or a look, or a circumstance" would lead anyone "to suspect for an instant that there was a particle more of familiarity between Mr. Jefferson and Sally Henings [*sic*] than between him and the most repulsive servant in the establishment."[22]

Jefferson's household staff—his cooks, his maids, his and his daughters' valets and butlers, and his seamstresses—consisted almost entirely of Hemingses. Five Hemings women, including both a young Sally Hemings and her mother, were among those in the room when Martha Jefferson died. As Edmund Bacon later described the family, "they were old family servants, and great favorites."[23] Jefferson was therefore inclined to trust Sally Hemings from infancy, and as she grew up and took care of his daughter he would have had the opportunity to watch her and assess her potential for prudence, tact, and sound judgment, which would be required for the purpose of remaining secretive. Also, not being able to foresee that his daughter Martha and her family would live permanently with him in his retirement, Jefferson also probably considered before getting sexually involved with Hemings that he might want a regular companion in his old age, placing Sally's mental capacity at an even higher premium. Aside, therefore, from any sexual feelings Jefferson had for her, the most important assets Sally Hemings had were that she was a Hemings and that she was intelligent. Her family affiliation and her personal characteristics would have to have been central to her having a sexual relationship with Jefferson and enhanced her appeal as both a sexual partner and a companion.

Jefferson becoming sexually involved with a Hemings had a certain irony built into it. Even though he knew the Hemingses better than any other family among his slave population, working in the house also made the Hemingses the most visible Monticello slaves to any guests. Discretion was therefore doubly important. Thomas Jefferson, though, apparently believed Sally Hemings possessed all the capacities he required. As Thomas Jefferson Randolph later recalled, perhaps revealing more than he intended about the connection between the Jeffersons and the Hemingses, his grandfather's "entire household of servants with the exception of an under cook and carriage driver consisted of one family connection and their wives. . . . It was a source of bitter jealousy to the other slaves, who liked to account for it with other reasons than the true one; viz. superior intelligence, capacity and fidelity to trusts."[24]

Taking into account the relative risks involved and the mutual considerations made by Thomas Jefferson and Sally Hemings when they embarked on their sexual relationship, Jefferson did not need to coerce Hemings physically to get her to exchange sexual partnership for privileges and her children's freedom. Given her options, Sally Hemings chose to return to Monticello, but when it came to making choices about her body and her children, those options were severely curtailed simply because she was a slave. In theory, she could have refused all terms of the proposed agreement with Jefferson and returned to Monticello without becoming his sexual partner. We will never know how Jefferson would have responded had she made this choice. Other masters might have beaten her, raped her, or sold her, but the position of Hemings family members in Jefferson's household and his personal tendency not to be especially violent or vindictive indicate that Sally probably would have suffered no harsh consequences. At stake in her decision to stay in France or return to Virginia, though, was freedom for herself and her children. This consideration was one she could not possibly ignore, effectively limiting her choices to two. She could stay in France and take her chances, risking an uncertain future and the loss of any significant connection to her family. Or she could enter into a sexual relationship with Jefferson. Here, she depended on his trustworthiness and health, but knew that he had the resources to offer her a life where work would be relatively light, where she would not have to worry about food or clothing, where she could live among the rest of her family, and where, most importantly, her children could eventually live as free persons in the United States. Only Thomas Jefferson decided whether Sally Hemings and her descendants would be free or enslaved in their home country. He did not need to point that out to her to be coercive. The situation was inherently so.[25]

This argument should not be taken to exclude the possibility that Jefferson and Hemings felt fondly for one another or that perhaps, over time, they even came to love one another in their own ways. Hemings, for her part, may have seen Jefferson the way many other women did — charming, handsome, talented, and intelligent, a man worthy of great admiration. Despite Jefferson's profession in the *Notes* that love among African Americans seemed to him to "be more an eager desire, than a tender delicate mixture of sentiment and sensation," Sally Hemings may have been able to prove to Jefferson that he was mistaken.[26] Perhaps he reciprocated her feelings in ways he might have not originally thought possible. Presuming they remained intimately involved even after they stopped having children together, it is hard to imagine such a personal relationship of more than thirty-five years where the parties did not feel at least some mutual affection.

However the couple's ties evolved emotionally, though, Thomas Jefferson and Sally Hemings carried out their relationship in an environment where her body was implicitly assumed not to be her own. Whatever negotiating power she may have had, the man she negotiated with already had the advantage of being her owner and provider. No matter what choices she had at her disposal, the consequences attendant to each of those choices demonstrate that she ultimately made her decision from a position of relative weakness to Jefferson, not from strength or even equality. Slavery in the United States could put people in peculiar positions. Even as masters owned slaves, both groups depended on one another and shared a greater daily intimacy than either might have liked to acknowledge. In this environment affection and tenderness could and did coexist with resentment and violence, but we should not delude ourselves when it comes to Thomas Jefferson and Sally Hemings. Whatever reciprocal caring there may have ever been between them, fundamentally their lives together would always be founded more on a deal and a wary trust than on romance.

From 1790 to 1794 Jefferson served as secretary of state in George Washington's administration and was away from Monticello between nine and eleven months of each year.[27] Before returning again to public life as John Adams's vice-president in 1797, Jefferson retired to Monticello. It was his wont throughout his life to entertain large numbers of guests, and during his brief retirement a constant stream of visitors made their way to Albemarle County. For a man so cautious in his private correspondence and one whose personal elusiveness remains notorious among historians, Thomas Jefferson's characteristic gregariousness made him particularly ill-equipped to conceal his sexual relationship with Sally Hemings. As early as 1796, a number of French visitors noted evidence of sex across the color line on Jefferson's resident plantation. The Duc de La Rochefoucauld-Liancourt mentioned "particularly at Mr. Jefferson's" slaves who had "neither in their color nor features a

single trace of their origin, but they are sons of slave mothers and consequently slaves." The Comte de Volney, also traveling during the summer
of 1796, similarly noted slaves at Monticello "as white as I am."[28]

These men could not have been describing Sally Hemings's children.
Although generations of oral history suggest that the child Hemings
conceived in France in 1789 grew up to become a man named Thomas
Woodson, the same DNA study that linked Jefferson to Hemings cast
significant doubt on such a possibility. Rather, it seems most likely that,
as Madison Hemings reported, Sally Hemings's first child "lived but a
short time." Hemings's second child, meanwhile, a girl named Harriet,
born in 1795 (and who herself would die in 1797), was just an infant
when these visitors made their observations.[29] Still, evidence of racial
mixing at Monticello must have been quite obvious, and no matter who
was involved or how discreet he was, Jefferson could not have hidden it
from guests. As a member of the Virginia gentry, Jefferson knew of similar affairs carried out in supposed secrecy and likely understood that
regardless of his best efforts, he could never hide everything or quash
every rumor. Still, he never anticipated James Callender, and in 1802
Thomas Jefferson's relationship with Sally Hemings became a rumor far
more widespread and far more public than he could ever have foreseen.

James Callender emigrated from his native Scotland to the
United States in 1793, fleeing British authorities he feared would charge
him with treason for his 1792 publication of *The Political Progress of Brit-
ain*, a pamphlet in which he attacked British political institutions and
advocated Scottish independence. Callender was a radical egalitarian
who detested the pretension and condescension he saw in wealthy and
powerful men. Once in the United States he was drawn to Jeffersonian
Republican politics for its antielitist, anticorruption, and anti-English
overtones. In late 1793 he began working for the *Philadelphia Gazette*,
reporting the proceedings of Congress. Most Republican party leaders
were ambivalent about Callender from the outset. They found his almost uncontrollably nasty journalistic style unpalatable, and moderates
feared his democratic extremism. But the Republicans of the 1790s were
a party struggling desperately to get into power, and in the words of his
biographer, Callender "could be guaranteed to diminish the public stature of his opponents."[30]

Thus, even after the editor of the *Gazette* fired him in 1796, party officials clandestinely continued to feed Callender information for anti-Federalist attacks. Callender struck his sharpest blow in 1797, when his *History of the United States for 1796* forced Alexander Hamilton to reveal an adulterous affair in order to counter allegations of his complicity in an illegal speculation scheme. Callender was thrilled with his own efforts, writing to Jefferson in September 1797 that Hamilton's embarrassing written reply to the *History of 1796* was "worth all that fifty of the best pens in America could have said against him."[31]

Jefferson and Callender probably first met in June 1797 at the Philadelphia printing office of Snowden and McCorkle, where Jefferson, then the vice-president, gave Callender $15.14 for copies of his *History of 1796*.[32] Callender thereafter repeatedly turned to Jefferson for financial support, and Jefferson gave Callender in excess of $200 — more money than he gave to any other Republican journalist — from his personal accounts over the course of nearly four years following their first meeting.[33] Jefferson rarely wrote to Callender. But he solicited others to subscribe to Callender's publications, and when Jefferson did write he indicated that he appreciated Callender's efforts and encouraged the journalist to continue writing and publishing. In October 1799, for example, after seeing some pages of Callender's soon-to-be-published *The Prospect before Us*, a relentless political and personal attack on President John Adams, Jefferson sent his congratulations and assurance that "such papers cannot fail to produce the best effect. They inform the thinking part of the nation."[34]

In 1798, the Federalist-dominated Congress passed the Sedition Act to stifle Republican newspaper criticism of Adams and his administration, using the threat of imprisonment against anyone publishing sentiments deemed hostile to the government or the president. Afraid of being arrested and prosecuted under the new law and uncertain that even his fellow Republicans would stand behind him, Callender promptly fled Philadelphia and ended up in Richmond. Callender became increasingly suspicious of and hostile to most Republicans in 1798 and 1799, perceiving quite accurately that they looked down their noses at him, used him when he served their interests, and left him to confront Federalist hostility alone when his work got him into trouble.[35] Even as Callender's anger toward the Republican Party grew, however, he became increasingly attached to Jefferson, the one man who seemed to offer the support and respect that he felt he deserved. In letters to Jefferson during 1799 and 1800, Callender began to use the pronouns "us," "we," and "our" when discussing Jefferson's chances at winning the presidential election of 1800.[36]

In June 1800 James Callender's fears came to pass. He was tried under the Sedition Act, primarily for his excoriation of John Adams in *The Prospect before Us*. Justice Samuel Chase found Callender guilty and sentenced him to a $200 fine and nine months in the Richmond jail. Republicans turned Callender into a political martyr, publishing the minutes of his trial as a campaign document for Jefferson, and Callender continued to write both political pamphlets and letters to Jefferson from prison. Paying his fine mostly out of his own pocket nearly forced Callender into bankruptcy, but Jefferson won the election of 1800, a victory in which Callender, not entirely unfairly, believed he had played an important role. By the time he got out of jail in March 1801, he had already made entreaties to Jefferson about a remission of his fine and about a job as a postmaster in the new administration.[37]

By the time Callender had served his sentence, however, Jefferson no longer needed him. Callender's antagonistic and provocative style was highly effective for an opposition party, but for a party in power it might prove more a liability than an asset. In addition, there was always the risk that Callender's extremism would turn him into a critic rather than a supporter of the party, most of whose members he distrusted anyhow. On assuming the presidency, Jefferson pardoned all Republican journalists who had served time in jail under the Sedition Act, including Callender, and he promised to remit all fines. But he had no intention of offering Callender a patronage position. While in prison, Callender had already sensed that Jefferson might be freezing him out, and when the remission of his fine was delayed and he still heard nothing from the president, Callender quickly became impatient.[38] Desperate for money and suffering from an illness he contracted in prison, Callender wrote a hostile letter to Jefferson in April 1801. He expressed his disgust that Jefferson had failed to help him retrieve his fine or give him a federal job, both of which he took as personal slights. He denounced the Republicans for having abandoned him once he had helped them achieve victory and regretted that he had ever devoted himself to any single cause when all he received in return was betrayal.[39]

Several weeks later, with Jefferson continuing to ignore him, Callender appealed instead to James Madison, the secretary of state and Jefferson's closest political ally. Subtlety, never Callender's strong point, had now left his writing entirely. He utterly failed to understand how Jefferson, who "repeatedly said that my services were considerable," could cast him out after winning the presidency, although he also claimed that he had always suspected Jefferson might turn on him. Callender also threatened the president in his missive to Madison, warning that he would reveal to the Federalists what he believed to be Jefferson's duplicity respecting the fine. More ominously, he hinted that he had items of even greater significance to bring to light. "I am not the man," Callender asserted, "who is either to be oppressed or plundered with impunity. . . . [S]urely, sir, many syllogisms cannot be necessary to convince Mr. Jefferson that, putting feelings and principles out of the question, it is not proper for him to create a quarrel with me."[40]

Jefferson, who surely heard about Callender's threats from Madison, would not submit to the journalist's intimidation. But he also knew that Callender relished tearing apart public figures in print and did not wish to antagonize the man further. Accordingly, in the hope that it would give Callender some immediate satisfaction and assuage his anger, Jefferson asked his personal secretary, Meriwether Lewis, to call on Callender and give him $50 to tide him over until the rest of the fine could be recovered. Callender responded with an even more overt attempt to blackmail Jefferson than that contained in his letter to Madison. According to Jefferson, who described the encounter between Callender and Lewis in a letter to his friend and Virginia governor James Monroe, Callender "intimated that he was in possession of things which he could and would make use of in a certain case: that he received the 50. D. not as a charity but a due, in fact as hush money; that I knew what he expected, viz. a certain office, and more to this effect." Insulted and appalled at Callender's temerity, Jefferson canceled all financial assistance he had authorized, and assured Monroe that Callender "knows nothing of me which I am not willing to declare to the world myself."[41] Whether Jefferson suspected that Callender's threats entailed revealing his relationship with Sally Hemings is uncertain, but with such an unequivocal rejection of Callender's blackmail he effectively chose to let whatever information Callender possessed appear in the newspapers.

Considering what he published in the fall of 1802, Callender himself probably alluded to the liaison when he told Meriwether Lewis he had damaging "things" to write about Jefferson. Callender almost certainly had heard rumors of the relationship between the president and Sally Hemings by the spring of 1801. Although Callender would be the first editor to put any specifics of the story in print, he was not the proximate source of the information, which had been bandied about by Virginians and others for a number of years before Callender ever published it. Jefferson's political enemies hinted at the affair even before the election of 1800, with William Rind, editor of the *Virginia Federalist*, claiming in the spring of that year that he had "damning proofs" of Jefferson's "depravity." Presumably, Rind had heard the gossip from others, and he probably told others the details, in this way serving as a conduit for the rumor and intensifying the suspicion of Jefferson's private life without ever running his speculations in print.[42] In September 1801, more than a year before Callender's reports appeared, a story in the *Washington Federalist* indicated that a prominent politician referred to as "Mr. J." had "a number of yellow children and that he is addicted to golden affections."[43] Vulgar poems intimating Jefferson's sexual involvement with black women appeared in newspapers months before Callender directly linked the president to any particular woman.[44] Shortly after Callender published his report of the story, the *Gazette of the United States* announced it would not print the story without greater corroboration from its own sources, but acknowledged it had "heard the same subject freely spoken of in Virginia, and by Virginia Gentlemen."[45] Although the Jefferson-Hemings story can hardly be said to have been common knowledge by the time Callender got hold of it, some people, especially in Virginia, clearly had already ground it in their gossip mill.

James Callender detested African Americans and found the notion of sex across the color line repulsive.[46] Once he reported the Hemings story, he described Hemings herself in the most racist terms, calling her a "wench" and "a slut as common as the pavement," accusing her of having "fifteen, or thirty" different lovers "of *all colours*," and referring to her children as a "yellow litter."[47] When he had held Jefferson in esteem, Callender discounted the Hemings rumor. Callender later wrote, for example, that he had first believed the hints emanating from Rind's *Federalist* to be "absolute calumn[ies]." In prison, however, feeling himself falling out of Jefferson's favor, he began to turn against the man he had once admired. After his release he made inquiries on his own, some of which confirmed what he once refused to believe. Now he had ammunition.[48]

Callender's fine was remitted in June 1801, but it was too late to restore his good opinion of the president. Callender had been run out of one city and had served nine months in jail in another. All of his work in the United States had been as a Jefferson supporter and once Jefferson made it clear that the relationship would not be reciprocal, Callender wanted revenge. In February 1802 he began writing for the *Richmond Recorder*, a Federalist newspaper, but he used the paper less to support Federalist policies than to blast the Republicans, who taunted him mercilessly in their papers for his misfortunes.

By May 1802 a full-scale newspaper war had broken out between Callender at the *Recorder* and his former employer, Meriwether Jones of the *Richmond Examiner*. Jones accused Callender of apostasy for turning against Jefferson and baited him to reveal whatever damaging information he claimed to have on his erstwhile patron.[49] For his part, Callender hurled epithets and accusations of his own, including the claim that Jones entertained a black mistress in his home whenever his wife was away.[50] The personal salvos flew back and forth and escalated in the degree of their vitriol. Editors of newspapers in other major cities soon entered the fray. On August 25, 1802, William Duane, editor of the *Philadelphia Aurora*, accused Callender of infecting his wife with venereal disease, and of getting drunk in the next room while she languished and eventually died and while his children went hungry. This charge was too cruel even for Callender. In the next issue of the *Recorder*, under the heading "The President Again," he wrote that it was "well known that the man, *whom it delighteth the people to honor*, keeps, and for many years past has kept, as his concubine, one of his own slaves. Her name is SALLY."[51]

Because standing sexual affairs between white men and black women in early national and antebellum Virginia were nearly always open secrets but only dangerously scandalous if widely publicized, whites involved in such liaisons had to rely on others to adhere to the cultural code of public silence. Such reliance, though, made exposure the ultimate weapon for anyone with an ax to grind against a white participant in interracial sex. Callender publicized Thomas Jefferson's sexual relationship with Sally Hemings because he had a personal grudge against Jefferson, one rooted in a relationship five years in the making and unmaking between the two men. The writer wanted recognition for his work and the financial security that a patronage job could provide. If Jefferson refused to comply, then Jefferson would have to pay. In the early republic, vicious personal enmity was frequently integral to and inseparable from partisan politics. It is therefore only fitting that James Callender thought releasing a humiliating story about the president's personal life would destroy Thomas Jefferson's political career.[52]

What, though, did Callender really know about Thomas Jefferson and Sally Hemings? The crux of the matter, as Callender reported in his original article, was that Thomas Jefferson and a house slave named Sally were involved in a sexual relationship; that Sally had gone with Jefferson to France along with his two daughters; that the two had "several" children together, including a ten- or twelve-year-old son named Tom; and that "President Tom," as Callender sarcastically called this boy, bore a striking physical resemblance to Jefferson. Two weeks after the original article, Callender brought specificity to the number of Sally's offspring, writing that she and Jefferson had exactly five children.[53] By presenting so many specifics about the relationship, Callender tried to establish from the outset that his charges, far from being concocted, were grounded in verifiable fact. He challenged Jefferson's supporters to refute them, writing that "if the friends of Mr. Jefferson are convinced of *his* innocence, *they* will make an appeal. . . . If they rest in silence, or if they content themselves with resting upon a *general denial*, they cannot hope for credit. The allegation is of a nature too *black* to be suffered to remain in suspence. We should be glad to hear of its refutation. We give it to the world under the firmest belief that such a refutation *never can be made*."[54]

Callender probably obtained most, if not all, of the information for his first round of articles directly from individuals who lived in Albemarle County, and he may have even traveled there after being released from prison, as suggested by a toast made in his honor at Richard Price's Albemarle tavern just over a month after he got out of jail.[55] Callender certainly implied that people in Jefferson's county were his sources when he claimed there was "not an individual in the neighbourhood of Charlottesville who does not believe the story; and not a few who know it."[56] Callender correctly reported not only the story's outline, but also some significant details. He identified Hemings by her first name, and he knew both that she had been in France with Jefferson and that she worked at Monticello as a house slave. That Hemings had had exactly five children was also true in 1802. In addition to the infant conceived in France and the first Harriet, she had given birth to a son named Beverley in 1798, to an unnamed daughter who was born and died in 1799, and to another girl named Harriet in 1801.[57] The accuracy of this informa-

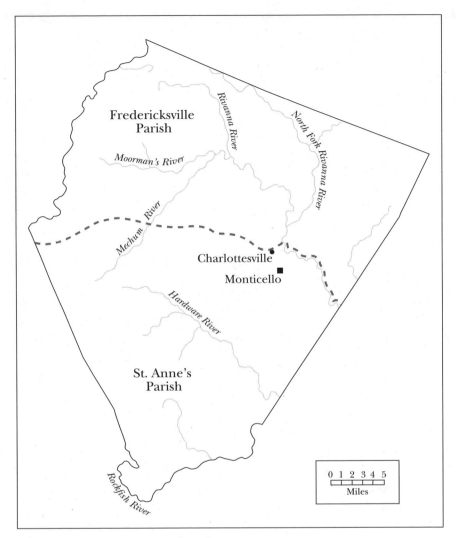

Map 1. Albemarle County, 1780–1800

tion strongly suggests that some of Callender's informants had, or knew people who had, extensive familiarity with domestic life at Monticello over the course of at least a dozen years.

The original source of the information easily could have been slaves in Albemarle County. Everywhere in the South, enslaved African Americans had kin and community networks that extended across vast distances. Slaves at Monticello knew of the association between Hemings and Jefferson and had greater access to details about their relationship than nearly anyone else. Recall Thomas Jefferson Randolph's report that other slaves envied the treatment afforded the Hemings family and suspected ulterior motives, "account[ing] for it with other reasons than the true one." Israel Jefferson, meanwhile, a Monticello slave who worked as a postilion, scullion, and waiter, confirmed that Jefferson and Hemings were sexually involved based on his "intimacy with both parties."[58]

Given Callender's disgust for African Americans, however, it seems unlikely he spoke directly to any Albemarle slaves. He claimed in print to have collected evidence from a large number of people, even asserting in December 1802, in response to repeated denials of the Hemings affair by Republican journalists, that he would happily meet Jefferson in any court and "prove, by a dozen witnesses, the family conviction, as to the black wench and her mulatto litter."[59] If he was serious about this challenge, his witnesses would have to have been white. He would have acquired his information from the most likely places to hear local gossip in Albemarle, as in any Virginia county—taverns, markets, the steps of the courthouse, other social gatherings. He probably relied especially on members of the Virginia gentry from Albemarle for what he believed to be his most reliable evidence. These men—and they were almost certainly men, given the significant breach of etiquette it would have been for a woman to discuss sexual matters with a man not her husband— might have overheard their slaves discussing the Hemings story. They also would have been the whites most likely to have visited Jefferson at Monticello, to have been inside the house (and thus to have seen Sally Hemings and perhaps her children), and to have heard the prevalent gossip about Jefferson and Hemings in elite social circles. Callender also may well have received some reports from other whites who might only have been at Monticello briefly if at all but could see Jefferson or his slaves when they came down from the mountain to town. Some sources were more reliable than others, but anyone who lived near Jefferson was a possible source of material. As Henry Randall wrote in private correspondence in 1856, Callender "was helped by some of Mr. Jefferson's *neighbors*."[60]

For five weeks after the middle of September, Callender added no new information to the Jefferson-Hemings story. The story was an evolving one, however, and once it appeared for the first time in print, new sources—possibly but not necessarily from Albemarle—reached Callender in Richmond to feed him more information or to correct errors he had published. That Callender changed the number of Sally Hemings's children from "several" to "five" in the two weeks between September 1 and September 15 is likely an example of just such a dynamic. Similarly, on October 20 Callender wrote that a few days after the original article ran, "a gentleman" came into the district court in Richmond and offered to bet anyone present a suit of clothing or any amount of money that the story was true, except for one small detail, namely that Sally Hemings had not actually gone to France with Jefferson but had joined him later. Callender corrected this mistake (Jefferson left for France three years before Sally Hemings's arrival), but used the correction as an opportunity to emphasize the reliability of his information, writing, "if we had been mad enough to publish a tale of such enormous, of such inexpressible ignominy, without a solid foundation, the Recorder, and its editors must have been ruined." Callender did not identify the man in the district court but noted that no one would take the bet, because the man was known both to be very wealthy and "to have the best access to family information."[61] Whether or not the courtroom drama actually took place, there is little reason to doubt Callender's description of his source, for the correction the man called for not only was accurate but was such a tiny detail that only someone unusually familiar with the Jefferson family — the events in question having taken place fifteen years earlier — could have known it.

In the first few months after Callender published his original story, people started bringing him as much misinformation and innuendo as fact, some of which he printed. On November 10, for example, Callender wrote "it is said, but we do not give it as gospel" that one of Sally Hemings's daughters, presumably fathered by someone other than Jefferson, was a house servant currently working somewhere in Richmond.[62] This story was patently false, because no such daughter of Sally Hemings ever existed. That Callender printed the story at all indicates that despite all he did know, there were some important things about Hemings he did not, including her age. In 1802 Sally Hemings was just twenty-nine years old, making the possibility of her having a daughter old enough to be a house servant unlikely.

That Callender made this mistake is not to say that he became careless or that he lacked the ability to distinguish fact from fiction. On the contrary, in the same November 10 article he reported that Jefferson had freed Sally Hemings's brother, who had an "infirmity" in one of his arms and had been seen selling fruit in Richmond. Here, Callender was almost certainly referring to Hemings's older brother Robert, who in fact had been freed by Jefferson in 1794 and had subsequently moved to Richmond, where he lost a hand in a shooting accident.[63] Callender did not catch every error he made in reporting the Jefferson-Hemings story, but he was a journalist very familiar with dealing with personal gossip about public figures, and he had a good sense of when a story might be inaccurate. Hence, he purposefully indicated that the story about Sally Hemings's daughter was only a rumor while publishing the story about her brother, for which Callender must have felt he had more reliable information, without qualification.

Yet it may be no coincidence that although he continued to hammer away at Jefferson for his relationship with Hemings for another month or two, Callender printed no new information about Jefferson and Hemings after November 10. By then, of course, the midterm elections had passed, limiting the utility of continuing to develop the story. But it is also possible that his sources dried up. There was, after all, probably very little anyone could have added to what Callender had already published. Similarly, by November Callender may have suspected that the rumor mill had begun to spin wildly and that the stories he now heard contained more falsehoods than truths. Before September 1, the story circulated mostly in private among people relatively close to the original sources of information. After September 1, though, so many people in so many places had heard the story that it became impossible to tell where the various pieces of gossip originated anymore. Callender was concerned with accuracy, and when he ran out of useful material, he stopped publishing additions to the story.

It is hardly surprising that Callender's reports contained some inaccuracies. White informants with the most intimate knowledge based their suppositions not on anything Jefferson told them directly, but on deductions and inferences from what they had seen at Monticello or in Charlottesville. Even Israel Jefferson, who lived at Monticello and saw both Jefferson and Hemings frequently, acknowledged that he could not "positively know" about Jefferson and Hemings's relationship but that he was certain of it "from circumstances."[64] Most people who knew the story had probably heard it secondhand, at best. Callender's information, then, came to him through at least one other person and more likely through two, three, or four. The more people the story passed through before it got to Callender, the less likely that all the facts would be correct. People who knew about Sally Hemings's children, for example, might not have heard that three of the five had already died by 1802.

The detail that Hemings and Jefferson went to France in two different ships a few years apart could easily have been collapsed into a single ocean voyage or, alternatively, Sally could have been confused with her brother James, who had in fact been on the same ship as Jefferson when he first left America.

Callender's most significant and most persistent error was his insistence that Jefferson and Hemings's oldest child, who was probably deceased in 1802, was in fact very much alive, named Tom, resembled the president, and could still be found at Monticello. Callender probably never corrected this mistake because no one told him that he was in error. To the contrary, even Jefferson's supporters never denied there was a "President Tom" (although they obviously claimed Jefferson was not his father), and Callender's informants clearly believed that there was such a child living at Monticello.[65] It remains somewhat of a mystery why these informants insisted they had seen a boy around twelve years old born to Jefferson and Hemings. Hemings's children were well known to resemble Jefferson. Perhaps Callender's sources conflated four-year-old Beverley Hemings with some older light-skinned enslaved boy at Monticello, thus creating "President Tom."[66] To those who did not claim to have seen the boy purported to be Sally Hemings's oldest child, however, that there was such a person would have seemed very plausible. Would not the story have more credence if Sally Hemings's first child was still alive, looked like Jefferson, and bore his father's name? How many people had enough access to Monticello to confirm or deny that particular element of the story? Not knowing which of Sally Hemings's children had died, most people would presume that Hemings's first child was still alive, and not hearing he had been sent away or disappeared, where else would he be if he were not at Monticello? We are all aware of rumors with grains of truth that get embellished to the point that they nearly lose their truthfulness altogether. Especially regarding a story of this nature, the possibilities for hyperbolic exaggeration as the Jefferson-Hemings story passed from person to person and then to Callender were enormous. That Callender got so much of the story right is remarkable testimony to the extent and transmission of social knowledge about private interracial sexual affairs in Virginia communities.

Not everyone in Albemarle had information for Callender because not everyone had heard the story, but Callender's assertion that nearly everyone in the county he mentioned it to believed it is persuasive.[67] Given what Virginians already knew about sex and slavery in their society in general, they hardly needed details about Jefferson's relationship with Sally Hemings to believe he might be sexually involved with her. Even Meriwether Jones, who tried to defend Jefferson in the pages of the *Examiner*, conceded that "in gentleman's houses every where, we know that the virtue of unfortunate slaves is assailed with impunity."[68] Of course, not every slave owner conducted himself in this fashion, but enough did that the allegations about Jefferson's participation would not have been implausible. Jefferson's particular actions and associations also gave residents of Albemarle County reason to believe the Hemings story. First, there was the significant presence of "white slaves" at Monticello, commented on since at least the 1790s. Second, John Wayles's sexual affair with Betty Hemings had been well known in Albemarle, the Hemings family still filled the most prominent roles in Jefferson's household in 1802, and Jefferson had already freed not one but two of Sally Hemings's brothers, having emancipated Robert in 1794 and James in 1796.[69] Third, Jefferson may have had other close relatives who engaged in interracial sexual conduct. In an 1858 letter, Jefferson's granddaughter, Ellen Randolph Coolidge, picking up on the family story told by her brother Thomas Jefferson Randolph, blamed Jefferson's nephew Samuel Carr for the paternity of Sally Hemings's children, accusing him of being a "master of a black seraglio kept at other men's expense." Genetically, neither Samuel Carr nor his brother Peter could have fathered Sally Hemings's children. They nonetheless might have been selected as the Jefferson family scapegoats because they were known to participate in sex across the color line.[70] Finally, and perhaps most tellingly, Jefferson was already known by 1802 to have facilitated the interracial sexual relationship of another of Betty Hemings's daughters. In 1792 Jefferson had sold Sally Hemings's oldest sister Mary, at Mary's request, to a white man named Thomas Bell, and the couple lived together with their children on Main Street in Charlottesville's downtown.[71] Many people who lived in Jefferson's neighborhood, then, believed the Hemings story because Virginia's slave owners and Jefferson himself had prepared them to believe it. Over the course of the antebellum period, they only saw additional reasons to accept the rumor as fact.

The Hemings family continued to hold important household roles long after Jefferson and Sally Hemings returned from France. It is hard to determine precisely what "extraordinary privileges" Jefferson bestowed on Sally Hemings herself. She continued to serve as Mary

Jefferson's personal attendant, probably until Mary married in 1797, but Hemings also worked in the house and did some sewing. She received rations of finer clothing than most Monticello slaves in the 1790s, but so did her sister Critta and her niece Betsy, which likely reflected these Hemingses' visibility in the house rather than any unusually favorable treatment for Sally. Both Madison Hemings and Isaac Jefferson recalled that Sally Hemings cleaned and maintained Jefferson's chamber and his wardrobe. She probably performed this duty until Jefferson's death, a trust in which she had access to Jefferson's most private space, granted practically to no one white or black.[72] Edmund Bacon remembered that Sally, along with a number of other Hemings women, was also responsible for airing out the house.[73]

Scattered evidence, though, suggests that Sally Hemings's workload may have been especially light. The *Frederick-town Herald*, which claimed to have its own sources on the relationship, wrote in December 1802 that Hemings was "an industrious and orderly creature in her behaviour," that she had a room of her own at Monticello, and that she was "treated by the rest of his house as one much above the level of his other servants."[74] Madison Hemings recalled that his mother did "light work," while Bacon claimed that, regarding the Hemings women generally, he was "instructed to take no control of them. They had very little to do."[75]

Jefferson and Hemings had two more children, both sons, after 1802 — Madison, in 1805, and Eston, in 1808. Jefferson gave Sally Hemings the opportunity to spend a great deal of time with her children, as indicated by Madison Hemings's recollection that he and his siblings "were always permitted" to be with their mother. Sometimes Jefferson made provisions to ease Hemings's time of lying in after childbirth, as he did on occasion for other enslaved women. In 1796, for example, Jefferson noted in his farm book that a young enslaved girl named Edy had moved in with Hemings, presumably to assist her in taking care of the first Harriet. A girl named Aggy briefly replaced Edy, and this caretaking arrangement was repeated in 1799, when a girl named Thenia briefly lived with Hemings during the life span of her unnamed daughter.[76]

Direct evidence of Jefferson's feelings and actions toward his enslaved children while they were very young is sparse. The names of the children may have reflected Jeffersonian choices — all except Madison, whose full name was James Madison, bore Randolph family names — perhaps indicating that Jefferson wished to reinforce his genetic bond with one of nomenclature. But these names might just as easily have been chosen by

Sally Hemings herself as part of an effort to tie her family more overtly to the other Jeffersons.[77] Madison recalled that in their youth Sally Hemings's children had very little in the way of work to occupy them. Jefferson allowed them to linger about the house, and they occasionally ran some errands and performed minor tasks for their mother. Generally Madison remembered that in childhood he and his siblings "were free from the dread of having to be slaves all our lives long, and were measurably happy."[78]

Madison Hemings noted that Jefferson's "general temperament was smooth and even; he was very undemonstrative. . . . He was not in the habit of showing partiality or fatherly affection to us children. We were the only children of his by a slave woman. He was affectionate toward his white grandchildren."[79] The year 1809, when Madison was four years old, marked a significant turning point in both the structure and functioning of the Jefferson household, fundamentally shaping how Thomas Jefferson would interact with Madison and his siblings until Jefferson died. In that year, Jefferson ended his second term as president and retired permanently to Monticello. Simultaneously, Martha Jefferson Randolph and her entire family moved in with her father. If Jefferson failed to treat his children with Sally Hemings with the same kind and degree of regard as he did his own grandchildren (who were of the same generation as the Hemings children), it surely reflected the intricacies of being the master of a household comprising both his black and white families.

It is nearly inconceivable that Martha Randolph failed to realize the nature of her father's involvement with Sally Hemings. Notwithstanding the capacity of white southern plantation women for denial respecting their husbands' infidelity with enslaved women, if the master of the household and one of the most visible house slaves had four living children, especially children said to look strikingly like their father, only a blind woman could have not noticed it.[80] Martha Randolph frequently spent summers at Monticello with her family prior to 1809, and she had been humiliated by the appearance of the Jefferson-Hemings story in the newspapers in 1802.[81] She must have understood even before moving to her father's house that Jefferson had an ongoing sexual relationship with Sally Hemings.

Martha Randolph was not married to Thomas Jefferson, which may have reduced the tension so often resulting from the sexual triangles in other plantation households between a white man, his wife, and his enslaved mistress.[82] Martha assumed the dominant managerial position in the household on moving to Monticello, meaning she and Hemings had to associate with one another on a regular basis. Martha Randolph had known Sally Hemings (who was also her half aunt) since birth, and the Hemings family had been the Wayleses' and the Jeffersons' most trusted slaves since before Martha was born. We need not assume that acrimony characterized Martha's relations with Hemings. But Randolph's permanent residence at Monticello still presented a situation that can be described generously as a delicate one that required an accommodation among Martha, Thomas Jefferson, and Sally Hemings.

Their accommodation was achieved through silence, the pretense that Jefferson's white family was his only family. For Jefferson to acknowledge openly that he had two families sharing Monticello and to have treated them equally would have been intolerable, both a violation of the unwritten code governing slave-master relations in the South and an affront to the sensibilities of his white family, who demanded the respectability and exclusive partiality that legitimacy entailed.[83] Instead, Jefferson's familial life in retirement suggests a balancing act. He tried to prepare his enslaved children for the freedom he had promised to grant, but he avoided acting in ways that others might see as indications he had any unusual connection to them. As Madison Hemings pointed out, even to the Hemings children themselves Jefferson would only rarely demonstrate emotionally that such treatment owed itself to familial affection or a biological relationship. He probably never did so in the presence of anyone else, and certainly not in front of any other white person.

Beverley, Madison, and Eston Hemings were all trained as carpenters in their teenage years by their uncle John Hemings, and Harriet Hemings worked as a spinner and a weaver. All four began working a few years later in their lives than did most Monticello slaves, giving them extra time before being forced to face the rigors of adulthood, although Edmund Bacon remembered that even on becoming a teenager Harriet Hemings in particular "never did any hard work." All three boys could play the violin, Jefferson's instrument, a skill at which Eston was known to be particularly proficient. Few people not living at Monticello would have suspected anything unusual about the treatment of the Hemings children. That they started work later in life than most children owned by Jefferson was a subtle distinction and would only have been noticeable to people who knew both that the children were related and their exact ages. Musical abilities could have been acquired within the slave community. Madison Hemings noted that he had to coax white children (probably Jefferson's grandchildren) to teach him to read, suggesting that Jefferson failed to educate his enslaved children in any formal way.[84]

Both Beverley and Harriet, though, eventually married whites of "good circumstances" and "good standing" in Maryland and Washington, D.C., respectively, without their spouses' families ever suspecting they had been born into slavery. After a stay in Ohio, Eston Hemings moved to Wisconsin with his wife, where both designated themselves as white. Individually, none of the provisions made for the Hemings children was in and of itself necessarily indicative of the children's relationship to Jefferson, but the end result was that they had learned to maneuver as whites in white society. Their mother, who had spent much of her life in the presence of whites and had likely observed a great deal, could have taught them the necessary behavioral codes to do so. But it is hard to imagine that their father did not play at least a managerial role in their upbringing, choosing the paths he believed would be the most valuable after he freed them. Such training must have been comforting to and perhaps even requested by Sally Hemings, who would have wanted repeated reassurance — in deeds if not in words — that Jefferson still intended to uphold his end of their deal and that her children would have the chance to thrive in freedom.

Jefferson could have acted toward and treated the Hemings children in their youth and adolescence differently than he did. Some men in Virginia openly embraced their interracial families in their homes and raised their multiracial children as they would have any white child. Ralph Quarles, one of the largest landowners in early nineteenth-century Louisa County, for example, belonged to a gentry family. He and one of his slaves, a woman named Lucy Jane Langston, had their first child in 1806, and Quarles freed both Lucy and their daughter together that same year. By 1809 Quarles and Langston lived openly as a couple, and had three more children by 1829, including John Mercer Langston, who would grow up to become a prominent lawyer, politician, educator, and diplomat. Quarles's children worked on his plantation, but he also taught them to read and write as well as some plantation management skills. On his deathbed in 1834, Quarles ordered that when Lucy died, she was to be buried alongside him.[85] Similarly, Henry Ferry, a man born into slavery on a plantation near Danville, remembered that his owner, despite being married to a white woman, had an open and ongoing affair with an enslaved woman named Martha, and that he treated his and Martha's son Jim "jus' like his own son, which he was. Jim used to run all over de big house."[86]

Conversely, Jefferson could have sold Sally Hemings and her children away from Monticello when the Randolph family moved in. Numerous ex-slaves recalled white men who had children with enslaved women making such a concession to their white families. Liza McCoy, who had been enslaved in Virginia, remembered that her Aunt Charlotte had a "white baby by her young master. Dats why de sold her south." Mary Wood remembered being told that her grandmother's sister Fannie lived on a plantation near Fork Union. Fannie's owner's wife caught her husband engaged in sexual relations with Fannie, only to exclaim, " 'Yes, I jes knowed you and Fannie been doing that all the time! Them three brats of hers is jes like you!' " Fannie's owner sold her the following week.[87]

Each of these choices, though, had consequences. Ralph Quarles found himself socially ostracized, at least in part because of his unconcealed relationship with an African American woman and his treatment of their children as if they were parts of a "legitimate" family. Henry Ferry's owner's actions brought his wife utter and constant humiliation and emotional suffering. Ferry recalled one day in particular when the local minister stopped by the house. Seeing young Jim running down the stairs to meet him, the minister "took de little boy up in his arms an' rubbed his haid, an' when Missus come, tol' her how much de boy look like his father and mother. 'Course it favors its father most,' de preacher say, tryin' to be polite, 'but in de eyes, de lookin' glass of de soul, I kin see dat he's his mother's boy.' Miss Mamie shooed de child away an' took de preacher inside. Never did let on it wasn't her chile. Was pow'ful mad 'bout it though. Never would let dat boy in de house no' mo'." Selling an enslaved mistress and her children away, meanwhile, could easily touch off a burst of gossip, as could freeing slaves, which required the creation of legal documentation. Manumission after 1806 brought an additional danger, namely that under the provisions of Virginia law a slave freed after that year who did not get explicit permission from the state legislature to remain had to leave Virginia permanently within one year of emancipation.[88]

Jefferson was in no way "trapped" by his society to act in any particular way toward Sally Hemings and her children. Slave owners involved in sexual relationships across the color line had many options with respect to their African American families, and their actions ran the gamut from love to cruelty. Jefferson, though, selected a course designed to minimize all the potentially dangerous consequences of his actions either for himself, his daughter, or the Hemings family. He would never risk sacrificing his positions as president, senior statesman, or eminent member of the Virginia gentry. Martha Randolph could not have felt the excruciating pain of a wife whose husband philandered with women said to be racially inferior, but her father's failure to make at least an effort at concealment could have cost her own social respectability and status. Given the long-standing nonsexual family relationship between the Jeffersons and the Hemingses, it seems unlikely that Martha would have asked her father to sell Sally and her children, even presuming she had enough clout to do so. In any event, such an action would have broken Sally Hemings's trust and shown callousness uncharacteristic of how Jefferson seems to have felt about his enslaved family, despite Madison Hemings's suggestion of emotional ambivalence. Formally freeing the Hemingses, particularly Sally Hemings, would have only renewed attention to the family and its relationship to Jefferson. Formal emancipation also might not have been in the best interests of the Hemings children, because legal documentation of their enslaved past could have hindered their efforts to move in white society. In short, Thomas Jefferson could have interacted with his enslaved family in any number of ways. His particular method was a choice, not a trap.

Beverley Hemings ran away from Monticello late in 1821 or early in 1822, when he was around twenty-three years old. Harriet Hemings left around the same time. She was twenty-one years old.[89] As Jefferson neared the end of his life, he provided in his will for the freedom of Madison and Eston Hemings on their turning twenty-one, and asked the state legislature to grant the two permission to remain in the state near their families. Madison Hemings was already twenty-one when Jefferson died in July 1826. Eston Hemings, according to his brother, was "given the remainder of his time" by Jefferson's heirs and freed sometime before he actually turned twenty-one in 1829. As Madison later put it, all of Sally Hemings's children "became free agreeable to the treaty entered into" by their parents. Jefferson never mentioned Sally Hemings in his will. But she was protected from sale at the posthumous auction of most of Jefferson's slaves, and Martha Randolph informally freed her sometime after Jefferson's death. By 1830 Sally, Madison, and Eston Hemings lived in a rented house in downtown Charlottesville, and the census taker that year listed the entire Hemings family as white. In 1833 Sally Hemings appeared in the census of "free Negroes & Mulattoes" for Albemarle County. She died in 1835. Her burial site remains unknown.[90]

Emancipating the Hemings children cost Jefferson and his family financially. Twenty-one-year-old skilled slaves were valuable assets, and Jefferson's white family inherited his debts, amounting to over $100,000. Here too, though, Jefferson balanced the commitment he made to Sally Hemings over thirty years before his death with the interests of his white family by concealing publicly the nature of his relationship with the Hemingses. He facilitated the emancipation of Beverley and Harriet Hemings without ever taking legal responsibility for having done so. Beverley simply ran away and was never pursued. According to Edmund Bacon, Jefferson gave Harriet, the first and only female slave he ever freed, $50 and had her put on the stage to Philadelphia. By having Harriet board a stagecoach in Charlottesville Jefferson risked gossipy murmurs, but he probably believed it foolish and perhaps dangerous to let a young woman wander off the plantation and fend entirely for herself.[91]

Jefferson failed to make similar arrangements for Madison and Eston Hemings, but he may have chosen to free them through formal legal channels because neither had any desire to leave the state. Much of their family remained in Albemarle County, and their mother, who was already in her fifties when Jefferson died, may have wished to live out her life where she had grown up, under the care of her two youngest children. Only after her death did Madison and Eston Hemings follow the path of many free African Americans out of Virginia to Ohio. Jefferson's public request that Madison and Eston be allowed to remain in the state, then, may have been a final favor to Sally Hemings. Jefferson made the same request for the three other slaves he freed in his will. But the request made for Madison and Eston Hemings was distinguished by the fact that it completed the project of enabling every one of Sally Hemings's children to live their entire adult lives in freedom. No other enslaved woman at Monticello ever accomplished so much.

Despite making a public overture on their behalf, nowhere in his will did Jefferson acknowledge that Madison and Eston Hemings were his children. Jefferson, in fact, left no explanation for freeing Madison and Eston at all and made no financial provisions for them. Instead, he apprenticed them as a sort of gift to their uncle, John Hemings, until they turned twenty-one.[92] The pretense of linking their freedom to John Hemings would have been transparent to anyone familiar with the Hemingses because Madison was already of age when Jefferson wrote his will, but Jefferson tried to divert attention from suspicions about his connection to the children of Sally Hemings to the very end. He may have known that some people would see right through the convolutions of his will. When it came to interracial sexual relationships in antebellum Virginia, though, pretenses protected reputations, and Jefferson smartly wore the mask of propriety.

If we can believe his own words, from the time he wrote the *Notes on the State of Virginia* until the day he died Thomas Jefferson maintained an utter distaste for sex across the color line. He wrote to James Monroe in 1801 concerning his belief that blacks needed to be colonized if freed. Jefferson expressed concern that such a colony, even if placed in South America, might be incorporated by the United States if the nation expanded. He raised the potential problem of white Americans sharing a language, laws, and a government with another race of people and could not even "contemplate with satisfaction either blot or mixture on that surface."[93] In 1814 Jefferson wrote to Edward Coles, an Albemarle County neighbor, that African Americans' "amalgamation with the other color produces a degradation to which no lover of his country, no lover of excellence in the human character can innocently consent."[94] In January 1826 Jefferson returned to the subject of colonization in a letter to his friend and fellow Virginian William Short. He still maintained that no colony should be located in a place that could become contiguous with the United States. He instead suggested the Virgin Islands "as entirely practicable, and greatly preferable to the mixture of colour here. To this I have great aversion."[95]

Jefferson's writings indicate that he was not entirely unaware of the contradiction between participating in sex across the color line even while claiming to be repelled by it, and that he tried to rationalize his actions. Interracial sex was to be avoided, but Jefferson clearly saw it was also inevitable whenever blacks and whites shared space. No white man or woman, perhaps, should have consented to such behavior, but Jefferson accepted as a given that it would happen in an interracial society. In conjunction with his expressed belief that African Americans would seek revenge for slavery, his thoughts on white supremacy, and the need to maintain purity of blood, his opinions on the realities of human sexual relations in a biracial society help explain why he felt blacks and whites simply had to be separated if either was to survive.[96]

Jefferson surely considered himself a "lover of human excellence," however, and simply believing that sex between blacks and whites was unavoidable was probably not enough to convince him that he was not regularly violating his own principles. Possibly Jefferson maintained his own sexual relationship with Sally Hemings because he could tell himself that Sally Hemings was somehow not really black. One of Hemings's grandmothers was African, but her other grandmother and both grandfathers were of European descent. Thomas Jefferson Randolph claimed that Hemings was "light colored," while Isaac Jefferson remembered she was "mighty near white" and that she had "long straight hair down her back."[97] Because people inherited status maternally, physical appearance had no bearing on an individual's freedom or slavery. It was not unusual in Virginia to encounter enslaved people of some African descent known, like some of those individuals observed at Monticello, as "white slaves" or "white negroes."[98]

Jefferson's letter to Francis Gray in 1815 suggests that Jefferson may have tried to use the ambiguity of race to his psychological advantage as a means of rationalizing his relationship with Sally Hemings. Gray had asked Jefferson what, by Virginia law, constituted a "mulatto." Jefferson had responded to Gray but believed he had misstated the case and wrote again to explain. What followed was a mathematical discourse on how the descendants of Africans might become white. Jefferson argued, as was true under Virginia law at the time, that a person with one-quarter "negro blood" — someone like Sally Hemings, for example — was technically considered a "mulatto." If such a person had a child with a white person or with any person of at least some white ancestry, however, the child would be considered white. Jefferson pointed out that the child would not necessarily be free because of the law of descent, but if "emancipated, he becomes a free *white* man, and a citizen of the United States to all intents and purposes."[99]

With this explanation, Jefferson simultaneously justified enslaving people who were legally white and found a way for them to become American citizens. He also implicitly, and conveniently, made the case that his children with Sally Hemings were in fact not black at all. And if his children with a woman of some African descent were white, then who was to say for certain that sexual relations of this sort even really qualified as sex across the color line? Moreover, if he set those children free and they became white citizens, then who was to say he had not made the most personal of contributions, if only in a small way, toward ending slavery and its "unremitting despotism . . . and degrading submissions"? Despite his professed opposition to slavery, nearly the only way Jefferson found in his life to free any slaves was literally to make them white, thus overcoming the "unfortunate difference of colour" he saw in the *Notes* as "a powerful obstacle to the emancipation" of African Americans.[100] Jefferson's devotion to white supremacy clashed with his belief that slavery had to end. Perhaps only "white slaves" could ever be free.

Jefferson's children with Sally Hemings undeniably appeared white to many people, as suggested by the marriage partners of both Beverley and Harriet Hemings and the racial designation given Madison, Eston, and Sally Hemings herself by the 1830 census taker. Edmund Bacon described Harriet Hemings particularly as "nearly as white as anybody," and Ellen Coolidge, taking note of the slaves freed by Jefferson, pointed out that "they were white enough to pass for white." Although a writer for the *Daily Scioto Gazette* in Ohio indicated that Eston "had a visible admixture of negro blood in his veins," Eston Hemings lived in a free black community in Ohio, and people where he lived knew that Thomas Jefferson had formerly enslaved him. They had good reason to assume he was black and saw his physical features and skin color in that context. Eston seems to have had little difficulty passing for white once he moved to Wisconsin, where he likely concealed much of his past.[101]

To argue that it made it easier for Jefferson to have children with Sally Hemings if he could convince himself that he actually was enabling her children to become free white citizens is not to accept the argument that Jefferson freed Sally Hemings's children because they were light-skinned. Ellen Coolidge made this claim in 1858, contending that Jefferson always let slaves leave the plantation who were "sufficiently white to pass for white men." Because travelers observed the presence of numerous light-skinned slaves at Monticello before Sally Hemings even had a child who survived past age two, and because we have no evidence that

Jefferson freed these slaves either formally or informally, this assertion holds little water.[102] But the whiteness of Sally Hemings and her children could easily have shaped Jefferson's thinking on his own sexual conduct.

Perhaps Jefferson's writings about sex across the color line were utterly unreflective and unselfconscious. White men could easily both be racists and the sexual partners of black women. Perhaps with regard to this aspect of his life Jefferson's words and his actions may have just failed to mesh. Maybe he saw his relationship with Sally Hemings as an exception he granted himself to his general rule. But in 1815, as Jefferson wrote his note of explanation to Francis Gray, Beverley Hemings, the former president's and Sally Hemings's oldest living child, was seventeen years old. Jefferson may have realized that the terms of his arrangement with Beverley's mother were coming due, and he may have begun to think about how the young man might survive and where he might go once he was set free. That Beverley could pass into white society surely brought his father some comfort.

James Callender's revelation of Jefferson's relationship with Sally Hemings failed to have its intended impact. By early 1803 the newspapers in Virginia for the most part had ceased discussing the matter, and the story was little more than a footnote in the 1804 national presidential election campaign, which Jefferson won in a landslide.[103] For several reasons, even in Virginia Callender's articles failed to do the damage he had hoped. For some people in Virginia the Jefferson-Hemings story was an old one by 1802, and Callender's claims were unlikely to change whatever opinions they already held. Other Virginians were unlikely to believe anything written by James Callender given his undisguised motives and his usual methods. Still others who strongly admired Jefferson might have simply refused to accept that he might have sex with an enslaved black woman, who was by race and status as debased as Jefferson was revered. For these Virginians, as Jefferson's granddaughter later argued, there were "such things, after all, as moral impossibilities."[104] In addition, in July 1803 James Callender, stumbling drunk through the streets of Richmond, fell into the James River and drowned. Other newspapers had picked up the Jefferson-Hemings story, but their editors had neither the network of informants nor the desire for personal vengeance that animated Callender. When Callender died, a significant portion of the energy behind the story died with him.

Finally, and perhaps most importantly, Callender misunderstood white attitudes toward interracial sex in Virginia, and thus failed to foresee that although his allegations might embarrass Jefferson and his white family, they were unlikely to provoke any larger consequences for his career or standing. To be sure, few white men would publicly voice their approval of sex across the color line. Children of mixed race confused the ideally bifurcated racial order and, as Jefferson himself noted, sex with black women was thought to degrade whites. As Callender observed, "it is only doing justice to the character of Virginia to say that this negro connection has not a single defender, or apologist, in Richmond, as any man, that even looks through a spyglass at the hope of a decent character, would think himself irretrievably blasted, if he had lisped a syllable in defence of the president's mahogany coloured propagation."[105]

Callender misread the silence among white male Richmonders. Because the systematic sexual abuse of enslaved women helped bolster slavery, because slaves followed the condition of their mothers, and because what a man chose to do with his own slave property was for the most part his own business, their silence did not necessarily signify outrage or disgust. Rather, white Virginians were of at least two minds about interracial sex, and a story about a white man — no matter who he was — having sex with his own female slave could hardly be expected to elicit universal indignation.

No great tumult was likely to occur when it came to Thomas Jefferson particularly, not only because of who he was but also because of how he conducted himself in his relationship with Sally Hemings. In the slave South, ethical norms governed even activities not generally perceived to be intrinsically ethical, such as interracial sex. Jefferson could never prevent people in his community from gossiping about his relationship with Hemings, but so long as he kept his affairs discreet — which entailed never acknowledging rumors about his sexual behavior, never demonstrating that he cared for Hemings, and never treating their children as legitimate blood relations — no one was likely to say anything about it in his presence.[106]

Callender, perhaps recognizing these realities, did try to make the case that Jefferson exacerbated the depravity of his sexual relationship with a black woman by disregarding the feelings of his white family. In his original article, for example, Callender hoped his readers would find Hemings's presence in Paris alongside Jefferson's white daughters particularly galling, writing that "the delicacy of this arrangement must strike every person of common sensibility. What a sublime pattern for an American ambassador to place before the eyes of two young ladies!"[107] In the weeks that followed, Callender continued to insinuate that Jefferson aggravated the contemptibility of his sexual behavior by granting Hemings a position of domestic legitimacy, referring to Jefferson as "Sally's husband" and to Hemings as "Mrs. SARAH JEFFERSON."[108] But however accurate Callender's factual reports may have been, when it came to characterizing the ethical nature of the Jefferson-Hemings relationship, he was mistaken. Discretion guided Jefferson's every interaction with Hemings and her children. From 1789 until the day he died, he never directly addressed the rumor of his relationship with Hemings, and he never accorded Hemings or his children by her the kind of respectability and legitimacy that might have suggested he viewed them as family members. And in the end, those pretenses put Jefferson's sexual behavior largely outside the bounds of public scrutiny, even to those who may have believed it possible that Jefferson and Hemings had children together. If there was ever such a thing in white eyes as the ethical amalgamator, Thomas Jefferson was the prototype.

Just as he failed to appraise accurately how most Virginians were likely to respond to his revelations about Jefferson, Callender never understood that in Virginia there were honorable and dishonorable ways of sharing information about the interracial sexual affairs of elite men. Consequently, he never foresaw that even people who considered Jefferson's sexual behavior less than admirable might also condemn Callender for publishing the story. The *Frederick-town Herald* from nearby Maryland, for example, believed Callender's reports, and thought the entire affair to be a subject of great hilarity. But its editors also called Callender a "sad fellow" and claimed they would not pursue the story. "Modesty," the paper argued, "orders us to drop the curtain. . . . We therefore assign it over to less scrupulous hands, confessing at the same time, that there is a merriment in the subject, which we should be graceless enough to pursue at the President's expence, were it less offensive to serious and decent contemplation."[109] Virginians may have found Jefferson's sexual behavior delightful for gossip. Some even fed Callender information, knowing he would print it. But no one, not even Callender's informants, would ever say anything to Jefferson directly. To do so not only would have been extraordinarily insulting, but also would have been a challenge to Jefferson's honor as a gentleman. As one hostile letter writer to the *Recorder* castigating Callender asserted, "He has no character, no honor, no sensibility."[110] By moving the rumor of Jefferson's interracial sexual affairs from private gossip to public discourse, Callender touched off whole new rounds of discussions about the president all over the country, but he also succeeded in cementing his own reputation as a scoundrel, a judgment that has lasted for two hundred years.

In Charlottesville on October 10, 1802, Mary Hemings and Thomas Bell's daughter Sally Jefferson Bell married Jesse Scott, the son of a Native American woman and a white man. Nearly twenty-five years later, at Thomas Jefferson's estate sale in January 1827, over one hundred slaves were auctioned. Jesse Scott purchased a woman named Edith Fossett and her two youngest children. Edy Fossett's husband was Joseph Fossett, an enslaved blacksmith at Monticello and one of only five slaves freed by Jefferson in his will. Scott's purchase of three Fossetts held both their families together, because Joe Fossett was Jesse Scott's brother-in-law, the older half brother of Sally Bell and a son of Mary Hemings born before she began her relationship with Thomas Bell. On June 14, 1832, Eston Hemings married Julia Ann Isaacs, the daughter of a white man and a free black woman who lived cater-corner from the Bell-Hemings-Scott family. James Scott—Jesse Scott's son and Mary Hemings's grandson—officially witnessed the ceremony.[1]

As this complex set of relationships suggests, when Thomas Jefferson sold Mary Hemings to Thomas Bell in 1792, he did much more than enable the development of one particular interracial family. The sale of Hemings to Bell was the first important moment in the evolution of what soon became a burgeoning multiracial community in downtown Charlottesville. The boundaries of this community extended beyond the town's borders and held together free and enslaved Virginians of European, African, and Native American descent through marriage, extended family ties, and mutual economic support networks. Mary Hemings lived to be at least eighty-one years old, and she served as a central link between the town and the countryside until her death sometime after 1834.

For Thomas Bell's part, he knew well at least one other white man in Albemarle County (aside from Thomas Jefferson) who was involved in an interracial sexual relationship. On September 6, 1796, Thomas West, aware of the illness that would kill him just a few months later, wrote his

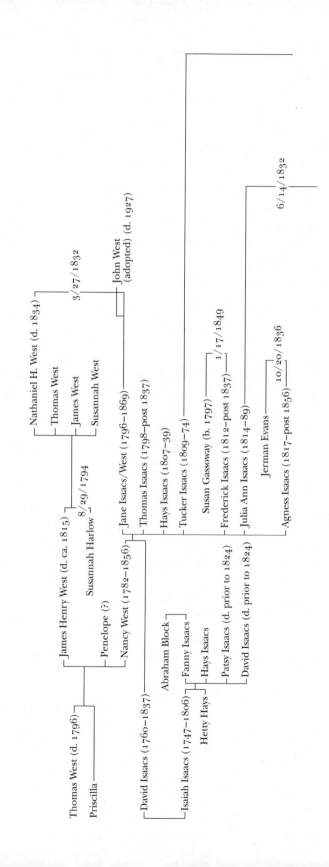

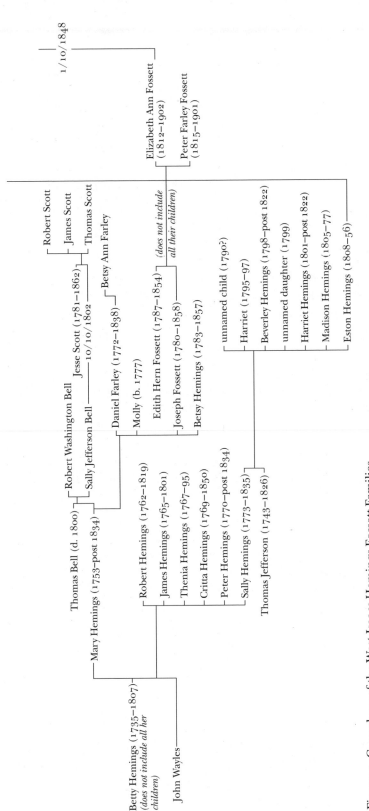

Figure 1. Genealogy of the West-Isaacs-Hemings-Fossett Families

last will and testament. West, a white blacksmith, owned land in both Amherst and Albemarle Counties, including ten half-acre lots in Charlottesville, amounting roughly to one-fifth of the town at the time of his death. In his will, West named two of his children — James Henry West and Nancy West — as heirs. Both children were free people of color born of a relationship between the elder West and a woman named Priscilla, who at one point in her life had been his slave. West left all of his land, his livestock, his furniture, and his eight slaves to James Henry West and James's family. Nancy West, fourteen years old at the time of Thomas West's death, was left just the annual interest on forty pounds until she turned twenty-one, at which time she would receive the principle. Thomas West requested in his will that Thomas Bell manage Nancy West's inheritance until she came of age.[2]

In the early twentieth century, R. T. W. Duke, who had been a commonwealth's attorney and a judge from Albemarle County, recalled that the Bell-Hemings family lived unmolested by their neighbors until Bell's death in 1800. "With the rather 'easy' morality of those early days," Duke remembered, "no one paid any attention to a man's method of living and Col. Bell lived openly with the woman and had two children by her."[3] Nancy West would discover over the course of her lifetime that not every interracial family was always so fortunate.

2

Notorious in the Neighborhood
An Interracial Family in Early National & Antebellum Virginia

Among the witnesses to Thomas West's will was David Isaacs. Isaacs, born in 1760 in Frankfort-am-Main, Germany, had immigrated to the United States and moved sometime in the early 1790s to Charlottesville from Richmond, where he and his brother Isaiah had been traders in Cohen and Isaacs, one of the city's largest mercantile firms. Both Jewish, the Isaacses lived in downtown Charlottesville on land rented from Thomas West.[1] While David Isaacs had a direct economic relationship with Thomas West for the few years he lived in Charlottesville before West's death, he had a more significant, lasting, and unusual relationship with West's daughter Nancy. Between 1796 and 1817, David Isaacs and Nancy West had seven children together. By the time of Isaacs's death in 1837 he and Nancy West (who occasionally, though rarely, used Isaacs's last name) had maintained a familial relationship for over forty years and had lived in a single household for seventeen of those years on Charlottesville's Main Street, where Isaacs owned a mercantile business and West ran a bakery. Between them the couple amassed substantial wealth. By 1850 Nancy West owned real property valued at $7,000, enough to make her the richest nonwhite person in Albemarle County.[2]

Interracial sex per se was not illegal in early national and antebellum Virginia, but laws prohibiting interracial marriages had been in place since the colonial era, and antifornication laws punished all sex outside of marriage whether or not it crossed the color line.[3] In this legal environment, a stable, successful, and familiar couple like David Isaacs and Nancy West never should have existed but nonetheless thrived. An investigation of their financial dealings, land transactions, and courtroom encounters provides a rare glimpse at how an interracial couple operated and even prospered at the margins yet mostly within the legal and social boundaries of a Virginia that discouraged their sexual activities and frowned upon their family, but which lacked either the motivation or the power to end their relationship.

The story of David Isaacs and Nancy West adds valuable details to the historical portrait of multiracial families and their peculiar positions in early national and antebellum southern communities.[4] In particular, it reveals how intricately and inextricably connected the couple's domestic and financial arrangements were, and how their economic position influenced precisely when some members of the white community in Charlottesville chose to revoke the toleration they usually demonstrated for West and Isaacs's relationship. Additionally, West and Isaacs's story shows their ingenious ability to turn laws of race, gender, marriage, and property designed primarily for legally married white couples to their distinct pecuniary advantage. What stands out most about Isaacs and West's sexual association is that, relative to the law, it was less directly subversive than it was startlingly ambiguous. When the couple altered their domestic arrangements around 1820, for example, they threatened both the moral sensibilities and the economic interests of some whites. But when they were subsequently accused of violating Virginia's laws against illicit sex, not even the highest court in the state would find them susceptible to criminal prosecution. Cautiously and at some risk but with a consistent strategy, David Isaacs and Nancy West exploited their unique status by slipping through legal loopholes to protect their own economic interests and the financial welfare of their children.

The life Nancy West and David Isaacs built together was hardly an unqualified success story. They had friends and supporters among local whites, and they found that the white community in Charlottesville generally left them alone. But no matter how financially successful they became, nearly being branded as criminals reminded them that they were perpetually vulnerable to legal harassment by whites. Although West and Isaacs never faced the possibility of criminal charges again, the same kinds of jealousy and resentment toward the couple's economic success that played central roles in provoking their original legal troubles seethed well into the 1840s. There would always be some whites who would try to take advantage of the idiosyncrasies of the couple's relationship in pursuit of their own economic gain. Rather than indicating the strength of interracial families in Virginia before the Civil War and the protections afforded to them, the experience of Nancy West and David Isaacs actually highlights the ultimate fragility and tenuousness of their status. That the couple managed to evade each obstacle placed before them is a testament not only to their shrewdness, intelligence, and foresight, but also to their enormous luck. Property and wealth can bring power, stability, and security. They can also provoke envy, greed, and hostility. For Nancy West and David Isaacs, they brought both.

On October 11, 1822, the grand jury sitting at the Albemarle County Court, on evidence provided by two witnesses, presented David Isaacs and Nancy West on the charge of "umbraging the decency of society and violating the laws of the land by cohabitating together in a state of illicit commerce as man and wife."[5] There are no extant descriptions of the testimony that brought about the presentment, but presumably the most germane facts were simply that the couple lived in the same house and acted as a married couple. Nineteen months later, on May 13, 1824, the court found the facts of the evidence against Isaacs and West to be true and asked the couple to show cause why Jonathan Boucher Carr, the local commonwealth's prosecuting attorney, should not bring an indictment against them for the crime of fornication. West and Isaacs's lawyer argued that, even conceding the facts in the presentment, the language used by the grand jury did not accuse the couple of violating any particular statute, and he questioned whether the state could even prosecute them on a fornication charge at common law. This legal strategy baffled the county court. Uncertain "whether, admitting the facts presented by the Grand Jury to be true, an Information will lie for the said offence at the suit of the Commonwealth," the court determined the case had to be sent to the General Court in Richmond. West and Isaacs objected, probably because they hoped the county court would simply dismiss the case, but were overruled.[6] In November 1826, their case finally worked its way onto the docket of the General Court in Richmond, where the justices ruled that the state of Virginia could not prosecute David Isaacs and Nancy West on any charge as presented by the grand jury.[7] On May 8, 1827, nearly five years after the original presentment, the Albemarle County Court dismissed all cases against Isaacs and West.[8]

The two witnesses who appeared before the grand jury in 1822 would have had to have been white, because David Isaacs was not black and Virginia law recognized the testimony of people of color only against other people of color. A fire in 1865 burned nearly all the original case papers of the General Court, precluding any precise knowledge of the witnesses' identities, but even without such specific information it seems extraordinarily curious that anyone would air a sexual grievance against Isaacs and West in 1822. Charlottesville was a small town with just 260 residents in 1810, and it had grown little by the early 1820s.[9] Much of the town's population lived within a few blocks of the couple. By 1822 a significant percentage of Charlottesville's residents must have known that David Isaacs and Nancy West were carrying on a long-term sexual relationship. The couple had already had all seven of their children, the oldest of whom (their daughter Jane) was twenty-six years old. Clearly Isaacs and West were and for years had been acting in violation of anti-fornication laws that prohibited sexual intercourse between unmarried persons, yet no one had chosen to do anything about it for more than twenty-five years.

David Isaacs's own economic clout and that of his business colleagues, many of whom were also prominent in local social and legal circles, might have prompted hesitation among people tempted to complain publicly about his relationship with Nancy West. Isaacs was a successful merchant and an esteemed member of the local business community. Among his associates were merchants John Kelly, John Winn, Twyman Wayt, James and Samuel Leitch, and John R. Jones, all of whom had been appointed by the county court as commissioners during the 1810s to assist him in his capacity as executor of the will of his brother Isaiah, who died in 1806.[10] In addition to being a merchant, Kelly was described as "a man of sterling integrity and a decided christian gentleman." In the 1820s he was also a founder of the town Presbyterian church. Winn owned the enormous Belmont estate, traded in real estate, and served for a time as town postmaster, a position in which Twyman Wayt succeeded him. Jones, who was later noted for leading an exceptionally "energetic and industrious life," served as a county magistrate beginning in 1819, acted as the financial agent for numerous local planters, and eventually became the first president of the Albemarle branch of the Farmers' Bank of Virginia.[11]

David Isaacs also counted Opie Norris and Alexander Garrett among his close friends in town, naming both as coexecutors of his own will.[12] Norris drew especial respect from Charlottesville residents, one of whom wrote after his death that he was "a man of mark . . . and as useful and beneficial to this community as any man that ever lived here." A merchant who also served as a county magistrate, Norris was a town trustee for many years, secretary-treasurer of a local turnpike company, and at one point in his life the owner of a blacksmith shop as well as a popular tavern. Garrett, meanwhile, dealt in real estate and spent most of his life in public office, serving as deputy sheriff and then as clerk for both the county and circuit courts. He also became the first bursar of the University of Virginia, married the daughter of one of Thomas Jefferson's nephews, and was named an executor of Jefferson's estate in 1826.[13] In addition to having influential friends in town, Isaacs had prominent customers throughout Albemarle County, not the least of whom was Jefferson himself, who bought all sorts of items from Isaacs ranging from meat, butter, and cheese to books and a horse. Jefferson's nephew, Dabney Carr Jr., had been a friend of Isaiah Isaacs, serving as a witness to a codicil of his will. Jefferson also made purchases from many other local merchants, but the long-standing patronage of prominent planters like him helped establish David Isaacs as a worthy, reputable, and respectable businessman.[14]

As a Jewish immigrant, however, David Isaacs would always be somewhat of an oddity in Charlottesville. Around 2,700 Jews lived in the United States in 1820 out of a total population nearing 10 million, and only 300 or so lived in Virginia. A few Jews other than David Isaacs lived in Charlottesville in the early nineteenth century, including merchant Isaac Raphael and lawyer Nathaniel Wolfe, but two-thirds of Virginia's Jewish population lived in Richmond.[15] Being a Jew in antebellum America meant numerical near insignificance but also often entailed cultural marginality and social prejudice. The anti-Semitism Jews faced in the antebellum United States paled by comparison to that confronted by Jews in Europe and was tempered by political, economic, and religious tolerance. Nevertheless, bigotry was widespread in America. Throughout the country the word "Jew" was used both as a generic pejorative and specifically as a synonym for a cheat. Overt hostility and violence toward Jews was rare, but Christian churches consistently preached that Judaism was an inferior religion. Jews were unusual and therefore exotic and interesting, but most gentiles also viewed Jews suspiciously and stereotypically as untrustworthy and avaricious. As historian Jacob Marcus writes, early nineteenth-century Americans were ambivalent toward Jews, and tolerance and acceptance frequently coexisted with rejection and a strong sense of Jewish difference. No matter the precise position of Jews in the United States, they "resigned themselves to the inevitable; there would always be a dividing line between Jews and Christians."[16]

David Isaacs's position as an outsider among white Christian society may have made his relationship with Nancy West — who, as a free woman of color, was herself an outsider — less offensive to other whites than had her partner been a white gentile. In the 1820s most Americans believed Jews were probably racially white, and Jews were treated as white under Virginia law, but the racial position of Jews was never entirely fixed due to centuries-old European folklore and stereotypes about distinct Jewish physiognomy.[17] In addition, Isaacs's religion certainly distanced him from many of his white Christian neighbors. They might not have expected him to adhere to as high a moral standard as that to which they believed they held themselves. If a distinction of faith helped at all in keeping David Isaacs and Nancy West out of a courtroom, however, such a distinction also meant that regardless of his economic standing, Isaacs could never completely integrate himself into Charlottesville's business and legal communities, which were held together as much by familial as by financial links. Samuel and James Leitch were brothers. John R. Jones's brother-in-law and his first business partner was Nimrod Bramham, another merchant and a man who later became legally entangled with David Isaacs. After parting ways with Jones, Bramham joined fortunes with his son-in-law, William Bibb. John Kelly's son-in-law was none other than Opie Norris, while John Winn and Twyman Wayt not only were partners but also had married two sisters from the same family. John Winn's oldest son Benjamin would grow up to marry the daughter of Ira Garrett, Alexander Garrett's brother.[18] Without access to these sorts of connections, David Isaacs could be deeply immersed in Charlottesville's mercantile world yet he would never be entirely of it.

It seems most likely, in fact, that one or more of Isaacs's fellow merchants instigated court proceedings against him and Nancy West in 1822. While changes that the couple made to their relationship in 1819 and 1820 may have prompted some complaints based on moral concerns, a closer look at the accusations brought against them suggests that economic interests played a significant role as well. Nancy West's economic position suddenly and dramatically improved beginning in 1819. Members of the merchant class frequently shared the same economic concerns, but they were also in competition with one another, which could breed jealousy and vindictiveness, especially when finances got tight. In the wake of the Panic of 1819, merchants finding it very difficult to collect debts even as they tried to pay off their own balances would have felt particularly vulnerable. Certainly it is not hard to imagine their antagonism toward the economic success of a free woman of color at such a time, especially when they perceived her as having procured that success in large part through an illicit sexual relationship with a white man. Perhaps some of the local mercantile elite felt it was time to remind the couple that they lived free of social and legal harassment mostly at the sufferance of the white community, and that there were limits to what they could and could not do.[19]

During most of the first two decades of the nineteenth century, Isaacs and West carried on their relationship and continued to have children while living in separate homes and owning their own independent businesses. In 1799, Nancy West turned seventeen. After convincing Thomas Bell to forward the forty pounds left to her by her father, she purchased a half acre of land—lot number 46 near Charlottesville's southern boundary—from her brother, James Henry West (see Map 2). She probably took up residence there around the time she turned twenty-one in 1803, and began raising her family and establishing herself professionally as a baker.[20] Isaacs himself lived just one block north and two blocks west on Main Street's lot 36, which he had purchased in 1802. A two-story wooden building on the property served both as his home and his store.[21] On the 1810 census, Nancy West and David Isaacs are listed as heads of different households. Isaacs lived alone, and West lived with five other free people of color, four of whom were probably the children she and Isaacs had at the time—Jane, Thomas, Hays, and Tucker.[22]

This arrangement changed beginning in December 1819, when Nancy West put her land up for sale.[23] Six months later, she purchased the bulk of lot 33, which was on Main Street just a few lots east of where David Isaacs lived, and she began renting out the property to assorted businesses.[24] In addition, the 1820 census reveals that Nancy West was no longer the head of a household, but that David Isaacs suddenly had ten free people of color living in his home.[25] As many as eight of these individuals were Nancy West and the couple's children, who now totaled seven after the births of Frederick, Julia Ann, and Agness between 1812 and 1817. West began running her bakery out of this building as well, next to David Isaacs's storefront. Less than two years later, the grand jury brought its presentment against the couple.

For more than twenty years after having their first child, then, David

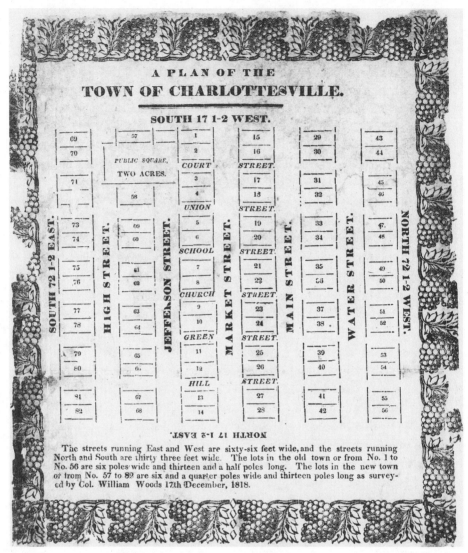

Map 2. The Town of Charlottesville, 1818 (courtesy of the Albert H. Small Special Collections Library, University of Virginia Library, Charlottesville)

Isaacs and Nancy West had maintained separate households. Technically, they even lived in separate parishes of Albemarle County.[26] It seems that so long as the couple kept their relationship a strictly illicit one and at least maintained the illusion that it did not exist, Charlottesville's white community let it go unchallenged. Only when the couple and their children started living together as a family did some members of the community find their arrangement unacceptable. Isaacs and West's sudden public pretense to being a family thus probably played some role in provoking the accusations against them. When the grand jury presented Isaacs and West, it also presented two other couples (at least one of which was also interracial and cohabiting) for fornication, which suggests that Isaacs and West's case may have touched off or been part of a small crusade by whites intent on rooting out sexual relationships that to them represented, in the words of Albemarle County judge Archibald Stuart, offenses "against good morals."[27]

Probably not coincidentally, the other interracial couple lived on lot 26, property owned by David Isaacs just two blocks west of where he lived with Nancy West. Joshua Grady was a white blacksmith who lived with a free woman of color named Betsy Ann Farley. Farley was the daughter of a free man of color named Daniel Farley, who lived at the east end of Main Street and was himself probably the oldest son of Mary Hemings. Hemings still lived on lot 23, cater-corner from West and Isaacs, and she shared her home with her daughter Sally Jefferson Bell and her son-in-law Jesse Scott. Thus, when Isaacs and West began living together, they not only presented themselves to Charlottesville as a legitimate family, but they also bolstered an interracial community on Main Street which had been growing for thirty years. Their presence may have brought the size of that community to a critical mass that finally provoked one or more Charlottesville whites to take action against it by striking at its newest and therefore most vulnerable members.[28]

It is impossible, however, to discount the significance of Nancy West's improved economic position, which was coterminous with her new living arrangements. For the first two decades of the nineteenth century, she was marginalized within the Charlottesville community spatially, socially, and economically. West was a free woman of color who owned property and a business, and who carried on a sexual relationship with a white man, but at least she was peripheral to the public gaze. She may have lived just a few blocks from David Isaacs, but her land sat at the edge of town. As late as 1820 her original property, including the structures on it, was valued at just $400, at a time when most lots nearer the court-house, even those just a block closer, were worth at least three times that amount. Before 1820 Nancy West posed no serious or visible threat, literally or figuratively, to the economic standing of other members of the white community. After that year, however, she not only lived openly as the wife of a white man, but she was accumulating capital and occupying valuable, centrally located real estate alongside other whites. The lot Nancy West purchased on Main Street in 1820 was practically across the street from her original location, but it was worth nearly $1,900, giving her economic strength on a completely different scale than that she had previously enjoyed. For some Charlottesville residents, Nancy West and David Isaacs had crossed the boundaries of acceptability in numerous ways. It was time to call them on it.[29]

The Albemarle County grand jury, however, seemed confused as to how to proceed against West and Isaacs, a confusion that was especially apparent in its failure to specify the precise nature of the charges it wanted the court to bring against the couple. The language of the presentment alleged that the couple violated "the laws of the land," but it did not specify which laws, and it contained what appeared to be contradictory accusations. On the one hand, Isaacs and West supposedly had committed the crime of engaging in the "illicit commerce" of a sexual relationship outside of marriage, with the legal implication that they were in violation of antifornication statutes. Yet simultaneously, according to the presentment the offensiveness of their relationship lay in their "cohabitating together . . . as man and wife" — that is, acting as if they were married. Given their respective races, this phrasing could be interpreted as an accusation of another crime altogether, namely that of racial intermarriage.

In its opinion on West and Isaacs's case delivered in November 1826, the General Court refused to entertain the vagaries of the presentment. In a case it had only recently decided, the court held that a single act of fornication could not be prosecuted at common law without other circumstances that in and of themselves would qualify as misdemeanors.[30] If, for example, a couple had sexual intercourse in public, the court argued that it "would be indeed an enormous indecency, and so grossly offensive and shocking to the feelings of society, as to entitle it to severe legal animadversion." Such circumstances, though, did not attend to West and Isaacs's case, and the Albemarle County grand jury never claimed that they had. The General Court suspected that the grand jury had included language about the couple living together to intimate that by sharing a household, the couple made their offense against society particularly outrageous. The grand jury presumably meant to imply that when West and Isaacs made the nature of their relationship so obvious, they "aggravate[d] its malignity." For their part, though, the justices of the General Court felt that the facts that the couple "occupied the same chamber, ate the same board, and discharged towards each other the numerous common offices of husband and wife" were "in themselves harmless and inoffensive." In short, the court determined that a couple living together as husband and wife — even an interracial couple — could not be said to be acting contrary to public morals. At least at common law, antifornication statutes could be used to punish flagrant and public acts of sexual indiscretion but not, regardless of a lack of formal validation from the state, a marriage-style relationship. If the Albemarle County grand jury wanted to charge Nancy West and David Isaacs with violating the state law against fornication, which technically had nothing to do with the egregiousness of the circumstances surrounding the sexual behavior, it could try. Under the presentment before the court, however, the justices held that the couple had committed no recognizable crime.[31]

In part, the leniency shown to West and Isaacs can be explained by the specifics of their case as it related to the judicial interpretation of the common law, the principles of which easily gave the General Court a defensible rationale for not punishing an interracial couple guiltless of either flagrantly fornicating or being legally married. The Albemarle County grand jury badly bungled its presentment, partially because the white community as a whole had failed to do anything about West and Isaacs for so long. Whites in Charlottesville allowed the couple to carry on their relationship unchallenged so long as the couple did not pretend it was legitimate. Once Isaacs and West did suggest legitimacy by openly living together, however, it was too late to find a court that would do anything about it. Also, while the presentment ostensibly attacked violations of both racial and sexual mores, it effectively attacked neither. To claim there had been a criminal violation of the racial order meant acknowledging the semblance of marriage in which West and Isaacs lived, but to attack the violation of the sexual order required challenging that very acknowledgment. In other words, Nancy West and David Isaacs either could be married or could be fornicators, but they could not be both. The General Court, presented with this legal and social conundrum, chose to leave the relationship alone.

Still, even though the General Court reasonably rejected the validity of the charge against West and Isaacs, the couple escaped mostly on a technicality. In other cases involving interracial sex, high courts across the South did sometimes demonstrate a willingness to override common-law traditions to express their own or the community's disgust. Had sex across the color line truly appalled the justices of the General Court, surely they could have broadened their interpretation of common law to envelop the Charlottesville case and thereby closed the loophole that enabled even the most thinly veiled interracial sexual relationships to go unchecked. That they refused to do so in part suggests a judicial lack of motivation to take action against sexual activity between white men and black women in Virginia, especially when conducted entirely in private. More specifically, there were relationships like that of Isaacs and West all across Virginia, some of which surely involved more prominent individuals than a Jewish merchant from a small hinterland town. Had the judges deemed interracial sex behind closed doors susceptible to prosecution in this instance, no one could predict how many other white men might be embarrassingly exposed to similar charges.[32]

The decision of the General Court still begs the question of why the Albemarle grand jury did not present the couple as being in violation of some specific statute. Surely a statutory case, either for fornication or for interracial marriage, might have held up better in court. Prosecuting the couple for violating the statute against interracial marriage would have done the most severe damage to West, Isaacs, and their family. In 1822, the white party to an interracial marriage faced six months in jail and a $30 fine, and any member of the clergy performing a marriage ceremony between people of different races had to pay a fine of $250.[33] But proving a charge of interracial marriage here probably would have proved exceedingly difficult. There is no evidence West and Isaacs ever married, and given the potentially severe legal repercussions of such an act it would have been foolish for them to have done so. Additionally, their marriage would have been a violation not only of state law but of Jewish law as well, since Nancy West was not Jewish.

It is worth observing that even if the couple had been married, ambiguities surrounding Nancy West's status might have made it difficult to bring a case of a racial nature against her and Isaacs. To be defined as "mulatto" under Virginia law in 1822, a person had to have at least "one-quarter" African ancestry.[34] Thomas West was white and presumably descended entirely from Europeans. To use the fractional language of the time, his daughter therefore would have been, at most, "half black." But perhaps she was even less than that. Whites in her community certainly appear to have known her ancestry, and in numerous documents she is described as a "free mulatto woman." Yet when she registered as a free person of color with the county court in 1837, she was described as being of "light complexion."[35] Her brother James legally married a white woman, Susannah Harlow, in Albemarle County in 1794, suggesting that his (and Nancy's) mother's ancestry may have been mixed enough for her children with a white man to become legally white.[36] Had a case of interracial marriage been brought against West and Isaacs, then, proving conclusively that West fell within the guidelines of the racial definition statute making her a mulatto perhaps could have been accomplished but it might have been complicated. Once the "blood" aspect of her racial identity became an admissible legal question, then how the white community treated her would have played a role in determining her status. At least two of her children — Tucker and Frederick — were educated with white children in local schools, and one local man testified in a separate lawsuit that her nieces and nephews (the children of James Henry West and Susannah Harlow) were "esteemed, received and accepted as white men, were educated with white children and required to perform and did perform Militia and other duties, required only of white men, and allowed to intermarry without objection on the score of blood, with white women."[37] Perhaps a case could be made that Nancy West, too, was effectively a white woman. In antebellum Virginia, race may have seemed fixed in law, but it was far more malleable in practice. The limitations of the public record make it difficult to speculate about how Nancy West and her family envisioned their own racial identities, but West's color, ancestry, and local standing all could have clouded the possibility of using race against her in a prosecution for racial intermarriage.[38]

Proving a case of statutory fornication, on the other hand, should have been relatively easy and straightforward. That the couple had had sexual intercourse was evident, and even the General Court conceded that from the evidence presented by the grand jury "the existence of a statutory offence may be inferred."[39] It is not entirely clear why the Albemarle County grand jury chose not to pursue a charge based on an infraction of the antifornication statute. Possibly it was just a tactical legal mistake. But perhaps the grand jury wanted to use its presentment to express a broader sense of moral outrage than was suggested by the language of the fornication statute, which included nothing specifically about race. From this perspective, bringing West and Isaacs up on charges was less about punishing them than about publicly rebuking and humiliating them with a reminder that although they might consider their family legitimate, the white community did not.

Ultimately, even if West and Isaacs had been found guilty of violating antifornication laws, their punishment would have been mild, just a $10 fine.[40] Despite the revulsion white Virginians expressed publicly toward sex across the color line, there was very little the law could do to stop it. Because West and Isaacs were not married and there were no laws that imposed strict penalties for illicit sex of any sort, no one could really prevent the couple from living together and building a family—unless the community was willing literally to run them out of town. When confronted with interracial sexual relationships, however, whites in Charlottesville, like whites generally across the state before the Civil War, seem to have had no inclination to take such extreme action.[41] Even if some people were so inclined, West and Isaacs probably had enough support from other members of the white community to prevent it. More than anything else, the presentment issued against Nancy West and David Isaacs demonstrates that their family was always vulnerable to legal harassment and that its legitimacy could always at least be called into question. The case brought against them was mostly a psychological ploy, intended to anger and instill insecurity precisely at a time when West, Isaacs, and their children were trying to build a new sense of familial intimacy by sharing a household. Ironically, with its decision the General Court effectively, if not legally, recognized the relationship of David Isaacs and Nancy West as what we might call a common-law marriage. No statutory case of fornication was ever made against them, but living under the duress of pending criminal charges for nearly five years may well have wrought psychological damage upon the couple and their family nonetheless.

Surely David Isaacs and Nancy West knew that attempting to live openly as husband and wife and establish adjacent businesses might arouse the hostility of some of their neighbors and possibly even invite criminal prosecution. The question remains why they made such a move. Certainly Isaacs and West wanted to live together with their children because they were a family. Moreover, immediate practical concerns may have played a role, because David Isaacs's house was much bigger than Nancy West's, which likely was very cramped with as many as seven children—at least two of whom, Jane and Thomas, were actually adults—sharing a relatively small space. In fact, between 1802 and 1833 David Isaacs added one-story wings onto either side of his home, no doubt in part to make room for the increasing numbers of residents.[42] Yet it is clear the couple also had long-term concerns about their family's economic stability and security, concerns that could be alleviated considerably through their new arrangement. Solidifying their relationship as domestic partners was part of a conscious effort to strengthen the security of their respective — and, subsequently, their collective — finances. That they did so successfully solely because of the illegality of their relationship could only have antagonized their white accusers even more.

By 1820, if David Isaacs's economic position was established, it was not necessarily secure. As a merchant, he could prosper if he were smart and careful, but the assumption of debt and extension of credit that accompanied his enterprise also entailed a great deal of risk. Misfortune or carelessness could produce financial ruin. David Isaacs fully understood the vagaries of the market, having sued at least seven different people for debt between 1810 and 1822 alone.[43] In addition to the uncertainties inherent to David Isaacs's own business, when Isaiah Isaacs died he left behind not only an estate of real and personal property but also four young children, for whom David took primary responsibility. Although two of Isaiah's children had died by the early 1820s, David Isaacs's entanglement of his own financial responsibilities with those of his deceased brother and his surviving niece and nephew made his economic situation even more precarious than that of other merchants.[44] With no bankruptcy laws in Virginia in the 1820s, what a man in David Isaacs's position needed perhaps more than anything else was a form of insurance — a knowledge that he had somewhere to turn for support and assistance should catastrophe befall him.

As a free person of color, Nancy West also needed security above anything else. In some ways, by 1819 she was fortunate. Both capital and land were typically beyond the reach of free blacks in Virginia, most of whom lived in dire poverty at the very bottom of the socioeconomic ladder. Free women of color in particular confronted severely restricted employment opportunities, but throughout her life Nancy West had been able to rely on white male patrons — her father, Thomas Bell, David Isaacs — to help shield her from trying economic circumstances. Still, her relationship with Isaacs was tenuous because it lacked legal sanction, meaning that she could be assured of Isaacs's protection only so long as he lived. Despite having some resources of her own, had David Isaacs died anytime before 1819, Nancy West would have been left heavily dependent on his estate for survival. The debts inevitably accrued by Isaacs as a merchant and as an executor would have to be paid in the event of his death. There was therefore no guarantee that West could rely on inheritance for financial stability.[45]

Nancy West's financial interests, in turn, were inseparable from those of her children, for if she could not survive economically, neither could they. Free women of color frequently had to raise their families alone, because they generally outnumbered free black men and were usually too poor to purchase enslaved spouses. Again, West was in a privileged position so long as David Isaacs lived, but in 1819 he was nearly sixty years old and five of the couple's children were still under age thirteen. Jane Isaacs, the couple's oldest daughter, was twenty-three and a milliner, and perhaps able to assist her mother both financially and as a secondary caregiver if necessary, but without Isaacs's support the entire family would have had to struggle like so many other free families of color.[46] In addition to their individual interests, then, David Isaacs and Nancy West shared collective concerns regarding their children. Together they faced the anxieties of continuing to support their offspring until they all reached maturity, as well as of guaranteeing the security of their children's futures as they came of age.[47]

The structure of Isaacs and West's relationship after 1819 nicely served their mutual financial interests and concerns. For David Isaacs, having Nancy West by his side both domestically and economically meant that he had some financial security should disaster strike. He could rely on her as an outside source of capital to vouch for him, provide security in case of debt, and even support him if he went completely bankrupt. Living, working, and owning land alongside David Isaacs, meanwhile, operated to Nancy West's distinct advantage as well. She gained access not only to greater wealth and potential income but, more significantly, to some degree of independence. If anything were to happen to David Isaacs after these maneuvers, Nancy West would still have sufficient means to support herself. This improved financial relationship also served the interests of the couple's children. If Isaacs lost his money or died or both, West was in a better position to support the couple's children as they grew. Finally, by increasing her wealth and landholdings over time, West would be able to pass some or all of that wealth on to her children as they got older and needed financial footholds of their own.

Throughout her life Nancy West always acquired land from members of her own family or that of David Isaacs, and Isaacs himself repeatedly facilitated West's economic mobility by helping ensure that she had significant resources independent of his own wealth. Like the property she had procured in 1803, the property West bought in downtown Charlottesville in 1820, lot 33, was land that had originally belonged to her father. Thomas West had rented the lot to Isaiah Isaacs during his lifetime and bequeathed it in his will to James Henry West's four children, each of whom held one-quarter interest. Between 1817 and 1819 David Isaacs purchased three-quarters of the lot from Nancy West's nieces and nephews. Just over a year later, Isaacs sold his entire share to Nancy West for $600, and West herself purchased the final quarter from her niece Susannah in 1823.[48] By the time West bought Isaacs's portion of the property in 1820, she had sold her land on the outskirts of town to a free man of color named William Spinner for exactly $600, but there had been legal complications in the exchange. Consequently, she had not yet received any payment, and would not until 1829.[49] She was earning her own money as a baker, but it still seems unlikely that West could have had $600 saved from her own income alone to pay Isaacs for the land. Instead, it appears that David Isaacs purchased most of the land in pieces, specifically for the purpose of then transferring it to Nancy West, with her purchase money then either given or loaned from him. At the very least, it was an unusual exchange, one made much easier for West by Isaacs's intervention. In his will, despite the fact that he had already sold the land legally to West, Isaacs made a specific point of relinquishing "all the right, title, interest, claim or demand" he had in the property. Presumably this was to be certain that no one would question the land transfer or suggest that Nancy West's land was in reality still owned in any way by Isaacs or paid for with his funds. It was important that anyone who asked know that this property belonged exclusively and entirely to Nancy West.[50]

In 1824 West paid $400 for the northern half of another lot, number 19, directly across the street from the land she had purchased in 1820. By this time it is certainly possible that she had enough money saved both from her business and from rents and profits collected on her other property to conduct the transaction entirely on her own accord.[51] Yet David Isaacs mediated this exchange as well, because the seller was his nephew Hays Isaacs, for whom David continued to be partially responsible as executor of his brother's will.[52] West no longer needed David Isaacs's financial backing, but this familial connection gave her privileged access to land she might not have had otherwise. Finally, in 1827 West purchased another Charlottesville property, lot 25, directly from Isaacs, who himself had bought it from a member of the Taliaferro family, who in turn had purchased it from the estate of Thomas West.[53] David Isaacs did not have to sell land to West at all. But the couple astutely realized that dividing accumulated wealth between them ultimately was more stable and secure than simply aggrandizing Isaacs's estate. The only other time Nancy West ever acquired land was when David Isaacs bequeathed her in his will partial interest in his property, some of which she eventually purchased outright from his estate.[54]

Obviously, every free family, white or black, worried about its finances, and many of both races kept property ownership within their extended families. In this respect there was nothing unusual about David Isaacs and Nancy West.[55] The couple was unusual, however, because even as antebellum Virginia law deprived them of an official marriage, effectively not only were they married but the law enabled them to stabilize their finances and hedge against economic peril in ways few white couples could ever have. In most Virginia families, married women had practically no authority to hold or dispose of property until 1877. Instead, by law every wife became a *feme covert*, meaning that upon marriage a woman surrendered ownership of all her personal and real property to her husband. A husband could not sell his wife's real estate entirely at will, but he could use it as he chose and keep all profits derived from it. That same property, though, could be lost by both parties to a marriage in the event that creditors came calling. One of the few ways for a married woman to retain any property rights was to have a trust established for her in equity by someone else, usually by her father. But almost invariably, a trust came with conditions that restricted its use. The legalities of trusts were so complicated that, over time, the equity system yielded increased litigation.[56]

Yet because of the unusual nature of their relationship, Nancy West and David Isaacs effectively circumvented and subverted the restrictions of Virginia's property laws. West could never claim a dower right in Isaacs's estate as a legally married woman might, but because she and Isaacs were not married she eluded the restrictions of coverture. Even more valuable than a dowry, she could own her own property outright without interference or conditions on its use and thus did not need the protection for legally married women that a dowry provided. Race and gender barriers in antebellum Virginia should have both worked against the possibility of Nancy West accumulating thousands of dollars of real estate, but with regard to property rights Virginia law made her position stronger precisely by the means it attempted to restrict her. She was a free black woman who, specifically because she was "married" (in fact but not in law) to a white man, had more economic independence, strength, and mobility than nearly any married white woman. Furthermore, while white families could protect a married woman's property from creditors through equity, the delimited conditions of its use restricted the free flow of capital both for families and for the larger society, and almost always precluded strategies of cooperation that might otherwise maximize a couple's and their family's economic potential through more flexible and collective uses of capital. Nancy West and David Isaacs were not bound by any such fetters. Many white couples, in fact, may have wished they could have enjoyed the economic dynamics of this relationship. That West and Isaacs could structure their financial lives so advantageously even as and, ironically, because they lived and worked together but stayed unmarried must have been especially galling.[57]

Nancy West's and David Isaacs's financial arrangements would be put to the test even before the General Court handed down its opinion in the state's case against the couple. In the spring of 1826, a number of Charlottesville merchants sued Isaacs for debts they believed he owed them in his capacity as executor of his brother's will. By the mid-1830s, more than half a dozen Charlottesville business owners sued Isaacs in three different lawsuits that dragged on through the courts for twenty years, past the time of Isaacs's death. As the suits progressed, the various plaintiffs demonstrated their willingness to use West and Isaacs's relationship against them in order to head off the couple's defense. That they tried at all demonstrates again how white men in conflict might use evidence of an interracial sexual relationship instrumentally, as a means of attack in pursuit of a larger goal. That they failed reinforces the notion that while whites might have some success in legally harassing an interracial couple, they had greater difficulty in achieving more tangible benefits.

When David Isaacs's nephew Hays Isaacs turned twenty-one in February 1824, he came into his full inheritance from his father Isaiah. It seems he celebrated by going on a spending spree, mostly in Charlottesville. Local merchants and tradesmen familiar with both the young man and his financial situation willingly extended him credit, and Hays accumulated debts at more than half a dozen establishments totaling well over $1,000. Unfortunately, Hays was financially inexperienced and irresponsible, more comfortable with buying and spending than with saving and accounting. By the end of 1824, some of the Charlottesville merchants tried to collect, only to have Hays refuse to pay, claiming he had no money. Nimrod Bramham and William Bibb consequently sued him for debt in Richmond, where he had also purchased some items from that branch of Bramham and Bibb's mercantile firm. In March 1826 a court in Henrico County ruled in favor of the plaintiffs. Hays Isaacs promptly left Virginia and never returned.[58]

Just a month later, Joel Yancey, another Charlottesville merchant, filed suit in chancery in Albemarle County against David Isaacs. Yancey believed that as executor of Isaiah Isaacs's estate, David Isaacs still held a large sum of money for Hays Isaacs. Because Hays owed Yancey more than $400 but was unable or unwilling to pay his debts (and, for that matter, could not even be located), Yancey's suit maintained that David Isaacs ought to be held responsible for paying his nephew's creditors. In June 1826 the merchant John R. Jones, who owned a store directly across the street from Isaacs and Nancy West, filed a lawsuit similar to Yancey's, and their cases were eventually joined together. In 1830 Bramham and Bibb, along with five other men to whom Hays owed money, sued David Isaacs as well.[59]

John Jones filed a statement that detailed his individual claims but also addressed complaints that all the creditors had about how Isaacs had administered his nephew's inheritance. Hays had signed away to David Isaacs all claims to his inheritance very soon after he came of age. Jones argued, however, that Isaacs had hurried his nephew—who in any event was "totally without experience" in analyzing financial accounts— through the release process, even paying an attorney $100 just to get Hays's signature quickly. David Isaacs, Jones alleged, had mishandled the accounting for his brother's estate and wanted to procure his nephew's release "for the purpose of closing the door to any investigation" into the accounts. Furthermore, Jones claimed David Isaacs knew that Hays had amassed substantial debts. By getting Hays to relinquish his rights, the elder Isaacs hoped to avoid having to fulfill his nephew's obligations and instead keep what remained of Hays's inheritance himself. Jones demanded that Hays's debts to him be paid from David Isaacs's accounts.[60]

Isaacs responded in March 1827. First, he argued that he had never wanted to be his brother's executor at all. The other men named as executors "declined incurring the trouble and responsibility." As Isaiah's only brother and closest relative David Isaacs felt a "sacred duty" to take the job himself, but claimed he "indulged no hope or expectation" that it would be "either safe or profitable to him." Isaacs further claimed that he had never cheated his nephew out of what rightfully belonged to him. He explained that Hays "was and had been unsettled and itenerant" and was considering leaving Virginia when he turned twenty-one. In addition, the accounts of Hays's inheritance suggested to both uncle and nephew that when Hays came of age, the amount being held for him would be roughly equivalent to bills that still had to be paid and to money owed David Isaacs in his capacity as executor. Consequently, they had mutually agreed that Hays would release his claims and let his uncle work out the details. David Isaacs insisted that the $100 paid to his attorney was for services rendered and not merely to obtain Hays's signature, as Jones's suit alleged. Furthermore, David Isaacs maintained he had wanted to make a final settlement of Hays's accounts because he feared he might become responsible for the young man's future entanglements and possibly suffer "loss and, probably, great injustice." Rather than using any "undue means" to procure Hays's release, trying to swindle his nephew, or avoid investigation, David Isaacs contended he had tried to end his financial connection to Hays precisely so he would never have to face the kind of lawsuit he now confronted. So far as he was concerned, his dealings with Hays Isaacs and his inheritance were complete, and he maintained that he could not be held responsible for any additional debts Hays had incurred.[61]

Witness testimony in the case centered on two issues. The first was Hays Isaacs's alleged financial incompetence. V. W. Southall, David Isaacs's lawyer, testified that Hays had seemed satisfied with his uncle's handling of his accounts. Although he did not know Hays very well, Southall believed the young man capable of making his own financial decisions, but he conceded that Hays did not "take time to examine the items composing the account." The merchant Isaac Raphael testified that Hays would not do blindly whatever David Isaacs told him to, but that Hays was also not "capable of investigating complicated accounts and of making judicious contracts about his property." Daniel Keith, Charlottesville's constable, lived one block from David Isaacs and was asked whether he thought Hays capable of handling money or property. Finding Hays generally to be "foolishly extravagant," Keith answered: "I knew him well. And think him incapable of managing either."[62]

As the plaintiffs' lawyer probed these witnesses for their assessments of Hays Isaacs, he also hammered away at David Isaacs's relationship with

Nancy West and their daughter Jane. Opie Norris was asked if Nancy West and Jane Isaacs were "both members of the family" of David Isaacs, "the first in the character of wife, and the second as daughter." Norris, giving an honest but disingenuous answer, probably in an effort to protect his friends, replied that Nancy and Jane lived in Isaacs's house but that he did not know for certain "that Nancy West is the wife of the defendant Isaacs or Jane Isaacs the daughter — only from public rumor." Daniel Keith, meanwhile, said that he knew Nancy and Jane and that "Nancy lives with [David Isaacs] as wife and Jane is called the daughter." Keith, Norris, and Isaac Raphael all also testified that they believed that around the time Hays turned twenty-one Nancy West had purchased his house and land in Charlottesville and that both Jane and Nancy might have received some slaves from him.[63]

David Isaacs and Nancy West had had their grand jury presentment dismissed just six months prior to the testimony in the Yancey and Jones lawsuit, only to find themselves caught in an antebellum catch-22. Their original legal troubles involved the accusation that they were not a legitimate family. Now Yancey and Jones argued that Isaacs's financial transactions were of questionable legality because he and Nancy West *were* in fact a family. The point of clarifying that David Isaacs's relationship with Nancy West was that of husband and wife was never overtly made in the case papers, but the implication was obvious: David Isaacs had taken advantage of his unusual relationship with Nancy West to acquire real and personal property from his nephew for himself. By making West the purchaser, the argument went, Isaacs was trying to avoid the charge of a conflict of interest that might arise had he purchased the property directly, but because West was effectively if not legally Isaacs's wife he could still enjoy the benefits from its use. Similarly, while Jane Isaacs nominally owned some of the slaves once belonging to Hays Isaacs, in reality David Isaacs had merely boosted his own holdings through his daughter's ownership. These transparent ruses, Yancey and Jones suggested, were clear abuses of David Isaacs's power as executor of Isaiah Isaacs's estate. He had exploited his own inexperienced nephew sheerly for his own financial enrichment.

It is impossible to know how well or how poorly Hays Isaacs understood his financial affairs or, for that matter, how much of an effort David Isaacs made to keep his nephew informed. At the very least, several aspects of the situation looked suspicious. David Isaacs's own lawyer admitted that Hays hardly glanced at his uncle's accounts before relinquishing his claims. That Nancy West and Jane Isaacs purchased land and may have procured slaves from Hays in December 1824, just as Bramham and Bibb were filing a suit against the young man in Richmond, suggests that David Isaacs and Nancy West indeed colluded to protect Hays's assets from being lost to pay off his debts. These transactions were certainly a conflict of interest for David Isaacs, because, even if they were undertaken at some level to protect Hays, any economic improvements in the lives of Nancy West and Jane Isaacs were improvements in David Isaacs's life as well. Jones and Yancey had a point when they drew attention to the peculiarities of the Isaacs-West family finances.[64]

David Isaacs's defense only weakly responded to the accusations made against him. Undoubtedly, he honestly wanted to be rid of any financial responsibility for his nephew. Hays's reckless spending placed David Isaacs at enormous risk, and we have already seen how much the elder Isaacs valued security. Ultimately, though, David Isaacs's only substantive response to the charges of Hays's creditors was a demand that the letter of the law be upheld. Regardless of what others might think of Hays's fiscal capacities, David Isaacs argued, he had never coerced Hays into signing anything. He and Hays Isaacs had a legally binding agreement between them, and no third party ought to have the authority to challenge its legitimacy. As David wrote in response to Bramham and Bibb's lawsuit against him, elaborating on an argument made in his response to Yancey and Jones, Hays had never attempted to retract his agreement to the arrangement between them, nor had Hays ever intimated that he believed he might have made a mistake. Consequently, David Isaacs claimed he could not "see the principle of equity which authorizes other and third persons to impugn or question the right and authority of a legatee or distributee . . . after their arrival to age, upon considerations sufficient to themselves, to release and acquit an executor or guardian of any claim."[65]

The Albemarle Circuit Superior Court of Law and Chancery ruled against David Isaacs on May 16, 1834. Based on its own readings of Isaacs's accounts, the court found over $2,500 still owed Hays as an inheritance. It ordered that the young man's debts be paid from this sum and that David Isaacs turn over to Hays directly whatever money remained. Essentially, the court accepted the claims of Yancey, Jones, Bramham and Bibb, and Hays's other creditors, all of whose cases the court ruled on together. Hays Isaacs's release to his uncle was technically legal, but the court ruled it could not be construed to have a negative impact on any parties aside from David and Hays Isaacs. David Isaacs, the court agreed, had procured his nephew's release "as a protection against the claims of the creditors." Additionally, the court took David Isaacs to task for his handling of his nephew's estate, suggesting he had misled his nephew for his own convenience and probably his own gain. David was not guilty of any criminal activity, but the court asserted that Hays's release was "not founded an actual settlement, in which every thing is explained; but obtained, as it would seem, with the view of preventing the necessity of such a settlement." The court mentioned nothing about David Isaacs's relationship with Nancy West or the financial transactions between her and Hays Isaacs.[66]

David Isaacs immediately prepared to appeal the court's verdict. In order to do so, however, he had to have someone post security equivalent to at least double the amount of the judgment issued against him. If Isaacs lost his appeal and then had insufficient funds to fulfill the court's decision, whoever posted security for him would be obliged to pay. Nancy West was available to assist, as was Jane, who now went by Jane West after having married her cousin Nathaniel H. West in 1832. On June 27, 1834, Nancy, Jane, and Nathaniel West all entered into a bond with David Isaacs, Hays Isaacs, and his creditors. The Wests collectively pledged over $7,000 as security, the entirety of their estates. Once again, David Isaacs and Nancy West proved their relationship invested them with financial strength and a kind of mutual reliance unavailable to others. Yet because they derived their strength only from being inextricably connected to one another, their fortunes still rose and fell together. The Wests' gesture entailed enormous risk.[67]

The same day that Isaacs filed his appeal, Hays Isaacs's creditors jointly filed a bill of exceptions with the Albemarle court claiming that the security posted by the Wests was invalid. First, they argued that Nancy West, though a "woman of colour," was "the wife *de facto* of David Isaacs . . . now living, and for many years having lived with the said David Isaacs as his wife, and which connection is notorious in the neighborhood in which they reside." Second, they alleged that any property West claimed to own in reality belonged to Isaacs. She may have purchased the land herself, but they asserted that she did so entirely "with the *funds* of the said David Isaacs." The creditors further tacked on the claims that Jane West could not enter into a valid contract, because she was a *feme covert* consequent to her marriage to Nathaniel West, and that Nathaniel West, in turn, was himself "notoriously insolvent" and owned no property at all. Taken as a whole, the intent of these objections was to head off David Isaacs's appeal of the judgment by accusing Isaacs of trying to post security for himself, because all the pledged money really belonged to him. Being from Charlottesville, Hays's creditors knew that David Isaacs's most realistic sources of sufficient security lay with his own family. If they could demonstrate a reason for the court to reject the legitimacy of the Wests' security, David might well be unable to find another person to put up any money in their place. He would have to start paying off his nephew's debts immediately.[68]

Nathaniel and Jane West paid no land taxes in Charlottesville in 1834 and could have contributed little to David Isaacs's security. The crux of the matter, then, was whether Nancy West actually controlled an estate legally distinct from that of David Isaacs. The objections specifically addressing her shared the claim that she did not. In the first, the creditors claimed that Isaacs and West lived as husband and wife, and while their relationship could not be recognized in law as a marriage because it crossed the color line, in this instance it ought to be treated as if it were a legitimate union. If Nancy West was therefore a married woman, she could not possibly post security for David Isaacs because her estate was legally his estate. Realizing that these grounds for objection might carry little weight with any court, because the fact remained that the couple could not be and was not legally married, the creditors filed their second objection. Here, they claimed that any property Nancy West appeared to own was merely a ruse designed to conceal David Isaacs's holdings.[69]

Hays Isaacs's creditors had good reason for wanting their money quickly. Whether or not Nancy West actually owned her own property, they had seen how David Isaacs relied on her whenever he got into financial trouble or looked for some economic advantage. What would happen if Isaacs fell into new legal difficulties while he appealed the judgment in this case? By the time a court ruled on the creditors' lawsuit, Isaacs and West could both lose their fortunes, leaving the men to whom Hays Isaacs owed money no possibility of collection, at least not without additional legal proceedings. Each of the objections to Nancy West's posting of security was logically sound, and they reflected the effort by Hays's creditors to object on every possible ground. When placed together in a single document, however, they were logically inconsistent. In the first objection the creditors asked the court to acknowledge the legitimacy of West and Isaacs's domestic partnership on equal footing with a legal marriage, thereby invalidating Nancy West's property ownership. In the second objection, meanwhile, it was taken for granted that the relationship could not be legally recognized. The point here was not that Nancy West *could* not own property, but that in fact she *did* not. In the same document, then, Nancy West was both married to a white man and not married to a white man. She both owned property and yet could not own property. Having all these claims be true was impossible, but the creditors cannot be blamed for trying. The failure of state law to define the relationship of West and Isaacs effectively meant that any attempt to confront the couple legally would be absurdly slippery. Nancy West and David Isaacs fell through the cracks between the laws and exploited them. Without explanation, the Albemarle court rejected the bill of exceptions, the Wests' posted security was accepted, and the appeal proceeded. After all, as the General Court had determined seven years earlier, little could be done about David Isaacs and Nancy West without raising a host of other difficult and uncomfortable legal issues.

David Isaacs died in 1837. In his will, he provided that Nancy West could continue to reside in the house in which his family lived and worked for as long as she lived, and he directed that it be sold on her death and the proceeds divided into seven portions for the couple's children. He allowed West to select any items of personal property from the estate she wished to keep and ordered that most of the remainder then be sold at public auction, with the proceeds to be given to a charity selected by his executors. She chose some cooking utensils, a few tables and a dozen chairs, a bureau, a bed and bedstead, an expensive metal clock, and David Isaacs's sleeve buttons and watch chain. At public auction in April 1837, Isaacs's son Tucker purchased some mugs, bowls, and other kitchen accessories, and his daughter Julia Ann's husband Eston Hemings bought some similar items. Numerous members of the Scott family, who were neighbors, family friends, and distant relatives by marriage, also made some purchases, including Isaacs's copy of the writings of Thomas Jefferson.[70] Little if any of the proceeds from the estate sale went to charity. David Isaacs's estate had a fair number of debts, no doubt compounded by the Panic of 1837. Isaacs's administrator, Egbert R. Watson (Isaacs's chosen executors had failed to qualify), spent more than a decade slowly paying off his liabilities, mostly by collecting debts still owed Isaacs and through rents, profits, and sales of property owned by his estate.[71]

In some ways, the late 1830s and early 1840s were years of great success for Nancy West. David Isaacs's death undoubtedly was painful and there were financial difficulties attendant to settling his estate. West, though, was able to sell and transfer property to the couple's children and their families, bringing to fruition what had likely been her and Isaacs's long-term goal of insuring self-sufficiency in adulthood for their offspring. As David Isaacs neared and then passed the end of his life, and West entered her later years — she was fifty-five by the time of Isaacs's death — this goal became increasingly imperative. In 1836, Nancy West gave a portion of lot 33 to Jane "in consideration of the natural love and affection which she bears to the said Jane West."[72] Nancy probably lived with her daughter for a number of years on this spot as well, because in September 1837 she arranged for a five-year rental of the house she and David Isaacs had lived in, most likely to help pay off Isaacs's debts. Although Isaacs had "loaned" West the property, rental fees accrued to his estate, which technically continued to own the property.[73] Back in her own house in 1842, Nancy West sold the property next door (lot 35) to Eston Hemings, and the following year Tucker Isaacs purchased a small piece of land from his mother on lot 33 next to his sister Jane.[74] By the end of 1843, Nancy West still lived in the house she had shared with David Isaacs and paid taxes on the land, but because Isaacs's estate still retained control over the property she no longer owned anything outright.[75]

Whatever pride came from being able to foster her children's independence, Nancy West still had her own lingering fiscal responsibilities. In early 1846, the Richmond Court of Appeals rejected David Isaacs's appeal from the Albemarle chancery court, but by this point the assets held by Isaacs's estate were not nearly enough to cover the sums owed to Hays and to the numerous merchants of Charlottesville. With accumulated interest and inflation over more than a decade, the debts now totaled around $5,000. It was only a matter of time until Egbert Watson let Nancy West know he had no option but to ask her to auction off her house. In June 1846 she consented to the sale, but given her own pledge to pay Hays's debts if David Isaacs could not, she really had very little choice. Refusing to relinquish her family home, she bought most of the property back herself for $2,300, while Tucker, who was also acting by this year as his mother's financial agent, bought a small piece of the property for himself.[76] As the time drew near for her to make her first payment for this purchase, however, Nancy West found herself low on funds. If she could not make the payment, the property would be resold, and if the purchase price failed to cover the debts owed by Isaacs, West would still be held accountable to pay what remained.

Even as the decree of the Court of Appeals placed Nancy West in a vulnerable position yet again, it simultaneously provided her with the means to overcome it. The court ordered David Isaacs's estate to pay all of Hays Isaacs's debts, and in keeping with Hays's apparent tendency to borrow money from nearly everyone he knew and not pay it back, he had still had an unpaid loan from Nancy West. In November 1846 Nancy West sued Hays Isaacs in chancery. The story she told in her deposition to the court went back to her land purchase from Hays in the 1820s. As discussed earlier, Hays had sold West half of lot 19 in Charlottesville in 1824. The other half of the lot belonged to Isaiah Isaacs's living daughter, Fanny. In 1825 or 1826, West recalled, Hays offered to buy out his sister's interest and sell the rest of the property to West, but he needed to borrow some money to make the purchase. West loaned him $200, but he never made the purchase, never returned her money, and, by the 1840s, had long since left the state. West believed at the time of her statement that he lived in Arkansas, leaving her no prospect of collecting directly from him.[77] With more than twenty years of accumulated interest added to the $200 Hays owed Nancy West, his debt would go a long way toward helping her cover the price of her home, and she practically begged the court to grant her lawsuit. It was her only chance to recover her money. The Albemarle chancery court granted the case, and West and Egbert Watson (who, as administrator of David Isaacs's estate, also administered Hays's accounts) settled out of court in 1850. Finally, David Isaacs's debts were paid, and Nancy West kept her home — barely.[78]

Undoubtedly, Nancy West felt somewhat desperate when she filed her plea to the court in 1846. She herself very nearly crashed financially right along with her deceased husband, and her personal holdings were always at least partially conditional on his financial circumstances. But while she would have had to move from her home had she been unable to scrape together the money to pay for it, it is unlikely that Nancy West would have been relegated to the poorhouse. David Isaacs assisted her in procuring assets independent of his own both so that she could survive financially without him and so that he might depend on her if he needed to. Nancy West implemented precisely the same strategy in the next generation. Because she had already transferred so much of her own wealth to her children, by the 1840s West had established a safety net both for them and for herself. A blend of insecurity and stability thus inhered to Nancy West's position throughout her life in Charlottesville, both domestically and financially. She was effectively married and raised a large family, but the legality of that marriage, and consequently the legitimacy of that family, was always in doubt. She attained wealth and passed significant amounts of that wealth on to her children, but her personal fortunes depended on the financial strength of David Isaacs, which in the end was unsure. Always, the dynamics that obtained in the domestic and the financial overlapped and were integrally related.

In 1850, Nancy West sold almost all the land she still owned in Charlottesville and shortly thereafter moved to Chillicothe, a town in Ross County, Ohio, and the home of many free people of color who had emigrated from Virginia. She died there late in 1856.[79] For much of her life, Nancy West's economic stature and her domestic relationship with David Isaacs seem to have meant that the legal and social hostility facing free people of color in Virginia did not greatly affect her desire to remain where she had been born. In 1832, for example, even as the Virginia legislature passed a series of restrictive laws against free blacks and slaves and gave specific permission to the trustees of Charlottesville to limit the ability of free blacks to gather within town limits, West and her son Frederick started and ran a newspaper known as the *Charlottesville Chronicle* from a building she owned. If Nancy West ever thought about leaving Virginia before David Isaacs died, her actions do not indicate she had any intention of doing so, and at least for some years after his death her transfer of property to her children implies that she assumed they would stay in Charlottesville as well.[80]

Surely the changing political, legal, and social environments for free people of color in Virginia in the late 1840s and the 1850s influenced West's departure. Amid growing sectional tensions, the General Assembly passed new legislation further constraining the activities and movements of free people of color. These restrictions included a tax on free blacks to pay for their own colonization to Liberia, which both Frederick and Tucker Isaacs paid in 1850, and a renewed effort to uphold the 1806 removal law. Despite a long tenure in her community and having been born a free woman, in 1850 Nancy West found herself before the Albemarle County Court along with dozens of other free people of color and asked to prove that she was born free and was a legal resident of Virginia. Having to make this appearance must have been humiliating, and Nancy West may have accepted Virginia's clear invitation to leave the state.[81]

More than the generally hostile legal environment, the migration of Nancy West's children probably played the greatest role in her decision to move. Eston and Julia Ann Hemings had lived in Ohio at least part of the time since the late 1830s. By the late 1840s Virginia law stripped free people of color of the right to return to the state if they left, clinching Eston and Julia Ann's decision to remove to Ohio permanently, which they had done in any event by 1845. Tucker Isaacs and his wife Elizabeth Ann had also sometimes lived in southern Ohio with her parents, former Monticello slaves Joe and Edy Fossett, since the early 1840s. In 1850, while Nancy West successfully demonstrated her right to remain in Virginia, Elizabeth Ann Fossett Isaacs's circumstances were less clear. Born enslaved, she had been manumitted in 1837, but she had never received permission from the legislature to remain. It does not appear from the public record that Elizabeth Ann was ever told she had to leave the state, but she and Tucker nonetheless soon left Virginia for good. In the early 1850s Agness Isaacs, Nancy West's youngest daughter, also moved to Ohio with her husband Jerman Evans, a free man of color from Charlottesville whom she had married in 1836. By the end of 1850 Nancy West was nearly seventy years old. Her husband had long since died, and his accounts were finally settled. Three of her children had departed a Virginia that no longer wanted their presence, and she too decided to live out her days elsewhere.[82]

In the end Nancy West and David Isaacs had achieved much. They had maneuvered through the labyrinths of their local community and of Virginia law to build and maintain a forty-year relationship that should have been impossible. They established themselves as landowners, businesspeople, and parents, and had utilized their own success to place their children, whose lifetimes would traverse the Civil War and Reconstruction, in positions where they too might succeed. But each in turn would ultimately have to do so on different terms and in different circumstances and social environments than their parents, and they each chose to follow different paths. Among David Isaacs's and Nancy West's children, only Jane West remained in Charlottesville by the onset of the Civil War, and she died there a wealthy woman in 1869. Thomas Isaacs's whereabouts for much of his life are unknown. Hays Isaacs, the couple's second son (not Isaiah Isaacs's heir), died a young man in 1839. Frederick Isaacs removed to Wythe County in southwestern Virginia, where he had such difficulties with debts in the late 1830s that he ended up in jail before finally filing in 1837 for bankruptcy under recently passed Virginia laws. Agness Isaacs inherited her mother's home and property in Chillicothe and lived out her life in Ohio. So did Tucker Isaacs, whose house, according to family oral history, served as a station on the Underground Railroad. Tucker Isaacs would also bring suit against an Ohio hotel after the Civil War for refusing to rent him a room. Julia Ann Isaacs moved to Wisconsin with Eston Hemings in the early 1850s. The couple changed their last name to Jefferson and became white persons.[83]

Early in March 1837 David Isaacs's son Tucker and his son-in-law Eston Hemings mounted a wagon, drove Isaacs's corpse from Charlottesville to Richmond, and buried him in the Jewish cemetery on Shockoe Hill in the capital's north end, as provided for in his will. There is no record of who attended David Isaacs's funeral. He had not lived regularly in Richmond for over forty years, but the service surely drew some who knew Isaacs more by name than by association. Before David and his brother Isaiah moved from Richmond to Charlottesville, they had both been instrumental in founding the capital's first synagogue, Beth Shalome. Isaiah Isaacs lived in Charlottesville a dozen or so years before he died, and both he and David maintained their connections to Richmond and its Jewish community. The elder Isaacs returned to the city repeatedly for both business and social visits before his death and, with Charlottesville having no local synagogue, both men remained members of Beth Shalome and, by extension, the Jewish community of Richmond throughout their lives.[1]

If any of the funeral attendees were of suspicious minds, the men who accompanied David Isaacs's body and were said to be his family may have appeared peculiar, even out of place. Most in attendance at the funeral, though, likely were familiar with the story of Isaacs's family through gossip and other communications that traveled between communities in Richmond and Charlottesville, a social network that David Isaacs himself helped maintain. As a grocer in a hinterland town, he received many of his goods from larger firms and importers in the city and probably made the trip back and forth from Albemarle County to Richmond many times over the decades. These visits served social as well as business purposes, as Isaacs would have taken the opportunity of his presence in Richmond to visit old friends and acquaintances. If he found himself in town on a Saturday, he may have even attended services at the synagogue. No evidence exists to suggest Isaacs wanted to keep his familial ties in Charlottesville a secret from people in Richmond, a task that in any event would have been impossible, especially after his and Nancy West's criminal case came before the General Court in the 1820s.

If Nancy West herself traveled from Charlottesville for Isaacs's funeral, anyone in attendance confused by the appearance of Tucker Isaacs and Eston Hemings would have immediately been able to fit together the pieces of the puzzle, for while interracial families may have been out of the ordinary in antebellum Virginia they were far from unheard of, something at least a few of Richmond's Jewish citizens knew full well. A number of David Isaacs's longtime colleagues or members of their families surely came to see him buried, some of whom had very personal knowledge of such circumstances. Members of the Judah family, including Manuel Judah, an auctioneer and liquor trader who had helped found the synagogue, were surely at the funeral. Manuel's brother Isaac Judah had, like David Isaacs, been a merchant and a founder of Beth Shalome. He had also been the congregation's first minister.[2] A lifelong bachelor, Judah died in 1827 and provided in his will that two female slaves, Maria and Betsey, be hired out by his nephew for fifteen years, at the end of which time both women would be freed and given all the money earned during their hiring period. Either Maria or Betsey or both seem to have been Isaac Judah's sexual partner, for "on consideration of their attachment and fidelity" and his "natural regard for them," Judah proceeded to leave tracts of land in Richmond and hundreds of dollars apiece to two "free mulatto boys," Philip Norborne Wythe and Benjamin Wythe. Philip and Benjamin were brothers and Judah's sons, suggested not only by the language of Judah's will expressing his attachment to the two but also by one of the will's other provisions. Judah, aware of the possibility that one or more of his white family members might challenge the will, stipulated that any legatee who tried to interfere with the arrangements for Benjamin and Philip Wythe or for Betsey and Maria would have his or her legacy stripped.[3] As merchants and prominent Richmond Jews, David Isaacs and Isaac Judah shared much in business and in their social networks. The similarities in their families could have only bolstered their personal and professional connections.

Also undoubtedly attending David Isaacs's funeral were numerous members of the Myers and Hays families, whose presence dominated Beth Shalome's membership list in the 1830s. Particularly notable in the crowd would have been Gustavus A. Myers, Richmond's most prominent Jewish citizen from the 1830s through the Civil War. Born in 1801 to

Samuel Myers, a wealthy merchant and importer, and Judith Hays Myers, a member of an affluent New England Jewish family, Gustavus Myers became a lawyer and had one of the largest legal practices in antebellum Richmond. By 1827 he held a seat on the Richmond City Council, which he retained until 1855, serving from 1843 to 1855 as the council's president. In 1833 he married the widowed daughter of a former Virginia governor, and before he died in 1869 Myers helped found the Virginia Historical Society, contributed to several literary journals, was a prominent Mason, directed both the Richmond, Fredericksburg, and Petersburg Railroad and the Mutual Assurance Society, and served in Virginia's House of Delegates.[4]

Gustavus Myers also presided over an extremely complex interracial family occupying multiple households in Court End, Richmond's wealthiest and most elite neighborhood, just north of Capitol Square. In 1822 Myers, twenty-one years old and then still a bachelor, had a child with Nelly Forrester, a free woman of color living in the home of Gustavus's relatives Moses and Sally Myers. The child, Richard Gustavus Forrester, was raised in the household of Gustavus's aunts, Catharine and Slowey Hays. After Slowey Hays's death in 1836, Gustavus Myers, who was now married and living around the corner from his aunts, sent his fourteen-year-old son to Canada for an education. Also shortly after Slowey Hays died, Narcissa Wilson joined Catharine Hays's household. Wilson, the daughter of Ellen Wilson, a free woman of color, and Judah Touro, a wealthy New Orleans merchant and a man who had courted Catharine Hays early in life in addition to being her cousin, married Richard Forrester in 1840 in Canada.[5]

At the time of David Isaacs's death in 1837, Gustavus Myers was rich, politically powerful, well known and respected by Jews and gentiles alike, and the head of an extended family deeply immersed in interracialism. Perhaps better than any of David Isaacs's other acquaintances, Myers understood just how important and how complicated interracial relationships could be for families in Virginia. In turn, the Myers-Hays family helped Isaacs develop his own personal understanding of the social landscape of central Virginia, where connections to Virginia's capital opened doors not only to larger worlds of religion and commerce, but also to a larger shared experience of interracial family links. Just as interracial sexual relationships helped tie communities of slaves, free blacks, and whites together between Virginia's countryside and its towns, so too did they help join those who dwelled in towns to the cities.[6]

The existence of extended households shared by individuals of multiple racial backgrounds in Richmond—like those of the Myers or the Judah families—was also important in tightening the integration of small towns and rural farms with the economic and political spheres of urban areas. Interracial sexual connections helped networks of blacks and whites envision worlds outside their immediate surroundings. But Richmond's urban setting also provided an environment distinct from the surrounding countryside for the cultivation of interracial sexual associations and relationships. Given the socioeconomic organization of a city whose population comprised an ever growing and constantly fluctuating mass of whites and blacks, men and women, rich and poor, native-born and immigrant, and freemen and slaves, such sexual transgressions were inevitable, even integral to the everyday functioning of Richmond's social and economic life.

3

The Church and the Brothel Are Only Separated by a Pane of Glass
Sex and Race on the Streets of Richmond

Over the course of the antebellum period Richmond evolved into the most important city in the Upper South. By the 1850s Richmond was the regional center for the processing and manufacturing of tobacco, the milling of flour, and the smelting of iron, as well as being the largest slave market. Because of its location at the falls of the James River, Richmond also was a natural entrepôt for all river traffic of goods to and from western Virginia, and for considerable national and international trade. The building of the James River and Kanawha Canal and the expansion of railroads enhanced Richmond's natural riparian commercial advantages with those created by man.[1]

As the economic and political center of antebellum Virginia, Richmond was also a population magnet for whites and blacks alike. Middle- and upper-class white men saw opportunities for increased wealth and power by investing and participating in the city's shipping, railroad, and manufacturing industries, capturing a part of the growing legal business, and getting involved in local politics and in cultural organizations. Poorer white men, including many German and Irish immigrants, came to the city looking for work, perhaps on the docks or in a factory. Others opened small businesses. Single poor white women might find work as domestics or in the sewing trades. Free people of color, who, with some exceptions, had few if any opportunities for economic mobility in farming areas, gravitated to Richmond as well, sometimes joining other family members who had already established themselves and sometimes struggling on their own to escape rural poverty. Free women of color in particular dominated the laundry business in the city, but they also often worked as domestics.[2]

Slavery took on unusual characteristics in antebellum Richmond. As elsewhere in the state, slave labor was integral to nearly every important sector of Richmond's economy. Many industries used slave labor, especially tobacco, where workers at practically every stage of production were predominantly enslaved men and women. Enslaved men also worked in iron foundries, flour mills, coal mines, railroads, tanneries, and bookbinderies, and as carpenters, blacksmiths, plasterers, shoemakers, and textile workers. The riverside economy teemed with slave laborers as canal bateauxmen, ship towers, fishermen, porters, stevedores, and drivers. Enslaved women, meanwhile, like free black and some white women, labored in many white and black households, mostly as domestic servants. What made the urban context unique was less the pervasiveness of slave labor than its residential patterns: slaves in Richmond, especially enslaved men, often lived away from their owners in the countryside, who sent them to the capital to be hired out when they were not needed in the fields. Slaves in the city were able to negotiate some of their own labor conditions through self-hire, a technically illegal but generally unprosecuted offense. They frequently had cash in their pockets, part of their earnings that masters allowed them to keep in order to live and eat in the city. Most importantly, slaves often could escape constant supervision by whites and use their leisure time as they saw fit. Some slaves in Richmond did not work at all. Instead they were runaways from across central and southern Virginia who came to Richmond hoping to find family and friends who would conceal them, and hoping to lose themselves amid the crowded streets and in the city's nooks and alleys.[3]

While one race or another predominated in certain antebellum Richmond neighborhoods and in certain occupations, most residential areas housed blacks and whites alike, and in some workplaces slaves, free blacks, and whites worked side by side. In addition, this diverse population unavoidably and constantly mingled together in the streets. Many of Richmond's hotels, banks, markets, and businesses (including its slave traders) lay clustered along roughly ten blocks of Main and Cary Streets, although this activity always included some distant areas—such as the Rocketts docks in the city's southeast and Penitentiary Bottom to the southwest—and expanded with the urban economy over time to encompass parts of Franklin, Grace, and Broad Streets (see Maps 3 and 4). The docks and the canal basin bounded this busy hub to the south, and the capitol building and the governor's home lay just a few blocks north. At night, the heart of downtown Richmond became a primarily, though hardly exclusively, working-class leisure scene marked by the mingling of male and female workers, sailors, gamblers, brawlers, thieves, and prostitutes of multiple racial backgrounds and states of bondage. Such intense interracial interaction in a society preoccupied with race as a signifier of status created a volatile environment. The mixture could breed cooperation and friendship, but it also commonly produced antagonism and violence across the color line. Frequently, both the cooperation and the antagonism had sexuality and sexual tensions at their core.[4]

For the most part, legal authorities found they could do little about sexuality on the streets of Richmond. Having a multiracial work force was imperative to the functioning of the city, and allowing slaves, free blacks, and whites to work out their own labor arrangements and commercial dealings without overzealous regard for the specifics of the law helped the city grow. Allowing such informality during the working day but trying too severely to restrict and punish the personal activities of the population after hours would have been impractical, somewhat self-defeating, and probably impossible even had Richmond's city authorities had the resources for a sufficient police force and for the necessary legal mechanisms to do so. Instead, as exemplified by rare Mayor's Court records from the late 1830s, for much of the antebellum period individuals involved in sexual activities across the color line were dealt with almost wholly in a reactive fashion. Rather than developing any consistent plan to address the problems interracial sex potentially posed for the racial order of the city, the police and the courts in Richmond handled situations in conflict with the law as they arose and mostly when they threatened to violate spatial and temporal spheres reserved for "respectable" classes of white Richmonders.

The geography of interracial sex in Richmond as well as the attitudes of local elites, however, changed as the city developed from a small riverside town and trade depot into a burgeoning metropolis. Begrudging acceptance of and even indifference toward interracial sex and its consequences, seen from the 1790s through the 1840s, evolved, in ways particularly evident in the 1850s, into an intensified desire among both legal authorities and many white citizens to rein in such sexual behavior altogether. This new attitude was just one part of a more general tightening of control over interracial interaction in Richmond, adopted to make the urban environment more responsive to both the fears and the hopes of its white residents. As the city limits expanded and suburbs developed, people found that vice followed them from downtown. Both the economy and the population of Richmond boomed in the 1850s, simultaneously provoking new fears regarding the slave and free black populations and a desire by local boosters to improve the city's image. An increasingly reformist mind-set yielded new attitudes toward urban crime, especially prostitution. Concerns about abolitionist activity and the underground railroad also roused Richmond's authorities to try to constrain resident free blacks and slaves, and their abilities to mix with whites. By the time of the Civil War, Richmonders with legal, social, and economic power were clearly more concerned than they ever had been about sex across the color line among the working classes. Whether they could actually control it was another matter.

Richmond grew rapidly in the decades after it became the political capital of Virginia in 1779 and was incorporated three years later. The relocation of the state government brought both people and business to the city, which was just over a square mile in size and housed around 1,000 people in 1782. By 1790 roughly 3,700 people lived in Richmond. Half the population was black, and over 90 percent of the black population was enslaved. By 1810 Richmond had expanded to 2.4 square miles—a size the city would remain until after the Civil War—and had seen its population explode to nearly 10,000.[5] The heart of Richmond's economic expansion was along its riverfront, especially after 1800 when the James River and Kanawha Canal connected the river to a large basin a few blocks south of Capitol Square. By enabling the passage of goods around the falls of the James, the basin enhanced Richmond's status as a trade depot for Virginia's hinterland and provided, along with the adjacent area to the east near the original warehouses, a primary location for the city's emerging interracial work and leisure environment. During the day the riverfront bustled with blacks and whites working on ships, on the docks, and in small craft shops and mercantile businesses. At night, the area abounded with taverns, tippling houses, gambling dens, and brothels, where slaves, free blacks, and whites, both male and female, often mixed.[6]

Not all nocturnal activities on the docks mixed races and genders, but when black and white men and women congregated in locations where alcohol and dancing provided the entertainment, houses frequently became "disorderly." That interracial sexual activity accompanied the goings-on at these underground haunts often is implied more than overtly stated in legal presentments. The grand jury of Richmond's Hustings Court, though, saw interracial sexuality as a problem as early as 1795, complaining to city authorities of "the numerous evils which result from the toleration of such a number of vagrants, beggars, free negroes, & runaway slaves as daily infest the streets and by night plunder the inhabitants, & among other things seeing allmost hourly proofs of the increasing corruption of morals and other injuries flowing from the permission of negro dancing where persons of all colours are too often assembled." In 1797 the grand jury complained again that "laws for promoting good order" went ignored and unenforced throughout the city.[7]

Regardless of the persistent complaints by some Richmonders, only on rare occasions and in response to particularly traumatic events did the police, the courts, or the urban upper classes who controlled municipal politics show even the semblance of an interest or effort to bring racial or sexual order to the city. In 1800, for example, the threat to slavery posed by Gabriel's Rebellion prompted both the city of Richmond and the Virginia General Assembly to take some action against the easy intermingling of whites and blacks, and free people and slaves, that had helped make planning the proposed uprising possible. In the capital, the Public Guard—a quasi-police company of the state militia—was created to patrol Capitol Square and the city's arsenals at night. Other laws passed early in the century cracked down on slave gatherings, and in 1808 the practice of hiring out slaves (Gabriel himself had been hired out) was made illegal altogether.[8]

Similarly, when a fire destroyed the Richmond theater in late December 1811 and killed more than seventy people, public discussion quickly turned from lamentations for the dead to a larger examination of the supposed moral consequences of urban frivolity. To their enemies, theaters in American cities in the early nineteenth century were notorious places. Crowds, though seated in separate sections, crossed race and class boundaries, and sexuality flourished. Establishments in many cities had a third tier of gallery seats primarily to service individuals who came less to see the play than to drink and socialize with the prostitutes who roamed the tier, plying their trade or arriving at prearranged meetings with customers. Given that both blacks and prostitutes were relegated to the galleries, the interracialism of the sexual atmosphere only heightened the sense of perversity many white Americans perceived there. Institutionalized interracial prostitution in Richmond's theaters was remarked upon as early as 1802, when in the pages of the *Recorder*, James Callender accused Skelton Jones, one of his political enemies, of going to the theater, where "he went into that corner assigned for girls of colour. . . . His heart found itself at home in the midst of African prostitution."[9]

Ministers across the country, whose words were printed in pamphlet form and sold in Richmond, used the conflagration to denounce the ungodliness of theaters and the sexual atmosphere they bred. Reverend William Hill of Winchester, Virginia, for example, called upon city and country folk alike to repent of their sins and declared himself "an enemy to the amusements of the theatre, as they are in use in our day," believing them to be "little better than schools of vice" and the habitat of "the most abandoned and licentious wretches and prostitutes."[10] A commentator from Baltimore dwelled especially on the sexual nature of theaters, writing that considering "how many painted strumpets are stuck about the theatre in the boxes, the galleries, and the avenues . . . it will, I think, be difficult to imagine places better adapted . . . to teach the theory and practice of fashionable iniquity." Hammering away at this theme, the author deplored theaters as "the very exchange for harlots," rhetorically asked if there was "a loose, debauched, depraved, ungodly man or woman" who did not attend the theater, and questioned the character of actors and actresses altogether. Even theatergoers who considered themselves "respectable" citizens might be corrupted by the plays themselves, which usually consisted of "love intrigues, blasphemous passions, profane discourses, lewd descriptions, filthy jests, and of all the most extravagant rant of wanton, profligate persons of both sexes, heating and inflaming one another with all the wantonness of address, the immodesty of gesture, and lewdness of thought that art can invent." It was unclear how someone who detested theaters so intensely knew so much about them, but the author asked rhetorically if activities so rife with carnality could possibly "form an amusement lawful for Christians."[11]

One historian has argued that the Richmond theater fire was a decisive moment for members of Richmond's elite, turning them to evangelical Protestantism and arousing a new sense of civic culture and of the need for racial, sexual, and economic order in their growing urban setting. Given that most of the people who died in the fire were members of the white upper class, including more than fifty women and children, Governor George W. Smith, and Bank of Virginia president Abraham B. Venable, such a response would have been understandable. Indeed,

Richmonders determined to build a church on the theater site as a monument to the dead, the Common Council passed resolutions in the wake of the fire banning "public dancing" and "any public show or spectacle" for four months, and no theater opened again in Richmond for a number of years.[12] Crime rates generally declined between 1811 and 1819, and the War of 1812 and its aftermath brought economic "flush times" to Richmond. To accommodate the continually growing population, entrepreneurs began a wave of building and improvements in some of Richmond's first suburbs. Real-estate speculation fueled high land prices, and the value of farm products increased as well.[13]

Despite a legal and cultural environment that might have indicated a growing intolerance for such activities, however, interracial mixing in Richmond's streets, docks, taverns, gaming houses, and houses of prostitution remained a regular part of life in the capital long after the supposed backlash in the wake of Gabriel's failed plot and long after the Richmond theater fire. Just as they had before Gabriel's Rebellion, Hustings Court grand juries complained that law enforcement was utterly incapable, unwilling, or incompetent to control the racial disorder of the urban environment. In 1809 they presented the whole night watch "as entirely useless, because we believe there is a want of energy, activity, and vigilance in the members thereof." In 1813 the grand jury accused a number of policemen, particularly the police captain, of taking bribes and letting suspected criminals walk free, while in 1815 it asserted that the city needed more constables for patrol. Also in 1815, jurors noted that they had seen "tumultuous assemblies of negroes in the streets of our City on Sundays which they conceive ought to be prevented, wherefore they respectively suggest to the Court to take such measures as they may deem best calculated to put a stop to this abuse and to produce generally greater vigilance in the police of the city."[14] As early as 1806 Richmonders saw the Public Guard as such a ludicrous military unit that they debated its abolition in the newspapers.[15]

Racial intermixture in particular remained a popular subject of discussion, and some Virginians recognized it as simply endemic to city life. In August 1812, for example, the *Virginia Argus* printed a letter from a Lee County man, writing under the pseudonym "Philo," who discussed the evident variety to be found in skin color among Richmond's inhabitants. Philo ridiculed the notions floated by some urban elites that phenotypic diversity had anything to do with Richmond's natural setting, its climate, or its proximity to the sun. Neither, he added, alluding to the theater disaster, did the spectrum of dermal hues result from "the curses, damns, and hell-fires dealt out in Richmond." Instead, "the true cause of this strange appearance" was that physical contact between blacks and whites was prevalent in a large and crowded city, more so than in the relatively thinly populated countryside. "In the city," Philo argued, "where all is hurry and bustle, it will be only strange that it occurs so seldom. — Where business, balls, routs, birth-nights, anniversaries, assemblies, plays and religious worship constantly call such crowds of both races of people together; where they are every moment liable, thro' inadvertence, to jostle and rub, without thinking of, or caring for the pernicious consequences." If Richmonders were serious about solving the problem of racial intermixture, Philo suggested they look not to pseudoscience or divine intervention but to themselves, particularly to reforming the white men who prowled Richmond's streets at night. Sarcastically discussing the nocturnal wanderings of Richmond's "gentlemen," Philo warned the "polite inhabitants of Richmond to be careful not to touch, or rub against the yellow sort, at places of public resort, or elsewhere — not to stumble upon them in the dark, nor knock their heads together in narrow lanes & dark passages."[16]

It was entirely unrealistic to expect that white and black Richmonders would not "jostle," "touch," or "rub against" one another in the streets. The professed efforts of white elites to reform themselves and their city after 1811 could never effectively end or even significantly curtail urban interracialism so long as their economic interests rested in a work force environment requiring whites, free blacks, and slaves to work and, in many cases, live together. Sexual interaction was no more and perhaps even less subject to control than the workplace, and if anxiety about urban living ever eased after 1811, it surely returned by the end of the decade. The real-estate bubble of the boom years popped with the Panic of 1819, bringing Richmond's economic growth to a near standstill. Buildings stood unfinished and many of those recently completed remained unoccupied. Planned suburbs were undeveloped, and streets scheduled for clearing or filling in stayed forests and ditches. Flour and tobacco prices plummeted. Richmond's economic base would not significantly recover from the panic until the 1840s.[17]

By 1830, whether because crime among free workers and slaves had increased in the wake of economic panic or because the population (which then stood at just over 16,000 people, slightly more than half of whom were African American) had simply grown too large, Richmond's small police force had become ineffective and the Hustings Court was no longer capable of adjudicating all criminal activity in the city.[18] In May 1830 the Common Council restructured both the police and court systems of the city, concentrating authority in the position of the mayor and effectively reducing his duties to that of chief law enforcer. The council created a "Mayor's Court" (sometimes referred to as the "sunrise court" because of its meeting time) to serve as a filter for the Hustings Court. Here, the mayor would sit each day and hold hearings on individuals rounded up for suspected criminal activity during the previous night. In criminal and civil cases falling under the city's jurisdiction valued at less than $20, the mayor could hand down sentences or order the accused sent before the Hustings Court grand jury for further investigation. The council also authorized the mayor to appoint between sixteen and twenty people to serve as night watchmen, who would walk the streets of Richmond from sundown to sunrise each night, and created a series of watch districts to enable more efficient monitoring of the city.[19]

Richmond newspapers saw no need to report regularly on local events or on crime until the early 1850s. Most of the activities of the Mayor's Court between 1830 and 1852 have therefore been lost, but one docket remains in existence covering the years 1836 to 1839, the end of the thirteen-year tenure of Joseph Tate. The activities of the court covered in its pages do not reflect a comprehensive list of individuals arrested by the night watch in those years. Many suspected drunks, prostitutes, and gamblers were apprehended, but the mayor took care of some cases before court at one of the two watch houses, sending the criminals on their way. White criminals especially could be disposed of in this fashion, because whites convicted of misdemeanors were subject primarily to fines, which could easily be collected on the spot if the accused had access to the money. By contrast, standard punishment for both slaves and free blacks consisted of lashes, meaning that in most cases when they were caught committing a crime they were held over to appear before the mayor in the morning. Despite its race and class biases, the docket nonetheless offers a vivid sense of the rough and often riotous texture of Richmond's interracial streets, and indicates how deeply sex and sexual tensions across racial lines were interwoven with everyday life in Virginia's capital.

Sexual banter and insults filled the air in Richmond in the 1830s. Women threw sexually laden insults at men, but most commonly they derided the sexuality of other women.[20] In 1838, for example, a white woman named Mary Fulcher accused Betsey Randal, a slave, of using "violent and insolent language" toward her on Independence Day. Fulcher found much of Randal's language too vulgar to repeat to Mayor Tate, but did mention that Randal called her a "liar whore." A woman's honor resided in her sexual purity, and for anyone looking to direct the most stinging invective toward another woman, nothing was more calculated than an attack on her chastity. A slave challenging a white woman in such a fashion served the purpose especially well, although it was also especially dangerous. A woman named Ann Thomas testified that she never heard Randal call Fulcher names, but Mayor Tate still ordered that Randal receive ten lashes.[21]

Perhaps the only way a woman could deepen her verbal offense against another woman was to add the implication of racial intermixture. When a white woman named Nancy Abrahams complained to the mayor about Letty Hamilton, a free woman of color, she claimed Hamilton had called her "a nasty poor bitch." Abrahams reported that Hamilton had also claimed that she "had a white man for her husband which was more than she (Mrs. A.) had." Hamilton's choice of insults, presuming she actually delivered them, was brilliant in its comprehensiveness, tying race, class, gender, and sex together in a brief outburst. Hamilton impugned the racial purity of Nancy Abrahams's husband, thus effectively accusing Abrahams of sleeping with black men, and asserted her own superiority through her sexual association with a white man. Whether Hamilton actually believed sleeping with a white man elevated her own status or whether she simply played to her perceptions of Abrahams's mind-set is uncertain. What is clear is that white and black women in Richmond in some measure understood that their sexuality and sexual affiliations were crucial to their own standing relative to one another. Confrontational language followed accordingly.

It seems possible that Letty Hamilton's insults struck a chord with Nancy Abrahams because they contained some truth. On being informed that she would have to appear at City Hall to testify if she wished to press her charges, Abrahams refused, saying "'twas the last thing she would like to do, and that if the woman conducted herself properly in future she would not press her complaint." When parties to a conflict appeared before Mayor Tate, he often questioned them in an effort to determine the cause of the dispute. In this case, he surely would have probed into Nancy Abrahams's life and the racial background of her husband, which might have forced Mrs. Abrahams to admit embarrassing racial facts publicly.[22]

Personal involvement in or knowledge of one another's sexual lives frequently lay behind confrontations among women in antebellum Richmond. In June 1837, for example, a white woman named Elizabeth Fowler complained that a black woman named Maria Moore had used insulting language toward her and had threatened physical violence against Fowler's child. In the end, Fowler decided not to prosecute her case, but Mayor Tate noted to himself that Elizabeth Fowler suspected that her husband William and Maria Moore were "too intimate."[23] A few months later, a white woman named Susan Parker complained that another white woman, Susan Butler, used "abusive & slanderous language charging her with being intimate with coloured men &c &c." The mayor, as he often did in cases where white women bickered, advised Parker to ignore Butler's remarks, but noted that William H. Parker, Susan Parker's husband, had "gone off with another woman."[24]

Slavery was inextricable from many sexual conflicts in Richmond. Most instances of sexually wrought verbal volleys involving enslaved and white women probably did not end up in the Mayor's Court at all and were handled within the household instead. But occasionally they became public. In one instance, a white woman identified only as the wife of Robert S. Redford charged Martha, a slave hired to another white man named Patrick Lyddane, with using "provoking language to her." The mayor listened to testimony from Mrs. Redford, Mrs. Lyddane, and a woman named Nancy Browning. In the course of her testimony Mrs. Redford seemed determined to report the story behind her battle with Martha. She claimed that Patrick Lyddane "was or had been *intimate with*" Martha when she went with him away from home, and that Martha had told Redford that as a consequence Mr. Lyddane "would not flog her." On hearing Mrs. Redford tell such a story, Martha denied both sexual intimacy with Mr. Lyddane and ever having had such a conversation with Mrs. Redford. Claiming that Mrs. Redford lied, Martha thus provoked Redford's complaint. Nancy Browning and Mrs. Lyddane both denied that Mrs. Redford had any conversation with Martha about her relationship with Mr. Lyddane. Both her "temper" and the urgency with which she insisted on telling her story led Mayor Tate to believe that Mrs. Redford was lying and that she held a grudge against both Martha and Mrs. Lyddane. He dismissed the case, but if he accurately assessed the scenario Mrs. Redford's story was well crafted to injure both Martha and Mrs. Lyddane had the mayor believed her. Martha would have been sentenced to receive lashes, and Mrs. Lyddane would have been publicly humiliated. In fact, to serve these ends the only person who really had to believe Mrs. Redford's story was Mrs. Lyddane, who would have been psychologically devastated and who surely would have had Martha severely punished. Race, sex, and slavery were inextricably linked, and women knew that when looking to injure, language was one of their most valuable and potent weapons.[25]

When men confronted one another (or when they had altercations with women), they were far more likely than women to attack one another physically or to assume an air of bravado. Here, race and sexuality came together too as white and black men jockeyed to display their masculinity. A white man named Jacob Mull, for example, charged a slave named Peter with using insolent language. Precisely what provoked Mull is not recorded, but on hearing Peter, Mull proceeded to beat the slave with his cane. Three white men testified to Peter's character "for submissive & humble & respectful behaviour to all & especially to white persons." Mull, however, brought two white witnesses of his own and insisted that even after being beaten, Peter continued to challenge him, impugning both his class and his honor by muttering that "no gentleman would have done that." The next day, a free man of color named Daniel Loney was hauled before the mayor by a white man for publicly "using seditious language." In reference to Peter's arrest for insolence and on hearing the details of his beating at Mull's hands, Loney was reported to have said "that before he would let any white man do him so, he would take a knife & cut his dam guts out." Physical aggression in response to provocative language was central to expressions of masculinity, and white and black men constantly insisted on asserting their own.[26]

Black and white men, like women of both races, sometimes loaded their language with overtly sexual implications. In June 1836 John Sacra, a white man, accused a free man of color named Thomas Kennedy of using "insolent and provoking language" by telling Sacra that he "would keep his wife as long as he pleased and that he had better not give himself any airs." Mayor Tate's description of this case was ambiguous. It is possible that Kennedy's wife was enslaved by Sacra, and Kennedy was warning Sacra that he would conduct his family life as he chose. But in the 1830s to "keep" a woman frequently referred to commercial concubinage. It seems more likely that Sacra had discovered that Kennedy was having sex with his wife or partner and had challenged Kennedy verbally, only to have Kennedy respond in an entirely unanticipated way. It is equally unclear whether it was Sacra or Kennedy who engaged in sex across the color line, but one of them did. In an environment like Richmond's, where white and black men and women constantly associated, for a white and a black man to battle over a single woman could not have been rare. Sexually and racially laden insults often had their origins in the sexual intertwining of black and white.[27]

Sex across the color line in downtown Richmond was available for almost anyone who wanted to procure it, especially if they had the money to pay for it. The bustling crowds that filled the city's commercial and industrial areas provided a semianonymity that individuals living in small towns and farming communities could never enjoy, and thus provided a perfect environment for commercial sex. In Richmond, an individual might be surrounded by people he or she knew in one part of town but could just as easily walk a few blocks to an unfamiliar neighborhood and see only complete strangers. Moreover, antebellum Richmond's population not only increased rapidly but also turned over with some regularity. Whites and blacks alike might stay in town for just a few days, a few months, or a few years before moving elsewhere.

The possibility of clandestine sexual encounters placed women looking to survive in Richmond's sex trade in an advantageous but ironic position. Such women, both black and white, had to be "public" women. Advertising their services in the newspapers was an unrealistic means of drawing customers. Instead, their occupation, or at least their location, had to be common enough knowledge to attract both regular visitors and random sojourners. Yet if they made their presence too evident by walking the streets or soliciting from windows and doorways of buildings, they risked arrest for disorderly behavior. A peculiar mixture of visibility and camouflage thus characterized prostitution, both within and across racial lines. Men had to know where to look, women had to make it clear how they could be found, and neither particularly wanted to get caught.[28]

As in other antebellum American cities, a hierarchy attended to prostitution in Richmond. At its bottom were women who walked the streets looking for customers. Among prostitutes, streetwalkers not only received the least money for their services, but they were also the most visible and thus most vulnerable both to arrest by the police and harassment from men who might be drunk and potentially violent. Both black and white women participated at this level of the trade, serving both black and white men. When Corian Carter and Nancy Johnson, both free women of color, were standing across the street from a tavern with a predominantly white male clientele, the police arrested them for "being street strumpets of evil fame" looking to "pick up men for bawdy purposes."[29] A white woman named Jane Blackburn, meanwhile, was arrested at least five times between 1836 and 1839 for drunkenness, disorderly behavior, and streetwalking.[30] Even enslaved women occasionally tried to earn money as prostitutes, such as Betsey and Martha, who were arrested for streetwalking near a theater on Fourteenth Street.[31]

Because they had no regular location from which to solicit or to which to bring customers, streetwalkers often found themselves caught by the police in compromising circumstances. Just a month before Corian Carter was arrested for being of "evil fame," she was hauled before the mayor for trespassing at the Bell Tavern on Main and Fifteenth Streets, where she was found in bed with the white occupant of room 18.[32] Another free woman of color, Mary Dungy, appeared before the mayor in the summer of 1837 on the charge of stealing $5 in North Carolina gold coins from a white man named John Brasington, who was staying in the boardinghouse of Lawrence Ryan. On examination, it was revealed that Dungy was in Ryan's house without his permission and was discovered by Ryan under Brasington's bed. She had none of the stolen property in her possession and reported that Brasington had picked her up, despite his assertions to the contrary, "for an improper purpose."[33] A year later, meanwhile, a white woman named Wesley Ann Smith was discovered, as Mayor Tate wrote, "*with* a man" in the Second Market House. The mayor had seen Smith before, when she was before him along with a sailor named Daniel Green for "indecent conduct & exposure &c. in view of the neighbouring houses" on Council Chamber Hill just east of Capitol Square. Tate would see Smith again in the future when she was convicted of "common drunkenness," by which point she was well known as a "strumpet — night walker at late hours to pick up men &c of any colour."[34]

Hardly all purveyors of commercial sex in Richmond openly walked the streets. Small groceries, run by both whites and blacks, dotted downtown Richmond. At night, many of these became sites of illegal trading (frequently in stolen goods) with slaves, underground tippling and gambling houses, and places where prostitutes might meet customers, as illustrated by the legal troubles of a number of white-owned groceries on

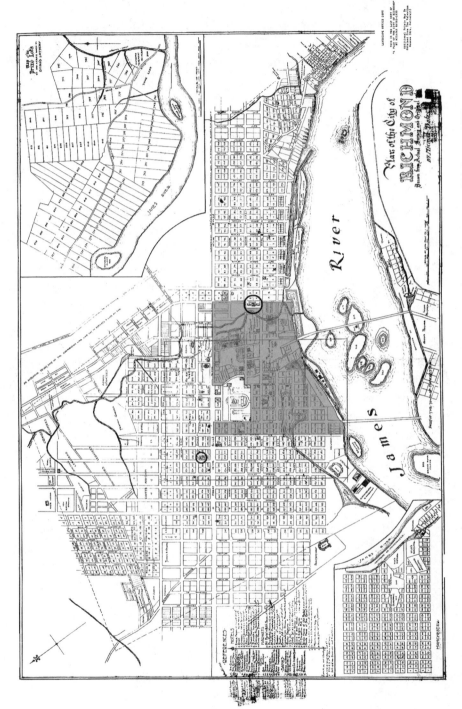

Map 3. Richmond, 1835 (map by Micajah Bates; photograph courtesy of the Valentine Museum / Richmond History Center)

Cary between Thirteenth and Virginia Streets.[35] At least four groceries sat on the block adjacent to the Columbia Inn, centrally located between Richmond's First Market three blocks east, the docks and mills two blocks south, the capitol district two blocks north, and the canal basin two blocks west (see Map 3). In July 1836 Rose Osiander, the co-owner (with her husband Philip) of one grocery, was charged by another owner, James Ballentine, with threatening to shoot him, a threat witnessed by the wife of a third owner, Mrs. Richard Burke. Mrs. Osiander in turn called on Elizabeth and Margaret Ann Kimberley, the former of whom ran the fourth grocery, as witnesses in her defense. The mayor put Rose Osiander on probation and ordered her to keep the peace, but this was hardly the end of the grocery owners' encounters with the law.[36] Just a few weeks later, all four were charged with keeping their businesses open on Sunday, the only day for many slaves to make commercial transactions. On another occasion, a slave named Frederick was arrested for receiving stolen coffee. He claimed to be on his way to Ballentine's to trade it for some chewing tobacco. Rose Osiander, meanwhile, was charged with allowing an illegal gathering of African Americans in her grocery in September 1836, and eight months later a free black woman named Maria Brack was brought in from the street drunk and claimed she had purchased liquor at the Osianders' store. Brack was also arrested on two other occasions for streetwalking, each time in the company of a white fellow prostitute. In 1837 the police raided a gathering of men and women drinking at the Osianders' shop. Among the company were Harriet Murray and Betsey Horton, both of whom were "women of ill-fame," the latter of whom ran her own brothel.[37]

The line between groceries where owners allowed prostitutes to cater to their customers and houses that served as brothels outright could be indistinct. Such establishments commonly sat in direct proximity to one another. Betsey Horton ran her brothel, for example, from a house on Fourteenth Street between Cary and Main, around the corner from the Osiander grocery, making it the perfect location for her and other women who lived in her house to meet prospective white and black clients.[38] Mayor Tate noted that Elizabeth Kimberley herself was a prostitute, as was her daughter Margaret Ann, who worked in the sex trade for a time while living at Mary Tucker's brothel, a house characterized as being "of the most infamous and debasd. character." Four of Mary Tucker's daughters, themselves "of notorious evil fame," and at least one free black woman, Mary Ann Lewis, lived in the brothel as well.[39]

Brothels in antebellum Richmond, reflecting the demography of the working population, were frequently places where men and women of both races mingled. Catherine Conway, a white woman, ran a disorderly house with her multiracial daughter, Cynthia, and two free black women, Susan Matthews and Matilda Finney, at Seventeenth and Broad Streets.[40] Nancy Johnson, a free black woman who had once been arrested for streetwalking, found herself in several interracial settings. The police took her into custody in 1837 for running a disorderly house on Franklin Street "to which white and blk. of evil fame &c. resort, quarrel, fight & use obscene language." In an effort to stay out of jail, she promised to abandon the house, only to be arrested two weeks later with another free black woman named Betsey Lewis for "disorderly and lewd conduct." Johnson apparently decided that running her own house was too much trouble, because by the following year she lived in an "extremely disorderly bawdy house" run by a free black woman named Betsey Isaacs. Among the others living in the house were Cora and Patsey Tucker, white women who no longer lived with their mother Mary.[41]

Even where white women seem to have constituted all the actual residents of a brothel, black men and women were constantly present. A number of white brothel proprietors either owned or hired female slaves or free black servants, usually to perform cleaning and laundry tasks in the house. Several white prostitutes who lived in houses and brothels on Virginia Street, for example, found themselves before the mayor consequent to their reliance on black labor. Ann B. Meredith, Polly McElligott, Ann Hansberry, and Elizabeth Kimberley, all white residents of Virginia Street (Meredith ran a particularly popular brothel), were charged with allowing their hired slaves to dump garbage and ashes into the street. Other brothel owners paid black musicians to perform at "balls" they threw to attract men who would pay for both liquor and sex. Three male slaves, one of whom was carrying a violin, were arrested in 1836 for being without a pass "at Ann B. Meredith's Virga. St. a brothel to play for the 'Ball,'" while on another occasion a slave named Tom Grimes was brought in on the same charge and "it appeared that Tom is a fiddler and fiddles at Houses of Ill-Fame." Brothels also relied on the services of black businesses to keep their houses running efficiently. Tom Griffin, a slave, and his wife, a free woman of color named Mary Bird, for example, got into trouble for keeping an illegal restaurant, or cookshop, in Exchange Alley, the northern terminus of Virginia Street. Mayor Tate noted that the shop was "a considerable establishment and furnishes suppers &c at all hours of the night to inmates of houses of ill fame."[42]

Women who became prostitutes did so primarily out of economic necessity or a desire to improve their financial circumstances. Few jobs were available for young single black or white women in the countryside, and circumstances could be particularly trying for poor women with limited or strained familial or communal ties.[43] When these women came to the cities, however, they found their options limited to working in factories, the sewing trades, or as domestics, all of which might bring them in contact with men who were economically as well as sexually exploitative. By contrast, prostitution often was more remunerative, gave working-class and poor urban women some choice over their sleeping partners, offered the opportunity to earn money in a business not controlled by men, and in any event was generally a temporary career in which most women remained for just a few years. In brothels, prostitutes also found women in situations similar to their own and could rely on them for protection as well as financial assistance. The Mayor's Court records are replete with cases of prostitutes who testified on one another's behalf in court and who bailed one another out of jail.[44]

Economically, although prostitution could yield a livable income, financial and other resources were scarce. Consequently, prostitutes frequently bickered with and assaulted one another. At Mary Weidmeyer's house, a large brothel, Harriet Branch filed a complaint against Fanny Butts for "beating her with a chair and with her fist in the face . . . and threats to kill her," while Elizabeth West brought fellow white woman "of ill fame" Caroline Fruitier before the mayor "for cowhiding her in the street."[45] When free black and white prostitutes fought, white women had the clear legal advantage, needing only to bring charges of abusive language against black women in the hope that the mayor would sentence them to physical punishment. Such a strategy worked sometimes, such as when Martha Detain, a white occupant of Amanda Loden's disorderly house on Main Street near the Bird-in-Hand Tavern, complained that Matilda Tankersley, a free woman of color, used "grossly abusive and provoking language" against her and dared her to fight. Mayor Tate sentenced Tankersley to ten lashes. On other occasions, though, the mayor chose to ignore the complaint, such as when Sarah Jane Trainum complained about the way Maria Willis, a free woman of color, spoke to her. The mayor, noting that the complainant was "an abandoned woman of the lower ord.," sent Willis on her way with a reprimand.[46]

Prostitutes sometimes battled over their primary resource, their customers, especially when a "kept" woman perceived that another woman was trying to pry away her "keeper." Mary Jane Henry, for example, a white prostitute living at Mary Weidmeyer's, went to Martha Gilliam's establishment on Main Street opposite the coal yards and threatened to beat Alice Newman, also a white prostitute, for being "intimate" with the man who kept Henry. Before the police could arrest her, Henry attended the theater and fought with Newman, bashing her in the head in the process. Similarly, Sarah Jane Harris and Eugenia Richardson, two free women of color, brawled over Henry Johnson, a black journeyman carpenter. Even though women had more at stake financially in their customers, men were not above fighting over women they kept, white or black, as evidenced when John B. Smith brought Edward B. Cook before the mayor for threatening to kill him. Cook, it seemed, held the "belief or suspicion that Smith was intimate with Delia Harris a mulatto girl kept by Cook" living in the brothel of Eliza Bradley, a free woman of color who kept a house on Twelfth Street between Main and Franklin.[47]

If they wished to control interracial sexual mixing, Richmond's authorities could have tried adopting aggressive patrol strategies or turning to the bevy of state and local laws designed to keep the slave and free black populations of the city tightly under control. The quotidian nature of arrests of blacks for being without passes or lacking free registry papers indicates the police had at least some desire to control the movements of African Americans. Moreover, the police commonly arrested white and black men and women who were obviously drunk or who participated in particularly raucous gatherings that could involve visible nudity and where loud music, fighting, and cursing disturbed the quiet that was supposed to reign after dark. For his part, Mayor Tate routinely sentenced black prostitutes to whippings when the police hauled them in, and ordered white prostitutes who appeared before him to post bond of $50 or $100 to be of good behavior, although he might financially penalize them substantially more. Those who could not afford to post bond went to jail. Some women in this situation managed to escape confinement by promising the mayor they would leave the city (many of these were empty promises, and the women appeared in the Mayor's Court again), but white prostitutes without financial support from other women or from men could get trapped in a revolving prison door. In some years, a prostitute might spend more time in jail than out.

Neither the mayor nor the police were indifferent to sexual disorder that crossed the color line, but neither did they try systematically to eliminate or even significantly curtail interracial licentiousness in antebellum Richmond. There were no sweeps of brothels and no ferreting out of tippling shops, and there appears to have been little real effort to keep blacks and whites apart at all. Even though Mayor Tate routinely noted that women lived at brothels or were of "ill fame," no one was ever actually arrested for prostitution or even for fornication. Instead, women in the sex trade only appeared before the mayor for crimes incidental to their occupation — vagrancy, public drunkenness, fighting, verbal abuse, and the vague but inclusive charges of "disorderly behavior" or keeping a "disorderly house."[48] In the 1830s the response of Richmond's legal authorities to sexual misbehavior emphasized controlling and containing its attendant excesses rather than eradicating the vice itself.

In part, the mayor and the police implicitly acknowledged that eliminating illicit sex in the city was simply impossible. Having a professional night police force in an American city in the 1830s was rare enough.[49] Still, there were only fifteen to twenty night watchmen in Richmond in the 1830s, not nearly enough to surveil all the streets, alleys, tenements, grocery stores with back entrances, basement tippling houses, and brothels in the city, and certainly not enough to keep thousands of blacks and whites sexually or otherwise discrete. Neither was it in the city's best interest to end sexual disorder, because vice was also integrated into and bolstered Richmond's "legitimate" economy. Money spent at brothels on alcohol, food, and prostitutes by local residents or by sailors and other visitors remained in circulation in Richmond, and nighttime illegalities boosted profits that kept businesses open during the day.[50]

The geography of disorder is still another key to the begrudging tolerance of commercial sex in antebellum Richmond. In the 1830s the heart of Richmond's sex trade still had relatively distinct boundaries. Most arrests of blacks and whites for disorderly behavior associated with prostitution occurred between Capitol Square to the north, the First Market house to the east, Eighth Street and the western edge of the canal basin to the west, and the James River to the south (see Map 3, area shaded gray). Occasionally, the police encountered problems in the eastern and southeastern edges of the city, but most misdemeanor-level criminal activity took place in Richmond's primary business district. In part, this pattern resulted from the locations of the headquarters and the beats of the night watchmen. The city's two market houses, on Seventeenth between Main and Franklin, and on the southeastern corner of Sixth and Marshall, doubled as police watchhouses after dark (see Map 3, circled buildings). Police surveillance seems to have been directed from the watchhouses to the west and south, respectively, thus both reflecting and shaping the locations of the city's rowdier areas. The police looked downtown because they knew that they would find brothels, illegal bars, and other white, black, and interracial illegal activity. Simultaneously, and perhaps more importantly, they tried to ensure that such activities would stay there. Most particularly, they wanted to ensure that urban disturbances would not spread to elite white neighborhoods north of the capitol on and near Shockoe Hill.

Not only place but time was crucial to why Richmond's authorities generally chose not to hound city residents for their illicit sexual activities. And the temporal factor, like the spatial one, was inextricably linked to the presumed economic and social class of prostitutes and their customers. During the day, the downtown area was Richmond's political center and commercial hub, housing large banks, prestigious hotels, and churches. The drunken and sexually charged interracial leisure scene emerged mostly after the sun went down, when the banks closed, the politicians retired to the hotels, and the wealthy went home. Elites were hardly ignorant of what occurred all around them, and Richmonders did not use space in an entirely dichotomous fashion based on time of day. Free blacks, whites, slaves, bankers, lawyers, factory workers, prostitutes, drunks, and thieves all walked the streets of Richmond during the day, and some rich white men and politicians undoubtedly returned to those streets—which were still generally within ten blocks of even the most elite homes—after dark or used more clandestine houses of prostitution that catered to a wealthier clientele. It is useful to think of antebellum downtown Richmond as a space that served multiple purposes, and a landscape that different populations tended to dominate at different hours. Occasionally, the crowd populating downtown at night overreached its boundaries, such as when Nancy and Patsey Tucker, sisters and prostitutes, were arrested at 3:30 on a Sunday afternoon on Ninth Street "for extremely disorderly conduct and vulgar language in the street whilst many persons, men and women, were passing to

Church." But so long as they stayed in the right parts of town, only pursued vice at the right times, and tried to keep quiet when they did, the police and the mayor largely left the blacks and whites who used Richmond's streets alone.[51]

American cultural attitudes toward prostitution in the 1830s made vigilance against the sex trade unlikely as well. In Richmond as elsewhere in the United States before the 1840s, few Americans saw prostitution as a problem deserving particular attention or the women participating in it as being in need of special protection. Instead, prostitution was just another form of vice that needed to be watched, kept within certain urban zones, and prevented from becoming too publicly visible. As historian Barbara Meil Hobson suggests, in the 1830s "brothels were looked upon by police as establishments where seedy characters and criminal types congregated, places not substantially different from gambling houses or rowdy taverns. The task of law enforcers was to maintain safety and order for the city's respectable citizens, not to regulate sexual morals."[52]

Richmond in the 1830s, then, was a southern city whose population was half African American and nearly 40 percent enslaved, and which had more interracial commercial sex than any city in the north (though perhaps less than other southern cities like New Orleans or Charleston), yet sex across the color line, when kept within the boundaries authorities deemed acceptable for it, does not appear to have been a problem worthy of unique attention or alertness. The foundation of Richmond's economy rested on its interracial labor force and the informal labor and living arrangements established by countryside masters, city employers, and hired slaves. Whites and blacks mixing across the color line after working hours could neither have been prevented nor seen as especially unusual. That such interaction would extend to sexual liaisons was part and parcel of Richmond's disorderly streets.

By the 1850s, however, Richmond's police, its newspaper editors, and its white citizens showed much less tolerance for urban disorder generally and for sex across the color line specifically. Legal changes, new approaches to law enforcement directed by a new mayor, and confrontations between blacks and white citizens on the streets all reflected growing discomfort with racial and sexual disturbances in the city. Changes in Richmond's urban geography, demography, and economy dovetailed with national political trends and cultural shifts to alter decades-old

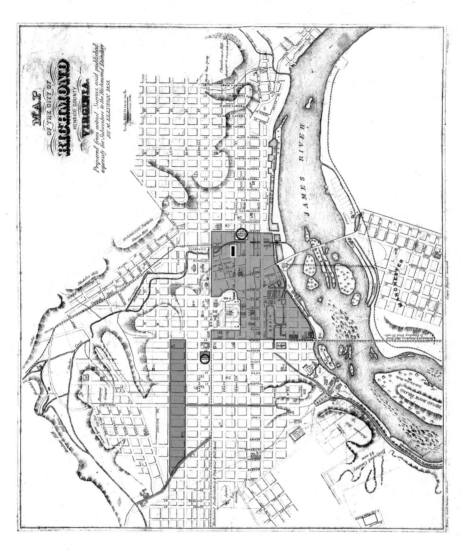

Map 4: Richmond, 1856 (map by M. Ellyson; photograph courtesy of the Valentine Museum/Richmond History Center)

attitudes toward interracial sex. By the eve of the Civil War, a certain paranoia in Richmond about the confluence of slavery, race, and sex had become obvious.

Richmond's population began to take off again in the 1840s and continued to do so until the Civil War. The population increased by over 35 percent from 1840 to 1850, when there were over 27,000 Richmonders, and by a similar percentage from 1850 to 1860, by which time there were almost 38,000 people in the city. While the black population continued to grow in numbers, the percentage of white residents increased, in large measure due to growing numbers of German and Irish immigrants. By 1860, there were over 11,000 slaves and more than 2,500 free people of color in Richmond, but the once-majority black population amounted only to around 37 percent in 1860, down from just under 47 percent in 1840 and just under 45 percent in 1850.[53]

Richmond's economy also began to boom in the 1840s and 1850s at a level it had not since the "flush times" after the War of 1812. The iron industry flourished, and Richmond became one of the largest producers of tobacco and flour in the world. The slave trade became more lucrative and active than at any other time in the antebellum period. New railroad lines extended from Richmond to the north and south, and out into Virginia's countryside, helping elaborate the city's connections to the rest of the state, the rest of the country, and the rest of the world. Suburbs began to fill with buildings and people, especially black and white factory and dock workers, craftsmen, and shopkeepers. Mostly white southwestern neighborhoods such as Sydney and Oregon Hill, the mostly black northwestern part of the city, which would later comprise Jackson Ward, and northeastern sections like Church Hill, Shed Town, and Union Hill all grew quickly. Building downtown increased as well. Granite fronts replaced wood and brick construction, and luxury accommodations such as those available at the American, the Exchange, and the Ballard Hotels attracted visitors and businessmen to Richmond. Local government and its activities and services expanded in the 1850s as well. The white, native-born, and wealthy businessmen, bankers, and lawyers who ran the City Council and boards of trade and commerce tried to see to it that major thoroughfares were repaired, kept clean, and sometimes paved, that the worst patches of Richmond's historically uneven and rough terrain were filled in and travel made easier, that gas lights illuminated some of the streets, that poor relief expanded, and that the city's overall aesthetic appearance improved.[54]

A spirit of boosterism and civic pride pervaded Richmond in the 1850s, and the city's newspapers joined efforts to promote the city. Newspapers commonly ran columns and editorials enthusiastically praising Richmond's economic prosperity and pleasant surroundings. Typical was an 1852 column in the *Daily Dispatch* — the city's first daily penny press and the first Richmond paper to report regularly on local events — entitled "Richmond and Its Prospects for the Future." The *Dispatch* drew attention to "the great increase of business on the principal streets, the scenes of new and elegant edifices which have been erected, the broad and finely graded streets, which have been laid out and lighted with gas." Taking special note of the railroads, steamship facilities, and canals that strengthened the connections between the eastern and western sections of Virginia, the paper further announced that Richmond's commercial prosperity was certain to continue for many years to come. The *Dispatch* also cited an article from the *Southern Literary Messenger* pointing out that Richmond lay midway between north and south and the mountains and the ocean, "in the position most favorable to health and long life." In conjunction with Richmond's moderate climate, the *Dispatch* felt that "for its size, Richmond is probably as healthy a city as there is in the world." With all its advantages, the paper concluded, "who would'nt live in Richmond?"[55]

Despite the best efforts of boosters to improve Richmond's appearance, the polish of the 1850s was in some ways a facade. Improvements were decidedly partial. Frederick Law Olmsted, traveling through the city in 1856, reported that while he found the capitol building, the city's singular architectural showpiece, visually stunning from a distance, up close the edifice was cheaply constructed and covered in stucco. He also reported finding that many shops, particularly those of German Jews, were "thickly set in the narrowest and meanest streets, which seem to be otherwise inhabited mainly by negroes." William Chambers, a Briton touring the United States, similarly noted that while there were attractive homes in elite neighborhoods north of the capitol, he found downtown that, "besides the principal thoroughfares, there are many narrow streets or lanes of a dismal, half-deserted appearance, generally dirty, and seemingly ill drained and ventilated. . . . The dwellings occupied by the lower classes of coloured people are of a miserable kind, resembling the worst brick-houses in the back-lanes of English manufacturing towns."[56]

Such scenes of squalor fit poorly with the new image Richmond's elites attempted to project in the 1850s to themselves and to the rest of the nation, as did the crime and disorderly behavior across sexual and racial lines that continued to plague the city. Not only were slaves without passes, free blacks without registers, and arrests for fighting, drunkenness, and illegal gatherings of African Americans still problematic, but newspaper reports also make it clear that sex across the color line remained an important part of the commercial sex trade in Richmond. Nancy Harris, for example, a free woman of color, was arrested for being in the city without a register in December 1856. Harris was also "said to be the proprietress of a den in the valley, where all sexes and colors assemble." The same day, a fourteen-year-old white girl named Hannah O'Brien was arrested for "associating with negroes." In court she claimed her parents had driven her from their house and that she was living with Harris "till she could do better."[57] Six months later, a slave named Lydia Brooks was "charged with keeping a disorderly and bad house, where whites and blacks congregate." Also arrested were Mary Crenshaw, a free black "inmate" of the house, and a white man named Charles Brooks. Brooks had previously been taken into police custody for beating a black woman with whom he had been cohabiting for a number of years.[58] In 1859, meanwhile, a woman named Betsy Oliver was arrested for "keeping a house of evil fame" in Shockoe Valley, a "vile den" where "black and white rogues assemble at all times."[59] Two days later a white woman named Mary Sullivan was charged with "associating with negroes."[60]

Men and women involved in sex across the color line in Richmond also continued to discover that their sexual choices potentially led them into confrontations and violence. In one instance, a white man named John N. Thornton and a free man of color named Robert Custello saw each other at an after-hours grocery on Brooke Avenue between Leigh and Duval Streets. After provoking a fight, Thornton, who had "the reputation of being a man of exceedingly bad character," stabbed Custello through the heart, killing him. As the newspaper revealed, "jealousy seems to have been the cause of the atrocious deed." It seemed that Thornton and Custello were both "on intimate terms with a low white wretch" who lived in the poorhouse, a woman named Sarah Lynn.[61]

Two years later three white men, all drunk, broke down the door of "a house of bad reputation" on Second Street belonging to a free black woman named Reubenetta Dandridge. On finding another white man inside, the men began beating him. Dandridge ran from the house but one of the intruders, Joseph Elam, caught her and stabbed her three times. Evidence produced at Elam's trial indicated that Elam had shown up at Dandridge's home a week prior to the stabbing, where two white men inside had refused him entrance. Infuriated, Elam threatened "to cut the throat of the negro woman for the treatment he had received." Reubenetta Dandridge hovered near death for over two weeks and survived, only to be arrested less than three months later for remaining in Virginia without a free register. A little more than four months after this second arrest, she attempted to commit suicide by swallowing an ounce and a half of laudanum.[62]

Anxieties about illicit sex had always been present in Richmond, but in the 1850s the willingness and desire to root out such activities both within and across the color line were apparent in ways they had rarely been previously. Where earlier in the century the Hustings Court grand jury and the mayor had been made aware of criminal sexual activity as the police discovered it or as neighbors complained about it, in the 1850s Mayor Joseph Mayo adopted far more aggressive strategies than Joseph Tate ever had. Shortly after Mayo took office in 1853, a free woman of color named Mary Tyree was accused of keeping an assignation house on Marshall Street between Eighth and Ninth, where "men and women of divers colors, and at different periods, do congregate for most unhallowed purposes." Evidence offered in the Mayor's Court was contradictory. The owner of Tyree's tenement, a white man named John Derricott, argued that Tyree's house only had one room, making its use for assignation purposes difficult. Derricott and a policeman claimed they never heard any complaints, but another police officer said he had warned Tyree about the noise in her house. A third claimed he heard the house was "one of ill repute." Mayo, probably looking to make an example of her, sent Mary Tyree's case to the grand jury, arguing that "assignation houses were, of course, kept quiet, and made as unobtrusive as possible; and therefore, being of the most secretly corrupting character, should be vigilantly ferreted out and broken up summarily." Later that year, the police arrested a black man named Patrick Maxfield, whose house on the corner of Twenty-fifth and Main, according to the *Dispatch*, was "represented to be the most disorderly and disgraceful in the city — a rendevous for negroes and whites — males and females." The paper also reported that instead of walking their usual beats for the previous week, the night watch had "devoted a large portion of their time in exercising a guardian supervision over Pat's premises." That law enforcement officials devoted such special attention to sites of prostitution and interracial sex marked an important departure from the past.[63]

New levels of concern not only about race and sex but also about interracial sexuality were apparent in the 1850s. In 1852 the City Council passed a regulation requiring blacks to allow whites passage whenever meeting on the sidewalks, even if that meant stepping into the street. The *Dispatch* noted occasionally in the early 1850s that crowds of African Americans on the streets ought to be dispersed. Beginning in the mid-1850s, however, the paper stepped up this criticism and repeatedly complained that the sidewalk law was not being enforced. In particular, the paper pointed out that white women needed protection from blacks of both sexes. During one week alone, the paper ran two stories on the matter. In the first, the mayor sentenced a free black man named James Booker to ten lashes for "impudence" to a white man. The man had cracked Booker over the head with his cane after observing Booker and another black man "walking leisurely along the sidewalk, and on meeting a lady . . . instead of giving her the walk way, rudely struck against her." Announcing that the mayor had instructed the police to arrest any African Americans violating the sidewalk law, the *Dispatch* wrote that it was "time to enforce the law, in defence of ladies who are now elbowed off the walks." A story later that week recounted the tale of a white man who severely beat a black man who had "wilfully jostled" a white woman off the sidewalk and "then became very impudent on being complained of." In 1857 the *Dispatch* reported that the mayor exhorted the police again to uphold the sidewalk law. This time, Mayo alluded "to the fact that ladies were frequently elbowed out of the way by well dressed mulatto women. . . . As Mayor of the city, he was determined to make all negroes and mulattoes know their places and obey the laws." Mayor Mayo repeated his complaint about mulatto women two years later and asserted that he was "bent on finding them out and giving them a few lessons in good manners."[64]

Scholars have largely tied shifting white attitudes toward sex across the color line to emancipation and its consequences.[65] Undoubtedly, emancipation accelerated antagonism toward interracial sex, especially between white women and black men. But important changes in white attitudes predated the Civil War, particularly in urban areas if not in plantation districts. By the late 1850s white men in Richmond had become noticeably afraid of black male sexuality, and they felt a pressing need to demonstrate the superiority of white women to black women, no matter how finely they dressed. All in all, they believed, white women ought not to touch African Americans of either sex with whom they were unfamiliar, even accidentally.

Apprehensions about sex across the color line in Richmond were parts of a larger sense of unease about the activities of the city's black population in the 1850s, a perception among legal authorities and white citizens alike that African Americans were getting out of control. Over the course of the decade, the City Council passed a series of regulations addressing the position of blacks in Richmond, finally codifying them all in a twenty-seven-part ordinance in 1859. The ordinance addressed long-standing concerns about slaves without passes, walking on any public grounds (such as Capitol Square), and purchasing and consuming liquor, while other sections dealt with the illegality of slaves hiring themselves out, boarding, and possessing cash. The ordinance also reaffirmed a set of restrictions designed to keep free people of color and slaves from associating with one another in public or private places, and to remind both groups of their inferiority relative to whites. Blacks were not only forbidden from gathering together in groups larger than five (except for church services), but they could not ride in a carriage or public hack, smoke tobacco in public, carry a cane, or maintain a cookshop of any sort. Still another regulation restated the illegality of any African American using "provoking language," making any "insolent or menacing gestures" or a "loud or offensive noise," or uttering "any blasphemous or indecent word" to a white person.[66]

Mayor Mayo was no less zealous than the City Council. On taking office, he ordered the police to sweep the city looking for slaves walking at large and for free blacks illegally living in Richmond. A few years later, Mayo gave two of his police officers horses "and ordered them to scour the by-streets, lanes, and alleys and break up the various gatherings of negroes who assemble every Sabbath day to pitch cents, bet at dice, drink and fight." Mayo also repeatedly used cases in his courtroom as opportunities to express his dedication to cracking down on black illegality. One white man arrested for having an unlawful assembly of African Americans in his grocery store, for example, found himself the subject of one of Mayo's tirades. The man listened not only to a personal scolding, but also to the mayor's generalized lament that "scarcely a morning passed that he did not have some drunken negro before him to dispose of. The trading with slaves," Mayo vowed, "was an illegal and reprehensible practice, and must be put a stop to."[67]

The *Dispatch* always spoke favorably of the mayor's approach and frequently asked him to go further, making it even clearer that whatever tolerance existed for disorder in the 1830s was rapidly disappearing twenty years later. The paper commonly grumbled that despite the efforts of the mayor and the police, illegal activities persisted on the city's streets. In particular, editorial commentary demanded that the slave population be kept both under control and away from association with free blacks and whites, where large gatherings only led to inebriation, theft, and the undermining of discipline altogether. On one occasion, the paper suggested that it was "a notorious fact that in this city there are hundreds of small shops, kept ostensibly as grocery stores and cook shops by negroes and white men, who sell daily to the injury and ruin of our colored population, quantities of liquid poison." Calling on Mayo to continue his policy of rooting out "these haunts of misery and degradation," the *Dispatch* called for special vigilance on Sundays, "when they attract and create, through the medium of liquor, throngs of noisy, drunken negroes." Other pieces complained of whites in the city who would sell to African Americans "anything they might desire," including guns, and warned about "night cribs" run by whites where slaves could sell stolen goods. Even the jails were places for dangerous associations, and in 1857 the *Dispatch* called for a new prison, because "in the city jail all sorts and colors of the same sex are mixed together . . . and the consequence is, that all are put in contact with the vilest and most corrupt."[68]

The City Council, the mayor, the police, and the newspapers all called for the strict maintenance of legal order, but when the law proved ineffective, Richmond's white residents sometimes took matters into their own hands. Troubled regularly by "frequent assemblages of negroes and white men" at a house kept jointly by a white and a black man, and believing "that the morals of their servants were suffering from the contaminating influences exerted upon them by designing persons," residents of Church Hill repeatedly complained to the police. In 1856 a group of slave owners and hirers, finding that their appeals had no impact on the gatherings, surrounded the house and hauled the African Americans present outside. After beating them, the white residents gave the white owner notice that he could leave the premises within five days or suffer the same punishment. The *Dispatch* warned of the dangers of vigilante justice, but added that "if any people in the world are justifiable in resorting to it, they are those whose slaves are being corrupted and ruined by cross road groggeries, where stolen goods are paid for in bad whiskey, and where the negro is taught to believe that to rob his owner is a virtue."[69]

In part, white Richmonders displayed such nervousness regarding the urban black population because it seemed the city simply was outgrowing the law enforcement capabilities of the municipal government. Richmond's last annexation of land before the Civil War was in 1810, when just under ten thousand people lived in the city. By 1850 nearly three times that many people lived in the same urban space, and between 1850 and 1860 over ten thousand more people moved to Richmond. The capital was rapidly filling by the end of the antebellum period. The population density downtown increased, and Richmond's suburbs hosted more and more residents each year, which limited both the range of the police force and the endurance of the mayor. In 1856 the *Dispatch*, noting the "rapid growth of our city and the consequent accumulation of police duties now devolving on the Mayor," called for police reforms designed to streamline the processing of criminals and to redistribute responsibilities for adjudicating civil and criminal cases in the city.[70] A year earlier, the paper had pointed out that the city was scattered "over a vast extent of territory" and advocated the regular placement of two daytime police officers (of which there were only five in total) on horseback, enabling them to cover more territory on their beats. Pointing to a practice earlier in the century where mayors personally rode horseback, "scouring the outskirts of the city every Sabbath day, and dispersing improper crowds of blacks and whites," the *Dispatch* admitted that Richmond in the 1850s was "too large now, and the duties are too complicated to expect the present Mayor to perform such service, but we have no doubt that he feels the necessity of such aid in enforcing the ordinances and the laws."[71]

White expressions of racial anxieties in highly sexualized ways also resulted from the increasingly large and congested urban population. The frequent complaints of white men and women in the 1850s about crowds of African Americans on the sidewalks generally reflected growing fears of black sexuality, but did so particularly in the context of Richmond's jammed streets. In addition, density decreased familiarity but bred contempt. The bigger Richmond got, the less likely people were to recognize others as they walked through the city, even in their own neighborhoods. The nervousness of whites about the city's black population, of whose faces they recognized fewer and fewer, reflected this anonymity. One brushed against the strange bodies of others continually in Richmond by the 1850s, and white apprehensiveness grew from a perception that public streets were contested and sexualized spaces more than they had been earlier in the century.

Not just the streets but entire neighborhoods became sexually contested areas by the 1850s. The geography of crime had clearly changed from earlier in the century. There had always been criminal activity beyond Richmond's downtown, but before the 1850s neither the day nor the night police appear to have paid very close attention to parts of the city where the population was scattered, because disorderly houses and other disturbances were less likely to irritate the neighbors there. In addition, because the goal of the police had been primarily to contain rather than eliminate the city's disorder, it made far more sense to patrol the edges of downtown and focus surveillance inward, toward the river, rather than outward. Reported criminal locations in the 1830s were almost all south of Broad between Seventh and Seventeenth Streets, with a few other pockets of crime in dockside areas like Rocketts. By the 1850s, though, there were fewer and fewer sparsely populated parts of town. New areas, especially to the west and northwest (which, not coincidentally, often were neighborhoods comprising large numbers of free people of color), joined downtown as hotbeds of vice and crime. Common sites included Brooke Avenue, Second Street, Clay and Leigh Streets, and "Pink Alley," which crossed behind the Second Market between Sixth and Seventh Streets and connected Broad to Marshall (see Map 4, area shaded gray). The prominence of arrests outside the heart of the city suggested that urban law enforcers were losing the battle they had fought throughout the first half of the nineteenth century to keep vice contained.

Controlling illicit sex across the color line had become an important priority for both Richmond's officials and its white citizens, and the sense of losing the battle to contain sexual disorder only made white Richmonders more determined to root it out wherever in the city it lay. In August 1854 the mayor fined a white woman named Jane Wright "for keeping a disorderly and ill-governed house" on Brooke Avenue, "where people of every sex and color congregate and associate by day and night."[72] This arrest did nothing to curtail the activities in the house, and five days later a free black man named Samuel Harris (also known as "Sam Patch") and Eliza Ann Bridgewater, a white woman, were arraigned for "associating improperly together" at Wright's, which the *Dispatch* called "one of the lowest and vilest dens of iniquity to be found in the State of Virginia."[73] By September, seeing that police efforts had failed to roust Jane Wright from her house, unnamed individuals simply tore the house down, leaving only the chimney, on which a citizen painted a portrait of Wright crying and standing next to a fiddle. Above the portrait the artist had sarcastically inscribed "We mourn these ruins." The *Dispatch* applauded the demolition, called for similar houses throughout the city to be destroyed, and wondered why the Hustings Court grand jury "suffers such sinks of iniquity to exist under the eyes of respectable families."[74]

Even downtown no longer seemed a tolerable location for interracial sex and other forms of vice in Richmond. The mayor began telling prostitutes near the First Market "that persons of their characters would not be allowed to reside in a populous part of the city," while the *Dispatch* started to argue that places where blacks gathered to drink and carouse "should not be allowed to exist in the very heart of Richmond."[75] The backlash against disorder downtown was partially a function of clashing class interests produced by the desire of city boosters to change Richmond's image. The city's downtown area, the *Dispatch* noted in 1853, was a strange conglomeration of buildings and activities. "The grog-shop and the temperance hall stand 'cheek by jowl.' The church and the brothel are only separated by a pane of glass or a narrow alley; the millionaire and the forlorn widow are parted by a few inches of brick or marble." Such a landscape was nothing new to Richmonders in the 1850s, and most residents of the city rarely took the time to notice it. "We in the city," the paper observed, "get hardened to these sudden contrasts by degrees."[76] This amalgam, however, hardly served as the appropriate showcase for attracting visitors and business to the city. As the *Dispatch* noted, the hordes of unfamiliar people — both black and white — who poured into Richmond needed to be monitored more carefully. "The vast increase in the trade of the city — the immense additions of goods and of treasure to its already magnificent resources — require that additional security be furnished the owners and other distributors of this wealth. Every member of society is interested in this protection. Our merchants, our store-keepers, our businessmen, our mechanics demand it."[77]

The movement toward a sanitized (what we might refer to as a gentrified) downtown reflected the crowding of the city as well. Since the 1830s, for example, a row of houses on Franklin Street just west of the First Market had been occupied primarily by prostitutes (see Map 4, in solid black). But unlike the row of similar houses on Virginia Street only a few blocks southwest, the Franklin Street houses had always sat on a relatively unpopulated section of the street. Vacant lots surrounded them to both the north and the south. The night watchmen used the market house as their watchhouse, but the row of Franklin Street houses drew little police attention despite its adjacency to the market. While the police surely knew what purposes the houses served, with little effort they could keep an eye on the prostitution taking place, and no one complained. The police's greater concern lay with making sure most criminal activity stayed south and west of the row, where it belonged. But as the *Dispatch* noted in 1853, "with the advance of time, that portion of Franklin street has become one of the most populous, business and public streets in the city. This change has made, what was at first comparatively a small grievance, at present one of no ordinary character." Fifty citizens petitioned the mayor to do something about the "den of infamy in their midst," and Mayo responded by hauling four brothel owners into court. "Gentlemen" witnesses (presumably they claimed to be neighbors rather than visitors) testified that the owners were "lewd women" and that the houses were "of ill-fame, name and reputation." Living in close proximity, they argued, left "respectable" citizens either exposed to the public nudity displayed by the women or suffocated from having to close their shutters. The newspaper felt confident that the prostitutes would "all desert their present premises, or change the character of their houses."[78] As people of varying social and economic classes filled in the city, came into closer contact with one another, and confronted one another in places they had not before, elites demanded that the urban authorities respond to sexual disorder in areas traditionally left largely untouched by the law.

Not just changes taking place within Richmond but larger cultural and political changes throughout the United States in the 1840s and 1850s account for shifting attitudes toward race and sex in Virginia's capital. The industrial revolution, immigration, changing gender roles, and evangelical Christianity all helped lead increasing numbers of native-born middle-class Americans toward a new ethos of family, respectability, and social and moral reform. At the heart of these changes lay fears of a world without behavioral restraints, especially one of unrestrained sexuality. Both public and private expressions of sexuality came under scrutiny. Antiprostitution efforts began as early as the 1830s but expanded rapidly by the late antebellum period. Middle-class reformers railed against men who patronized prostitutes and saw prostitutes themselves alternately as sexual temptresses who undermined the family and as poor and unfortunate "abandoned" and "fallen" women in need of protection and salvation. In cities and towns across the United States, particularly in the Northeast, police and reformers alike began to pursue prostitutes and their customers with new vigor.[79]

By the 1850s Richmonders clearly participated in the national preoccupation with sexual order. An 1852 editorial, for example, complained that northerners had begun bringing pornographic literature to Richmond and called on captains of steamboats and hotel owners to suppress the trade of the "obscene novels and books of the most disgusting character, both in their subjects and illustrations." The papers particularly feared the "pernicious tendency" such materials would have on families. Parents would find the "correct sentiments and virtuous principles" they taught "in one evil hour . . . overthrown and lost by such books"; young men reading them might find themselves consequently on a path toward "a whole life of misery and wretchedness to themselves, their parents, and friends."[80] Other editorials expressed sentimental sorrow for the fate of sewing girls — "helpless, unprotected, dependent" women — whose salaries could be so pitiful that "women sometimes depart from the path of rectitude and virtue, and become inmates of a brothel." The paper called upon "the ladies of the city" to help find sewing girls better work and wished that "every vile, unprincipled monster, who attempted to command their labor without a fair remuneration, could be held up to public gaze and universal scorn."[81]

Ironically, the same impulses to control and reform an industrial world that inspired antiprostitution efforts also provided the spark for abolitionism, which most white Richmonders feared rather than embraced amid the tensions of sectional conflict. Richmond's ocean and river traffic as well as its railroads provided many opportunities for slaves to escape to the North, and famous runaways such as Henry "Box" Brown and Anthony Burns reminded Richmonders that their city was vulnerable to underground railroad activity.[82] In 1857 the *Dispatch* warned Richmonders that the " 'underground railroad' is again in operation, and negroes are being persuaded to take passage on it for the North every week or two." The police tried to monitor transportation routes, but slaves nevertheless found ways to escape. One article suggested that slaves were leaving Richmond by hiding in fish carts headed to the York River. From there, they procured rides to New York on wood and oyster boats.[83]

New understandings of sex and sexuality meshed with fears of abolitionism and the underground railroad to make interracial sex an issue of special concern in Richmond. The destruction of Jane Wright's house indicates that local citizens as well as the police were willing to take active steps to crush interracial sexual vice, but whites sometimes even ferreted out and punished white men involved in interracial sexual liaisons, which rarely happened anywhere in Virginia before the 1850s. In 1856 a party of approximately fifteen to twenty white men gathered on Oregon Hill in Richmond's southwest. They marched as a unit to the house of Jordina Mayo, a free woman of color who lived on the banks of the canal near the State Armory and Iron Works. The men, some of whom were probably ironworkers at the Armory or the nearby Tredegar Iron Works, surrounded the house to keep anyone from escaping. Breaking through the front door, they found their target — Mayo's white male sexual companion, John McRoberts — as he was getting out of bed. Seeking to punish him "for his low associations," the men dragged McRoberts out of the house, tied a rope around him, and threw him into the canal. After dunking him three times and nearly drowning him, the men pulled McRoberts out, stripped him naked, and painted his entire body black "in order to make his paramour and himself the same color." They then released McRoberts, "with the assurance that they would call again . . . and repeat their treatment, if he did not vamose the city at once, which, on his knees, he pledged himself to do." Jordina Mayo, meanwhile, ran screaming from the house for someone to "save her husband," and when the mob had finished she "aided [McRoberts] in scrubbing off the coloring which had been applied to his skin, and kept him with her till morning."[84]

Calling the incident a "hydropathic cure for vice," the *Dispatch* found it an "amusing case of lynching," and reported that Jordina Mayo was "a sooty black free negro of bad character" whose house was an "annoyance and disgrace" to those in the neighborhood. The police had tried repeatedly to roust her but had been unsuccessful, prompting the men who attacked McRoberts to take action, claiming that they wanted "to rid the neighborhood of the dissolute and abandoned characters in it, which seemed to be beyond the reach of the law." The mayor sent the men to be indicted by the grand jury, but he also sentenced Jordina Mayo to fifteen lashes and held her to bail for keeping a disorderly house. John McRoberts swore he had only spent a few nights at Mayo's house since Christmas and that he only went there because she did his laundry. He promised that he would leave town. But witnesses testified that they knew him "to be extremely intimate with the dark object of his affections" and that he in fact lived with Jordina. Mayor Mayo sent McRoberts to jail.[85]

White men taking such demonstrative action against interracial sexual activities in their neighborhood, and particularly against the white male party to the activities, points to extraordinarily heightened levels of intolerance toward sex across the color line in Richmond by the 1850s.[86] In 1856 in Rocketts, a group of white men calling themselves the "Rocketts Regulators" made it their mission to rid the area "of all disgraceful characters by summary punishment." In their first publicly noticed act, the men met and determined to tar and feather a man who had deserted his wife and children for another woman. Not finding him at home, they decided instead to harass interracial couples for their club's evening activities. First they "visited a den in which a negro woman and [a] white man lived on most intimate terms." They dragged the couple outside, dunked the man in a creek and painted him (presumably in black), and gave the woman "a scrubbing." The Regulators then "called at another notorious shanty occupied by a white woman and a negro man." Here they took both their victims to the river, repeatedly dunked them, and "promised to repeat their visit if their associations were continued."[87]

Interracial sex particularly offended moral sensibilities and it threatened the "respectability" of neighborhoods. Moreover, it placed whites and blacks together in ways that could only undermine slavery and white supremacy, both of which needed bolstering by the end of the antebellum period.[88] The anxiety among whites that brothels were implicitly sites for politically subversive activities lasted beyond the antebellum period as well. It was perhaps no coincidence that middle-class Richmonders not uncommonly characterized the working-class women involved in the city's 1863 bread riot as prostitutes, or that beginning in 1864 Richmond women imprisoned for their involvement in the sex trade were sent to a jail also housing Confederate deserters, spies, Union sympathizers, and free people of color.[89]

The mixture of unfamiliar whites and blacks coming to and from a city that was also a feared locus of underground railroad activity in a cultural context of sexual moralism all fit together. Interracial sex became not only unpalatable to Richmonders but something that needed to be rooted out and prevented. No matter how vigilant white Richmonders came to be by the onset of the Civil War, however, they never effectively stamped out the interracial vice in their midst. They destroyed Jane Wright's home, but she either rebuilt or moved down the street. She reappeared before the mayor just a few months after her house was razed, on the charge of keeping another disorderly house, also on Brooke Avenue near Jefferson Street, this time with the help of a white partner named John Thornton. Two years later she appeared again on the same charge at the same house, where it was reported that "negroes and low whites assembled by day and night."[90] The mayor also frequently saw Jordina Mayo. As late as 1858 she got into a fistfight with Catharine Houston, a white woman and a fellow prostitute, to which the *Dispatch*, tired of hearing about Mayo, responded that her "behavior deserves, and should always receive just the punishment inflicted upon Jordina."[91] The police also knew Houston well, for she ran a house on the west end of the canal basin in an area known as "Buzzard Roost," a row of buildings where "blacks and whites assemble to violate laws and outrage public decency."[92]

Only after the Civil War did Richmond's authorities effectively rein in sexual vice. As in many other cities, Richmond's postwar officials forced the commercial sex trade into a red-light district. Appropriately, it lay downtown, between Fourteenth and Fifteenth Streets between Main and Broad. Even more appropriately, despite the appearance of the early stages of segregation within the district, black and white men and women walked the "streets, lanes, and alleys devoted to Negro prostitutes for white men . . . Negro prostitutes for colored men," and "white prostitutes for white men, some of whom secretly sold their favors to colored men."[93]

Interlude The Context for Lawmaking

Richmond's greatest significance lay in its being the political center of Virginia. The governor and the judges of Virginia's highest court lived in the city, and legislators stayed there for several months out of the year while the General Assembly met at the capitol. Early in the nineteenth century, many legislators resided at taverns near Capitol Square such as the Swan, located on Broad between Eighth and Ninth. Later, some were known to stay at the Powhatan House at Broad and Eleventh. By the 1830s, though, lawmakers had begun gravitating further downtown, south of the square, and they lodged in hotels that became increasingly luxurious over the course of the antebellum period. The Eagle Hotel on Main between Twelfth and Thirteenth Streets was popular until it burned in 1840. Within a few years, the Exchange Hotel opened on the corner of Fourteenth and Franklin Streets. Operated by John Ballard, the Exchange (and the Ballard Hotel, built late in the 1850s across Franklin Street and connected to the Exchange by a bridge over the street) came quickly to be known as "the center of society, business and of politics during the annual meetings of the Legislature." Legislators, wealthy planters, and businessmen — not mutually exclusive groups, to be sure — mingled in the hotel lobby and the bar discussing important matters of the day.[1]

Neither legislators nor any other political official could have failed to see that interracial sex and interracial sexual relationships were everywhere in Richmond. Each day, the mixed crowds of white and black men and women surrounded them as they walked from their hotels and homes to Capitol Square. If a slave trader ever persuaded them to come to one of the city's many slave auctions, legislators had only to walk down the street from the Exchange to see the center of Richmond's slave market, which, as one historian has recently observed, was also "suffused with sexuality."[2] The heart of Richmond's trade was probably the corner of Fifteenth and Franklin Streets, although private jails and offices of traders, agents, and auctioneers lined Fifteenth from Broad to Main as well as nearby thoroughfares like Wall Street and Locust Alley. The slave trade boomed especially in the 1850s in no small part from the common sale of "fancy girls" — light-skinned African American enslaved girls and women sold to white men as concubines.[3]

Perhaps some Virginia politicians even knew Robert Lumpkin, a slave jailer and sometimes trader so prominent that Wall Street, west of Fifteenth between Franklin and Broad, also went by the moniker of "Lumpkin's Alley." Lumpkin lived in a marriage-style relationship with an enslaved woman named Mary, had five children with her (at least two of whom he sent to Massachusetts to be educated), and named her executor of his will when he died in 1866.[4] Surely, many of Virginia's powerful political officials were familiar with Lumpkin's business colleague Silas Omohundro, one of Richmond's wealthiest slave traders. Omohundro spent extravagant sums of money on diamond jewelry and other items for an enslaved woman named Corinna, whom he considered his wife, and on gifts for his five children by her. On his death in 1864, Omohundro freed Corinna and her children, his only family, and left them his entire estate. One of Omohundro's executors was none other than the vigilant mayor of Richmond, Joseph Mayo.[5]

Virginia's legislators did not even have to leave their hotel to see whites and blacks trading in the overlapping and integrally related businesses of sex and slavery. The Exchange Hotel itself housed the offices of a number of agents dealing in slaves, as did the nearby St. Charles and City Hotels, and the Odd Fellows' Hall.[6] Behind and beneath the Exchange was a notorious illegal bar and gambling facility known as the "Underground Hotel." Mostly free and enslaved African Americans met here, including servants of the hotel, although whites sometimes joined the crowd along with "ladies (of a certain class) rustling in silks and as odoriferous as pinks or honey suckles."[7]

The social milieu of Richmond, as well as that of the district each man represented, formed the contexts out of which legislators passed laws and reached decisions on particular cases involving sex across the color line. The thinking of state judges and the governor on such matters was informed by the city streets as well. The prostitutes, drunkards, gamblers, and slave traders in Richmond influenced state-level politics and political decisions undeniably, if only subtly and indirectly, by forcing people in positions of power to realize the inevitability and pervasiveness of sex across the color line regardless of their personal opinions.[8] Society, politics, and law intersected in Richmond. Specific legal entanglements involving interracial sex from both the countryside and the city appeared before state officials, and those officials made policy and passed judgments that in turn were transmitted back into the hinterland. As was commonly the case in the capital itself, managing sex across the color line and containing its consequences, rather than undertaking any determined effort to eliminate it, formed the core of statewide policy.

4

The Strongest Passion That Can Possibly Aggitate the Human Mind
Sexual Violence, Slave Crime, Law, and the White Community

No visitor to the antebellum South could fail to notice that slave owners and other white men had sex with enslaved black women, and that they often did so by force. Harriet Martineau, for example, wrote in 1837 that "every man who resides on his plantation may have his harem, and has every inducement of custom, and of pecuniary gain, to tempt him to the common practice."[1] During her experience living on a Georgia plantation, Fanny Kemble believed it "notorious, that almost every Southern planter has a family more or less numerous of illegitimate colored children."[2] J. S. Buckingham, confronted with southerners' denials that masters had sex with black women or sold their own slave offspring, spoke to enslaved mothers of multiracial children. They convinced the Briton "that the practice, instead of being very rare, is unhappily very general!"[3] Travel narratives from the antebellum period are replete with references to children with light brown skin who bore remarkable resemblance to male members of their owners' families if not to the owner himself. Authors frequently drew attention to the hypocrisy of southern men who claimed during the day that their abolitionist political opponents supported "amalgamation" even as those same men crept through the slave quarters at night. White men with unrestrained sexual appetites, these writers argued, caused inestimable damage to the bodies and morals of female slaves, the psyches of white women, and the family lives of both black and white Americans.[4]

As suggested in an earlier chapter, a white man might reasonably believe he could act toward black women sexually as he chose. So long as he kept his affairs quiet and comported himself respectably before his neighbors and colleagues, no legal or public repercussions were likely to follow. Interracial sexual abuse reminded enslaved women that their bodies were never their own. It placed black men on notice that their families were insignificant and their pretenses to protecting their wives, daughters, mothers, and sisters from harm ultimately futile. White women, meanwhile, responded to the extramarital affairs of their spouses with a combination of resignation, denial, and displaced hostility and vindictiveness toward their slaves. If a slave owner recognized his black family in his will with emancipation or financial assistance, it often posthumously compounded the emotional and psychological injuries to his white family, who were compelled to confront what they may have been able to deny while their husband, son, father, or brother lived. From the colonial era to the Civil War, thousands of rapes of black women went unreported and thousands of rapists went untried, thousands of white wives maintained public silence while their husbands turned their private lives into a series of painful and tumultuous betrayals, thousands of neighbors whispered to one another behind closed doors, and thousands of black men stood by anguished while their loved ones were sexually assaulted.[5]

But not always. Violence can breed further violence rather than submission, and in the South white male brutality sowed the seeds of dissent among slaves. Sometimes African Americans retaliated with violence of their own. This chapter focuses on two cases in antebellum Virginia where sex between white men and enslaved African Americans had unanticipated consequences. In one, a slave man in 1818 murdered a white man who had sexual relations with the slave's wife.[6] In the other, an enslaved woman, with the help of a slave man she recruited, responded to the recurring sexual aggression of her master by ending the white man's life in 1830. The systematic exploitation of African Americans produced intense antagonism that constantly simmered just below the surface of slavery in Virginia, and perpetually threatened to boil over in moments of unchecked passion and rage. These two incidents of unrestrained hostility were occasions when the cold warfare between whites and blacks over the control of African American sexuality, described vividly by former slaves in their narratives both during and after slavery, became hot. The conflicts were not random outbursts of violence, but the product of daily skirmishes that culminated in bringing two sides to the field for pitched battle.[7]

A slave murdering a white man was not only a personal confrontation, but also a capital criminal act that had to be adjudicated in court, forcing white communities to confront the consequences of having ignored the brutal treatment some of their neighbors accorded bondsmen and -women. Whites dreaded slave unrest and especially the possibility of an uprising, yet they understood that even a slave might have cause to commit murder if provoked. White men realized that their sexual exploitation of black women was central to the maintenance of racial hierarchy, yet the cycle of violence bred by sexual abuse simultaneously threatened that order. Such paradoxes entailed larger predicaments than any particular trial. They were quandaries endemic to slavery in the South, and they would never be solved.

The state of Virginia demanded that slaves found guilty of murdering whites or blacks be sentenced to death by hanging, but whites in Virginia communities did not always agree that such punishment was either just or practical. Rather than snap to judgment, before, during, and after trials of suspected slave murderers, whites carefully considered the particular circumstances of the crime and the characters of all the individuals involved. Determining proper punishment also required self-examination by whites — of their own peculiar emotional blend of empathy, fear, and rage, and their opinions about mercy, justice, and vengeance. Whites negotiated between the state and their communities, between the demands of the law and the realities of life in their localities, between their emotions and their intellect, and between their intimate knowledge of the people involved in these cases and their broader attitudes about both race and gender. Even as they sorted through the specifics of each case, though, whites never saw a white man's murder as an opportunity to scrutinize the institution of slavery or to ask why they had to live perpetually with the threat of violence from the people they owned. Slave murderers implicitly challenged slavery, but for whites containing the threat rather than questioning the system always carried the day.[8]

The behavior described in the cases under investigation here was at turns cruel, sadistic, brutal, perverse, and tragic, but these were neither typical nor exceptional events. Surely, more horrific things occurred under slavery in Virginia than appear in the public record, and just as surely incidents like those discussed here did not take place every day in every community. Interracial sex between white men and slaves was not only one of the ugliest sides of American slavery, but it could be messy and dangerous as well. Ultimately, individual instances of slave resistance did nothing to topple the hierarchies of power and control in ante-bellum Virginia, and the forced silence of slaves and their families with regard to interracial sexual abuse generally contributed to the overall stability of the racial and gender orders of antebellum society. But some-times white men failed to understand that every individual had limits to what he or she would tolerate. A misjudgment or a misstep, slave owners sometimes found, provoked responses that were entirely unpredictable and that challenged the very stability and control to which they believed their actions contributed.

By Saturday, May 30, 1818, Manuel decided that he had had enough of Langford Harrison. That morning Manuel, an enslaved man belonging to William Jones of King George County, told a runaway slave named Moses hiding at Manuel's home that "Harrison had had connec-tion with his wife, and that he expected Harrison owed him a grudge and that he would seek an opportunity to kill him."[9] Hostility, it seems, had been brewing between Manuel and Harrison, a white man in the neigh-borhood, for some time. Later that Saturday, despite her warnings that Harrison wished to shoot him, Manuel told Cate, a slave who lived on a farm near that of Manuel's owner and who later testified at Manuel's trial, that he had "often given him [Harrison] the road but would not do it again."[10] Another slave named Harry testified that Manuel had told him in the past that Harrison "had a spate against him" and that he would carry a basket of stones to retaliate should Harrison ever attack him.[11] Whatever previous animosity there had been, however, harass-ment on a local byway and an exchange of verbal hostilities did not compare with the rage provoked when Harrison had sexual relations, forcibly or otherwise, with Manuel's wife. Whatever restraint he had previously shown, now Manuel was out for blood.

Over the course of the next four days, Manuel's anger intensified as he considered how to pursue his revenge. Later on the same day that Manuel talked with Moses, a white man named Daniel Coakley said he saw Manuel with an axe in his hand. To Coakley, Manuel reiterated that "he had often gave Harrison the road, but would never do it again." The next day, a Sunday, Manuel asked Abrella, a slave who lived on a farm very near that belonging to Harrison's father and uncle, when Harrison would pass that way again. Abrella, understanding Manuel's intentions, warned Manuel that Harrison wanted to beat him. Manuel responded that "he was not afraid of Harrison and that if Harrison troubled him again, he (Harrison) should never tell the Judges who hurt him." Also on Sunday, Manuel told Harry that if the two of them were walking and met Harrison on the road, Harry should keep going and not look back. On Monday, Manuel saw Cate again and announced that "he wished he might be damned if Harrison should not die before Saturday night." Manuel also had a conversation with a white man named John Rawlet. Rawlet averred to Manuel that he doubted Harrison really intended on hurting him, but Manuel adamantly maintained that "if ever Harrison troubled him on the road, he would kill him."[12]

By Wednesday evening, June 3, Manuel had determined his course of action. About an hour before sundown, Moses claimed he saw Manuel with a dogwood club and a table fork. Manuel, Moses reported, had also said that he would kill Harrison that same night. William Marders saw Manuel shortly thereafter, around sundown, with two dogs and what appeared to be an axe under his arm, walking in the direction of the tavern owned by William Coakley. Manuel had good reason to presume Harrison would stop at Coakley's. Not only did Coakley's home and tavern lay along the route to Harrison's home from where he worked, but Harrison was also married to the former Elizabeth Coakley, who was probably William Coakley's sister. Arriving at Coakley's, Manuel passed the time with Mary, one of Coakley's slaves. When he saw Harrison coming toward the tavern, he told Mary that "my man is coming." When she discovered he meant Harrison, Mary warned Manuel to go away, for if the two met one would surely be killed. Manuel assured her that "it would not be him," and swore "he would kill Harrison for he could get no rest for him."[13]

Just after sundown, Manuel left the spot from where he had watched Harrison and walked down the road past William Coakley's house. Harrison saw him pass and, in keeping with his past interactions with Manuel, chose to badger him, asking Manuel why he was in the vicinity and whether he had a pass permitting him to be out after dark. Manuel replied that he had one and he continued walking, muttering to himself. Harrison left Coakley's house about half an hour later and followed the path Manuel had traveled. He probably had no inkling that Manuel waited for him at a fork in the road below Coakley's tavern. When Harrison approached, Manuel sicced the two dogs he had with him on the white man, probably knocking him to the ground. It is not known whether Harrison was conscious when Manuel took the dogwood club seen by Moses, which likely had the table fork Moses mentioned affixed to its end, broke Harrison's jaw, and stabbed him through each eye. The wounds were three inches deep. They not only figuratively obliterated whatever images of Manuel's wife Harrison had seen, but they also penetrated Harrison's skull, entered his brain, and killed him almost instantaneously.[14]

Three different white men would testify that in the days following the murder they saw Manuel's clothing covered with bloodstains. Manuel told one man the blood was his own and came from briar scratches, told another that he got blood on his coat while branding some horses, and told a third that he had had a bloody nose. When Langford Harrison's body was discovered, it was brought back to the home of William Coakley for an inquest, at which Manuel was present. Manuel tried to pin the murder on Moses, telling Coakley that Moses had offered to shoot Harrison if Manuel continued to conceal the runaway in his home.[15] This strategy failed. On June 12, 1818, Manuel was assigned counsel and tried by a court of oyer and terminer specially convened at the county courthouse for the occasion. A panel of five local judges heard from black and white witnesses, found Manuel guilty of the crime of murder, sentenced him to hang on July 14, and valued him at $650 for the purpose of compensating William Jones for the loss of his property.[16]

Manuel was hardly the only male slave who suffered the anguish of knowing that a woman he cherished had sexual intercourse with a white man. In their narratives, formerly enslaved men from Virginia repeatedly told of the agonizing frustration of watching their families and friends victimized, physically and sexually, by whites. In most situations, there was little a man could do to protect his wife. Reverend Ishrael Massie, who grew up in South Emporia in Sussex County, told an interviewer in the 1930s that it was common for white men to assault slave women sexually. "Marsters an' overseers use to make slaves dat wuz wid deir husbands git up, do as dey say," Massie recalled. "Send husbands out on de farm, milkin' cows or cuttin' wood. Den he gits in bed wid slave himself. Some women would fight an tussel. Others would be 'umble — feared of dat beatin'. What we saw, couldn't do nothing 'bout it. My blood is bilin' now [at the] thoughts of dem times. Ef dey [slave women] told dey husbands he wuz powerless."[17] Similarly, Dan Josiah Lockhart, who had been a slave in Frederick County and then in Winchester before escaping to Canada, told of the beatings he witnessed of his wife and children and claimed that "the hardest thing in slavery is not the work, — it is the abuse of a man, and, in my case, of a man's wife and children. They were not punished severely, — but I did not want her whipped at all — I don't want any man to meddle with my wife, — I bothered her enough, and don't want anybody else to trouble her at all."[18]

The sexual exploitation of enslaved women not only violated and degraded the women themselves, but also humiliated and emasculated enslaved men and shattered even the pretense that they might shield their loved ones from harm. As both Massie and Lockhart suggested, the masculinity of slave men included a sense that they bore a responsibility to safeguard "their women" from the dangers that surrounded them, particularly those presented by the sexual appetites of other men. When white men demonstrated their complete disregard for slave marriages and slave families, the pain of recognition among male slaves that they too were being sexually exploited, if only indirectly, was especially sharp.[19] White sexual aggressors could not have failed to understand the havoc they wreaked on the spirits of slave men by sexually assaulting slave women. Sam and Louisa Everett, both born near Norfolk, told of their master who frequently enjoyed entertaining his friends by forcing slaves to copulate publicly. "Quite often," the Everetts reported, "he and his guests would engage in these debaucheries, choosing for themselves the prettiest of the young women. Sometimes they forced the unhappy husbands and lovers of their victims to look on."[20] Just as white men knew that raping a slave woman was an assault on her mind as well as her body, so too did they realize that crushing slave men psychologically by ravaging their families demonstrated dominance more effectively than any beating ever could.

Facing such repeated attacks on their families and their personal dignity, some enslaved men ran away. Isaac Williams, for example, who lived in slavery near the Rappahannock River, reported that the overseer on his master's plantation used to whip Williams's wife simply to spite him. When asked by another enslaved woman if he would ever leave his wife and children, he responded, "what's the reason I wouldn't? To stay here with half enough to eat, and to see my wife persecuted for nothing when I can do her no good. I'll go either north or south, where I can get enough to eat; and if I ever get away from that wife, I'll never have another in slavery, to be served in that way."[21] On one level, running away seems a cowardly reaction. It certainly was a selfish one, for even if a woman's husband escaped slavery, in and of itself a difficult and dangerous task, the assaults against her were unlikely to cease. Perhaps some men believed they could escape, establish themselves elsewhere financially, and return to save their families. Most, though, probably realized when they left the plantation that the odds they would see their kin again were slim, and that they might very well die before they ever achieved freedom. For these men, death might have been preferable to the particular forms of demoralization whites brought to their daily lives.[22]

Sometimes enslaved women tried to conceal from their husbands that they had been forced into sexual intercourse with a white man. Reverend Massie told of one enslaved man who sat in his cabin rocking his infant child in his arms when he realized some peculiarities about the baby. Calling his wife to his side, he pointed out that the baby had white fingernails and blue eyes, eyes that looked strangely like those of the plantation overseer. The man's wife responded by counting the months from conception, but she did so quickly and erroneously, confusing her husband into believing it had in fact been nine months since the couple could have conceived a child. Only after this explanation, Massie claimed, was the man "satisfied hit wuz his chile. De pint I'm at is, she wuz feared to tell on overseer den."[23] Here, an enslaved woman was afraid to tell her husband the truth for a host of reasons. First, she probably feared the wrath of the overseer and additional sexual attacks if the overseer discovered she had reported their encounter. Maybe she feared that her husband would blame her for the child's conception and turn his anger toward her. She may have loved the child regardless of its paternity and did not want to see her husband withdraw his affection and resources from the infant. Or perhaps she feared for her husband's life. If he knew of the child's origin, his wife may have anticipated that he would react violently against the overseer, placing his own life in danger.[24]

Indeed, some enslaved men, like Manuel, did place their lives on the line and met the violence of white men against their families with violence of their own. Robert Ellett of Hampton, for example, remembered one day when "a strange white man came down around our cabin and tried to get my sister out. Father jumped him and grabbed him in the chest. He pointed at the big house and said, 'If you don't git in that house right now, I'll kill you with my bare hands.' The white man flew."[25] Such resistance by enslaved men was rare, however, for reasons best explained by Charles Grandy, who told a story from when he lived on a plantation, like Robert Ellett, in Hampton: "Dere was an' ole overseer too, what wanted one o' de slaves wife. Started bothern wid her right fo' de slave's face. De colored man made at him an' he [the overseer] shot 'im wid a gun. Den de colored man come at him wid a hoe. He kept shootin' 'till de man fell dead in his tracks. Nigger ain' got no chance."[26]

Perhaps it seems obvious that Manuel too stood "no chance" when he walked into the King George County courthouse for his trial in June 1818. It does not appear that Manuel's owner tried to save his slave's life, but William Jones was not in a socioeconomic position to have brought much influence to bear in any event. Jones owned three slaves in 1817 and just two in 1818, and only 150 acres of land. Langford Harrison was not of the elite white population either, owning just four horses in 1817, of which he seems to have sold or traded three during that year to buy his first slave.[27] But Harrison was still white, Manuel was still a slave, and slaves simply could not expect to get away with killing white men. In his study of the law of slavery, Thomas Morris surveyed antebellum southern county court cases where one or more slaves stood accused of killing a white superior and found only one instance where all the slave defendants were wholly acquitted. The conviction rate for murder was nearly 100 percent, higher than for any other criminal accusation, including insurrection.[28]

When local courts in Virginia found a slave guilty of killing a white man, judges had little choice but to sentence the slave to death. Such a sentence, however, did not guarantee the slave would actually be executed. In accordance with legislation passed in 1801, the trial record of every capital case involving a slave that ended in conviction had to be sent to the governor's office in Richmond. Upon their receipt, Virginia's governor presented the court documents, along with any letters or petitions received from local citizens respecting the case or, occasionally, with the recommendation of the oyer and terminer judges that the slave be reprieved, to his Executive Council, which in turn made a recommendation. The governor could then respond in one of three ways. He could choose not to act, allowing the slave's execution; he could pardon the slave; or he could reprieve the slave from hanging and sentence him alternatively to be sold to a slave trader and transported out of the United States. Between 1801 and 1865, nearly one thousand Virginia slaves convicted of capital crimes saw their sentences reduced to transportation and were sent into exile. There was an option available to whites in King George County if they believed that Manuel ought to be punished but ought not die.[29]

The sentence of transportation served both economic and humanitarian purposes without sacrificing the dedication of white Virginians to punishing slave criminals. In the 1790s, whites had begun to suspect that execution failed to deter slave criminals effectively, a suspicion that Gabriel's Rebellion only enhanced. Moreover, executing a slave was costly, since the state compensated an owner for his human property but then destroyed the person for whom it had just paid. Transportation entailed nearly all the costs of execution, but the state was able to recoup a fair amount of those costs by selling the convicted slave to a trader willing to remove the felon from the country. Transportation also gave whites the opportunity to believe they appeared merciful to the slave population. In hundreds of cases over the course of the antebellum period, local judges and other members of white communities in Virginia argued the death penalty was unnecessary or inhumane. Either because the crime was perceived to be too petty or the criminal too young, insane, or coerced or provoked by others, because the slave had been of "good character" in the past, or because evidence found after the trial suggested the possibility of innocence, whites claimed that transportation would serve the same purpose as the original sentence. The inception of transportation as a punitive option thus gave whites the ability to eliminate a slave perceived as dangerous without increasing the burden on either their wallets or their consciences.[30]

Among slaves convicted of murdering whites in Virginia between 1785 and 1864, 197 hanged and 42 were transported.[31] Sometimes where a number of slaves were convicted of acting in concert to kill a white person, some slaves hanged while others had their sentences reduced. That over 17 percent of all slaves convicted of homicides of whites were transported, however, suggests that execution was hardly a guaranteed outcome and that judges, white community members, the governor, and his council considered the circumstances surrounding slave murders and the involvement of each slave individually when determining a sentence they believed suited the crime. Take, for example, the murder of Nathaniel Crenshaw of Pittsylvania County. Shadrack, one of Crenshaw's slaves, was tried, convicted, and sentenced to death for shooting his master and bashing in his skull with a large rock. But the governor received two different letters from Pittsylvania asking that Shadrack's sentence be relaxed, based on testimony that became available after the trial. The executive delayed Shadrack's execution pending the receipt of further evidence.[32]

Three separate communications reached the governor in the two weeks after Shadrack's temporary reprieve. Six white men reported that another of Crenshaw's slaves had confessed to the murder and that they believed Shadrack's insistence upon his innocence and his claim that he knew nothing about the murder until days afterward. The petitioners added that the charge against Shadrack was supported only by a single teenage female witness. Thomas Wooding, one of the judges who sat on Shadrack's trial, confirmed that a runaway slave named Squire had confessed to Crenshaw's murder and had insisted that Shadrack played no role in the slaying. Wooding added that a third slave named Joe also confessed his role and that a white man had been taken into custody on suspicion of instigating Crenshaw's slaves to murder him and rob his house. Twelve men, including eight Pittsylvania attorneys (one of whom assisted in Shadrack's prosecution) and the county jailer, wrote that they all believed at the time of Shadrack's trial that he was guilty. But they admitted he was convicted solely on circumstantial evidence. Furthermore, Shadrack's own contention that he was innocent and the trials and convictions of Squire and Joe had now convinced them that Shadrack was probably not guilty and certainly not deserving of capital punishment. Refusing to admit that they had made a mistake and nearly sent an innocent man to his grave, they asked the governor to exercise "the prerogative of mercy in favor of a man who *may* have been improperly convicted," and either to pardon Shadrack or reduce his sentence to transportation. The governor spared the slave the experience of the gallows and had him transported out of the country.[33]

In the hysteria that followed Nathaniel Crenshaw's murder, the court of oyer and terminer had sentenced Shadrack to death on evidence that was flimsy by its own admission. The judges and the white community could have let Shadrack die anyway, but they chose to ask that the governor spare his life for a number of reasons. Even if Shadrack had been involved with the murder, he had not been the principal actor. At most, he was merely an accomplice. In addition, as Thomas Wooding suggested, there was suspicion that a white man had instigated the crime, which somewhat shifted the guilt from the slaves who actually committed the crime. But, above all, it simply became clear that Shadrack was innocent, and the citizens of Pittsylvania County had no taste for hanging innocent men, enslaved or not. As soon as whites began to associate his name with the murder of his master, Shadrack probably was doomed to being implicated and punished, and it is unlikely he believed that the governor did him a favor by "only" shipping him out of the United

States, away from whatever friends, family, and community he had, for a crime he likely never committed. But Shadrack was not destined to die. Local courts at least undertook the pretense of carrying out justice and finding the truth behind a crime, even when a white man lay dead at the hands of his own slaves.

It is important to remember that although whites looked closely at the specifics of each case in which a slave was accused of murdering a white man, they did not all reach the same conclusions from the evidence. Neither did whites always stand up for slaves who appeared to be innocent. In March 1828, for example, a slave named Harry went on trial in Powhatan County for the murder of Elbert Mosby, who had been beaten and stabbed to death. Testimony in the case was confused and contradictory, with witnesses testifying (all from confessions they heard from Harry himself) to differing roles for Harry in the murder. It appears that a white man named Robert Mendum was the primary assassin, with Harry's possible role ranging from that of innocent bystander to active conspirator in Mosby's death. The court sentenced Harry to death by hanging, but the uncertainty about Harry's involvement and the presence of strong evidence against Mendum convinced three of the five judges on the panel to recommend Harry for transportation.[34]

Shortly after the trial record was forwarded to the governor, two petitions arrived from Powhatan County. One, signed by twenty-nine men, urged the chief executive to accept the recommendation of the majority of the court. These petitioners argued that Harry was young, that he was of "general good character," and that many members of the Mosby family, to which Harry belonged, were of "bad character." The petitioners added that Harry had "not been proved by any credible testimony to have borne an active part in the perpetration of the murder." Powhatan County, they claimed, was currently in a state of "popular excitement," with many individuals furious at the recommendation of the court, but the petitioners firmly believed that those seeking Harry's execution would later "regret that they had not listened to the dictates of mercy." The second petition, signed by forty-nine men, insisted that Harry hang. The evidence in the trial, these men argued, showed that he had been "rightfully condemned to die." They acknowledged that "humanity" had induced the majority of judges to recommend Harry to transportation, but such a recommendation, these petitioners argued, "was contrary to the interest of the public." Slaves murdering white men posed a threat to slavery so great that the "strictest justice" was required. The governor had to "make such an example of Harry as will deter other slaves from the repitition of similar offences." Harry had to die, in short, to ensure "the saifty of every master of slaves in the state." After recommending Harry five different times for respite from execution, the Executive Council finally determined to let the law take its course. Harry hanged.[35]

Compared with the cases of Shadrack and Harry, the circumstances behind Manuel's crime gave no local whites any obvious reason to speak out on his behalf. At first glance, in fact, his case does not appear of a sort that would even arouse the neighborhood controversy that Harry's did. When Manuel murdered Langford Harrison, he was the only assailant and had no accomplices. No white men encouraged him to kill Harrison, and although there were no eyewitnesses to his crime, the evidence against him was both consistent and strong. He had told or implied to seven different people that he intended to kill Harrison, a witness tied him directly to possession of the murder weapon, and three different men saw blood covering his clothing after the crime. Still, the extraordinarily tense sexual dynamics underlying Manuel's case suggest that some white men in King George County may have at least considered that he had been provoked by Langford Harrison to murder. Other murder cases indicate that, across racial lines, men in Virginia appear to have shared an understanding that having sexual intercourse with another man's wife could easily incite a profoundly dangerous and unpredictable kind of rage. The judicial sphere, no less than any other in the antebellum South, was a male-dominated one, and in criminal actions white men considered that even enslaved men felt a sting when sexual boundaries were violated.

On January 12, 1801, a slave named Ben belonging to the estate of William Ware of Chesterfield County went on trial for the murder of Joe Gooding, a free man of color.[36] At his trial, Ben tried to explain his actions, and he told one of the more harrowing stories that American slavery had to offer. Sometime in 1796 or 1797, Ben acquired the consent of Mr. and Mrs. John Bass to marry an enslaved woman, never named in the trial proceedings, whom the couple owned. Despite belonging to and working for Ware, Ben regularly lived with his wife on the Bass plantation for two or three years, until one day when John Bass ordered Ben not to set foot on his farm if he wished to avoid being severely beaten. Ben, believing he had no choice, stopped visiting his wife.

Shortly after his banishment, Ben began to hear that Joe Gooding "was very much in favor with Mr. and Mrs. Bass and had taken up with his wife." Gooding stayed "in favor" with the Basses for two years, during which time Ben ceased visiting his spouse and Gooding presumably continued to have sex with her. Whether he did so with her consent is not recorded. After two years, "it was reported in the neighbourhood that Bass and Joe Gooding had had a falling out." Ben, finally seeing an opportunity for reunion, approached John Bass one Sunday morning after church and asked if he could begin visiting his wife again. Bass indicated that now he had no objection to Ben returning to his spouse. But there was a catch. Bass, perhaps angry at Gooding for something related to their "falling out," wanted Gooding dead, and he told Ben that if he wanted to see his wife again, it would be a good idea "to put Joe out of the way" first. Bass reasoned with Ben that because Gooding had "taken his wife from him," Ben would be perfectly justified in killing Gooding. Bass further explained that the task could be executed easily with poison, which would be impossible to detect.

In the months that followed, Ben and John Bass had many conversations about the planned murder of Joe Gooding. Ben eventually agreed to the plan and procured "a dose of poison from a negro Doctor in the Neighbourhood." One evening in November 1800, he put the poison in a plateful of food that he believed Gooding would eat. But Ben had made an irreversible mistake. His wife accidentally ate the food intended for Gooding, and she died shortly thereafter. Enraged, anguished, and bent on vengeance, Ben stole his master's gun, and shot and killed Gooding. He then ran to the Bass home and confessed the homicide. The Basses promised not to reveal Ben's crime, and they did not until sometime in December, protecting themselves as well as Ben.

Despite the circumstances, the court of oyer and terminer sentenced Ben to death for murder. Ben's attorney made a motion that his client might be recommended for clemency, but the judges overruled the motion. Chesterfield County clerk Thomas Watkins forwarded the available record of Ben's case to Governor James Monroe. He wrote that despite the refusal of the judges to recommend Ben for transportation, John Bass and his wife had raised the hackles of the white community against themselves by withholding information about Gooding's murder for over a month, well after the inquest was performed on the dead man's body. "[T]hese circumstan[ces]," Watkins claimed, "united together with many reports now in circulation in [the] neighbourhood where the affair happened and the death of Ben's wife apparently by poison, have raised suspicions very much to the prejudice of Bass and wife and excites a general wish that Ben's life should be saved provided he could be sent out of the Country."[37]

John Bass trafficked in the sexuality of Ben's wife repeatedly for his own benefit, first by using her to cement a friendship with Joe Gooding and then by playing on the desire of her husband to see her again to effect Gooding's execution. While the judges who sat on Ben's trial failed to see these circumstances as extenuating, if we can believe Thomas Watkins, other Chesterfield whites certainly did, probably for a host of reasons. First, although Ben plotted to murder Joe Gooding, Gooding had violated Ben's marriage and repeatedly had sex with Ben's wife prior to the murder. Second, when Ben finally did kill Gooding he was driven by impulsive rage rather than premeditation. The tragedy of unintentionally killing his own wife, with whom he was so close to reunion after Gooding and Bass stole her away, perhaps was too much to expect a reasonable human being of any race or status to stand. Third, although Ben could not legally testify against Bass in court and Bass would never be held legally accountable for instigating a murder, in giving testimony at his own trial Ben effectively did implicate Bass, and whites in Bass's neighborhood believed the slave. Other whites in the community surely felt uncomfortable with the notion of one of their neighbors using slaves as contract murderers. Whatever the precise combination of factors entering the minds of whites in Chesterfield, they did not want this slave murderer in their community, but neither did they wish him dead given the exigencies of his crime. From the "motives of humanity" they pleaded for his life. Governor Monroe granted their request and reprieved Ben on May 9, 1801.[38]

Occasionally, members of a white community found the circumstances surrounding a homicide so exculpatory that even transportation was too harsh a punishment, and they instead asked the governor to grant a full pardon to a slave murderer. On August 5, 1818, Sam, a slave belonging to Thomas Young, appeared on the plantation of Thomas Thornton. Sam accosted a slave boy named Davy and told him to go get John, a slave who lived on a nearby plantation. Sam announced that he had come to fight with John to the death. Upon hearing this information from Davy, John immediately left his house. He confronted Sam and proceeded to beat him with a large stick, leaving Sam bleeding and unconscious on the floor. Sam was carried outside to a tree, under which he died from his wounds. At John's trial for Sam's murder, Thomas Thornton, who also owned

John's wife, testified that Sam had the habit of appearing on his property against his explicit wishes. Thornton further explained that he had been told by his slaves that Sam was "very intimate with John's wife and was informed by the prisoner that he had caught him (Sam) in bed by his wife, and this some time before Sam's decease." John was found guilty of murder and was sentenced to be hanged, but the court, "in consequence of the uncommon good character of John previous to the act for which he stands convicted," unanimously recommended that he be transported.[39]

The day after the trial, forty-four men from Caroline County, including the commonwealth's attorney who prosecuted John, three of the judges who sat on John's trial, the county sheriff and his deputies, and the county clerk and his deputy, signed a petition to the governor affirming their belief that John's good character made him worthy of a reprieve. But the petitioners went on, explaining other circumstances they believed ought to be taken into consideration. First, less than half an hour prior to his death, Sam had been seen in search of John, saying that he wanted to fight with him until one of them was dead. Second, Sam had been caught in bed with John's wife. This discovery, along with Sam's "uniform bad character," prompted Thomas Thornton to forbid Sam from visiting his plantation. But Sam kept returning, and John killed him less than sixty yards from his wife's cabin. Most importantly, John had a good reason for killing Sam. John, the petitioners claimed, "was prompted to commit the unfortunate act by the strongest passion that can possibly aggitate the human mind namely jealousy; It appearing from strong circumstancial testimony that the unfortunate deceased was constantly visiting the said John's wife and keeping alive the aforementioned angry passion." As men, those who petitioned the governor understood the anguish John felt and, as white petitioners in slave murder cases rarely did, they asked that John be fully exonerated for his actions. The governor and his council accepted their recommendation and pardoned John.[40]

What Joe Gooding and Sam had in common, of course, was their race, and in the minds of the white citizens of King George County, Langford Harrison's white skin ultimately may have been what mattered most when they considered Manuel's fate. In both Ben's and John's cases, whites in the community confronted the dilemma of whether to execute slave murderers or to show mercy to tortured men, but had Joe Gooding or Sam been white, there would hardly have been much of a dilemma at all. Whatever small degree of sympathy Manuel's case may have elicited from white men in his local community was overridden in significant measure because his chosen victim literally embodied dominance, and that dominance was not subject to such a brazen, decisive, and violent challenge. Between 1785 and 1864, however, slaves convicted of murder still hanged in nearly half the cases where their victims were other slaves or free people of color, and the cases of Ben and John suggest that a myriad of factors other than the race of the victim alone entered into the thinking of whites when considering where justice lay. These considerations could in turn help to mitigate a slave's punishment for murder.[41]

Manuel could claim none of those mitigating factors. Dozens of white men testified to John's good character, but not even Manuel's own master would stand for him. Ben could claim that his was a crime of passion borne of a situation a white man had forced him into if he ever wished to see his wife again, but Manuel had planned his crime for days and he had been thinking of it for longer. The only white man he talked to before he murdered Harrison, John Rawlet, told Manuel that he believed Langford Harrison was bluffing when he threatened to harm him. If anything, Rawlet was discouraging rather than inciting the violence he saw coming. In light of all these circumstances, then, Manuel indeed had no chance. But in New Kent County in 1830, three slaves conspired to kill their master, and their case demonstrates that one other crucial factor clinched Manuel's death sentence. Manuel was a man. While his masculinity might have enabled white men in King George County, however minimally, to recognize the rage of jealousy in a person of their own gender, ironically it was also Manuel's gender that worked together with his race to seal his fate.

John Francis, a white man in his fifties and the owner of around ten slaves, lived alone in a farmhouse in New Kent County between the Pamunkey and Chickahominy Rivers just east of Richmond.[42] In the middle of the night on Sunday, August 22, 1830, two of his slaves, a young man named Patrick and a young woman named Peggy, entered Francis's home. One held a large stick while the other carried an axe. They proceeded to attack their owner, bruising and slicing Francis in the head, stomach, back, and sides. Peggy and Patrick then left the house and set it on fire, burning it to the ground and decidedly ending John Francis's life. On September 10, 1830, Peggy and Patrick were brought into court on murder charges. Two other female slaves who had belonged to Francis before his death, Franky and Caroline, were charged as accomplices. The court dismissed all charges against Caroline, but found Peggy, Patrick, and Franky guilty and sentenced all three to death by hanging.[43]

During Peggy, Patrick, and Franky's trial, the details of the story behind John Francis's murder slowly emerged from witness testimony. Peggy, Patrick, and Franky themselves all pled not guilty, and all seemed to tell slightly different stories. As related to the court by John Royster, the committing magistrate, Peggy insisted that she had not killed her master but had only beaten him with a stick. Patrick, she claimed, had accompanied her and chopped Francis with the axe. As a means of explaining her actions, Peggy also mentioned that prior to the attack, Francis had threatened to beat her until she was practically dead and then to sell her. Patrick, meanwhile, said that he had carried the stick and that Peggy held the axe, and claimed that he had only stood by the door while Peggy hacked away at her master. Peggy and Patrick both agreed that the fire was already burning inside the house when they got there, while Franky, whom Royster believed "was disposed to lie altogether," said that Patrick had gone out of the house and returned carrying the fire with him. Franky also asserted that Peggy had approached her in a cowpen on the day of the murder and upon asking Peggy "what she was going to do," Peggy responded that she "was going to beat her master."[44]

Another slave, a man named Jesse, testified that he had been standing under a tree just a few feet from John Francis's home on the night of the murder. Sometime around midnight, he saw Peggy and Patrick enter the house, one carrying a stick and the other an axe. Shortly afterward, Jesse began hearing noises, including Francis crying out "O Lord have mercy." Franky and Caroline, who had been inside the house, ran outside, and Jesse proceeded to walk away as well. A short time later, Jesse swore that he, Franky, and Caroline returned to the house, only to see Peggy and Patrick each carrying a counterpane full of straw, which they placed in the house and set ablaze. Sucky, a slave girl around twelve or thirteen years old, had also been in Francis's house when Peggy and Patrick entered. She confirmed much of Jesse's account, while Henry, a young slave boy, added that he saw Peggy and Patrick shortly after the attack searching Francis's smokehouse for money. Finally, Richard Burnett, who lived half a mile from Francis, testified that he saw the light of the fire and ran to Francis's house. As the house collapsed, he saw a body in the corner of the dwelling and threw water on it to keep the remains from being entirely charred by the flames.[45]

Notwithstanding the testimony of the accused, that three enslaved witnesses placed Peggy and Patrick inside the home of John Francis, beating him and setting his house on fire, would seem unquestionably not only to have clinched the duo's guilt but also to have sealed their fates. Like Manuel, Peggy and Patrick seem to have carefully planned and carried out their master's violent execution. But additional testimony made it clear that extenuating circumstances, beyond the physical abuse cited by Peggy, provided a chilling explanation for the slaves' drastic and almost certainly suicidal actions. After testifying to the facts of the night of the murder as he witnessed them, Jesse said more about the peculiar relationship between John Francis and his slave Peggy. He said the two fought frequently and that Francis usually kept Peggy chained to a block and locked in the meal house. Jesse believed John Francis's lasciviousness lay behind both his treatment of Peggy and his subsequent demise, for Peggy would not consent to sexual intercourse with her master. Confirming some of Peggy's own testimony, Jesse claimed that he too heard Francis threaten "that he would beat her [Peggy] almost to death, that he would bearly leave life in her, and would then send her to New Orleans," but added that Francis did so because Peggy refused to have sex with him. Jesse also testified that Francis, frustrated with Peggy's noncompliance, had sworn that if Peggy continued to deny him he would have Jesse and Patrick hold her down while he raped her. For her part, Peggy was consistently unmoved, because John Francis was not only her owner but also her father. "Peggy said she would not yeald to his requests," Jesse asserted, "because the deceased was her father, and she could not do a thing of that sort with her father." Likely near the end of her rope and tired of his perpetual threats and mistreatment, Peggy enlisted Patrick to bring the terrorism of John Francis to a halt once and for all, even if it meant her own death. As she herself told John Royster, she reasoned that she was soon going to her grave one way or another, and that "she had as well die with the ague as the fever."[46]

That John Francis sought an incestuous relationship with one of his own slaves was apparently no secret to anyone, black or white, who lived in his vicinity. Hannah, another enslaved woman who shared the same mother with Peggy, testified that her mother always told her that Peggy was Francis's daughter and that Peggy considered him her father. Concurring with Jesse's statement, Hannah also claimed to know "the deceased wanted to cohabit with Peggy, to which she objected, and that was the cause of the difference between them. . . . [T]he deceased threatened Peggy to beat her almost to death and to send her off if she did not yeald to his wishes, and declared he would have her held if she did not consent."[47] Abner Ellyson, a white man who lived in the same neighborhood as Francis, swore that "it was currently reported in the neighbourhood that the deceased was the father of Peggy and that he wished to have illicit intercourse with her, to which she objected and that that was the cause of their disagreement."[48] Nathaniel White, another white witness, supported Ellyson's statement, while John Royster also said that Peggy was believed to be her master's daughter and that he had "heard, but did not know, that Francis wished to cohabit with Peggy." One of the local justices of the peace, William E. Clopton, who lived on land adjacent to Francis, concurred with Royster.[49]

The judges impaneled at the oyer and terminer court felt they had no option legally but to sentence Peggy, Patrick, and Franky to death for their crimes, but many white men in the community claimed that Peggy's situation prior to murdering her master was so horrifying that she and her accomplices deserved mercy. One hundred men, including one of the judges at the trial, the local sheriff and two of his deputies, the county coroner, and the town constable, signed a petition to Governor John Floyd asking for clemency for the three slaves. The petitioners expressed "the utmost abhorrence" at the crime but believed that the circumstances surrounding the case, "although not sufficient to justify the act," were enough to justify some mitigation of the punishment. Hanging, they believed, was unnecessary, and commuting the sentence to transportation out of the United States would "have the same good effect on Society, as the punishment by death."[50]

Unlike Peggy, in Virginia and elsewhere most enslaved women who suffered the sexual assaults of white men did so in silence, either believing there was little they could do to alter their circumstances or fearing the consequences of resistance. Bethany Veney, author of a published slave narrative, spoke to the sense of resignation and despair felt by most who confronted the power of white men under slavery. She asked her white northern audience to imagine her pained ambivalence as the new mother of an enslaved infant, especially since her newborn was a girl. Veney loved her baby, but "from her own experience she sees its almost certain doom is to minister to the unbridled lust of the slave-owner, and feels that the law holds over her no protecting arm." Veney claimed she "would have been glad if we could have died together there and then."[51]

Other enslaved Virginia women suggested a similarly shared sense of the futility of resisting white male aggression. May Satterfield, born in Lynchburg in 1861, remembered how her mother explained the existence of people of mixed ancestry to her, indicating that for most slave women, when it came to sex with white men choice was never even a remote possibility: "Dey ain't no 'cuse fo' it now, but dey was in slav'y time. My mama said dat in dem times a nigger 'oman couldn't help hersef, fo' she had to do what de marster say. Ef he come to de field whar de women workin' an' tell gal to come on, she had to go. He would take one down in de woods an' use her all de time he wanted to, den send her on back to work. Times nigger 'omen had chillun for de marster an' his sons and some times it was fo' de ovah seer. Dat's whar ha'f white niggers come from den."[52] Sis Shackleford of Brunswick County told of the time Tom Greene, who owned a plantation adjoining the one where Shackleford lived, wished to purchase her mother to be "his 'oman." Her mother was never sold, but while her owner and Greene negotiated she "jes' sits roun' jes' as sad an' cried all de time," perfectly understanding the fate that potentially awaited her.[53] Julia Williams of Chesterfield County told one of the more heartrending stories reflecting the powerlessness of enslaved women, relating the tale of a woman whom "all de men want[ed]," sold by her master on the auction block. Shortly thereafter, Williams saw the woman running down the road, singing maniacally. The wife of her original owner bought the woman back, but it was too late. The sexual assaults suffered in the brief interim she belonged to another master apparently had driven her insane. She could do nothing but work minimally in the house. Eventually the woman ran away and was never heard from again.[54]

As Sally Hemings seems to have done, some enslaved women tried to make material advantage for themselves out of being the subject of their master's overtures, accepting favored treatment — perhaps lighter work or better housing — in exchange for acting as an owner's mistress. It is difficult to document conclusively when a female slave and a master made such an exchange or even whether the parties involved were conscious that the crass barter of sex for material benefits had occurred. More often than not, this sort of agreement was probably unspoken. A slave owner might give a woman small gifts or hold her to a much lower standard of work performance than other slaves. For their part, slave women understood quickly the significance of such special treatment, and those who sought to take advantage of their owners' attention to serve their own interests or those of their children might respond as they knew their owners wished.

Across antebellum Virginia, there were also female slaves who did muster the courage to fight off the sexual advances of their masters, though rarely in so gruesome a fashion as Peggy. Works Progress Administration (WPA) narratives are littered with references to enslaved women who tried desperately to maintain some sort of control over their own bodies. A few women ran. M. Fowler from Chesterfield County, for example, remembered one evening when her master came home drunk, "an' I was waitin' on the table, an he look up an' see me, an he give me a funny look, an' I was scared an' showed it, an' that made him mad, an' he said to the overseer, 'Take her out an' whip some sense in her,' and I run. I run out in the night, an' kept a-runnin', but finally I run back by the quarters." When she returned to her mother's home in the quarters, she was immediately whisked away to Richmond for sale. She never saw her mother again.[55]

Other enslaved women simply refused to have sex against their will with white men. Like Peggy's owner John Francis, not every white man was willing to rape a woman who refused his advances. Perhaps these men feared they might lose in a physical struggle. Others, perhaps, like those who procured sexual favors in exchange for preferential treatment, insisted on the illusion of consent, an illusion impossible to sustain if they needed to force a woman to have intercourse.[56] Complete and true domination of slave women, these men likely believed, could not be achieved through sexual violence but rather through the ability to have sex with enslaved women because the women themselves at least appeared to desire it. Absolute control consisted in mastery over both mind and body, and only sex with "consent" and preferably with longing brought both.[57]

But white men who failed to achieve such control were not above using torture as physical punishment for a woman's refusal. John Francis chose confinement and threats of beatings and sale. Minnie Folkes, a slave in Chesterfield County, told of her mother's similarly excruciating suffering under slavery. An overseer on her family's plantation used to tie her mother's arms over her head while she stood on a block of wood in the barn. Once tied, the overseer kicked the block away, stripped Folkes's mother naked, whipped her while she dangled in the air, and poured salt water on her wounds. Folkes asked her mother what she had done to receive such treatment, and her mother replied, " 'nothin' tother t'dan 'fuse to be wife to dis man.' "[58] Fannie Berry, a slave in Appomattox County, claimed that she had successfully fought off the sexual advances of white men, but that other slaves were less fortunate: "Dese here ol' white men said, 'What I can't do by fair means I'll do by foul.' One tried to throw me, but he couldn't. We tusseled an' knocked over chairs an' when I got a grip I scratched his face all to pieces; an' dar wuz no more botherin' Fanny from him; but oh, honey, some slaves would be beat up so, when dey resisted, an' sometimes if you'll 'belled de overseer would kill yo'. Us colored women had to go through a plenty, I tell you."[59]

Like Fannie Berry, there were still other women who successfully staved off sexual attacks from slave owners and overseers without having to resort to the homicidal measures of someone like Peggy. Berry told the story of another enslaved woman named Sukie, for example, whom her master "was always tryin' to make . . . his gal." On one occasion, Sukie's master entered the kitchen where she was boiling three large pots of lye in preparation for making soap, and he insisted that Sukie take off her dress. The woman refused, whereupon her master tore the dress from her shoulders and began pulling her to the floor. "Den dat black girl got mad. She took an' punch ole Marsa an' made him break loose an' den she gave him a shove an' push his hindparts down in de hot pot o' soap. Soap was near to bilin', an' it burnt him near to death. He got up holdin' his hindparts an' ran from de kitchen." Sukie's master decided to sell Sukie, but he "never did bother slave gals no mo.' "[60]

The power dynamics between slave owners and enslaved women were never as simple as choices between submission, compromise, or resistance. In most cases, black women and white men constantly battled over who controlled the bodies of female slaves. Slave women capitulated when they believed they had no choice. They bargained when the calculus of available options suggested a means of salvaging something from their anguish. And sometimes they fought back rather than endure the physical and psychic torments of sexual assault. Such battles were never entirely won or entirely lost, producing situations where white men could believe in their own omnipotence even as slave women successfully maintained their own sense of dignity. Only when women like Peggy ended the battle with such a decisive blow as murder did other white men realize how tenuous their position might actually be.[61]

When Peggy and Patrick lit the flames that finally ended the life and the brutality of John Francis, suddenly the white men of New Kent County discovered that their perceived sense of absolute power could actually be contingent. They found that the resistance of slave women could assume deadly and uncontrollable proportions and that the sexual violence of slavery they knew existed but avoided discussing and confronting would not stay concealed forever. It seems curious, then, that one hundred county men might join together and ask that slaves such as Peggy, Patrick, and Franky, who threatened the stability of white male dominance in Virginia, be granted executive clemency. Hanging the three rebels should have been the easiest, fastest, and most forceful way to demonstrate who remained in charge. As Manuel's case demonstrates, slaves could not kill white men with impunity and not expect the severest punishment, no matter how traumatic the provocation.

We can never know definitively why the men of New Kent County pleaded for the lives of Peggy, Patrick, and Franky, but their expressed explanation deserves some examination. The petitioners claimed the circumstances of Peggy's life — the constant threats of rape and incest, the mistreatment and torture — could never exonerate her of the crime she and her accomplices committed, but somehow they mitigated it. Yet white witnesses who testified at the trial conceded that they and everyone in their neighborhood knew full well the environment in which Peggy had lived every day, and they said and did nothing. The petitioners' step from inaction to action therefore seems curious, their actions before and after the murder inconsistent.

The lack of intervention on Peggy's behalf before John Francis's death was in keeping with how white communities approached the treatment of slaves by their owners. In the South, racial slavery dovetailed with a man's preeminent property rights. The way a white man treated his slaves away from watchful eyes — whether he was unsparing in his use of physical discipline or whether he was a habitual rapist — was mostly his business, both by law and by community custom. Neighbors limited their criticism of unusually cruel treatment to disapproving gossip behind closed doors, or perhaps to a private chastisement of the offending owner.[62]

But once John Francis was dead, the perspective of members of the white community changed. They likely continued to believe that nothing could fully justify the killing of a white man by African American slaves and that white men, if they chose, could have sex with their slaves at will. They also, however, knew John Francis and how he had treated the slave who was simultaneously his daughter. Accordingly, they seemed to have understood that if John Francis did not exactly deserve the method of his demise, the especially distasteful form of sexual abuse he attempted to perpetrate could easily provoke an intense reaction. In this instance, the community's own sense of justice simply failed to coincide with the written law as executed by the court. The sympathy and pity of local whites prompted them to try and protect these slave murderers from the gallows. Perhaps John L. Poindexter, a judge who helped convict the three slaves and sentence them to death but whose signature was also the first on the petition to spare their lives, had a change of heart. More likely, though, he believed that while his position as a judge dictated one course of action, the sentiments of his own conscience and his own community dictated another.

It is also important to remember that once the court convicted Peggy, Patrick, and Franky of murder, the judges effectively stripped possession of the slaves from John Francis's estate and transferred it to the state of Virginia. Property rights still remained an issue, but in asking for leniency from the state the petitioners challenged the rights of no one they knew personally. As citizens, in fact, the white men who signed the petition challenged only themselves. They had voted for the governor to whom they appealed for reprieves. They paid the taxes from which compensation for Peggy, Patrick, and Franky would be drawn should the three be executed. John Francis's death very clearly altered the perceived moral and legal positions of his neighbors to the extent that their actions came to match their sympathies.

These humanistic, local, and legal explanations, however, fail to comprehend that when slaves rose up against their masters, regardless of the context in which they did so, they implicitly threatened all masters and all whites. The actions of Peggy, Patrick, and Franky, no less than those of Manuel, must have confirmed some of the worst fears whites had about slave uprisings. Surely every intelligent white man in New Kent County understood that showing any mercy to slave insurgents could be interpreted as a sign of weakness by other slaves, who certainly would hear of how the white men had handled the affair.

Here, though, whites in the community chose not to suspect that the individual actions of a few slaves under extenuating circumstances suggested anything beyond a localized and isolated incident. Manuel carried out his crime on a public road and he killed a white man who was not his owner. By contrast, the murder of John Francis occurred entirely within the confines of his household. He died on his own property and at the hands of his own property. Unlike Langford Harrison's death, the fatal assault on John Francis was both physically and psychologically a self-contained incident, enabling Francis's neighbors to distance themselves from him altogether as a representative slave master. They could consequently handle the aftermath of his death without exaggerating its meaning. Read this way, the decision of the white men of New Kent County to ask for mercy for Peggy, Patrick, and Franky was part of a process of convincing themselves that the murder of John Francis was an anomaly, perfectly understandable given the constellation of conditions surrounding it. Francis had acted irresponsibly and had abused his power egregiously, and he paid the price. That slaves might sometimes exact retribution in such extreme and unusual cases, though, did not suggest a larger sense of crisis for slavery.[63]

The petitioners of New Kent County, then, probably believed they acted beneficently and out of sympathy, but their plea for mercy was really not about mercy at all. The execution of Peggy, Patrick, and Franky could be carried out if necessary. The court's verdict demanded it, and there was never a guarantee that a petition, especially in this case, might be responded to affirmatively. Following the violence of the murder with the additional violence of vengeance, however, could suggest that white men in the county were deeply frightened more than either they wanted to believe or they wanted other slaves to believe. Showing mercy to the murderers of John Francis was a sign of strength rather than weakness. Whites believed in the importance of demonstrating to other slaves that they could handle individual slave discontent flexibly even as they maintained firm control over the rest of the slave population.

The punishment of transportation, in fact, can never be understood as an entirely merciful, beneficent action on the part of white Virginians, for the death penalty and transportation worked together to uphold slavery, not as distinct alternatives that suggested either strength or cowardice. In supporting the power of slave owners without ever requiring uniform death sentences, the flexibility in punishment of slaves for capital crimes in Virginia represents a classic example of the "hegemonic function of the law," to borrow Eugene Genovese's phrasing.[64] To maintain their own sense of stability and supremacy, and their slaves' sense of trepidation, white Virginians wanted to appear neither too bloodthirsty nor too lenient, but always secure, calm, and rational. As Philip Schwarz has argued, "whites might be impressed with the level of determined opposition to slavery that many condemned slaves represented; they might even see the humanity of slaves in the very men and women whom they categorized as the most dangerous. But they ultimately could rest assured that hangings and reprieves from hangings were but two sides of the coin that they used to help pay for making their world safe for slavery."[65]

Gender factored into how whites in New Kent County considered the fates of Peggy, Patrick, and Franky in significant ways as well. First, when enslaved African Americans resisted their masters in a criminal fashion, men were far more likely than women to do so with a violent physical attack. In most cases, women were physically weaker than their owners. When they wished to harm a master or his family, arson or poisoning were more typical weapons of choice. The simple rarity of female murderers, then, enhanced the notion that the murder of John Francis was an isolated affair and likely made it much simpler for the petitioners from New Kent to recommend the reduction of sentence in this case to transportation.[66]

In addition, the provocation for John Francis's murder was peculiar to slave women, and the petition sent to the governor from New Kent asking to spare the slaves' lives implicitly acknowledged the trying nature of these particular "circumstances." When interracial sexual abuse remained private, the gender-specific burdens of slave women remained their own, and white men recognized and took the advantage that black female vulnerability accrued to them. But whites did recognize this vulnerability. In other instances of slave crime, local whites demonstrated that they understood that sometimes enslaved women bore special consideration for their crimes because of their gender. In Southampton County on January 13, 1840, for example, a slave named Malinda belonging to Thomas Newsom killed Allen, another of Newsom's slaves, by stabbing him in the chest with a knife. The key evidence in Malinda's prosecution for murder came from a woman named Patsey Fogg, the only eyewitness to the crime. Fogg testified that Allen approached Malinda and put his hand on her shoulder. Malinda warned him to get away from her. He refused and continued touching her. As the two "went on further round," Malinda managed to cut Allen on the arm with a knife. Later that same day, Fogg saw Allen pressing his body to Malinda's up against a post. Malinda then stabbed Allen, who staggered off and died a few minutes later. The local court sentenced Malinda to death, but recommended that she be reprieved to transportation, a request the governor granted.[67]

The justices gave no explanation for their recommendation, but presumably they believed that Malinda killed Allen in self-defense. Malinda might not have had the same judicial luck had she stabbed her master, his overseer, or some other white man. But local judges understood that, at least against a fellow slave, an enslaved woman might have good cause to protect herself from a sexual predator. This argument is not intended to imply that the judges believed that slave women somehow possessed absolute rights to their own sexuality. Far from it; the law refused to recognize in Virginia or any other slave state that an enslaved woman might be raped. In Malinda's case, the court did not exonerate her for her crimes, but it did implicitly recognize that Malinda might have cause to fight off a slave man looking to assault her sexually, at least to the extent that she did not deserve to die for that defense. The difference in the race of her victim strongly distinguishes Malinda's case from that of Peggy, Patrick, and Franky, but Malinda's case demonstrates that sympathy for the perils slave women faced as women was not entirely beyond the comprehension of white men.[68]

If the role of gender was ambiguous in motivating the petitioners from New Kent regarding the death penalty, that the governor and his council considered it when they deliberated the request of the petitioners is undeniable. On October 23, 1830, after twice postponing a vote on the case, the Executive Council recommended that Peggy and Franky be spared execution, but that the sentence of death be carried out on Patrick.[69] The trial record as forwarded to the governor contains nothing to suggest that Patrick played a larger role in the crime than Peggy or Franky, and the petitioners from New Kent County made no distinction among the three criminals. Only that Patrick was a man can explain why the council insisted that he be hanged, which brings us finally back to the function of gender in Manuel's case. To white men, enslaved men like Patrick and Manuel were simply more dangerous than enslaved women because they were far more likely to commit crimes, and when they did, deadly consequences were more likely to ensue. Moreover, Manuel was not himself the direct victim of any sort of physical or sexual attack from Langford Harrison. Similarly, Patrick personally faced none of the assaults that Peggy had. His participation in the murder of John Francis, even on her behalf, could not be justified to the Executive Council by the circumstances particular to her life.

Still, we have seen that white men in Virginia were capable of sympathy for the rage of black men who looked to make reprisals against other African Americans who sexually interfered with their family lives. White men even sometimes forgave the sexual aggressions of enslaved men against white women, especially women who were poor, without white male protectors, and perceived to be of questionable sexual mores. In 1803, for example, Carter, an enslaved man belonging to William Boyd of King and Queen County, held an axe to the throat of a "free white woman" named Catherine Brinal, told her he would kill her if she did not lie still, and raped her. Brinal testified at Carter's trial, as did Billy, a slave who was with Carter the night of the rape. Billy swore that Carter broke down Brinal's door, and further testified that he heard sounds of resistance from inside Brinal's house and "the voice of the woman as if she was crying." Carter was found guilty of rape and sentenced to hang. Three of the judges at Carter's trial, however, wrote to the governor. They conceded that Carter probably did rape Catherine Brinal, but that Brinal was "a woman of the worst Fame" and that she had three children of mixed race "which, by her own confession were begotten by different Negro men." Furthermore, Brinal had "no visible and honest means of support" and she had previously had consensual sex with Carter. In combination with testimony that Carter himself "was proved to be a negro of tolerable good character, not inclined to be riotous but rather of a peaceable disposition," the judges believed he deserved a reprieve from the death sentence, which he received.[70]

As men, white men may have been able to recognize that even black men sometimes had honor relative to one another that had to be defended with physical violence. Relative to poor, unprotected, and sexually promiscuous white women, enslaved men could even benefit from the contempt in which such women were held by most of white society. Slaves were literally and figuratively perceived to be more valuable.[71] It is telling that the three judges writing to the governor on Carter's behalf noted not only that the enslaved man possessed a superior character to that of his victim but also that they considered him to be "of great value."[72] Relative to a white man, however, no matter who the white man was, enslaved men had no honor. White men, in fact, gauged their own sense of honor to a significant extent in contradistinction to their slaves, especially enslaved men. White men could identify with black men in certain contexts, and masculinity might be shared across racial lines. Ultimately, however, in antebellum Virginia, when black masculinity and white masculinity vied for supremacy, African Americans always were supposed to come up short. Recall that when Manuel saw Langford Harrison heading in his direction, he informed the enslaved woman next to him that "my man is coming." In his fury, Manuel looked for the first time in his life to "possess" a white man, just as Harrison had "taken" Manuel's wife. At an important level, though, Manuel's battle with Harrison was not even about Manuel's wife. It was about two men fighting over who held the upper hand relative to the other. Manuel either did not care or failed to realize until it was too late that neither Harrison nor any other white man could ever be "his" man. At least not if Manuel wanted to live.[73]

It might seem odd, then, that whites in New Kent County bothered appealing for Patrick's life at all, but when the word came back to the county that Patrick was still scheduled to hang for the murder of John Francis, local whites immediately drafted additional petitions. The governor and his council needed to know that with regard to Patrick there were extenuating circumstances even beyond those of the crime in which he was involved that demanded his reprieve. Eleven men petitioned the governor and claimed that it would be "both inhumane and unchristian" to execute Patrick, for Patrick was severely mentally disabled. Included with their petition was a certificate from Turner Christian, the county jailer, who attested to his belief from talking to Patrick repeatedly in jail that the slave was "scarcely one remove from an Idiot, and that he the said Patrick is not possessed of a sufficient degree of reason to be capable of Judging Between right and wrong and may be easily induced By a designing person to commit any act without knowing it to be morally wrong." Christian further argued that Peggy was that designing person. She was, the jailer believed, "a girl of unusual intelligence, and . . . I believe that she was the mover and author of the plot and conspiracy against the said John Francis which lead to his death." Given these circumstances, the petitioners argued, executing Patrick served no purpose. It "would not render the lives of the good people of this Commonwealth any more secure than his transportation and . . . it would have no more effect on the rest of the Community than the slaughter of a bullock or any other inferior animal."[74]

On receipt of this petition, the governor's council gave Patrick a respite and delayed his execution for one month. The next day, ninety-three men from New Kent began still another petition to the governor, reaffirming Christian's belief that Patrick was incapable of understanding his actions and that he "was used merely as an instrument in the hands of Peggy." If the principal murderer was to be reprieved, they argued, they saw no reason to hang an accomplice, especially one difficult to hold accountable for his actions.[75] Council members considered this petition and could reach no decision on Patrick's fate. They gave the governor no advice. A third petition arrived on Patrick's behalf just a few days later, whereupon the council finally relented and reduced Patrick's sentence to transportation. Still, one council member remained resolute in his insistence that Patrick ought to die.[76]

It is uncertain whether Manuel would have had his sentence commuted had he been a female victim of sexual assault who waited for Langford Harrison on that road in King George County, or if whites had been willing to testify that he was insane or mentally disabled in some way. The particular configuration of relationships in a given county at a given time, so difficult to reconstruct in its nuances and details, had as much to do with the outcome of a criminal case as any abstract ideas about justice, control of slaves, gender, or the disabilities of a criminal. But that Manuel was a sane slave man who placed himself above the law of white men for a single violent, murderous moment gave him little hope for reprieve. He was executed on July 14, 1818. Peggy, Patrick, and Franky disappeared from the state of Virginia. The state sold them to three traders along with twenty-one other slaves on April 29, 1831, whereupon they were shipped to parts unknown.[77]

Once the legal mechanisms of Virginia took Manuel, Peggy, Patrick, and Franky out of King George and New Kent Counties, life likely continued largely unchanged. Perhaps white men stepped a bit more carefully around slave women for a time and thought twice before assaulting them. Perhaps those white men who had already taken sexual advantage of slave women who had husbands, fathers, and brothers watched their backs and tried not to walk alone. Slowly but surely, though, the blanket of silence covering sexual violence against slave women, momentarily ruffled, returned to its original place of rest.

Interlude The Fate of Lucy Bowman

When John Winn of Lunenburg County died in 1821, he divided almost all of his estate among his wife, his two sons, his daughter, and his grandchildren. He made no provisions for freeing any of his slaves except one, a woman named Lucy Bowman. By the terms of Winn's will, after his death Lucy was to continue serving his wife Susanna. When Susanna Winn died Lucy Bowman would be a free woman, supported financially for the rest of her life by John Winn's estate and "not to be subject to the controal of any person whatsoever." Susanna Winn died in the summer of 1833, and later that year twenty-three white men and women from Lunenburg, including two local magistrates and ten members of the Winn family, petitioned the state legislature to grant Lucy Bowman an exemption from the 1806 removal law and allow her to remain in Virginia. The petitioners stressed not only that Bowman had "always borne an excellent character" and that she had "spent her life in the faithful discharge of all duties incumbent upon her," but also that she was more than fifty years old. Forcing her to leave the state was, as they put it, "impracticable." The legislature referred the petition to the House of Delegates' Committee of Courts of Justice, which found the request reasonable and drew up a bill for Bowman on February 3, 1834.[1]

Even as the legislature and numerous members of the Winn family acted on Bowman's behalf, other Winns sought to thwart her. Twelve of them filed a counterpetition demanding that Bowman's request be denied. They could do nothing about Lucy Bowman's freedom, but they asserted that Bowman had been anything but faithful and upstanding. On the contrary, they alleged that by her actions, "the pleighted faith [has] been Violated and the Hart of an helpless Female been made to bleed at every hoar." If Bowman had earned "any thing for her conduct," they concluded, it was exile from Virginia. These Winns left the details to the documents accompanying their protest and claimed in their petition only that their objections were entirely "of a morral character," rooted in no "pecuniary" or "sordid consideration." They had not seen Bowman's petition, for which they alleged the signatures had been gathered quickly and without their knowledge, but felt sure they "could confute the whole." Moreover, they felt certain that once the legislators read what Lucy Bowman had done, they would "spurn her petition with that contempt that it deserves from every lover of vi[r]tue."[2]

Among the documents sent with the Winns' counterpetition was an affidavit from John Winn's son James, who stated that he "knew that my mother Susana Winn, had to give up her bed, to Lucy, the negroe woman lett free by the will of my father . . . in [the] lifetime of my father for twelve or fifteen years." In her own affidavit, Charlotte Winn, the widow of John Winn's other son, also named John, claimed her husband told her while he was alive that the very day Susanna Winn died Bowman "demanded her freedom" and said she would no longer serve the family. The younger John Winn replied that if she "behaved herself" she would be treated well and that if she did not "he would make her remember what she had made his mother suffer." Charlotte Winn went on to state that shortly after this confrontation her husband got sick and died, as did his sister Priscilla. She believed Bowman had poisoned and murdered not only Priscilla but also both the elder and the younger John Winn, and that in the past she had poisoned to death a female slave belonging to one of Priscilla's sons as revenge for his having angered her. One of the elder John Winn's grandchildren added in still another affidavit that Bowman became obstinate after the death of Susanna Winn, demanding immediate receipt of the financial support guaranteed in John Winn's will and refusing to labor. Priscilla Winn had whipped her to get her to work.[3]

Richard May was a medical doctor, a delegate from Lunenburg County to the General Assembly, and a supporter of Lucy Bowman. At the end of February 1834 he placed a note in the file related to her petition. Addressed to no one in particular, presumably he wrote it as the man most familiar with the now confusing situation in an attempt to clarify matters for other legislators. The petition in favor of Lucy Bowman, May wrote, not only had been well known to the counterpetitioners in advance but had been "signed by highly respectable men." Furthermore, the facts in Bowman's petition were true. Bowman was indeed "of uncommon character, for a negroe." As a friend of the Winns for eighteen years, May often had seen Bowman interact with the family. He added that she had long served as the head housekeeper during John Winn's lifetime, "was on the best terms, then and since with her *Mis-*

tress and the *Family*," and had continued in her role as "keeper of the keys" until Susanna Winn's death. May had never heard anything like the charges made against Bowman in the counterpetition, and he believed its authors were motivated by financial interest. As he pointed out, every signatory to the counterpetition was a legatee of John Winn's will. Baffled by the impossibly contradictory information presented to them, the General Assembly took no action on Lucy Bowman's petition. The bill granting her permission to stay in Virginia died when the legislature adjourned.[4]

In 1835 Bowman tried petitioning the legislature again. This time, seventy-two men and women from Lunenburg signed on her behalf and asserted that she was not only old but also infirm. Any forced migration out of Virginia might very well kill her. Writing that her life "must in any event be but short" and that she would never need the state's money for support, they pleaded with the legislators to let her stay. David Street, a neighbor of John Winn's and a local magistrate at whose house the affidavits in the counterpetition had been taken, swore in an affidavit of his own that he had lived near John Winn for seventeen years and that the elder Winn had always spoken highly of Bowman. Moreover, Street had seen Susanna Winn many times before her death, stated that she always called for Bowman before calling for any other slave, and noted that to him Bowman "always appeared to be a very trusty servant." Street had never heard Bowman accused of poisoning anyone, but he had heard John Winn's grandson John P. Winn say that if the other legatees to the will "would let him keep Lucy, he would not oppose her petition before the legislature for remaining in the State." Edward Winn, meanwhile, swore in an affidavit that he had known Lucy Bowman for over fifty years, that the Winns always spoke well of her, that he had never heard her accused of poisoning anyone, and that he had heard "James Winn, the only surviving child of the said [John] Winn repeatedly say since the counter petition . . . that he never did believe the said Lucy was a poisoner, and did not give his affidavit to that effect."[5]

In its entirety, the story the counterpetitioners told about Lucy Bowman was as unbelievable as it was bizarre. According to them, she had carried on a sexual affair with John Winn for fifteen years. She then murdered him, waited twelve more years until Susanna Winn died, and then murdered two other members of the family because they refused to acknowledge the full extent of her freedom. The family's reaction in turn was not to bring Bowman to trial or even to accuse her formally of a crime, but only to ask that she be exiled from the state.

What really happened between Lucy Bowman and the Winn family? It seems unlikely that she poisoned anyone, but had she really been John Winn's sexual partner, which even her supporters never denied? Was there actually hostility toward allowing her to enjoy her freedom, and did that reflect antagonism accumulated over the years? Or was the sexual aspect of the story a lie as well? Instead, had Bowman's demands for the money due her while the family still grieved over the loss of Susanna Winn struck the Winns as ungrateful? Had Bowman angered the Winns by refusing to work and provoked both an argument with the younger John Winn and a beating from Priscilla Winn? Had the Winns been so furious, compounded by the deaths of both Priscilla and the younger John Winn in rapid succession, that they looked to make Lucy Bowman's freedom be a time of suffering? Or was the counterpetition simply about money? Does the language of the counterpetitioners claiming they did not object for financial reasons to Bowman's request indicate they protested too much? The offer from John P. Winn alleged by David Street suggests Winn intended on keeping the money due Bowman in his grandfather's will, but that he could make such an offer at all also suggests perhaps that other legatees wanted Bowman to be able to stay in Virginia. Why, then, did they all end up signing a petition against her? Did they hope her journey from the state would kill her, allowing them to split the money for her support among themselves? If she left the state and survived, did they plan on supporting her at all?

The battle for Lucy Bowman's residency in Virginia demonstrates not only that allegations of interracial sexual relationships might be used to injure the black as well as the white partner to the act, but also how difficult it could be sometimes — no less for the historian than for contemporaries — to sort out the truth and to determine with precision the interpersonal dynamics or the course of events that provoked the allegations. State officials, as seen with the governor's handling of cases involving slave crime and as will be seen in cases discussed in the next chapter where legislators confronted divorce petitions, hoped that people close to the circumstances could agree upon a proper course of action and could advise them accordingly. When no such common ground could be found, as was the case with Lucy Bowman, officials usually took the most conservative course of action. The Winns' counterpetition may have sounded a bit outlandish, but why risk rewarding a homicidal ex-slave? The General Assembly rejected Lucy Bowman's second petition.[6] Less than a year later, she submitted one final plea. Too weak to leave Virginia, perhaps with no place to go, and remaining in the state contrary to law, Lucy Bowman faced reenslavement. She asked the legislature "that if she is compelled to be sold, that an Act may be passed authorising her to make choice of a Master." The body rejected her petition. It is unknown whether Lucy Bowman died a slave or a free woman.[7]

5

To Be Freed from Thate Curs and Let at Liberty
Interracial Adultery and Divorce

In 1831 Thomas Culpepper of Norfolk County married Caroline Johnson. According to Thomas, he and Caroline lived together after their wedding in "utmost harmony" for six months, at which time Caroline "became dissatisfied and discontented" and left her husband. She began to have adulterous sexual relationships, leading Thomas to label her a prostitute. Moreover, her husband believed she undoubtedly "had carnal intercourse with black men or negroes." Thomas claimed that he pleaded with Caroline to return home "and deport herself as became" a proper wife, but she refused, apparently lacking regard for the "honor of her character and that of her sex." Eventually, Thomas Culpepper decided he could take no more. Arguing that Caroline had "rendered herself infamous and bankrupt in reputation, and unworthy of associating with the decent and respectable of the community," he petitioned the state legislature for a divorce in December 1835.[1]

Three years after Thomas and Caroline Culpepper wed, Elizabeth and Edmund Pannill married in King William County. Edmund quickly demonstrated that while he came from a "respectable family," he was not the man Elizabeth thought she had married. She asserted that although Edmund had been relatively poor before marriage, he had received a substantial estate through the couple's union. A few months after his wedding he nevertheless "commenced and pursued a life of profligacy, aberration and shameful adultery." Edmund entered into adulterous liaisons with many women, but particularly with a hired slave named Grace, whom he encouraged not only to speak to Elizabeth in "the most insolent language" but also to assault her physically. Edmund tried to run away with Grace in 1836, only to be caught and prosecuted for attempted theft of a slave. He avoided imprisonment on a technicality and promptly left the community, never to be seen again. By 1837 Elizabeth Pannill, "poor and pennyless," lived with friends in the neighborhood. She filed a petition with the state legislature in which she declared that "it is the desire of security from the intrusion, violence and tyranny of an abandoned husband which she now seeks to obtain through a Divorce from him. The past sufferings seem to entitle her to this, and such is, she believes, the opinion of all who have heard her story."[2]

Neither the acceptable grounds for divorce nor the official procedures for procuring one in Virginia were written into state law until 1827. In practice, Virginia's chancery courts had been granting separation agreements, also known as divorces *a mensa et thoro* (from bed and board), since the colonial era, but while these decrees separated a couple and freed them from many of the financial obligations and restrictions of marriage, neither partner could legally remarry. Only the state legislature could authorize a complete divorce, or divorce *a vinculo matrimonii*, which it did for the first time in 1803. Even after the General Assembly passed laws delegating increased authority over divorces to the courts, until 1848 the legislature retained sole power to grant complete divorces on the grounds of adultery. Before then, if Virginians like Thomas Culpepper and Elizabeth Pannill wanted divorces, they had to petition the legislature to pass a private act on their behalf. Upon receipt in Richmond, divorce petitions were referred to the Committee of Courts of Justice in the House of Delegates. Committee members sorted through the documents, discussed whether they believed the petitions "reasonable," and sent their recommendations to the entire House. The delegates considered the opinion of the committee and voted whether to draw up a private bill granting the divorce. The bill then had to pass both the House and the Senate before being enrolled into law.[3]

Although petitions such as those of Culpepper and Pannill, in which a white Virginian accused his or her spouse of adultery with one or more African Americans, were unusual in the early national and antebellum periods, they were far from rare. Between 1786 and 1851 (when a new state constitution ended the practice of legislative divorce altogether) over forty white Virginians (twenty-three men and twenty women) submitted petitions of this nature, amounting to roughly 9 percent of all divorce petitions received by the legislature. Of the legislative divorces granted by the General Assembly during the entire early national and antebellum periods, 17.6 percent (27 of 153) involved interracial adultery.[4]

These petitions are primarily important not for their numbers, but for what they reveal about how some white Virginians and their communities responded to interracial sex when it entered their lives, how they expressed themselves publicly about it, and how state legislators responded to the complaints of their constituents. Adulterous sex across the color line implicitly challenged early national and antebellum southern racial and gender orders, and it posed an explosive threat to the institutions of family and marriage. We might reasonably expect that when white Virginians discovered their marital partners engaged in such behavior, they would act speedily, determine they could tolerate no further emotional, legal, and financial entanglements with their spouses, reach a decision to make their domestic troubles public by petitioning for divorce, and lay heavy emphasis on the excessiveness of the outrage. In response, even legislators who generally opposed divorce might presumably realize that these cases were exceptional. No white man could be expected to remain legally connected to a white woman who had sexual relations with black men, and despite the silence that cloaked white male sexual encounters with black women, denying a white woman a divorce under the circumstances of interracial infidelity would suggest an awkward approbation of such practices. When adultery and interracial sex came together, divorce, especially for white men, would appear nearly a necessity in a society rooted in racial slavery and white male dominance.[5]

An examination of petitions containing accusations of illicit liaisons across the color line, however, indicates a more subtle relationship among adultery, race, and divorce. When petitioners complained of interracial adultery, it is clear that the racial element in the violation of marriage vows mattered. For some male petitioners particularly, the interracial element of their wives' infidelity was so shocking and appalling that it prompted immediate indignation and a demand that the situation be rectified via divorce. For many men and for most women, however, the solutions to their difficulties were less clear. In most cases, outrage and disgust were heavily muted by a reluctance to air publicly the turmoil that provoked those emotions. For white men, admitting that their wives found black men preferable as sexual partners was extraordinarily embarrassing and a potentially devastating blow to their egos and their honor. White women, in turn, likely restrained themselves in their complaints in part because they understood that white male infidelity with black women was common and usually went unpunished. This double standard meant that women's chances for successfully procuring divorces were not greatly enhanced by an emphasis on the interracial sexual activities of their spouses. In addition, for many women, turning this aspect of their marital strife into public knowledge only heightened the humiliation of what might already be a futile effort. The consequences of admitting that racial hierarchies had turned upside down in one's marriage, then, made many petitioners of both sexes couch their appeals to the General Assembly in terms that made race sometimes incidental rather than central to the complaint.

As these petitioners tried to understand how their marriages had gone awry, racial transgressions paled in significance when measured against how deeply the act of adultery itself and other marital violations undercut the potential for a stable and satisfying marriage. At the heart of most complaints citing interracial adultery were not appeals to the need to uphold white supremacy and to punish the crossing of racial boundaries. Instead, petitioners expressed larger concerns about marriage. White Virginians who asked for divorce revealed in different and gender-specific ways that they had expected certain types of behavior from their spouses and had anticipated finding happiness and fulfillment within marriage, but that those expectations had been disappointed and betrayed in intolerable ways. Petitions were legal documents and requests to legislators, and petitioners naturally phrased their pleas and described their marriages in ways they or their lawyers believed would be most effective in winning the passage of a private divorce bill. But divorce petitions were also personal narratives of marriages replete with accounts of long-standing and repeated psychological — and, where women were concerned, often physical — agony and of the struggle to hold a dying relationship together. When interracial adultery intruded on the petitioners' domestic lives, they insisted that they wanted to be married and retain their positions as respectable members of white society. But they also finally realized, usually slowly, amid great confusion, and with the help of friends, neighbors, and relatives, that a divorce was their only hope for a better future.

We do not always know why state legislators did or did not grant individuals their divorces. The outcomes of cases involving interracial adultery suggest, however, that legislators, like the petitioners themselves, struggled with the conflict between the desire to uphold marriage and the need to condemn improper actions within the institution. Legislators, like their constituents, had to reconcile their support for the marital relationship in an environment of proper gender and racial orders with the reality that that relationship and the insistence on absolute adherence to those orders could be unstable and unhealthy. While petitioners came to feel that only divorce could resolve the contradiction, members of the General Assembly demonstrated they were less certain.

In April 1829 Richard Hall of Orange County married Sarah Paul. Believing that Sarah was a woman of "respectable parentage and occupying a respectable standing in society," Richard "had flattered himself with the hope of acceding, by the union, to her and to his own happiness for life."[6] Other men who, like Richard Hall, eventually petitioned for divorce, made similar statements about what kind of women they had believed their brides were and about what they had expected to find in marriage. Isaac Fouch of Loudoun County, for example, wrote that when he married Elizabeth Beach in 1802, he understood her to be of "fair character and unsullied reputation," and that after the couple wed, they lived together for three years "in the strictest love, friendship and happiness."[7] Dabney Pettus of Fluvanna County, meanwhile, wrote that on his marriage to Elizabeth Morris in 1801, he believed she was "a woman descended from honest industrious parents, and of unspoiled character." During the four short months the Pettuses lived together, they did so "with all the affection and tenderness that could possibly exist between husband and wife."[8]

In the early national and antebellum South, marriage was no longer primarily about the economic union of two family fortunes, as it had been for centuries in Europe and had continued to be throughout the colonial period in America. Rather, as was happening in the North, men and women increasingly married because they loved one another, and because they believed marriage would bring them a lifetime of happiness and mutual affection. Isaac Fouch wrote of his deep attachment to Elizabeth, saying that he had "from his first acquaintance with her cherished the most ardent, tender affectionate Love and regard for her."[9] But this "companionate" basis for marriage did not mean that a woman's family and her personal reputation in the community were unimportant. As Hall, Fouch, and Pettus all noted, an acceptable wife had to come from a "respectable" background. It was helpful, of course, if a woman's family could provide a newlywed couple with financial security, but it was more important that her family be accepted by the community as reputable and honest citizens. If a woman grew up in such a milieu and also was herself "unspoiled" (which primarily referred to her virginity), she was a likely candidate for a man looking to start a lifelong happy family.

For some men, however, no matter how much they loved their wives, no matter how moral an upbringing they believed their partners had had, and no matter how harmoniously their marriages had begun, something had gone seriously wrong. A stable marriage in the early national and antebellum South depended not only on mutual affection and respect but also on monogamy. The twenty-three Virginia men who accused their wives of interracial adultery certainly had lost that sexual loyalty. Lewis Bourn of Louisa County, petitioning the General Assembly in 1824, maintained that his wife Dorothea had "lived for the last six or seven years and still continues to live in open adultery with a negro man a slave the property of one of your petitioners neighbors," and that she had borne two children by the "said negro man."[10] Thomas Cain of Frederick County wrote in 1841 that his wife Mary had given birth to "black children who could not be other than the fruits of an adulterous intercourse with a negro."[11] William Pruden of Nansemond County insisted in 1840 that his spouse Louisa—who had "been recently seen engaged in illicit intercourse with a negro man" in his house and on his bed—was not only a "notorious whore, accessible to all who choose to apply for her favors," but had also borne the biracial child of a free man of color.[12] Of the twenty other men who petitioned against their wives' interracial adultery, sixteen found what they believed to be irrefutable proof in their spouses having given birth to one or more children who clearly manifested African ancestry.

To white southerners, a woman who committed adultery acted in direct contradiction of her role as a wife. Richard Jones of Northampton County wrote in 1814 that his wife Peggy, who delivered a baby that "could not be the offspring of your petitioner or of any other white man," was a woman who had abandoned "every principle of virtue and chastity which ought to govern the conduct of a woman and a wife."[13] William Baylis of Fairfax County asserted that his wife Rebecca had become "notoriously infamous in morals" by living openly with a free man of color and bearing a child by him, while Joseph Gresham of James City County believed that his Sarah had acted "in violation of her marital vows, and the duties of a virtuous and faithful wife."[14] These wives, through their adultery, had in many ways entirely inverted the characteristics of the women their husbands thought they had married. The ideal wife was a paragon of "virtue" — chaste, devoted, and affectionate. These women had done little to fulfill that ideal but much to demonstrate their promiscuity and faithlessness. If they bestowed affection, they did so upon other men.

Southern wives were supposed to abide by the wishes of their husbands in all things domestic, including sexual relations, but in accordance with southern family ideals, men had marital responsibilities to meet as well. Men who petitioned for divorce often made clear that they had held up their end of the marriage bargain. Lewis Bourn, for example, insisted that before his wife's adulterous relationships began, he had "treated her with all the tenderness affection and respect which could have been asked at his hands as a husband and a man."[15] Similarly, Bryant Rawls of Nansemond County wrote that he had "endeavored to treat [his wife Rachel] as well as his circumstances in life would justify,"[16] while Isaac Fouch asserted that he had acted toward his wife "with all that tenderness and respect which the most upright and virtuous woman ought to expect."[17] If, above all, wives owed husbands sexual loyalty and obedience, husbands owed wives respect, financial support, and affection. Men like Bourn, Rawls, and Fouch made a point of telling the legislature that they had acted responsibly.

In part, men noted that they had acted as proper husbands to assure lawmakers that they were in no way responsible for the actions of their wives. If a man wanted a divorce, he had to demonstrate that he was the injured party and that he had not encouraged his wife's behavior.[18] This need for a husband to show his innocence of wrongdoing helps explain why Joseph Gresham insisted that he had "been liberal in supplying all the wants of his wife, peaceable, kind, and affectionate," and that his wife's "crimes and delinquencies . . . have been in no way induced by want, severity or unkindness."[19] But we should not overestimate the strategic element in a husband's proclaiming his guiltlessness. A husband asserting in a divorce petition that he had been wronged by his wife also marked one of the rare instances when a white southern man publicly acknowledged that he had been victimized at the hands of a woman. Through such an admission, men expressed not only their outrage but also their confusion, disappointment, and embarrassment at their wives' betrayal and refusal to abide by their husbands. Southern men who petitioned for divorce necessarily revealed a chink in their masculine armor. In the cultural environment of the early national and antebellum South, where honor was central to a man's identity, and where that honor importantly relied on white female sexual virtue specifically and the dependent position of married women generally, this insecurity had to be compensated for by a proclamation of masculinity.[20]

That men felt such a challenge to their maleness rarely appears overtly in divorce petitions. Ayres Tatham's petition, however, is one that lends itself to such a reading. Tatham married his wife Tabitha in Accomac County in 1793. Ayres was a laborer and claimed he expected little financial success, but he "had flattered himself with such portion of domestic happiness, as might reasonably be expected in his condition of life." With Tabitha, he thought he had found that happiness. The Tathams lived together for ten years "in harmony" and had three children, but in 1803 Tabitha delivered a child fathered by a black man. In 1804 she proceeded to abandon Ayres, only to be spotted later living in Philadelphia. "It is vain to describe the distress of your Petitioner on that occasion, or the shame and confusion of a woman, whom he had cherished with the kindness due to the relation which she stood to him," Tatham informed the General Assembly. "Suffice it to say, that shame and confusion soon induced her to desert the view of those, to whom she had been formerly known." While Ayres Tatham possessed intimate knowledge of his own distress, it is unclear that his wife actually told him of her "shame and confusion" before she abandoned him. Perhaps Tabitha was indeed ashamed of her adultery, but Ayres's juxtaposition of his distress with Tabitha's shame and his repetition of the phrase "shame and confusion" at least suggest that Ayres projected some of his own feelings onto his wife.[21]

David Parker of Nansemond County employed a similar rhetorical strategy when he wrote that his spouse Jane, who had "frequently had criminal intercourse with slaves or persons of color," had left the state and moved to North Carolina. In his words, Jane was "urged no doubt by a sense of shame and a consciousness of guilt." David Parker never seems actually to have heard his wife say anything of the sort but instead assumed it to have been the case.[22] Men whose wives committed adultery genuinely believed they had acted properly as men. Their complaint lay not with their responsibilities but in the humiliating and bitter reality that they had been denied the happiness and the full and proper expression of their masculinity they believed would come through the fulfillment of those duties.

Some men who accused their wives of extramarital intercourse with African Americans clearly believed that the interracial element greatly exacerbated the betrayal. Joseph Gresham, for example, stated bluntly that his wife's adultery was "aggravated by the fact, that it was committed and carried on with a man of colour."[23] Thomas Cain argued that Mary Cain's delivery of children of mixed ancestry made her adultery "of the most aggravated character."[24] Similarly, Leonard Owen of Patrick County offered the fact that his wife Nancy give birth to a biracial child as "such a horrid violation of the marriage bed" that he saw no need to elaborate further "upon his case as he is convinced it must be obvious to any person" that he deserved a divorce.[25] The reaction of these men to the activities of their wives is expected, given that interracial sex was perhaps the greatest legal taboo in the nineteenth-century South. The willingness of antebellum southern legislators to intervene in an area of private life such as sexual conduct was rare, and the laws against fornication and interracial marriages suggested a level of anxiety among white southerners about liaisons across the color line unapproached even by fears of other threats to the family such as incest and rape. White women having sexual relations with black men seemed especially likely to provoke antagonism, in keeping with the dedication of white southerners to the maintenance of white female sexual purity.[26]

In the complaints of most men, however, the influence of racial ideology on the gravity of the adultery was far murkier, as suggested by the multiple petitions of William Howard of Amherst County. When he first filed a divorce petition against his wife Elizabeth in 1807, Howard claimed that the couple had been married for nearly two years until Elizabeth "either by the ill advice and persuasion of wicked disposed people, or from her own natural perverse disposition . . . began to alienate her affection and duty from her legitimate husband." By the time William Howard asked for a divorce, Elizabeth had left home and she lived "constantly in the habits of adultery and lewdness with other people." Howard declined altogether to indicate the race of Elizabeth's adulterous partner or partners.[27]

Only when Howard failed to procure his divorce and filed a second petition in 1809 did he elaborate on the circumstances of his crumbled marriage. This time, he wrote that his neighbors informed him that whenever he left home Elizabeth used his money and his house to entertain "the idle, the Vicious, and disipated," and that she commonly engaged in "the most brutal and licentious connections, having no regard to persons of colour." Howard did not want to believe the reports circulating in the neighborhood but could no longer delude himself after he came home one night and discovered his wife naked and in bed with a free man of color.[28] Howard's avoidance of the racial issue in his first petition suggests how a white woman's adultery with a black man might have exacerbated a white man's embarrassment at the circumstances of his marriage. Simultaneously, however, Howard's failure to mention the interracial nature of his wife's infidelity indicates that he may have felt the race of his spouse's adulterous partner or partners to be less relevant to the procurement of a divorce than the simple fact of adultery itself.

Bryant Rawls's appeal points to similar confusion over the connections among adultery, race, and divorce. Rawls informed the General Assembly that Rachel, his wife of thirteen years and mother of his three children, "in violation of her marriage vow, and in opposition to every principle of known religion and morality has abandoned the bed of your petitioner, [and] has been delivered of a coloured child while living with him say about 2 years ago, which child was begotten by a negro."[29] Rawls's language is highly imprecise. His petition never indicates whether Rachel's abandonment, her adultery, or her sexual trespass across the color line was her most egregious sin. That Bryant Rawls failed to specify whether his wife's greatest crimes were of a racial or sexual nature is in some ways unsurprising. Southern racial and gender orders were inextricably linked, and when a woman violated both in a single act, neither race nor gender need necessarily supersede the other in offending the moral sensibility of a respectable white southerner.

Numerous scholars argue, however, that the participation of a white woman in interracial sex was so beyond the pale of morality that the social response was to ostracize the woman swiftly and automatically.[30] Presumably, the husband of a married woman guilty of such illicit behavior would, at the prodding of his community, try to exclude her as quickly as possible from the honorable institution of marriage. But as Virginia's divorce petitions show, the response of husbands to the discovery of their wives' adultery with an African American was not always swift or automatic. Some men did indeed act quickly and petitioned within months of discovering their wives' adultery, but many others waited years before doing so. The wives of Thomas Cain and Lewis Bourn had not one but two children with black men. Richard Hall's wife Sarah began a sexual relationship with a black man shortly before the Halls' marriage in 1829 and had her first biracial child just six months after her wedding. By the time Richard petitioned for divorce, it was 1838 and Sarah had borne three black children.[31] Clearly, most men were repulsed by their spouses' behavior, and even if they did not divorce their wives immediately they at least ceased cohabiting with them or procured legal separation decrees. But many of these men remained married for years afterward.

Hesitancy and delay on the parts of many petitioning husbands do not suggest a degree of tolerance for their wives' adultery, nor does it seem that many men secretly harbored a desire to forgive and reunite with their unfaithful spouses.[32] Some men likely waited to petition for divorce because they had no immediate wish to remarry or because they had to accumulate enough money to cover legal fees. The reality that one might collect the necessary funds and still not get a divorce must have caused some men to pause as well. But many probably delayed filing their petitions because getting a divorce in a society so devoted to the maintenance of the family was not a matter to be taken lightly. Even when a woman had committed adultery with an African American, the alternative of divorce was a weighty matter to be contemplated with great earnestness. Men accusing their wives of interracial liaisons could not in good conscience continue cohabiting with them, but just as living with a disloyal woman undermined familial stability and threatened a white man's honor, so too did the embarrassing public admission that one needed a divorce. Caught between two unpleasant realities, some men came to feel that divorce was the lesser of two evils.

Most men who finally made the decision to petition for divorce did so with the assistance of their communities. Accompanying petition after petition by men are affidavits and depositions of friends, relatives, and neighbors testifying that the facts were truly stated. Community members provided testimonials to the good character of the petitioner, such as the nineteen Amherst County citizens who endorsed William Howard's second petition and certified that he was "an upright, Honest, and industrious man."[33] Men and women alike affirmed that they had witnessed events as related by the petitioner. Midwives testified that they had delivered biracial children to women accused of infidelity, house guests swore they had personally witnessed acts of adultery, and neighbors stated that they had examined the infants of the accused women and believed the babies to be at least partially of African descent.[34] Although women frequently testified as to relevant events they witnessed, when it came to judging the character of the petitioner, women seldom had a public say. Certainly, women were important arbiters of local opinion, and behind closed doors likely brought influence to bear on what was said and thought about men. But in a public document, what women actually thought about the character of a man appears to have been irrelevant. Only men sat in the state legislature, and while they valued what women saw, they held women's opinions insignificant next to those of fellow men, who determined what made another man honorable.

Community members demonstrated their willingness and ability to support a man's petition, but they rarely encouraged a husband to divorce his wife. Neighbors appear to have known the intimate details of petitioners' lives, which amounted to local scandals and provided topics for gossip. Richard Jones, for example, reported that the fact that his wife's daughter had an African American father was "notorious in the neighbourhood."[35] Affiants for Richard Hall similarly noted that the African American paternity of Sarah Hall's children was "generally understood and believed in the neighbourhood," while fourteen men signed a statement on behalf of Lewis Bourn in which they noted that the fact that Dorothea Bourn had given birth to children of an enslaved man was "doubted by no person who knows anything of the parties."[36] It also seems likely that communities did indeed sometimes ostracize adulterous women. Enough petitioners indicated that their wives left the state to suggest that at least some unfaithful women literally became social outcasts.[37]

Other women, however, never left, and they stayed in the community regardless of what their neighbors thought. Numerous men wrote in their petitions that their wives still lived in the local community in a state of "open adultery."[38] The family was still in many ways a private enclave in the early national and antebellum South, and although neighbors might tell a man that they would support him if he chose to file for divorce, ultimately the decision was his and his alone. John Fleming, for example, offered to help his friend Lewis Bourn procure a divorce (for a price), but only after asking Bourn "what he was about to do with that woman" and hearing Bourn respond that "he wished to be divorced from her if he could."[39] In this way, neighbors acted more as informal monitors of community standards, keeping their eyes and ears open at all times, than they did as an active police force ensuring that all violations of the social order were ruthlessly punished.[40]

When men finally decided to petition for divorce, they justified their actions in several ways. Some couched their petitions in appeals to male honor. William Rucker of Allegheny County, for example, asked the legislature, "[W]ho wolde wish a man to be compeled to live with a woman who had a mellatter childe thair is none of yew bute wolde like to be freed from thate curs and let at liberty."[41] Isaac Fouch, meanwhile, was certain that reconciliation with his wife was impossible and that "to attempt to live with her again, would only insure the contempt and disrespect of the worthy and virtuous part of society."[42] Rucker and Fouch had reputations to uphold, and they appealed to the members of the General Assembly, as fellow men, to respect their need to do so. Other men suggested that the marriage relationship was a contractual one and that when wives failed to meet their obligations, husbands were entitled to be freed from the arrangement. Bryant Rawls, for example, argued that "no person ought to be compelled to support or recognize as a wife a woman so lewd as the said Rachel."[43] Richard Jones, meanwhile, reported that his wife had so forsaken the virtuous and chaste life a married woman was supposed to lead that he "finds it impossible to continue with her on those terms of harmony and affection which ought to subsist between those united by such intimate ties."[44]

Whether appealing to honor or to the notion that a contractual arrangement had been breached, men implicitly expressed their desire to mend what they saw as a tear in the social fabric of early national and antebellum Virginia. Some men made this connection explicit. Lewis Bourn hoped legislators would assist him and "embrace every opportunity to show their disapprobation of a practice and a state of things so directly against the spirit and policy of our laws; so injurious to the morality of the country, upon which must, in a great measure, depend civil liberty and the permanency of the land."[45] Bourn apparently failed to see the irony in waiting seven years and until his wife had given birth to two children of color before he began legal proceedings to rectify the "state of things" in his marriage. That his seemingly firm resolution finally to do so grew out of a long period of inaction suggests that divorce was a last resort for him, the only means he saw remaining to resolve the difficulty that his wife's actions posed.

William Baylis's petition to the Virginia legislature in 1831 neatly tied together the themes of threatened honor, violation of an agreed-upon contract, and the need to restore social order expressed by men who wished to divorce. Baylis wrote:

Your petitioner believes, that the institution of marriage is as honorable as it is ancient; and has for its object the promotion of happiness and a virtuous and lawful intercourse or connection, between the sexes: it inculcates domestic peace, and a firm and abiding confidence between the parties contracting, without which, instead of its being a source of domestic endearment and social affection, it becomes an irksome and disgusting tie, without respect, without confidence, without affection, the sure precursor of anarchy, confusion, and too often self-destruction. Your petitioner, seeking therefore (legitimately) that happiness and self respect, which every rational being *has a right to seek*, asks of your Hon. Body, the only means by which it is attainable under existing circumstances — that is to say, by divorcing him from the said Rebecca, and which were he not to ask, would be a lame and shameful submission on his part to a personal degradation scarcely before equalled in the annals of domestic life.[46]

Women who committed adultery with African American men threatened male honor. They laid bare their own lack of virtue as white women. They undermined any pretense to sustaining a marriage based on mutual loyalty and affection. Through all these violations, these women posed fundamental challenges to the foundations of southern society. Divorce in many ways demolished those foundations by entirely severing the ties between men and women in the family. Confronted with such a dilemma, however, some men decided that when so much damage had already been done to the marriage relationship, it was irreparable. Only its legal dissolution could allow people like William Baylis to rebuild their lives as respectable white men, perhaps married in the future to some more respectable woman.

Lucy Watts believed herself born "of the most respectable parentage." When she married James Watts in Amherst County in 1822, she did so "from no improper motives," but only with "sincere and ardent affection." She "had fondly hoped that similar feelings and similar affections warmed the bosom of her husband" and planned that "days and years of happiness and contentment would have been the lot of each."[47] Sopha Dobyns of Bedford County similarly recalled that at the time of her wedding "she enjoyed all the blessings which can result from parental tenderness, all the advantages which are derived from education, and all the benefits arising from the fortune and high standing in society of her deceased father." From her union with Jonah Dobyns, she expected nothing less than "a fulfillment, of those youthfull anticipations, of reciprocal attachment and blissful old age."[48] In many ways, women like Watts and Dobyns, who eventually petitioned for divorce from husbands who sexually crossed the color line, wanted from marriage precisely what men did—lifelong love and mutual affection. Women appear to have been proud that they possessed what men desired in a wife—a strong moral character and a respectable upbringing in an honorable family.

As Sopha Dobyns indicated, a respectable family often meant a relatively wealthy one. To poor or middling men, many women brought financial assets as well as virtue to a marriage, because a married woman's property accrued to her husband. Women who petitioned for divorce, however, did not necessarily point to the financial rewards marriage to them entailed as a suggestion that their husbands married them solely for their money. Rather, women from financially successful families were proud to be able to bring some of that success to their marriages. They believed that having money could only enhance the happiness of companionate matrimony. Charlotte Ball of Culpeper County neatly demonstrated the connection between financial stability and a healthy marriage in 1806 when she petitioned for divorce from William Ball, her husband of six years. "[P]ossessing a property," she declared, "very adequate with care and industry to their decent support, she had every reason to hope for as great a portion of happiness as most people enjoy in a married state." In this way, when women wrote of the property they brought to their marriages, their wealth supported their virtuous moral characteristics and bolstered their value as brides.[49]

As Charlotte Ball implied, the possession of financial resources did not absolve a husband of his responsibilities as a married man. The Balls began their marriage with property, but that property had to be managed with "care and industry." Married women wanted to fulfill the expectations of their husbands, but women had expectations of their own. In particular, women required men to be good providers. Even when women brought no property to a marriage, they believed they had a right to ask a man to work hard and help ensure his family's survival. As Sarah Robinson of Campbell County wrote in 1841, when she married her husband Samuel he was "poor having no property but as your petitioner then supposed sustained an honest and reputable character." Her family had little to provide the couple, but she hoped that despite Samuel's poverty, "by their united exertions a competency might readily be procured to enable them to sustain themselves in comfort, happiness, and independence."[50] Sarah Robinson's family was not rich, and she was willing to work, but she still believed, as did most women, that her husband had a duty to support the family. Just as men asserted they were industrious and looked for women of virtue, women maintained they were virtuous and looked for men of industrious character. Gender roles thus complemented one another in southerners' sense of the proper marital relationship.

Sadly for many women, southern men frequently failed to meet their responsibilities as loving providers. Many women who petitioned for divorce, in fact, argued that their husbands had never intended to play their proper roles as husbands at all. Instead, they had duped their spouses into marriage. Janet Hunter of Petersburg, for example, claimed that Samuel Hunter had "wormed himself into the good graces" of both her and her mother through ardent professions of piety. Once he and Janet wed, however, he "threw off the mask." Samuel not only informed her he had married her for her patrimony but he also "became the most abandoned and profligate of men and a scoffer and contumner of religion."[51] Elizabeth Harwell wrote in 1820 that her husband Hartwell had begun courting her when she was just twelve years old. Listening to his "warm Professions of ardent and never ending love," and to the advice of her friends who sang his praises and spoke of the glories of married life, Elizabeth accepted Hartwell's proposal. Within a few weeks of their marriage, though, Elizabeth "awoke, as from a delightful dream, to all the horrors of her unhappy State." Employing the same metaphor as Janet Hunter, Elizabeth Harwell recorded that "the mask of Hypocrisy in which her vile and profligate husband had too successfully hidden his real character, was thrown aside, and the ardent, tender Lover, became the cold senseless hard hearted Tyrant."[52]

Unlike men, who focused almost exclusively on their wives' adultery when filing their petitions for divorce, women usually leveled a litany of charges against their husbands. Most common were accusations that a husband was repeatedly and maliciously both verbally and physically abusive. Lucy Norman reported that within the first year of her marriage, her husband James rapidly "advanced from one step of dissipation to another and from acts of indifference and neglect to cruelty and violence."[53] Janet Hunter charged that Samuel Hunter "not only abused his wife frequently to her face in the most opprobrious manner; in terms grating to the ear of a virtuous woman, but he used the same terms against her frequently in the Market Place of the Town. He also beat her in the most severe and cruel manner, sometimes even with the Tongs, so as to cover her body with blood."[54] Ann Eliza Eubank of King William County complained that just a few days after she married her husband Alfred, she found an open knife in her bed. Alfred and Ann Eliza lived together for just three months, during which time he frequently told her he married her for her property. He also commonly beat her, choked her, threw her out of the house for hours at a time on winter nights, and generally inflicted the "most cruel, wanton and unprovoked corporal punishment" on her. Ann Eliza also reported that Alfred woke her up on several occasions while trying to suffocate her to death.[55]

Another complaint of many women, often compounding abuse, was that their husbands failed to support them. After Sarah Womack's spouse beat her, threatened to kill her, and finally chased her from their Halifax County home in 1843, she lived in the "most destitute condition" and was deprived "of her rights and of the means of support."[56] Mary Alvis was a widow in possession of several years' earnings when she married her second husband, Peter, in 1824. Ten weeks after their wedding, Peter took all the couple's money, abandoned his wife, and provided "no assistance whatever towards her support and maintenance."[57] Nancy Rowland's husband Washington squandered their estate and chased her and the couple's infant daughter from their home. They were left "to the protection of an aged father upon whom they are now dependant for present support and future provision." Nancy feared that she and her daughter would soon "be deprived of house and home and dependant on the charity of the world."[58]

Men were frequently not only abusive and irresponsible, but they were adulterous as well, in the above cases and others with African American women. Mary Terry's husband William, for example, abandoned her and five children, "took up with a free negro woman living in the neighborhood, and, with her, left the County and state."[59] Robert Dunlap came into possession of an enslaved woman named Milly when he married Ellen Shields. According to Ellen, he "was criminally unlawfully and carnally Intamate with and Keep her the said Nigroe Milly from the time your petitioner first married him untill she was from necessaty compelled to leave him" nine months after their wedding. Witnesses on Ellen's behalf testified that Robert frankly admitted to his sexual relationship with Milly, that he "took her in his own wifes Bed and there carryed his licenshious designs into opperration," and that Milly had recently given birth to a biracial child.[60] Lucy Watts reported that she and James lived together for three and a half years until he suddenly left her and their three children. James then enlisted for a five-year term in the army, where "he became attached to a free woman of color, and claimed her as his Wife, and carried her away with him when he left Lynchburg where he had enlisted as a soldier."[61]

The array of charges women directed against their husbands can be explained in several ways. One is that husbands beat their wives far more frequently than the reverse, and because married women could not own property, only husbands were in a position to ruin their wives financially. Women accused their husbands of multiple aggravations simply because men committed more of them.[62] In addition, although male adultery was certainly not viewed as acceptable behavior, a double standard nevertheless traditionally existed in European and American cultures that found a woman's adultery far more egregious than a man's. This perspective in turn helped shape attitudes toward divorce and suggested that men would be more likely than women to be granted a divorce on grounds of adultery alone. Awareness of this divergence in attitudes toward sexual violations of marriage vows may have prompted many women to describe their grievances more fully, rather than rely only on the crime of adultery as justification for a divorce.[63]

Women probably also detailed the full range of their complaints because in so doing, they demonstrated that their husbands had entirely failed to act as married men were supposed to in the early national and antebellum South. Men were heads of the domestic household, but they were expected to treat their wives with respect and to support them financially. In addition, although the need to protect white female sexuality meant that white male southerners made a woman's sexual purity central to her respectability as a wife, male adultery was not unimportant. A sexual double standard may have made such activity less distasteful to southerners (especially to male southerners), but male philandering still violated the sanctity of marriage. In the same way that a man accusing his wife of infidelity implicitly painted a portrait of her as the antithesis of a good wife, women detailed the crimes of their husbands to the same effect. Southern wives, no less than southern husbands, expected certain behavior from their spouses. For women who petitioned for divorce, their spouses had failed to act as anticipated.

Just as men made certain to indicate that they had not been at fault for the adultery of their wives, women repeatedly and consistently assured the legislature that they had in no way provoked their husbands' infidelity or abuse. Mary Terry, for example, wrote that her conduct while she and her husband lived together "was that of a dutiful and affectionate wife; and that the extraordinary conduct of her said husband has not been brought about by any neglect of duty or affection on her part."[64] Janet Hunter similarly asserted that she "performed the part of an affectionate, conciliating and virtuous wife and employed all the means of her power to render the said [Samuel] Hunter happy and contented, and she can with confidence say that it is not in the power of said Hunter or of any other person to prove aught against her character or conduct as an exemplary wife."[65]

Women, in fact, tended to go even farther than men in providing evidence of their willingness to act as proper spouses. Few men admitted that they would forgive or even tolerate their wives' sexual transgressions. Women, however, often averred that they tried desperately to get their husbands to cease their philandering and abide by the sanctity of their vows. Washington Rowland not only abused his wife and ran her out without reliable means of financial support, but just a few months after the Rowlands married he entered into a sexual liaison with one of his own slaves. He also regularly stayed in the same bed with his enslaved mistress, in the same room in which his wife slept. Still, Nancy Rowland wrote that for nearly two years "without complaint she submitted in silence to her husband's infidelity and attempted to reclaim him by caresses and obedience but in vain."[66] Witnesses for Lucy Norman reported that her husband verbally abused and physically threatened her, and that he was involved in a sexual relationship with an enslaved woman named Maria, whom he often embraced and kissed in the presence of his wife. Nevertheless, Lucy wrote that "not having despaired of the happiness which she had promised herself, by the connection . . . lost sight of no means to win his affections and reform his habits: She determined to exhaust every expedient at conciliation and friendship, and, under no circumstances, to permit herself to be provoked to any step which might serve him as a pretext for greater unkindnesses or improper excesses; but, in that spirit of 'charity' which 'hopeth all things' to 'overcome evil with good.' "[67]

In part, this effort by women to reclaim their husbands can be explained strategically. To obtain a divorce, women needed to prove not only that they were personally obedient and dutiful wives, but that they were virtuous even "in the face of provocation."[68] Endeavors by women to save their husbands from waywardness, however, also fit with their expected roles. Women were seen as repositories of virtue and were expected in marriage to tame the wild ways of men. This burden was one men did not have to bear. Nurturing a wayward husband may have been an onerous and painful task, but for a wife to acknowledge her failure was also potentially to admit that she was somehow inadequate as a woman. Married women petitioning for divorce took every opportunity to demonstrate that they had fulfilled each feminine duty their society required, precisely so they could show that their husbands bore sole responsibility for the unhealthy state of their marriage. By petitioning for divorce, women had to acknowledge that their unions had failed, but they would never concede that they had failed to act as respectable women.

If the importance of the racial element to adultery was unclear in the divorce petitions of men, it was even more so in the petitions of women. Undoubtedly, most women found their husbands' trespass across the color line especially grotesque, an inordinate aggravation of their violation of the marriage bond. Charlotte Ball, for example, wrote that she was "tortured" by her husband's "frequent criminal connections with the most abandoned of the human species."[69] Elizabeth Harwell was appalled not only that another woman had taken her place as the object of her husband's affections but also that the woman was "(shameful Truth) his own Slave." She asked the General Assembly rhetorically: "Was she to submit to all this?"[70] Janet Hunter, meanwhile, lashed out at her husband, who had become "habituated to the most open and shameless adultery, indulged in illicit intercourse even in his own house with the vilest blacks of the Town, and even openly boasted of the number of his black wives." She added that Samuel Hunter was sometimes "confined to his house by the most loathsome diseases contracted in his adulterous intercourse with negroes."[71]

Most women, however, while noting the race of their husbands' illicit sexual partners, placed little stress on the interracial element of the crime. Ann Eliza Eubank, for example, complained of her husband Alfred's "shameful, sinful and degrading intercourse with other women, white and colored" and of his frequent abandonment of "the marriage Bed to seek the Bed of a colored woman." But these complaints were brief and followed a detailed history of physical abuse that caused Ann Eliza to live "in great bodily fear of her life," and of Alfred's abandonment of her.[72] Mary Lawry of Culpeper County complained in 1843 that her husband, Newsome, had been imprisoned for trying to run off with his enslaved mistress, Cynthia, and for stealing a horse. In her petition to the legislature, however, Mary stressed that she was "poor and penniless and is the disgraced wife of a miserable convict," not that she was the spouse of a philanderer who strayed across the color line.[73]

Some women, while mentioning their husbands' adultery in their petitions, failed to indicate any interracial element to the crime at all. Sarah Robinson complained that her husband was lazy, neglectful, and intemperate, that he threatened her with physical violence, that he repeatedly committed adultery "with the basest prostitutes," and that he finally left the county with a "woman of ill fame," by whom he had two children. Only in the Campbell County court proceedings, required by state law before a Virginian could petition for divorce, did the jury note that Samuel Robinson "notoriously lived in habits of illicit intercourse with lewd women, both white and black."[74] In her petition, Sopha Dobyns detailed how Jonah gave her lashes with a stick, how he beat her father when he tried to intervene, how he wasted their money until he became "almost a vagabond," how Jonah pursued her and her three infant children wherever she tried to take shelter, and how her husband repeatedly threatened to kill her, often while holding a gun in his hand. Sopha mentioned nothing about adultery. She left that to Stephen Terry, who filed an affidavit on her behalf detailing how he witnessed Jonah Dobyns beating his wife. Terry added that "he heard the said Dobyns boast to his wife that in her absence he had taken one of his own negroe women into her bed and that he would do it again whenever it suited him."[75]

This lack of emphasis may have resulted from another double standard that existed for sexuality in the early national and antebellum South — the attitude toward sexual relations between whites and blacks. Interracial intercourse was nearly always frowned upon, but communities rarely exposed men publicly, and their wives frequently suffered in silence or remonstrated only in private. Women, therefore, may not have emphasized the racial element of their husbands' extramarital affairs because others in their social environment may not have seen it as an especially aggravating feature. Compared to the adultery itself, the beatings, and the financial ruin women cited, the interracial aspect of the crime may have been relatively minor. In a social and cultural environment where sex between white men and black women was neither entirely tolerable nor demonstrably intolerable, a woman petitioning for divorce probably found the racial element of her husband's crime worth mentioning but not worth emphasizing. A husband's financial neglect, habitual physical abuse, and withdrawal of affection generally were causes far more likely to galvanize a woman's community to back her petition for divorce.[76]

A few women, however, did detail their husbands' behavior with respect to black women. Often, those who did called particular attention to the intent of their spouses to degrade their white wives, in the belief that lawmakers would not tolerate such inversion of racial and gender hierarchies. In 1824, Evelina Gregory Roane of King William County reported that in addition to beating her frequently and preventing her from seeing her family, her husband Newman brought his enslaved mistress and his two children by her into the Roane house and treated them as his family. To Evelina's consternation, Newman "declar[ed] his strong attachment for the mother and stat[ed] that the two children were his and that he meant upon principle, to do more for them, than for his lawful children." Newman also forced Evelina to perform domestic chores, forbade her to scold his biracial children, and demonstrated in front of her "the tie of regard for this nigroe woman . . . in a strong discriminating manner — as if to encrease the unhappiness of your petitioner, by removing all doubt." Newman Roane, Evelina wrote, had utterly overturned his white wife's rightful position as the domestic head of a slave-owning household by reducing her to "the situation of a Slave who for some unpardonable offence, was constantly under the frowns of its Master."[77]

Similarly, Elizabeth Harwell wrote that her husband Hartwell had allowed his slave mistress to usurp "*her* empire over him." One witness swore to an instance when Elizabeth refused to return home with Hartwell Harwell unless he sold or hired out the slave. Harwell refused and fired back: "[D]amn you, if that sticks by you, I will bring her by here tomorrow in the gig by the side of me in stile."[78] Witnesses for Lucy Norman reported that her husband James often had Maria, his enslaved mistress, sit at the table and eat along with the Normans. On one occasion, Lucy told Maria that if she sat at the table she would be punished. James responded by telling Lucy that he would kill her if she laid a hand on Maria, whereupon Lucy burst into tears, turned to a guest seated at the table, and asked "if it was not too much for her to stand." On other occasions when Lucy Norman tried complaining of Maria's presence at the table, James told her that Maria "was as good and worthy as" his wife, and that if Lucy "did not like his course of conduct to leave his house and take herself to some place she liked better."[79]

It seems likely that many other women who filed for divorce in part based on their husbands' interracial adultery experienced similar humiliations. Most, however, left the details of these events to the imaginations of the legislators. Even if these women believed that describing such events would help their cause, the incidents either could not be proved (because men bore no mixed-race children) or were simply too traumatic and embarrassing to admit. Asking for a divorce and reporting that one's husband committed adultery with African American women was difficult enough, but detailing such experiences as those of Evelina Roane and Elizabeth Harwell was simply too painful for some women to bear. As Elizabeth Pannill confided, "many incidents of [her husband's] private domestick persecution, remain even now buried in the bosom of his unhappy victim, being of a nature too painful for recapitulation, and not susceptible of legal proof."[80] Those who filed affidavits on Lucy Norman's behalf gave some significant details of her husband's behavior, but Norman herself indicated they only "partially enumerated" James Norman's actions. There was still much more she could not bring herself to describe, and she hoped in her petition "to be spared the pain of further enumeration of them."[81]

Just as they supported men, white community members assisted women who petitioned for divorce. Just as neighbors testified to the good character of male petitioners, so too did they affirm the virtue of female complainants. Nancy Rowland, for example, procured the signatures of thirty-two Henry County men on a statement that "from her infancy to this time she had been reputed and held and believed by us to be a moral chastte and respectable woman, and that we feel for her present situation, and most earnestly recommend her as worthy of being relieved by the legislature of the commonwealth." When Rowland's first petition for divorce was rejected by the General Assembly in 1820, she resubmitted in 1821, this time with the support of sixty-one county men.[82] Men and women alike vouched for the truth of events as told by women in their divorce petitions — to beatings, verbal abuse, and adulterous liaisons they had witnessed or knew about. But just as male petitioners relied on other men for their opinions of the case, so too did it seem especially important for women to prove they had the respect and support of men in the community. A woman might proclaim her virtue and protest against her husband's treatment, but men were the primary public arbiters even of a woman's virtue.[83]

Community members supported women when they petitioned for divorce, but, as in the case of male petitioners, friends and neighbors rarely appear to have encouraged it. They sheltered women who had run away from their husbands for fear of their lives, who had been evicted from their husbands' homes, or who were left destitute by a dissolute husband. But marriage — especially for women, whose roles as wives dictated their dependence on and obedience to their husbands — was central to the moral foundation of the early national and antebellum South. Neither community members nor married women themselves wanted divorce to enter their lives. Confronted with the choice between misery and divorce, women, like men, sometimes waited many years after their mistreatment began before petitioning for relief.[84] Only truly desperate circumstances would sanction such action.

Desperation, in fact, seemed to characterize the reasoning of most women when they petitioned for divorce. Women couched their appeals in terms of their dependency, relying on the sympathy of state legislators for relief from their misery. But wives who argued that they deserved a divorce turned their ostensible position of weakness into a strength. Many women, in playing on the mercy of members of the General Assembly, simultaneously tweaked the lawmakers' sense of male honor. Both Janet Hunter and Elizabeth Harwell, who argued they had been tricked into marriage by their husbands, pursued the theme of their own frailty to the very end of their petitions. Hunter wrote that "she is with the Bitterest agony compelled to state that if there be a man in this State whose reformation in this life is utterly hopeless it is Samuel G. Hunter. Your petitioner therefore presents with confidence her claim on the magnanimity, the honor, and justice of the Virginia Legislature, fully believing that no case was presented to the Legislature where female endureance and female patience was ever carried further than in this instance."[85] Harwell, after finally being abandoned by her husband and forced out of penury to live with her mother, produced a truly inspired plea. She asked rhetorically: "What alternative is now left to your Petitioner, but to Resort to the Magnanimity Candour Liberality and Justice of the Legislature for Relief from accumulated Misery. Shall the voice of the wretched be heard in vain? shall helpless injured woman Plead, and to Virginians too without success? Your Petitioner cannot, she will not believe it."[86]

Women like Janet Hunter and Elizabeth Harwell had not spurned the roles of obedience and dependency they were expected to play in marriage. Rather, they protested that despite every effort to play those feminine roles, their husbands had declined to act as married men should. Even then, Hunter and Harwell did not cease behaving as respectable women. If anything, they wallowed in their dependence and respectability. They transferred the demand for honorable behavior from their husbands to the General Assembly. The offended wives concluded that if legislators were truly decent, upstanding Virginians, they would bestow mercy upon women who, in the process of trying to live up to the ideals of their own culture, were themselves so virtuous yet so mistreated.

In petitioning state legislators, Virginia women, like Virginia men, called upon those in power to rectify a difficult situation, to bear some responsibility for a set of social and cultural rules Virginians elected them to help uphold. Men and women alike suggested that they had wanted to stay married and had tried to act appropriately, but their spouses would not oblige. In demolishing whatever remained of the marriage bond, divorce was not a pleasant option, but it was the only equitable one petitioners believed available if they ever wanted to reassume their places as respectable men and women in southern society. As Evelina Roane wrote in an unusually eloquent appeal against Newman:

> It is in great apprehension she comes, tho with a mind firm in its purpose. . . . [I]n the sight of God and Man she would seek to learn if there is any ordinance of social and civilized man . . . which goes to perpetuate the marriage vow, under circumstances, allowing of no reciprocity and where the life of the weaker party is but a contingent event, leaning upon the aweful suspense of cruel rage and unrestrained violence. To the holy in mind who revere those institutions upon which the happiness of the human family is founded . . . she puts the precious question, who in the narrative of this case has prophaned the holy law. To those whom Philosophy guides, whose attribute it is to govern their species and estimate all human policy, she appeals they know well their responsibility.[87]

But Virginia's legislators do not seem to have always been sure just where their responsibilities lay. Of the twenty-three men who cited interracial adultery as a complaint in their divorce petitions, the legislature granted divorces to sixteen, just under 70 percent. Of the twenty women citing the same complaint, eleven, exactly 55 percent, received divorces.[88] During the early national and antebellum periods as a whole, the General Assembly granted divorce to 33 percent of both male and female petitioners, indicating that while both men and women had higher success rates when they reported their spouses' adulterous liaisons with African Americans, men were particularly successful.[89]

Such markedly high percentages of success for men might be taken to support the suggestion that southerners found white women having sex with black men so appalling that no man could be expected to stay married to such a woman. On occasions when the Committee of Courts of Justice's recommendations were recorded in the legislative journals or when the assembly explained its reasoning in the act of divorce itself, the presence of biracial children, whose existence supposedly proved the interracial sexual affair of a white woman, was sometimes the crucial factor in the divorce.[90] Similarly, if southerners indeed found white men's sexual straying across the color line more tolerable (and harder to prove) than white women's, it may help explain why the divorce rate for women was less affected by the interracial element. Even in cases where men filed against their wives, however, race does not appear always to have been the overriding concern of legislators. Had that been so, one would think that men leveling such accusations would have received their divorces almost automatically.[91] But in nearly one-third of these cases, men stayed legally married to their adulterous wives, a circumstance that, regardless of whether men actually cohabited with their spouses, effectively meant they could not marry again without becoming bigamists.

In cases of interracial adultery where petitioners were denied divorces, legislators did not reveal their reasoning.[92] The lack of any clear pattern in the decisions of the General Assembly may suggest that legislators were torn by contradictory impulses in making decisions about divorce. They wanted to maintain social stability, which required keeping as many marriages together as possible and dissolving them only in cases of absolute necessity. This desire for close supervision of divorce requests helps explain why the legislature retained complete jurisdiction over divorces until 1827 and over a substantial number of them until 1848, despite the growing numbers of petitions that prompted the overburdened Committee of Courts of Justice to resolve as early as 1815 "that it is expedient to pass an Act, investing the Superior Courts of law with jurisdiction to grant divorces in certain cases."[93] But even as they tried to contain the number of divorces they granted, lawmakers also had to acknowledge that they perpetuated demonstrably unhealthy and unstable domestic situations by forcing married couples to stay together when a man cruelly neglected and abused his wife or when a woman was sexually disloyal and challenged the preeminent role of her husband in the household. Sometimes, a divorce was necessary to maintain the moral integrity of the law in the eyes of white communities.

Two divorce cases from neighboring North Carolina, both heard by the state's supreme court in 1832, illustrate the kinds of tensions that could pull at southern state officials when they made decisions about divorces. When Marville Scroggins sought to divorce his wife Lucretia because she had given birth to a biracial infant, North Carolina chief justice Thomas Ruffin refused the request, noting that Scroggins knew his wife was pregnant when he married her. Ruffin expressed abhorrence at Lucretia Scroggins's behavior but held firm to the principle that "persons who marry, agree to take each other *as they are.*"[94] As Victoria Bynum has demonstrated, the state supreme court under Ruffin's leadership viewed divorce with great skepticism, as the justices saw themselves "as guardians of social stability who cherished the ideal of paternalistic harmony within husband-wife relationships."[95] But the Scroggins decision did not sit well with many white North Carolinians, and when a similar case appeared before the court just a few months later, Ruffin granted Jesse Barden a divorce from his wife, noting that his decision was "a concession to the deep rooted and virtuous prejudices of the community" against white women participating in sexual relationships across the color line.[96]

For Virginia legislators too, decisions on divorces were balancing acts. Just as each petitioner had to determine at what point asking for a divorce outweighed the need to act as a proper married man or woman, so did members of the General Assembly need to calculate the relative value of various factors in a confusing situation. Legislators had to balance the notion that women were supposed to remain obedient to their husbands with the idea that women were also entitled to male respect and support. They had to decide whether it was more important for men to stay absolute rulers of their households or whether a man who behaved so poorly and ruled so ineffectually that he had lost the esteem of and control over his wife required state intervention in his private affairs. Historian Peter Bardaglio suggests that southerners also had to deal with the tension between a family model of harmony, hierarchy, and

dependency and a more northern bourgeois model of family as a contractual relationship based on affectionate love.[97] The element of race
only complicated an already complex situation, as lawmakers had to
determine to what extent the taboo against interracial sex would influence their thinking.

It also has to be remembered that the state legislature was not a single-
minded body but a collection of individuals. Each legislator had his own
opinion on questions of family, gender roles, marriage, and divorce, and
how the legislature as a whole chose to resolve the tensions provoked by a
divorce petition depended in part on the particular composition of the
body. That the membership of the General Assembly changed from session to session ensured that voting patterns on petitions would change as
well, as new groups of state lawmakers confronted the issue of divorce.

Petitioners accusing their spouses of interracial adultery to justify
their pleas for divorce expressed concerns about marriage common to
Virginians filing divorce petitions for other causes as well, from adultery
with a white person to desertion, from physical abuse to drunkenness. All
petitioners wrote of expectations and betrayal, of hopes shattered, states
of confusion entered, and breaking points reached. For example, William Bartlam, a minister from Chesterfield County, wrote that during his
marriage to his wife Temperance "he had endeavoured to perform towards his wife in good faith all that he had promised in his matrimonial
vows, and he can truly say he loved her with all that affection which
should exist in this holy relation." Despite his warnings that she was not
comporting herself in a way he thought "proper in a virtuous woman,"
he discovered Temperance in bed with another white man. William tried
to win her back from her adulterous ways, but she continued her course
of action, and he finally determined in 1844 that "humanity cannot
always endure there is a point beyond which the stoutest heart would
cease to yield support, honour, good name had been forfeited on her
part." William Bartlam recognized that "her whom he cherished in the
soul of his hope and over whom his affections had hovered as the 'cloud
rest on the deep blue sea' is lost to him forever! aye forever." Bartlam
asked for a divorce.[98]

Women such as Polly Carver of Pittsylvania County wrote of how their
marriages had gone off track as well. Polly had married Hiram Carver
around 1812. During the short time the couple lived together, "she
manifested towards him a degree of affectionate kindness of which the
female sex so justly boast and which are eminent Traits of love and

devotion. She was influenced in her kind Treatment toward him by the most ardent and involuntary love and ventured to hope for a requittal or at least to find it reciprocated." Just two or three days after their marriage, however, Hiram "went off with a party of shewmen." He returned several weeks later for one night and then vanished, never to be heard from again. "The hopes of mortals," Polly wrote to the legislature in 1819, explaining why her attachment to Hiram had to be severed permanently, "are indeed fallacious. We immagine ourselves in actual possession of those objects in pursuit of which we have passed so many moments of anxious solicitude. We indeed feel ourselves engrasping and encircling the object of our most fond and pleasant anticipations and rest easy and contented when on a sudden and without notice we discover our fatal error and hence our most brilliant prospects forever blasted."[99]

Petitions involving accusations of interracial sexual liaisons differed little in their rhetorical content from other Virginia divorce petitions, but therein lies their value. Broadly, they yield insight into the language of divorce among petitioning Virginians, into the gender-specific marital expectations of love and mutual respect, and into the emotional devastation wreaked when those expectations were not realized. Specifically, the ways petitioners discussed interracial sex suggest that even when this issue interfered with their marriages and even when a white woman was involved, adultery with an African American provoked intricate responses from Virginians rather than reflexive, unthinking ones. Some petitioners expressed indignation and anger, but most chose not to emphasize that racial boundaries had been crossed in their marriages. Petitioners were revolted and knew their marriages could no longer continue as they had, but confusion and shame controlled the mind-sets of these Virginians as they pondered the significance of that understanding and the realization that rectifying their situations required a public airing of their problems. Often, it took years and the support of their neighbors and friends to sort through this set of issues in any final emotional or legal way. Legislators, in turn, reflected the confusion of their constituents. As they considered the justice of these petitions before the law, they faced conflicts of their own between the need to uphold white male supremacy and the need to maintain the institution of marriage. The sexual confounding of the color line, rather than uniformly stirring calls for the strict maintenance of racial boundaries, instead confounded the lives of all those it touched.

On February 13, 1836, Thomas Culpepper was denied his divorce. The Committee of Courts of Justice recommended that the legislature reject his petition, and the House of Delegates accepted the committee's decision.[100] Two years later, on April 9, 1838, the General Assembly passed a private bill on behalf of Elizabeth Pannill and granted her a divorce.[101] She could begin the process of digging herself out of poverty and rebuilding her life. If she chose to remarry despite Edmund Pannill's mistreatment, perhaps her new husband fulfilled the "hopes of happiness and protection" she had sought all along. Thomas, meanwhile, would never be allowed to remarry. Legally he remained attached to Caroline Culpepper, regardless of her activities as "a woman of ill-fame." But perhaps Thomas ignored the decision of the state legislature. Maybe he and Caroline simply resolved to live their lives as if they had never had an association with one another. Many couples in antebellum Virginia, too poor or too impatient to wait for the General Assembly to determine their fates, likely went their separate ways without the legal sanction of divorce. Happiness, after all, was hard to find.

When Lewis Bourn filed for divorce, he claimed that his wife Dorothea lived in "open adultery with a negro man a slave." The affidavits accompanying Bourn's petition indicate that the enslaved man in question was named Edmond, and a number of witnesses testified that Edmond was a "mulatto." Others, however, introduced a curious phrase to describe him. Wilson Sayne described Edmond as a "white slave," as did Thomas Pulliam, who called Edmond a "remarkable white slave." Edmond's owner, John Richardson, swore that Edmond was "as white as white men generally are." Thomas Sayne noted that "this slave is nearly or quite as white as Lewis Bourn's wife," while Thomas Anderson pointed out that "this slave is so bright in his colour a stranger would take him for a white man."[1]

Slavery passed down through an individual's mother and, as the children of Thomas Jefferson and Sally Hemings made abundantly clear, skin color had very little bearing on slavery. Inherited status trumped appearance. When individuals like Edmond or the Hemings children were free, however, they caused all sorts of difficulties for white Virginians looking to categorize them racially. In the mid-1820s, for example, John Carlton, a white slave owner from King and Queen County, made out his last will and testament and left his entire estate to two of his children, Mary and Thomas Carlton. John Carlton made no mention in his will of either his wife Sarah or the child with whom she was pregnant at the time of the will's writing. Sarah gave birth to William Carlton just six months after her husband wrote his will, but John Carlton never altered its terms. By the end of the 1820s, John Carlton had gone insane and died. The King and Queen Circuit Court ordered that Mary and Thomas Carlton each receive one-third of their father's land and slaves. The court ordered the remainder of John Carlton's estate to be rented and hired out until a decision was reached as to whether William Carlton could legally claim a share as his father's son. In 1829 Mary Carlton, now married to William Watkins, sued in the Superior Court of Chancery in

Richmond, claiming that her purported brother William was in fact not John Carlton's son at all, but rather was of mixed race. He had been born while Mary Watkins's parents were married and living together, but had an African American father, was therefore illegitimate, and was not entitled to any portion of the Carlton estate.[2]

William Carlton was not at the chancery hearing, but the court heard depositions as to whether he "appeared by his features, hair and complexion, to be a mulatto." The chancellor ordered the case back to King and Queen County for the court there to determine three issues: the race of John Carlton, the race of William Carlton's father, and finally whether John Carlton was William Carlton's natural father. The chancellor further suggested that William himself be shown to the jury so that they might visually inspect him. After a change-of-venue request from William's guardian and some jurisdictional confusion, the case was tried in neighboring Essex County in 1837, by which point Sarah Carlton had died. At trial, the plaintiffs attempted to call local witnesses to testify that John and Sarah Carlton had both been white and that William Carlton was of mixed parentage. They also endeavored to bring to the stand "a physician of eminence in his profession" to testify that "according to the laws of nature" it was impossible for two white persons to have a multiracial child.[3]

William's lawyer, R. T. Daniel, objected to both of the plaintiffs' strategies. He argued that according to the law of presumption regarding illegitimacy, if John and Sarah Carlton were legally married, unless the plaintiffs first brought evidence that John Carlton was impotent, that the Carltons lived apart, or that John Carlton had no sexual access to his wife around the time William Carlton was conceived, then William was the Carltons' legitimate child. His physical appearance and how anyone assessed it were irrelevant. The court sustained the objection, and excluded both the local and medical testimony. The jury accordingly found that "John Carlton of King and Queen County and Sarah Carlton his wife . . . were white persons and that Wm. Carlton the defendant was born during wedlock of said John and Sarah and that according to law and the evidence introduced that the said defendant Wm. Carlton is the legitimate child of the said John Carlton and Sarah his wife." Eleven months later the court ordered a division of the estate between all three Carlton children. William's share amounted to more than $3,500.[4]

William and Mary Watkins appealed to the General Court of Virginia. Essentially, they argued that the lower court's rulings on admissions of evidence interpreted the legal presumption of legitimacy far too narrowly. The logic behind the legitimacy presumption was that if a married man could not possibly have had sex with his wife when she conceived a child, then the child was a bastard and not the husband's legal responsibility. Here, the point of an impossible conception was precisely the same, even though the reasoning behind it was unusual. By the logic of the lower court, because a white man possessed his full reproductive capacities and had sexual access to his white wife when she conceived, the presumption of legitimacy was so powerful that no evidence could be introduced demonstrating either that the child was of mixed race or the scientific implausibility of such a birth to a white couple. In excluding such evidence, the court had also made it impossible for the jury to address all the issues before it as ordered by the original judge in the case. They could not determine whether William Carlton had a white or black father because no witnesses were permitted to speak to the matter. Without any evidence as to William's race they had no alternative but to find that he was the legally legitimate son of John Carlton even though William was undoubtedly not white. "The white and negro races," the Watkinses argued, "were distinguished by natural marks not to be mistaken. And the mulatto bore on his face distinct and certain indications of his mixed parentage: the hair, the complexion, the features, all betrayed the truth."[5]

R. T. Daniel replied to the Watkins appeal with the unusual gambit that evidence of appearance was absurdly vague and that "there was great variety in the hair, complexion, and features, of persons of unmixed race, and yet greater variety in persons of mixed race." Additionally, since a "mulatto" had to have at least one-quarter "negro blood" to qualify as such under Virginia law, Daniel claimed it would be difficult if not impossible to tell the difference between a person of mixed race and a white person because "it was always [a] matter of opinion, founded on inspection." In this case particularly, because opinions as recorded in the original (excluded) depositions conflicted, William Carlton ought not to be declared illegitimate "by the admission of evidence in its own nature so uncertain." To the claim that it was impossible for two white persons to have offspring of color, Daniel introduced the folk belief that if a white woman looked at a black man while pregnant, it could alter the appearance of her child. Ultimately, Daniel called for the court to adhere strictly to the rules of presumption in cases of disputed paternity, which the General Court in a previous case had explicitly held precluded wide-ranging "indecent enquiries" into the sexual dalliances of men in order to maintain "public decorum." To allow a full exploration of William Carlton's parentage would obviously involve introducing evidence regarding the sexual activities of men not her husband with Sarah Carlton.[6]

In January 1840, the General Court directed that a new trial be held on the three questions raised by the original judge in chancery, admitting both witness testimony as to William Carlton's race and evidence "of professional men" that two white people could not have a mixed-race child. The jury in the original case had answered the first question in its verdict — John Carlton, it held, had been white. The jury had spoken to the third question only indirectly, since its verdict was that John Carlton was in law, though not necessarily in fact, William's father. In any event, the General Court held that the second question — regarding William's biological father's race — was the most important, and the jury had ignored it altogether. The General Court chose to interpret the spirit rather than the letter of the law of presumption in cases of illegitimacy and argued that the law intended simply to bastardize a child if the husband of the child's mother could not possibly have been the father, for whatever reason. In the minds of the justices, a child of mixed race could not be the offspring of two white persons, and at the very least a jury had to be allowed to listen to evidence and determine William's racial extraction for itself.[7]

In August 1840 the children of John Carlton decided to settle their case out of court, and they divided their father's estate three ways.[8] Whether John Carlton really was the father of William Carlton is unknown, and that it remains unknown exemplifies the conundrum William and other people of ambiguous race presented to white Virginians. No one knew William's racial ancestry for certain. His sister and brother-in-law, along with their medical professional, felt sure they could tell just by looking at him that he was not white. Those deposed in the lawsuit were less convinced and collectively split their judgment. R. T. Daniel asserted that racial characteristics varied greatly from person to person and that race was often little more than a matter of opinion. For much of the early national and antebellum periods, in fact, Daniel was right. Virginians had engaged in sex across the color line since the earliest days of colonial settlement, and by the late eighteenth or early nineteenth century ancestry became so entangled that for some people racial definition was imprecise. Incorporating individuals like these to Virginia's legal and social orders was imperative, for in Virginia no one could be without race. Yet fitting such persons into some racial schema was also a dicey proposition. Who decided who was white and who was black in Virginia before the Civil War and how did they decide?

6

Let There Be but Two Races among Us
Mixed Bloods in Early National and Antebellum Law and Society

Black, very Black, perfectly black, uncommonly black, quite black, slick black, rusty black, low black, real black, nearly black, not quite black, not entirely black, rather light black, smooth and dark but not black, dark though not very black, dark, tolerable dark, not very dark, chockolate, copper, brown copper, Tawney colour not quite black, Tawny, bright mahogany, gingerbread, light gingerbread, dark gingerbread, very dark gingerbread, high gingerbread, rather brown, light brown, Brown, dark Brown, dark Brown (not a mulatto), Brown approaching a mulatto, Brown neither black nor mulatto, between black and mulatto, dark mulatto, rather dark mulatto, brown mulatto, red mulatto, mulatto, bright almost a mulatto, Bright mulatto, pretty bright mulatto, tolerable bright mulatto, very bright mulatto, bright mulatto very white for a slave, dark yellow, Yellow, yellow not mulatto, bright, tolerable bright, light, very light, sallow, coloured, light coloured, half white, two thirds white, nearly white.[1]

White Virginians describing runaway slaves to the Richmond police in the 1830s and 1840s demonstrated that collectively they knew at least sixty-one different ways to describe the skin tones of those they held in bondage.[2] The General Assembly made its first formal attempt to inscribe such pigmental diversity into just a few distinct racial groups in 1705 by creating the intermediate category of "mulatto" between black and white to describe anyone with at least one African parent, grandparent, or great-grandparent.[3] The legislature addressed the issue of racial classification again in 1785 and 1833, each time altering and refining the original criterion of ancestry as the fundamental determinant of race. Yet the laws defining the color line never made clear provisions for categorizing free people with some but very distant African ancestry, whom white Virginians commonly called "mixed bloods" by the end of the antebellum period. If such individuals were neither black nor mulatto — which was an entirely descriptive category legally indistinct from black — it would appear they had to be white, since Virginia's legal order was designed for racial duality rather than racial multiplicity.[4] But Virginia's lawmakers generally addressed the problem of racial liminality by avoiding it. Instead of clarifying the law, they left much of the power to determine the whiteness or blackness of racially ambiguous persons in the hands of local white communities.

In those local communities, meanwhile, whites acknowledged that the extent of African ancestry mattered in determining whether someone was white or black, as did a person's physical appearance. But even a person who appeared to be white and who legally had a claim to whiteness by ancestry might not be received as such by the white community. A set of other considerations, including a person's associations, actions, and loyalties, was also crucial in helping other whites determine whiteness. Color and ancestry were necessary but not sufficient qualities for an individual of mixed race to become white. Above all, for a person with distant African ancestry, what mattered was whether the people already accepted as whites in his or her locale recognized his or her whiteness. As Martha Hodes has argued, determining an individual's racial classification sometimes required an investigation of "the person's entire way of living. This meant inquiring into comings and goings, his or her companions, reputation, treatment by neighbors, and manner of self-presentation. It meant, in short, inquiring into a person's precise footing in a community."[5]

Legal conflicts in local communities whose resolutions depended on determining the racial status of one or more individuals periodically appeared before Virginia's General Court. The justices of Virginia's highest tribunal did not know personally the individuals of uncertain racial identification they discussed in their cases. Whether or not they used a case to establish legal precedent and offered judicial opinions that discussed how a jurist might attach conclusiveness to indeterminate racial situations, they generally recognized that white community members and local courts were in far better positions than they were to determine who was black and who was white. The law, then, both as written and as interpreted, provided broad guidelines for separating black from white in early national and antebellum Virginia, but individuals who were not clearly either found their racial status determined mostly by their neighbors. People known to have some "negro blood" could be and occasionally were white. Whiteness did not always require the mythical "purity" it would later entail.

Even during the antebellum period, however, some white Virginians found the idea of people of any African descent being or becoming white problematic. Especially by the 1850s, white preoccupations with "blood," racial purity, and a strict color line escalated amid the intensifying sectional crisis and the efforts of people of mixed ancestry to exploit racial ambiguity to their advantage. Especially in Richmond, editors and municipal authorities began calling for the attachment of new and extraordinary levels of exclusivity to whiteness in law, and state lawmakers joined the public debate. Could access to whiteness, with the heightened social and civic status it entailed, really stay open to people of "mixed blood"? If not, was it possible that such people were something other than black, as some of them claimed? By the mid-1850s, a crisis of racial ambiguity was at hand in Virginia. To resolve it, even before the Civil War white Virginians considered the wisdom of the "one-drop rule" that became the standard for defining the color line in the twentieth century.

Virginia criminalized sex across the color line because the very act blurred the boundaries between black and white, and slave and free. When such sexual encounters produced offspring of ambiguous appearance, those individuals had to be forced into a legal racial category or the boundaries threatened to disappear altogether. For much of the early national and antebellum periods, white Virginians designed the racial walls of their society to have a small but significant degree of flexibility, much like modern engineers design buildings to withstand the tumult of an earthquake. Shortly before the Civil War, some white Virginians started to believe that such flexibility had become a flaw rather than an important precaution. They looked to the law to provide more rigid materials that they thought could better endure the tremors they sensed. Despite these changes over time, however, white Virginians' ideas about race were nearly always bifurcated. They consistently found ways to draw racial distinctions in case after case that might have confounded their efforts, forcing people of mixed ancestry into categories of black or white. It is hardly reasonable to expect them to have done anything other than reify race. Early national and antebellum white Virginians had a great deal invested in the existence of a color line.

Without anyone on the other side, being white hardly mattered, and if being white hardly mattered, little else in the socioeconomic order would have made much sense.[6]

Colonial legislators did not reveal why they chose ancestry as the primary legal criterion for determining race and drawing the color line in 1705. Perhaps it seems an obvious choice. The law was designed to address the problem of free individuals with at least one African ancestor but a majority of European ancestors by codifying at what point, if at all, African ancestry ceased mattering enough to consign such people to inferior status.[7] But given the variations in appearance individuals of mixed race could manifest, phenotypical appearance might have made a more logical choice as the guiding principle for determining race. The legislature could have passed a law, for example, indicating that shades of skin tone and texture of hair, to use some commonly noted markers, decided a person's race. Laws based on ancestry, in fact, were somewhat shortsighted. A moment's consideration should have made it clear to lawmakers that eventually, as an individual's most proximate ancestors were neither European nor African but both, disentangling pedigree with precision might prove extraordinarily difficult.

In part, theoretical legal concerns led legislators to settle on ancestry for the 1705 law. Ancestry already framed the mind-set of Virginia's lawmakers in thinking about the acquisition of status, because the status of one's mother distinguished free from slave. Classifying appearance, in establishing a different standard for separating black from white, would have been somewhat inconsistent and could have raised questions about the inheritability of slavery. Practical concerns were probably equally central in the legislators' minds, because putting appearance into law might only have heightened some of the problems the 1705 act was intended to resolve. Laws based on appearance would essentially have to make a subjective phenomenon such as perception into something people could universally agree upon. Crafting such a law that could work effectively likely would have been impossible. No matter how finely detailed the descriptions, laws based on appearance were bound to yield wrangling over who looked like what to whom. The legislature's job with respect to race in the early eighteenth century was not to bring subjectivity into the courts but to bring order out of the potential chaos wrought by intermixture and to find what legislators believed to be a reliable, simple, and objective legal mechanism for distinguishing black from white. Ancestry may have been deceptive in its apparent simplicity, but it was laughably easy compared with the prospects of fixing appearance in law.

The selection of ancestry helps explain the legal foundation for the color line in Virginia but hardly explains its precise placement. To use the mathematical language on which Virginians would come to rely, it is not entirely clear why the colonial legislature settled on one-eighth African ancestry as the dividing line between black and white. For biological reasons, the fraction had to be an even number, but why not one-half or one-fourth or one-sixteenth? Both concerns about slavery and the desire to correlate ancestry with appearance, at least roughly, were important in setting the boundary. Marking the color line at one-half would have made a vast number of slaves legally white and thus challenged the developing racial rationale for slavery.[8] It also would have been counterintuitive, making "white" many individuals whose African ancestry was still quite evident. Conversely, using one-sixteenth (or less) as a guideline would have proved relatively useless at the time, because in 1705 few Europeans or Africans could have been in Virginia for more than four generations. Additionally, such a strict definition of whiteness might have made some people who appeared white into mulattoes, which could be especially problematic for colonial elites seeking the allegiance of lower classes behind a racial banner. Bacon's Rebellion was not so distant from the memories of legislators, and forcing too many people to be anything other than white begged for trouble. At the time, using one-eighth as an indicator as opposed to one-fourth essentially made anyone with any African ancestry a mulatto and thus struck the proper balance between white and black so as to prevent the threat of insurrection. Moreover, it prevented the maximum number of people from falling into a category that belied their appearance.[9]

The colonial color line in Virginia remained in place until after the American Revolution. But in 1785, a new law changed the boundary between white and mulatto to one-fourth African ancestry (meaning a person had at least one African grandparent) from one-eighth, where it would remain until well after the Civil War.[10] This piece of legislation is utterly baffling. The free black population was growing in the 1780s in Virginia as a consequence of the liberal manumission act of 1782. Increasing the allowable amount of African ancestry a person could have and still become legally white effectively widened the category of whiteness precisely at a time when more individuals might be eligible to claim membership in it who would otherwise have been free people of color. By 1785, Europeans and Africans had been in what was now the United States long enough that, despite the added difficulties of enforcement, if white Virginians wanted freed slaves still to be black, raising the barrier for whiteness — say, to one-sixteenth African ancestry — would have made much more sense than lowering it.

It is possible that the increasing numbers of free people of African descent in the state in the late eighteenth century was precisely the factor that led state legislators to alter the law. Surely, lawmakers could not have wanted large numbers of formerly black people to become white, but in keeping with the fears of their colonial predecessors, they may have worried that denying citizenship to too large a percentage of the population raised the possibility that those denied might ally with one another and perhaps even with slaves. Opening whiteness to some free people of color may have been undertaken as a means of dividing the interests of the free African American population. Additionally, the quandary of supposedly white citizens becoming mulattoes if someone chose to make an issue of their ancestry may have persisted from the colonial era as well. Lowering the amount of "white blood" necessary for whiteness should also have helped alleviate this problem.[11]

Even as legislators shifted the location of the color line, they do seem to have intended to assert consistently that no matter what specific degree of extraction made the determination, there were two, and only two, races of free people in Virginia: black and white. It is not even entirely clear, however, that the original creation of legal categories in 1705 really established fixed racial positions for everyone in Virginia, or that in changing the boundaries of race in 1785 the General Assembly actually bestowed whiteness on any more people. A close reading of the 1785 legislation indicates that it failed to be very definitive at all. The text of the act read: "Every person of whose grandfathers or grandmothers any one is, or shall have been a negro, although all his other progenitors, except that descending from the negro shall have been white persons, shall be deemed a mulatto, and so every person who shall have one-fourth part or more of Negro blood shall, in like manner, be deemed a mulatto."[12] Most obviously, the act (like its colonial predecessor) contained no means of enforcement or verification. If people wanted to claim that they were not mulattoes — that they had less than one-quarter African ancestry — how could they do it? Could they take their case to court? Did they have to come to the legislature directly? Was there some other legal channel to go through? Even if the appropriate jurisdiction was discovered, what kind of proof did people need and how could they get it? Proof of parental marriage was clearly out of the question because interracial marriages were illegal. Direct maternity might be provable, but paternity could easily be questioned. Beyond the proximate generation, how could anyone of mixed race prove anything about his or her ancestors? The most important ambiguity left in both the 1705 and 1785 laws was the issue of what people of less than one-eighth or one-fourth African ancestry actually *were* racially. Implicitly, of course, in Virginia everyone who was not black had to be white. But the laws never specified that. Instead, legislators were content to state categorically that most people of mixed race were black and thus to clear up some confusion, but they were unwilling to affirm absolutely that everyone else was white.

Answers to these questions may have been left purposefully vague by the lawmakers. They may have wished to let the courts sort out the problems. In addition, legislators may have understood that what mattered most in the daily lives of people of uncertain racial background was far less their specific pedigree and far more how they looked and how whites in their local communities understood their racial identity. But because they left the precise mechanism for racial determination unspecified, legislators really only decided the theoretical rather than the actual boundary between black and white. Effectively, the laws of 1705 and 1785 did not so much establish a single color line as draw a set of parallel lines. On one side were whites, on the other side were mulattoes and blacks, but in the middle lay a group of people who did not really fit into Virginia's legal racial order at all.

Examining how the General Assembly dealt with the issue of racial distinctions in 1833 points up the limits of the law and underscores just how many questions previous measures had left unresolved. In 1832, partially in response to the burgeoning abolitionist movement and to the 1831 slave uprising in Southampton County known as Nat Turner's Rebellion, the legislature passed a series of laws imposing new restrictions on free people of color, including the provision that for most crimes all blacks, free and unfree, would be punished as if they were slaves. This change meant most importantly that instead of paying fines for minor criminal activities, all people of color now could be punished with public beatings.[13] In January 1833, Delegate John Murdaugh of Norfolk County introduced a resolution calling on the General Assembly to exempt "Indians and other persons of mixed blood, who are not free negroes or mulattoes" from the penalties and restrictions against free people of color. Basing his plan on the framework whereby free people of color carried freedom papers from their local courts, Murdaugh asked the legislature to authorize any county court to grant a certificate to mixed-race individuals declaring and able to prove their exemptions.[14] In March 1833 the assembly adopted Murdaugh's resolution, empowering the county courts "upon satisfactory evidence of white persons being adduced" to "grant any free person of mixed blood resident within such County, not being a white person nor a free negro or mulatto, a certificate that he or she is not a free negro or mulatto; which certificate shall be sufficient to protect and secure such person from and against the pains, penalties, disabilities and disqualifications, imposed by the law upon free negroes and mulattoes, as free negroes and mulattoes."[15]

On its surface, the 1833 law made no sense at all. The laws restricting free blacks and mulattoes applied to free blacks and mulattoes. Free people who were not black or mulatto should have automatically been exempt from the restrictions — because they would have been white. The "not a negro" act of 1833 explicitly indicated that there were some people whose exemption had always been questionable — people who were not black but who were not white either. Legally, until 1833 such individuals did not exist. If the 1785 legislation really had successfully made all Virginians either white, mulatto, or black, it would have been impossible to be something else, but it turned out that the law had never actually made a binary division of free Virginians entirely clear. Theoretically, then, some Virginians had been legally raceless.

The 1833 law may have been an attempt to give these raceless Virginians a formal legal status even as it allowed them to escape the new restrictions on people of color. If so, it only compounded the uncertainty left in Virginia's racial order by earlier legislation. The law did resolve the problem of jurisdiction over racial determination that was left unclear in 1705 and 1785. The legislature, however, not only still failed to settle many of the legal questions raised by people who hovered around the color line but raised new questions in the process. The 1785 act had been silent as to the specific status of people of ambiguous race. So in 1833 lawmakers tinkered again with the idea that racial identity was rooted in ancestry and made very clear that such people fell outside the established ancestral guidelines that might have made them black or mulatto. But instead of deciding that this class of persons was white, the

General Assembly implicitly recognized a third racial category without giving it any distinct content. Individuals who fell within the boundaries of this category were not slaves and they were not subject to the special restrictions faced by free people of color. The legislature gave permission to any court to issue such people pieces of paper saying they were not black. Nothing in law seemed to distinguish them from whites, but the law also specifically included language that they were not. What were these people? The only answer was that they were "not a negro."[16]

The absurdity of defining a racial category based on what it was not rather than what it was is an irony that perhaps we only can appreciate with hindsight. By the end of the antebellum period the odd emptiness of such a category infuriated some white Virginians. But in 1833 the legislature's action marked both an acknowledgment and an evasion. The body acknowledged that there were men and women in Virginia who fell outside the definition of blackness but simultaneously refused to cover such persons automatically with the blanket of legal whiteness. The General Assembly evaded the question of what actually separated such "mixed bloods" in practice from whites and instead gave only ancestry as a broad framework for local communities to find places in the social order for these people. In those communities, though, ancestry was only part, and not even necessarily the most important part, of the complex story of racial definition.

In January 1833, just weeks before the General Assembly began considering the "not a negro" law, fifty-one white men from Stafford County signed and sent a petition to the legislature asking that five former slaves — William, Lemuel, Barney, Nancy, and Lewis Wharton — be permitted to remain in the state. The Whartons had been enslaved by John Cooke (who was dead by 1833), but a few years prior to the petitioners' plea had purchased their own freedom and had lived peacefully in Stafford County until the previous term of the county court. There, they were presented for the crime of residing in the state contrary to the provisions of the 1806 removal law. Many petitions from newly freed African Americans asking that exceptions to the law be granted them to remain in Virginia included certificates of support from local whites, who swore that the free people in question were of sound character and were hardworking individuals who performed valuable services for the community. In this respect, the Stafford County petition was unexceptional, with the petitioners vouching that the Whartons were "persons of excellent character, some of them are pursuing trades, and all are industrious and useful."[17]

The Wharton petition, however, also contained a more unusual argument. The citizens of Stafford County claimed that the Whartons were free but were not people of color at all. True, they had nominally been enslaved by Cooke, but the petitioners argued that the Whartons were all whites. Their claim rested on a series of considerations. First, according to the laws of descent, the petitioners agreed that "more than three fourths" of the Whartons' "blood is derived from white ancestors." Also important was that the Whartons were "all white persons in complexion." Third, despite knowing both their racial heritage and their former enslaved status, the white community in Stafford County allowed the Whartons to exercise "all the rights of free persons in the acquisition of property and otherwise without interruption." Fourth, the Whartons' most intimate social connections were only with local whites. The petitioners asserted that the family had "no association with coloured persons," that a number of them had married whites, and that "their partialities are decidedly for the whites." One Wharton in particular helped capture a man in Washington who had stolen several Stafford slaves, while another apprehended a number of local runaway slaves in New York. Finally, the petitioners argued that to force the Whartons to leave the state made little sense, because all of them could move to another state, become white citizens, and move back to Virginia. The removal law, the petitioners claimed, did not apply to people like the Whartons.[18]

Stafford's petitioners mentioned the Whartons' ancestry and their appearance only in passing, but they called attention to both factors before getting into details about any other aspect of the Whartons' existence. The petition was a remarkable one, for its authors claimed that people in Virginia could go directly from being enslaved to being white, drawing attention to the literal reality of white slavery in the state.[19] Eyebrows were sure to be raised in the legislature, and to hope their petition would be successful the petitioners had to ensure the lawmakers that the Whartons qualified to be white both legally and phenotypically. The Whartons were treated as whites, but if they failed to meet the legal ancestry requirement, an argument that they were in fact white was likely to fall on deaf ears. Similarly, although most of the legislators had never seen them, it worked to the Whartons' favor for the lawmakers to know that they looked white and that a decision on their behalf would be consistent with common sense.

Appearance and ancestry alone did not make the Whartons white, though. The Whartons were white because they acted white: they carried out the civic activities that helped define whiteness, their chosen social associations and marriage partners were all from white families, and they performed specific acts showing they bore no allegiance to the enslaved community of which they had once been a part. In racial determination cases in antebellum courtrooms across the South, judges and juries considered evidence such as documented ancestry, appearance, and, by late in the period, scientific definitions of race in order to determine a person's whiteness or blackness, but evidence of reputation and of "performing whiteness" just as persuasively proved white status. Stafford County's petitioners presented precisely such a diversity of information.[20]

No single piece of evidence brought by the Stafford petitioners in and of itself conclusively established the Whartons' whiteness. In 1811, for example, when nine members of the Dean family petitioned the legislature to remain in the state after being emancipated, fourteen white men from their community in Amherst County signed a statement indicating that the Deans were all "so nearly white that they would not be taken to be mulattoes where they were not known." Perhaps the Deans could have met the legal ancestry requirement for whiteness, but no one made such an argument on their behalf. Regardless of how they looked to others, in their own neighborhood, the petitioners suggested, whites saw them as mulattoes and treated them as such. The Deans looked white, but they were still black. Their petition was rejected outright.[21] Similarly, attestations on behalf of free people of color frequently included mentions of their allegiance with whites on matters related to slavery as proof that they were unlikely to join or provoke an insurrection. In 1825 Dillard Gordon, a free man of color from Essex County, petitioned the legislature on behalf of his wife that she might be permitted to remain in Virginia. Fifty-five local white men signed a statement of support wherein they noted that Gordon was "vigilant and prompt in detecting thefts &c. in slaves." Dillard Gordon was safe on slavery but that hardly made him, or his wife, white. The legislature rejected his petition as well, legally exiling his wife from the state.[22]

The petition for the Whartons can be read as a coded message to the General Assembly. Each form of evidence served a distinct purpose, and cumulatively all the pieces of evidence added up to whiteness. Ancestry meant that the Whartons fulfilled the legislature's sole qualification for being white. Appearance meant that anyone who did not know them would assume the Whartons were entirely white. Social reputation proved that the people in their own community said they were white. In conjunction with the rest of the material, evidence that the Whartons demonstrated their loyalty to slavery implied that in some instinctive and essential way the Whartons really were white. If the legislature, the community, and the rest of the nation said the Whartons were white, and the Whartons themselves showed they bore allegiance to whites, then surely they had to be white.

Of course, evidence of social reputation itself rested entirely on circular logic. According to the whites who signed the Stafford County petition, the Whartons were white because they married white people and because they carried out the civic activities that white people did. But they could only have acted in those ways if they were already white. Whiteness neither preceded nor followed these social behaviors. Instead, they were all of a piece. At bottom, what evidence of social reputation really proved was that the Whartons were white because the other people accepted as whites in their community said they were. This testimony was conclusive enough for the state legislature. The body approved the Stafford petition and on March 9, 1833, declared that all five Whartons were "not negroes or mulattoes, but white persons, although remotely descended from a coloured woman."[23]

White Virginians were not always so solicitous of individuals who posed questions for the color line as they were of the Whartons. Local understandings of a person's position in a community were critical in determining whiteness and blackness, but those understandings were not always commonly shared. In lieu of written documentation, ancestry might be differently remembered by different people. When Stephen Saunders sued Hezekiah Chaney in Wythe County in 1811, for example, white witnesses provided contradictory testimony as to whether John Rose was competent to testify in the matter, differing in opinion over whether Rose's maternal grandfather, Nicholas Smith, had been black.[24] Similarly, appearance, a wholly subjective category to begin with, could easily be disputed, as demonstrated by the deponents who disagreed over whether William Carlton looked to be a person of color. Social acceptance by whites, meanwhile, could depend on whom you asked. In one 1847 case from Culpeper, the Circuit Court had to determine the race of two brothers from whom goods had been stolen before the brothers could testify against the accused white thief. Witnesses agreed that the brothers had a white mother, but the race of their grandparents was crucial. Testimony as to their grandmother was "contradictory; though she was probably white." Important in determining the race of their grandfather, meanwhile, was whether he had been "a respectable man."[25] Whites in Virginia repeatedly demonstrated in case after case that they had a capacity for living with racial indeterminacy in their midst for many years if not for generations without difficulty. Whites knew who racially ambiguous persons in their communities were, although they did not necessary agree about what such persons were.[26]

People of ambiguous race were wholly suspect individuals when they were not grounded in a local community at all and when whites did not personally know their family background and social standing. Take, for example, the case of William Hyden. Late in 1833, the seventeen-year-old Hyden made the unfortunate mistake of walking through Prince William County. He was a stranger, and when people saw him they asked questions about who he was, where he came from, and where he was headed. He told local residents he was a free man of color from New York. He had lived in Ohio in a free black community for the previous three years, but the state had recently been enforcing strict residency laws with which he could not comply.[27] Hyden, with little choice but to leave Ohio, decided to return to New York. He took a circuitous route and passed through Virginia on the way, but he carried no free papers. Unfamiliar with Virginia laws that forbade any free person of color from entering the state, by the time he realized his error it was too late. Instead of peacefully returning to his native state Hyden found himself arrested and held in prison. Because Hyden had no written proof of his freedom, the Prince William County Court ordered that he be treated as a runaway slave. Accordingly, advertisements of Hyden's capture were placed in the newspaper, and when no one came forward to claim him, he was publicly offered for sale on the auction block.[28]

On January 1, 1834, Basil Brawner, a deputy sheriff in Prince William, sold Hyden for $452 to Robert Lipscomb, the county jailer and a local agent for a slave trader who promised that the trader himself would arrive in a few days with the money. As scheduled, Lipscomb's trader arrived at the jail, but on seeing Hyden he refused to pay for him. Frustrated, Brawner tried other means of selling Hyden. He turned to James Fewell, a local man who was already planning a trip to sell slaves of his own, and asked if he would take Hyden and sell him if he could. Fewell agreed and offered Hyden both publicly and privately in Fredericksburg and Richmond, but reported he "could not sell him at any price." Fewell returned Hyden to Brawner, and Brawner again endeavored to sell Hyden at auction on court day in the town of Brentsville. A number of slave traders were present and all refused even to bid on Hyden. While Brawner exercised his options in a desperate attempt to find someone willing to pay for Hyden, Hyden escaped from prison. He was never found.

Brawner had no choice but to report this situation back to the Prince William County Court, which ordered the sheriff's office to pay the expected proceeds from Hyden's sale to the commonwealth, as required by law. Now Basil Brawner had a serious problem. The state auditor of public accounts charged what Brawner termed "a large sum of money" to Michael Cleary, who had been the sheriff of Prince William when Hyden was originally taken into custody. But Cleary was no longer in office in 1835, leaving Brawner bearing full financial responsibility for Hyden.[29] Brawner petitioned the state legislature to be forgiven the debt, claiming that he could never get a court to issue a judgment against Robert Lipscomb to pay the amount of his original bid and that, in any event, Lipscomb did not have anywhere near the personal financial resources to make payment. Brawner himself claimed it was unfair to make him pay back the state because in this case the laws respecting runaways could not be enforced. William Hyden was a man who could not be sold in Virginia. Brawner had tried, and no one would buy him.

Primarily (and ironically), despite his purported partial African ancestry, no one bought William Hyden because of the color of his skin. Fewell could not find a buyer in Richmond or Fredericksburg because all alleged "that he was too white," that in fact he was "so bright that he might easily escape from slavery." Back at the court day auction in Brentsville, the traders present similarly agreed "that his colour was too light and that he could by reason thereof too easily escape from slavery and pass himself for a free man." It was not Hyden's skin color alone that warned potential buyers away. It was also his carriage. As soon as anyone talked to Hyden they sensed that he was not and never had been a slave. James Fewell claimed to have quizzed Hyden on New York geography and trade, asking him about cities, towns, rivers, and the kinds of vessels used for transporting goods. Hyden answered each question correctly. These responses, in addition to "his dialect, and education," gave Fewell no doubt that Hyden was a free person. M. B. Finelain, who wrote the legislature in support of Brawner's petition, concurred with Fewell that Hyden was freeborn, his belief founded on Hyden's "representations."

Brawner himself wholly believed Hyden's story, asserting that talking to Hyden was enough "to convince any person that he was born, raised, and educated and migrated, as he the said Hyden himself represented."[30] That Brawner believed Hyden's story did not prevent him from trying to sell the man.

Given his bearing, his appearance, and probably his ancestry, had William Hyden actually been born and raised in Prince William County, the same whites who tried to enslave him might have been equally likely to give evidence that he was white. Had William Hyden been female, the same potential purchasers who shied away from owning him might have paid a very high price for such a "fancy girl."[31] As it was, though, William Hyden was male and a stranger in Virginia. If he escaped, he effectively could become a free white man and leave the state, which he probably did. Color and status never correlated precisely in antebellum Virginia, which made free blacks generally so troublesome. But Hyden personified how sex across the color line could ultimately destabilize slavery altogether. That he eventually eluded his captors so successfully proved why no slave owner in Virginia wanted anything to do with him. In adjacent counties less than a year apart, the Whartons went from being slaves to being white and William Hyden very nearly became a slave despite looking white. That people who probably did not appear dramatically racially dissimilar to most Virginians faced such diametrically opposed fates points up that appearance was only the first, and not even always the most important, determinant of status for racially ambiguous free individuals at the local level.

Obviously, whites were not the only people who determined the race of individuals like the Whartons or William Hyden. In part, the Whartons became white because they wanted to be white, and Hyden was treated as a runaway slave because he told white Virginians he was a person of color. But because the law never established precisely what people like Hyden and the Whartons were racially, local white communities and local courts were the primary arbiters of racial privilege and bore the greatest responsibility for determining the status of individuals of mixed race. Even the justices of Virginia's General Court recognized this reality. Their decisions in two cases mentioned earlier illustrate this point. In the 1811 case from Wythe County, the local court determined that John Rose was not a competent witness against Hezekiah Chaney and refused to read his deposition to the jury. The court apparently chose to believe witnesses who testified that Rose's grandfather was black, which, under the 1785 legislation, made John Rose a mulatto and incapable of testifying against a white man in court. Without Rose's testimony, Stephen Saunders lost his case against Chaney and appealed to the District Court. Here, Chaney again objected to the admission of Rose's deposition, whereupon "a great variety of viva voce and written testimony was introduced to impugn, or support, the competency of John Rose to be a witness against a white man." This time, though, the court ruled that Rose was a competent witness and read his deposition to the jury, which found Chaney guilty and ordered him to pay Saunders $450, prompting Chaney to appeal to the General Court.[32]

In *Chaney v. Saunders*, the General Court overruled the District Court's verdict and upheld that of the local court. This decision effectively meant that John Rose was legally black, but that consequence, while unlikely to give the justices pause, had little to do with the court's reasoning. The justices, in fact, insisted that they were "not deciding, absolutely, upon the weight of the evidence" regarding John Rose's grandfather, which was "extremely contradictory, and emphatically involved the credibility of the witnesses." The justices of the General Court really had no knowledge of John Rose or his ancestry at all, but they did feel that the county court "had lights, arising from the manner of giving testimony, and other extraneous circumstances, which neither this court, nor the District Court, in its appellate character, possessed in an equal degree." Essentially, the General Court argued that without an evident procedural error in the original lawsuit, the local court could determine better than any other court whether or not John Rose was a mulatto. The judges at the local level probably knew some if not all of the witnesses who testified on both sides, or knew people who did. At the very least they understood the nuances of relationships in their community more intimately than any General or District Court justice would. The local judges weighed the witnesses' opinions, and decided John Rose could not testify against Hezekiah Chaney, which was entirely satisfactory in the eyes of the General Court.[33]

In the 1847 case from Culpeper County, a white shoemaker named Dean was tried for stealing unnamed goods worth less than $10 from brothers William and John Ross. Dean claimed the Ross brothers could not testify against him because they were "mulattoes." The Circuit Court for Culpeper heard witnesses provided both by the state and by Dean, and from their testimony "it appeared certainly" that although the

Rosses' grandfather may have been a mulatto the brothers themselves "had less than one fourth of negro blood." The court consequently ruled that their "impurity of blood" did not disqualify them from testifying against a white man. Dean objected and asked the court's permission to present his evidence regarding the racial ancestry of the Ross brothers directly to the jury, which was denied. Dean was convicted. He appealed to the General Court, claiming that the Circuit Court should never have allowed the Ross brothers to testify, that if they did testify he should have been allowed to present evidence of their ancestry to the jury, and that there was insufficient evidence in any event to convict him.[34]

In *Dean v. Commonwealth,* the General Court unanimously agreed with the Circuit Court that individuals with some but less than one-quarter "negro blood" could testify against a white man, and six of the nine justices agreed that the Circuit Court justifiably refused Dean's request to present evidence regarding the racial ancestry of the Ross brothers to the jury. Nonetheless, five of the justices believed that Dean should be retried. Two argued he had been convicted with insufficient evidence, while three held that the Circuit Court had erred "in excluding the evidence of negro blood" from the jury. Six of nine justices, then, believed that in handling the evidence of the Ross brothers' racial background, the local court had acted correctly and in accordance with the law. Possibly the three justices who dissented on this aspect of the case felt that no one with any "negro blood" should be allowed to testify against a "purely" white man. Other white Virginians might very well have agreed, but the vague language of the 1785 racial determination law gave the judges no solid legal foundation to create such a strict color line. Instead, they may have hoped that a jury who heard what the Ross brothers were racially would see the case their way. Whatever the rationale for dissent, it is clear that all the justices felt that whites at the local level—whether on the bench or on a jury—ought to have the authority to decide how to treat people like the Rosses in their community.[35] On retrial, the Ross brothers lost. Dean was found not guilty by the county court in October 1847. It is unclear from the trial record whether the jury received knowledge of the Rosses' racial ancestry or, if it did, whether that information made the difference.[36]

Neither *Chaney* nor *Dean* had major legal, social, or economic ramifications for Virginia, but some cases of racial indeterminacy did, especially when they involved slavery. One of the most significant appellate decisions made by Virginia's General Court before the Civil War was

Hudgins v. Wrights. In October 1805, an enslaved woman named Jacky Wright and her three infant children sued Holder Hudgins, their owner, for their freedom. The Wrights contended, contrary to Hudgins's claims, that they were descended not from women of any African ancestry but from free Native Americans. The case first appeared in the Superior Court of Law and Chancery in Richmond, presided over by George Wythe, where a series of witnesses testified as to the racial ancestry of the Wrights. Cumulatively, they traced the Wrights' genealogy back to a woman named Butterwood Nan. A witness named Robert Temple did not seem to know anything about Nan's mother, but he swore her father was Native American. Another witness described Nan as "an old Indian," while others testified that Nan's daughter Hannah had "long black hair, was of the right Indian copper colour, and was generally called an Indian by the neighbours, who said she might recover her freedom, if she would sue for it." Still others claimed that Hannah's brother John had brought a lawsuit for his freedom and that Hannah herself "made an almost continual claim as to her right of freedom, insomuch that she was threatened to be whipped by her master for mentioning the subject."[37]

When making his decision, Wythe personally inspected Jacky Wright, her mother, and her youngest daughter and found that there "were gradual shades of difference in colour" between the three. The child in particular he found to be "perfectly white," given that her complexion, hair, and eyes "were proven to have been the same with those of whites." Between what he saw with his own eyes and what he heard from the witnesses before him, Wythe held that the Wrights were entitled to their freedom. Wythe further stated that his ruling accorded with the premises of the first clause of Virginia's Bill of Rights, which declared that "all men are by nature equally free and independent." Consequently, Wythe reasoned, any time an enslaved person claimed legally that he or she ought not to be a slave, the burden of proving the individual's status lay with the putative owner.[38]

It is worth noting that while Wythe did believe the legal presumption ought to be for freedom, if he wanted to set the Wrights free he also had no choice but to make an argument as to why the burden of proof lay with Hudgins. Despite witness testimony suggesting the Wrights might be legally free, the evidence provided did not prove anything conclusively one way or another. Robert Temple's testimony was particularly problematic. Suspiciously, he knew who Butterwood Nan's father was but knew nothing about her mother or, for that matter, about Nan's own appearance. One of the justices of the General Court, in fact, distrusted Temple, believed it probable that he had a personal stake in seeing the Wrights go free, and thought he was not telling all he knew. "His memory," wrote Justice Spencer Roane, "seems only to serve him so far as the interest of the appellant required." Most judges recognized that personal concerns could often be inseparable from testimony about interracial sex and its outcomes.[39]

Wythe's decision was extraordinarily clever. If the justices of the General Court, to whom he surely knew Hudgins would appeal, affirmed his decision, they placed the law in a position to threaten slavery significantly. Slaves would certainly hear about the decision and swamp courts across the state with suits for freedom, which anyone could see they would stand an excellent chance of winning given the complications of tracing slave ancestry with absolute clarity. Any slave might claim a free female ancestor and go free unless his or her owner could absolutely prove otherwise. Conversely, if the justices overturned Wythe's decision, they threw the burden of proof onto the Wrights and thus doomed them and other "perfectly white" individuals to slavery. Hudgins's lawyer saw the problem and noted on appeal that the Wrights' skin color had nothing to do with their freedom. "The circumstances of the appellees' being white," he argued, "has been mentioned, more to excite the feelings of the Court as men, than to address them as Judges."[40]

Had *Hudgins v. Wrights* appeared in court twenty years earlier, when many white Virginians were sympathetic toward ideas about black liberty, Wythe's opinion might have stood a chance of being upheld in its entirety. As it was, the General Court handed down its decision in *Hudgins* in November 1806, thirteen years after Eli Whitney invented the cotton gin, six years after Gabriel's Rebellion in Richmond, and the same year that the reactionary removal law undermined the easy manumission act of 1782. The revolutionary spirit was clearly waning in Virginia, and the value of slavery could not be underestimated. Neither could the value of whiteness. The General Court ruled that the Wrights were indeed entitled to their freedom, but they rejected Wythe's reasoning on legal presumption in similar lawsuits. Instead, they successfully escaped Wythe's logical trap by differentiating between causes for freedom, in the process inextricably correlating physical appearance and status in a way the law as written never thoroughly did. If individuals suing for freedom appeared to be white, the General Court held, the legal presumption was that they were free and the burden of proof lay with the person claiming them as slaves. If those suing for freedom appeared to be black, they were legally presumed to be slaves and had to prove that they were not. As Justice St. George Tucker argued in rejecting the crucial element of Wythe's opinion, the Virginia Bill of Rights "was notoriously framed with a cautious eye to this subject" and was intended to protect free citizens, not "by a side wind to overturn the rights of property, and give freedom" to African Americans. Contrary to the claims of Hudgins's lawyer, the Wrights' whiteness was very much relevant to their case. White people were supposed to be free, the court held, and black people were supposed to be slaves. The chances of anyone of visible African descent successfully suing for freedom were significantly constrained within such a legal framework. By locking black skin and slavery together so explicitly, the ruling simultaneously bolstered both slavery and white supremacy.[41]

The ruling also assumed that a strictly binary system of race existed in early nineteenth-century Virginia. The justices wrote their opinions almost entirely in terms of black and white physical appearances, and for all intents and purposes the General Court collapsed the Wrights and others of Native American descent into the category of whiteness. But even though at least one of the Wrights looked "perfectly white" to George Wythe, their case quite obviously raised the question of what to do in other cases of racial indeterminacy. If the court wanted to rule there were only whites and blacks in Virginia, it consequently had the opportunity, if not the responsibility, to delineate some means for courts to tell the difference between the two in uncertain cases. Justice Tucker admitted that he knew very little about "the natural history of the human species," but his ignorance was no obstacle to a brief discourse on how to distinguish black from white. Tucker believed that even when the color of a person's skin was unclear, people of African descent had "two characteristic marks . . . which often remain visible long after the characteristic distinction of colour either disappears or becomes doubtful; a flat nose and woolly head of hair." Tucker claimed that hair texture in particular passed down from a person of African descent to his or her child and that it was impossible to confuse white or Native American hair with black hair. A judge could determine race accordingly, either from witness testimony as to appearance or "upon his own view."[42]

Tucker's opinion hardly addressed the problem, because he was only willing to extend his argument absolutely so far as instances "where the party is in equal degree descended from parents of different complexions."[43] In other words, if a person had an African parent and either a European or Native American parent, Tucker argued he or she would invariably have "woolly" hair. Tucker evaded the reality that racial intermixture in Virginia was usually far more difficult to disentangle than the hypothetical case he offered. He claimed that the follicular and nasal characteristics of Africans could be seen even beyond the first generation of mixture, but aside from this vague assertion he was silent on how judges and juries were supposed to sort through those more complicated situations. Justice Roane offered a different perspective on distinguishing between the races. He, too, believed that "the different species of the human race are so visibly marked, that those species may be readily discriminated from each other by mere inspection only." Unlike Tucker, however, Roane also acknowledged that when "these races become intermingled, it is difficult, if not impossible, to say from inspection only, which race predominates in the offspring." Furthermore, even in a case where a person was obviously of mixed descent, it was certainly impossible to tell of which race his or her mother was in particular.[44]

Roane made no pretenses that the *Hudgins* decision conclusively answered questions about people of indeterminate race. In suits for freedom, he believed that where there was no suggestion the person in question might be of "mixed blood," a judge or jury member might make a racial determination by visual inspection just as well as he could from witness testimony about appearance. He could then assess the burden of proof for freedom. But Roane went on to assert that "where an intermixture has taken place in relation to the person in question, this criterion is not infallible; and testimony must be resorted to for the purpose of shewing through what line a descent from a given stock has been deduced."[45] In indeterminate cases, Roane argued, one had to hear testimony from witnesses familiar with the individuals under discussion in order to have any idea what they were racially. Roane only mentioned explicitly the need to hear evidence on appearance and ancestry, which for people held in slavery were the only factors that really mattered when it came to suing for their freedom. When the background of free people was at issue, whites considered a number of additional factors in assessing race. But the broad principle laid down by Roane held true. How could judges, especially those on higher courts, possibly figure out the ancestry or status of people of mixed race just by looking at them? White people who lived in communities with people of ambiguous race could speak to who was white and who was black and what made them so far more reliably than most public officials ever could. St. George Tucker may have thought he could distinguish race in most instances simply by inspecting an individual. Spencer Roane was more honest. Physical appearance always mattered, but Roane's approach of taking into account the sentiments of the community toward racially mixed people carried the day in Virginia for much of the early national and antebellum periods.

In the decade before the Civil War, some white Virginians began to perceive great danger from having any flexibility at all on the matter of racial intermixture. Abolitionist attacks and mounting political conflict over slavery expansion to new territories provoked a regional defensiveness in the South. Amid the perceived need to bolster slavery against external assaults, white southerners developed an understanding of slavery as a positive good, where previous defenses maintained the institution was a necessary evil. Given the crucial linkage but still inexact correlation of whiteness with freedom and blackness with slavery, a larger sense of racial anxiety accompanied this support for the peculiar institution. By the 1850s Virginia, like many other southern states, stepped up restrictions on the activities and freedoms of free people of color in an effort to treat them more and more like slaves. In light of this effort to strengthen the connection between whiteness and liberty, the notion that some people of color might still cross the color line was infuriating. More than ever before, white Virginians believed they needed to know for certain who was black and who was white.[46]

Natural scientists and physicians fed the appetite for racial clarity in the 1840s and 1850s by floating the hypothesis of "polygenesis" — a theory that races were created as entirely separate species and that blacks were naturally and permanently inferior. Within such a framework, racial intermixture between whites and blacks was not only a blending of superior with inferior individuals but was unnatural and produced freakish monstrosities. Ironically, "race scientists" inadvertently contributed to white racial insecurity, because even as they argued — and many whites believed — that one could always detect the moral and physical characteristics of "negro blood" after many generations of intermixture, some white Virginians surely knew that such might not be the case. They looked to the law for reassurance that the color line was impassable.

Instead, to their dismay whites found that the law enabled some people known to be of African descent to claim legitimately that they were not black at all.[47]

In late August 1853, Richmond police arrested a teenage boy named George Drew on the charge of stealing $6 from an enslaved woman. Mayor Joseph Mayo attempted to treat Drew legally as a free black man, but B. B. Minor, Drew's lawyer, objected. Drew's mother was "a bright mulatto" and his father was "said to be a white man." Accordingly, Minor argued that Drew had "less than one-fourth part negro blood in him, and therefore was entitled to a different character of trial to that of a free negro." Mayo asked Minor to show him a certificate from the Hustings Court "declaring the prisoner to be a person of mixed blood — neither negro nor white." Minor responded that his client had no such certificate yet, but that the Hustings Court just the previous week had taken testimony on the spot regarding a defendant's ancestry and determined "that the party accused was a person of mixed blood — neither white nor negro in the eye of the law." He demanded that Drew be accorded the same opportunity. Mayo was uncomfortable hearing such testimony and preferred to leave consideration of the matter to "a higher tribunal," but he agreed to listen. A white woman named Susan Ann Beveridge testified that she had known Drew from birth, that her mother had told her that Drew's maternal grandmother was white, and that the man said to be Drew's father was white. The mayor determined to try Drew as a free person of color nonetheless, found him guilty, and sentenced him to thirty lashes.[48]

In the 1850s, individuals previously considered to be and treated as free people of color increasingly tried to use Virginia law to elude the growing legislative hostility toward people of African descent.[49] Especially in Richmond, where strict city ordinances that constrained the freedom of free people of color added additional burdens to those imposed by state laws, anyone who could tried to lay claim to being "not a negro" in order to avoid being persecuted and prosecuted as a free black, which frequently entailed physical punishment. The "not a negro" law allowing for such a claim had been on the books for twenty years before George Drew tried to use it, but cases like his were rare before the 1850s, at least in Richmond. As the *Richmond Daily Dispatch* noted in 1852 when two girls claiming to have "less than one fourth of negro blood in them" successfully persuaded the Hustings Court to grant them a certificate of their racial status, their application itself was "somewhat peculiar in its character."[50] Few whites, in fact, may have even realized such a law existed. The *Richmond Enquirer*, for example, wrote of the "not a negro" law in 1853 as "a recent act of the General Assembly."[51]

Whether or not editors in the state capital knew how long the law had existed, by the fall of 1853 they understood they had a problem on their hands. If a person could claim to be neither black nor white, then what were they before the law? Being "not a negro" seemed to shelter a person from the special penalties free people of color faced for having some African ancestry but, as the language of George Drew's case suggests, such individuals were not white either. With racial purity and racial control at a premium, such ambiguity seemed especially pernicious. Edward Gentry's application to the Hustings Court for a certificate declaring him "not a negro" just two weeks after George Drew's trial provoked the first of many calls for legal order amid the potential chaos. According to the *Dispatch*, there were many "mixed bloods" in Richmond who had never claimed to be anything other than free people of color until recently, when the "vigilant enforcement of the law against free negroes," especially as regarded freedom of travel, had prompted individuals to "continually annoy" the courts with applications for certificates that they were "not a negro." Such certificates, however, effectively showed that people who held them belonged to "a class of persons which could be reached by no criminal law of the Commonwealth" because the criminal code only recognized slaves, free blacks, and whites. The only alternative to such vagueness seemed to be to pronounce these individuals white persons, especially because the "not a negro" law never precisely specified the "disabilities" from which they were exempted. Invoking the specters that would haunt white southerners for another century and beyond, the *Dispatch* felt sure that the legislature never intended to allow "mixed bloods" to exercise all the privileges of whiteness — "to become governors, judges, jurors, soldiers or lawyers . . . to exercise the right of suffrage, or marry with white persons." But because the law had no "fourth *status*" for "mixed bloods," the *Dispatch* concluded "we can conceive of no reasons for granting them exemption from the penalties and liabilities to which free negroes are now subjected."[52]

Concerning Gentry's case, the *Dispatch* took issue with the very idea that he could prove "with any degree of certainty, what amount of negro blood" he possessed. Evidence offered in the Hustings Court proved that Gentry was born in Hanover County. His mother was "about two-thirds white" (an unusual fraction even by the contortions of antebellum racial arithmetic), his grandmother was white, his grandfather was a "brown skin negro," and his father reputedly was white. The paper, however, argued that Gentry's mother herself had started the rumor that her son's father was "a white gentleman of the neighborhood," and that it "circulated from neighbor to neighbor, and from house to house" until people believed it. Only white persons could testify as to Gentry's ancestry, but the paper argued that the court might just as well have let Gentry's mother testify herself, because at least she might be cross-examined, whereas her neighbors could only repeat what they had heard.[53] The *Dispatch*'s reasoning indicates the growing intolerance among white Virginians even for the small amount of malleability regarding race accepted just a generation earlier. In cases of racial determination, it had never mattered before where rumors of racial ancestry originated. All that mattered was whether white people familiar with the local situation believed them to be true. Now, the *Dispatch* argued, it did not even matter whether whites thought they knew the backgrounds of mixed-race people. More reliable evidence than common neighborhood understandings was required. Without birth and marriage records, though, procuring such evidence might very well be impossible. The Richmond Hustings Court rejected Edward Gentry's application.[54]

Richmond's editors pleaded with the General Assembly to take action on the problematic "not a negro" legislation. The *Dispatch* believed Edward Gentry's case surely would force Virginia's lawmakers to see "the importance of an immediate repeal or amendment of this law."[55] The *Richmond Enquirer* concurred and asserted its own hope that applications like Gentry's "may be rejected here as well as throughout the State." Unlike the *Dispatch*, which interpreted the law to give "not a negro" certificate holders some unrecognized, and therefore legally untouchable, position, the *Enquirer* consistently and emphatically believed such documents would effectively "place the applicant upon the footing of a white man in many respects."[56] When police arrested a man named Richard Bradley for causing a disturbance during a theater performance, he claimed to be Native American rather than black. Bradley's claim in particular elicited mockery from the newspapers, which used his physical appearance to ridicule the "not a negro" law. The *Enquirer* wrote that Bradley's "appearance shows that there is just about as much affinity between him and the Indian race as there is between a full-blooded horse and an adulterated jackass." The *Dispatch*, meanwhile, called Bradley a "mongrel darkey," a "wooly-headed Indian," and a "grape-haired Indian," and again called on the legislature to give the laws affecting "mixed bloods" an "overhauling." "Let there be but two races among us," the *Dispatch* proclaimed, "whites and blacks — so that we shall see no more 'wooly heads' applying to the Courts for certificates pronouncing them other than negroes."[57]

Shortly after the legislative session opened in December 1853, House of Delegates member Travis H. Epes from Amelia and Nottoway Counties moved that the body's Committee of Courts of Justice investigate changing the racial definition law of 1785 so as "to declare all persons to be negroes who may be known or proven to have negro blood in them."[58] Epes's resolution, which if approved would also repeal the "not a negro" act, had radical implications for the ways white Virginians thought about and treated individuals of mixed race. Neither white nor black, throughout the antebellum period Virginians of ambiguous race had led ambiguous lives. Their appearance and their ancestry mattered, but so did the local context. Whites in their communities treated them and acted toward them in different ways depending on any number of factors, including how "mixed bloods" presented themselves, the dynamics of a particular situation, and the white person with whom they interacted. Some whites might treat people of mixed race as if they were white in certain circumstances, whereas others might treat them as if they were black in others. Epes's framework, essentially a proposal for what became known in the twentieth century as the "one-drop rule," incorporated none of those subtleties. Appearing to be white no longer mattered. Neither did treatment in the community by other whites. The only significant factor in determining whiteness or blackness was whether a person had even the most distant African ancestor. Epes rooted his proposal in an obsession with racial purity and a demand for racial absolutism few white Virginians would have entirely understood thirty or forty years earlier.

In January 1854, the Committee of Courts of Justice reported it "inexpedient" to change the "not a negro" law. There is no recorded reason for its rejection of Epes's proposal. First and foremost, though, it seems probable that while few legislators liked the idea of people of mixed ancestry possessing the rights of whites, most realized that the "not a negro" law did not necessarily invest them with such rights. The 1833 law gave "mixed bloods" some special protections not afforded to most blacks, but it did not include explicit provisions for their possession of positive civic rights such as suffrage or office holding. These privileges were specifically reserved for whites. Men like Epes and the editor of the

Enquirer exaggerated when they claimed "not a negro" certificates effectively made their holders into white persons, although the legislature itself enabled this confusion when it revised the Virginia Code in 1849. Probably in an effort to simplify the legal language of the "not a negro" law, the 1849 version took out the words "not being a white person, nor a free negro or mulatto" used to describe those eligible for "not a negro" status and replaced them with the briefer "any free person of mixed blood." The spirit of the law was no different in 1853 than it had been in 1833, but without specific language indicating that "mixed bloods" were not white, the letter of the law could be read as a suggestion that they might be.[59]

The Committee of Courts of Justice probably also rejected Epes's resolution because its members realized that a color line as rigid as Epes called for was unenforceable and in many cases unprovable. Any African ancestry would make a person black by the provisions of Epes's rule, but how far back could the law really expect a person to be able to trace his or her ancestry? Even presuming the state could root out everyone with a hint of blackness, Epes's proposal would make hundreds if not thousands of "white" Virginians of all classes (and perhaps even some of the legislators themselves) into "black" Virginians. As one Virginian wrote to the *Enquirer*, arguing the foolishness of changing the law, "I doubt not, if many who are reputed to be white, and are in fact so, do not in a very short time find themselves instead of being elevated, reduced by the judgment of a court of competent jurisdiction, to the level of a free negro."[60] Additionally, such a change in the position of the color line would undermine long-established social norms and legal principles vesting great importance in physical appearance when determining whiteness and blackness and freedom and slavery. Finally, Epes's proposal might have established theoretical legal clarity but held the potential for new forms of social chaos. By the 1850s, white Virginians already understood that light-skinned runaway slaves sometimes pretended to be white in order to travel north undetected.[61] In Epes's formulation of race, however, a free person who appeared to be white but who was legally black because of some small amount of African ancestry might very well leave his or her community and "become" white elsewhere. In urban areas, such people might not even have to travel to pull off such a trick. Epes wanted every drop of "black blood" to be traceable and accounted for, but in reality his proposal potentially made "blackness" more elusive than ever before. In Virginia, the phenomenon of surreptitious "passing" still in parlance was born out of laws such as that suggested by Travis Epes.[62]

On January 10, Epes rose in the House of Delegates to move that the entire body vote to change the language of the Committee of Courts of Justice's report to read that it was "expedient" to alter the laws of racial definition. He addressed the House to defend his original proposal, drawing the delegates' attention to the social damage he saw resulting from the "not a negro" law. As reported in the *Richmond Whig*, Epes argued that "the strong tendencies to ultimate amalgamation which it favored, showed the great evil of such a law, as it sanctioned the introduction of this new class into the same social arena with the white race, extending to them equal privileges in all the social relations of life." The members of the Committee of Courts of Justice were all absent from the floor and could not defend their position, but because a vote in favor of Epes's motion only sent the matter back to the committee to draw up a bill, the issues could be discussed when the committee made its next report. Epes's motion passed.[63]

On January 19, the Committee of Courts of Justice presented its bill, which, according to the House journal, declared "all persons, having negro blood in them, mulattoes," and repealed the "not a negro" law. The bill, however, really did no such thing. As first reported to the floor, the bill did repeal the "not a negro" law but rewrote Virginia's law of racial definition as follows: "Every person who has one sixteenths of negro blood shall be deemed a mulatto or negro, and the word 'negro' in any other section of this, or in any future statute shall be construed to mean mulatto as well as negro."[64] The members of the committee may have seen their proposed bill as a compromise with Epes. Perhaps he was right that using one-quarter as a racial guideline was too generous and admitted too many people of mixed race to whiteness, or at least to something other than blackness. But while a one-drop rule extended racial purity to its logical extreme, it also exposed its absurdity. A line drawn at one-sixteenth would mean that anyone with at least one black great-great-grandparent would still be black. In most cases, going back further than that just could not be accomplished. As a body, though, the legislature did not feel a change to the ancestry laws was necessary. The bill was read and engrossed, but the General Assembly never took action on it. When the legislative session closed in March 1854, the bill died.[65]

With the "not a negro" law still in place, people of mixed race continued to try and use it when they believed holding such an ambiguous status might protect them. Two cases that appeared before Richmond's Mayor Mayo at the end of August 1858 indicate that while they tried to use the vagueness of the law to their advantage, it might also very well work against them. On August 24, William Ferguson appeared in the Mayor's Court on the charge of assaulting a free man of color with a brick. Ferguson had a "not a negro" certificate from the Hustings Court, and when black witnesses came to testify against him, his lawyer objected. Ferguson, the lawyer argued, might not be white. But he was certainly not black, and black witnesses could only testify in court against other blacks. Ferguson's lawyer "confessed that he knew but two classes in Virginia—whites and negroes." He did not wish to argue the merits of the "not a negro" law but insisted that the mayor "had no right to construe it in any other light than as laid down in the law books." Mayor Mayo responded that if there were only two races in Virginia, then Ferguson was "a free white citizen, to all intents and purposes, and as such could vote and be voted for, to fill any public station in the state, however high." Surely, he felt the legislature had not intended that such a construction be given to the law. Mayo announced he would reserve judgment until he reviewed the law.[66]

The next day, the mayor heard the case of Andrew and Agnes Cosby. Agnes accused Andrew of beating her, but the Cosbys' neighbors testified Agnes was "a perfect virago," while Andrew was "an ill-used and much-abused individual" and a man known to be of good character. Suspicion of abuse now turned against Agnes. Andrew Cosby was a free man of color, but when Agnes was asked where she was born and how long she had been married to him, she said they had been married six years, and produced a certificate from the Hustings Court declaring her to be "not a negro." Perhaps she had hoped the certificate would preclude the admissibility of witness testimony, but in fact she had trapped herself. If she wanted to be treated as a white woman, "according to the interpretation given to the State law," then she was guilty of violating laws against racial intermarriage. The mayor held her case over until he handed down the interpretation of the laws related to "mixed bloods" that he had promised in the Ferguson case.[67]

On August 31, Mayo announced that the "not a negro" law made persons of ambiguous race little other than free people of color. They might be exempt, he claimed, from carrying free papers, from being sold into slavery for nonpayment of taxes, from restrictions on leaving and reentering Virginia, and other "regulations of that character." But the General Assembly, Mayo believed, "had never intended to make white persons of this class, or to create a third class in the State, and until overruled by an appellate tribunal, he should look upon them as free negroes and treat them as such." In other words, as the *Dispatch* reported in its description of a case a few weeks later, Richmond's mayor felt that people who were of African descent but were not mulattoes were "*privileged* free negroes." The "not a negro" law never stated from just which "disabilities" such people were exempt, and they tried to capitalize on the law's lack of clarity to escape prosecution as free people of color. The mayor had hoped the legislature would resolve the problem in 1853–54, but it took no action. Without making people of ambiguous race either black or white, Mayo felt he could not run his courtroom, and he refused to accept the possibility that they were white. Accordingly, he filled the legal gap as he saw fit. "By pursuing this course with that class of persons who have certificates stating that they are not negroes," the *Dispatch* wrote, the mayor "hopes to get the higher courts to fix their status, and thus relieve him of a most perplexing subject."[68]

Outside of Richmond, meanwhile, the refusal of the legislature to change the laws of racial definition meant that white communities continued to position people of ambiguous race as they always had. Sometimes even a person of African ancestry could for all intents and purposes be white, suggesting that anxieties about interracial sex and the maintenance of racial boundaries in the 1850s may have been more pronounced in urban than rural parts of Virginia. In 1858, for example, twenty-three men from Lancaster County petitioned the General Assembly regarding property owned by James Corsey. Corsey, whom the petitioners referred to as "a free coloured man," had held one-third interest in a tract of land but had died intestate. When Edward Payne, a white man who owned the rest of the tract, died, the entire plot was put up for sale, and a county official instituted the legal proceedings to have Corsey's interest in the land escheated, or reverted, to the state. The Lancaster County petitioners asked the legislature to forgo its right to the property, for while James Corsey had no legal heirs, he did have children whom the petitioners believed ought to receive the proceeds of the land sale.[69]

The petitioners explained that James Corsey had been "at least three fourths white" and "much esteemed and respected" by whites in Lancaster. He was of good character, and he "associated mostly with the white people of his neighbourhood." He had entered into a sexual relationship with a white woman, the couple had lived together as husband and wife, and they had had numerous children. Corsey and his wife had never married because interracial unions were illegal in Virginia, but "they lived together it is believed in entire conjugal fidelity to each other." After Corsey's death, the petitioners continued, his "wife . . . if they may so call her" and children lived together as a family and conducted themselves with so "much propriety, virtuously and respectably, that they all now pass as white people and are recognized as such with and among those with whom they associate." One of Corsey's daughters had already married a white man, and the couple still resided in the county. The white citizens of Lancaster County understood that the Corsey children could not inherit their father's estate automatically because they were illegitimate, but "justice requires that they should have it, that if there was any fault committed by their father . . . it was not their fault and they ought not to be made to suffer for the sins of their father." If the Lancaster petitioners ever really believed James Corsey committed any "sins" by "marrying" a white woman, they seem to have done very little about them. A family like the Corseys was unusual, to be sure, but still a part of the white community who deserved that community's help if its members could give it. Legislators were not so understanding. They ignored the request.[70]

Interlude *Toward a New Racial Order*

On the last day of 1853, as the Committee of Courts of Justice debated whether to address the issue of racial definition in Virginia, the *Richmond Enquirer* insisted that the law had to be changed. For its part, the paper approved of Travis Epes's resolution because the law as it stood was "certainly unwise and inconvenient." The very idea that a person of "mixed blood" might be entitled to the status of a white person was intolerable, for an individual could "have less than 'one-fourth part of negro blood,' and yet betray in his physical and moral organization the essential character of the negro." The *Enquirer* called for the law to accord with the feelings of white citizens, for regardless of the status of a person of mixed race in law, the paper believed whites could never accept anyone with "black blood" as a social equal. There should be, the paper concluded, "no such conflict between law and society. The law should be the expression of the will of the community, and not do violence to its feelings, usages and principles. Unless we mean to encourage amalgamation, the Legislature should draw the line of distinction between the races with the utmost precision and rigor. The blood of the Caucasian cannot continue pure and undefiled, while the law compels a fellowship with negroes."[1]

A few days later, a man signing his name only as "A Lawyer" wrote the *Enquirer* a letter sharply disagreeing with the paper's position. Not only had the "not a negro" law been in place for twenty years but even when created it had changed nothing in practice from the 1785 law of racial definition. Because a person was only black or mulatto in law if he had at least "one fourth of negro blood in his veins," no one ascertained to have less than that percentage had ever been subject to restrictions against free people of color in Virginia. The "not a negro" law was designed only to save time and energy by allowing courts to issue certificates that relieved their holders of having to prove their ancestry every time they came to court, and by giving prosecutors advance warning of a suspect's racial status before mistakenly trying him or her as a "free negro or mulatto." Whether or not the law as it stood was "unwise," the man wrote, "it is certain that such has been the law of the State for sixty-eight years, and nobody before has proposed to change it."[2]

No one had made such a proposal, "A Lawyer" continued, because the suggestion that "not a negro" certificates made people holding them either legally or socially white pointed to "a strange misapprehension of [the law's] object, and inattention to its express language," and simply was absurd. "If such, or any thing like such, consequences legitimately flowed from the law, it is strange they had not been discovered before this." A man, for example, who had "nothing of the physical organization of a negro" would be unlikely to apply for a certificate declaring him to be "not a negro" in the first place. If he did for some reason and a court found him not to be of "mixed blood," it would not and could not by law give him a certificate, because he would be white. It was only in the event that a person "does betray something of the 'physical organization' of a negro," the man argued, "and is in fact of mixed blood" that he or she would apply for and receive such a certificate. "Not a negro" certificates, then, not only did not make their holders white, but that they needed such a document drew attention to the very fact that they were not white at all.

"A Lawyer" conceded that where to draw the line of exemption from restrictions against people of color was a debatable issue. But wherever the line was drawn, it made no difference in terms of the social relations between blacks and whites. "It is not likely that a person having the physical organization of the negro, would gain admission to a fashionable party with or without his certificate, unless he should go without invitation to a mask-ball; and the exhibition of such a certificate would certainly exclude or expel him thence." Furthermore, the idea that the "not a negro" law somehow encouraged interracial sex was hysterical. "The process of *amalgamation*," the letter writer concluded, will not "be more apt to be resorted to by any one, because he knows that his progeny in the third, or even the second generation, may be able to get a certificate that they are not negroes."

The *Enquirer* and its "lawyer" correspondent talked right past each other on the question of racial ambiguity, mostly because each incorporated slightly different assumptions about the relative power and importance of legal edicts and social regulation in controlling the racial order. The *Enquirer* believed that the times demanded complete certainty on racial definitions and hard-and-fast rules about whiteness and blackness that only the law could establish. Even the possibility that "not a negro" status opened the door to legal whiteness (and even a generous reading of the law pointed to some ambiguity between black and white) to anyone eligible to apply for it was frightening. For the *Enquirer*, the priority of a rigid racial order and the need to root out supposedly white persons who, somewhere deep inside, might still have the "essential character" of blacks, trumped the claims of individuals with some very distant African ancestry who might still have a legitimate claim to whiteness.

For his part, "A Lawyer" contended that because "not a negro" status by no means made a person white, creating an absolutely strict color line in law both challenged the legal rights of some "white" citizens and threatened the prerogatives of white communities to control access to whiteness. When it came to the treatment of people of mixed race, the "will" of white communities well before 1853 had sometimes allowed people of mixed ancestry to exercise some if not all the social and legal privileges of whites. "Society" had long accepted the "hybrid recruit" in rare cases at its own discretion, and by leaving some room for that possibility, the laws already accorded with society. To change the law would mean that some people recognized as socially white in a community suddenly had no legal rights as white persons, thus creating more problems than it solved. Most whites had never thought in terms of "Caucasian blood" continuing to be "pure and undefiled," because it never had been since the earliest days of colonial settlement. Attitudes and language were in flux in the 1850s, though. "Blood" may have been the dominant metaphor of race since the colonial era, but only in the 1850s did some white Virginians begin to make the case that it was the only one.

The real conflict between law and society, one that had been deeply ingrained in Virginia for centuries, was that the law militated strongly against sex across the color line, yet whites had long understood that such activities were part and parcel of the Virginia in which they lived. Some flexibility regarding people of mixed race helped to conceal and to manage that disjunction. The *Enquirer*, though, wrote in the language of a new racial understanding, and held up as the ideal society an unyielding one where whiteness could be purged of blackness and Europeans entirely separated from Africans. In a way, the *Enquirer* and its sympathetic white readers looked not forward but backward for an opportunity to start over in a new America where race brought the absolute order it was designed to instill and where they could pretend whites did not need blacks so desperately as the threats to slavery made painfully and frighteningly obvious. When the Civil War obliterated the southern socioeconomic order, they got their chance.

Epilogue

In November 1857, a white woman calling herself Mary Medor and claiming to be from Charlotte County boarded a train for Richmond, attended by a black man named John who she said was her slave. The train's conductor noticed the couple, suspected that something was out of the ordinary, and began asking questions. Mary Medor said she was on her way to Norfolk to see her relatives. Her father, she claimed, had left John to her in his will, but she did not wish to sell him and therefore brought him along on the train. The conductor talked to John as well, but felt that John's story differed in important ways from Mary's. The police examined Medor's and John's baggage when the train arrived in Richmond and, finding the couple's clothing mixed together in a single bag, took them to jail. The pair confessed. John admitted that he was the property of Lucy Harris of Mecklenburg County and that he had run away at the prompting of Mary Medor, whose real name was Susan Percy. Percy, for her part, at first insisted that searching her bags had been a violation of her rights and that John had lied. Eventually, she admitted that she had been living and working with Mrs. Harris for two or three years, "that an intimacy had grown up between her and the servant, John, and that a short time since, they two had determined if possible to make their escape to a free State, she to hide her shame, and he to secure his freedom."[1]

The next day, Susan Percy and John appeared before the mayor of Richmond, whose courtroom was packed with spectators wishing to get a glimpse of what the *Richmond Daily Dispatch* called the "disgusting exhibition" of the couple. John claimed that Percy had instigated the entire scheme, urging him to steal a horse late one Sunday. The couple, John continued, then rode through the night to Nottoway County and hopped on the train the following morning. The mayor determined to send the two back to Mecklenburg County, where John would be returned to his owner and Percy would be tried for stealing a slave. The stagecoach on the way back to Mecklenburg overturned, nearly killing

Percy and delaying her return to prison. On arriving back in his home county, John was released from custody, but the *Dispatch* reported that "it is said he will be rearrested on a charge having its origin in his intimacy with the woman, and which, if satisfactorily established, will cause him to swing."[2]

As Richmond hurtled unknowingly toward the Civil War, whites began to chafe at sex across the color line, and they felt a need for vigilance to keep blacks and whites sexually discreet. That so many people came to see the spectacle of Susan Percy and John and that the newspaper declared that such a "singular depravity" ought to result in John's hanging points to a particular concern in Virginia in the 1850s about sex between black men and white women. The Mecklenburg County Court, however, seems to have thought the bloodthirsty sentiments of Richmonders somewhat of an overreaction. John was indeed rearrested (for an unnamed offense), but in December 1857, on the recommendation of the local prosecutor, the court dismissed all of the commonwealth's charges against him. Susan Percy, meanwhile, who was indicted for "a felony," appears never to have been tried. In February 1858 her case was carried over to the next term of the court. It then vanishes from the public record.[3]

Still, that both Richmond's legal authorities and editors responded so suspiciously and so viscerally to the sexual association of Susan Percy and John suggests that the racial sensibilities and sexual anxieties of white Virginians were in the midst of significant shifts from the days of Thomas Jefferson. For most of the seventy-five years before the Civil War, whites met the discovery of sex across the color line with disapprobation but also with equanimity. They recognized that exploitative, familial, commercial, and adulterous interracial sexual liaisons were all unavoidable in a multiracial world, especially where "our family, white and black" served as one of the central metaphors for understanding social and economic relations in that world.[4] Accommodation of such illicit sexuality was not without its consequences, foremost among which were the instabilities wrought by the emotional suffering of members of white and black families alike, the bitter tensions and ferocious violence provoked by the systematic sexual abuse of African American women, the periodic dissolution of marriages, the blurring of the line theoretically separating black from white, and the existence of individuals and families who seemed beyond the reach of the laws designed to make their lives difficult and dangerous. But bending to the winds of social and legal contradiction helped keep early national and antebellum Virginia from breaking. Moreover, the presence of slavery guaranteed white supremacy, enabling white men in positions of power and authority at both the local and state levels to respond to situations involving interracial sex requiring their intervention without consistently making the enforcement of laws that demanded rigid racial and sexual boundaries their sole or even their top priority.

In the 1850s, some white Virginians began to ask whether policing those boundaries more consistently might be necessary, especially in urban areas where local social and demographic changes dovetailed with the threats to slavery whites perceived from the escalating sectional crisis. Emancipation decidedly answered that question in the affirmative for white Virginians throughout the state. In a number of ways, in fact, the case of Susan Percy and John foreshadowed the white sexual paranoia about black men characteristic of the post-emancipation South. Before the Civil War, local context significantly helped determine white reactions to interracial sexual activities, but Susan Percy and John were on a train moving across Virginia's landscape. They arrived in Richmond without a context, arousing the curiosity of the train's conductor. Moreover, it is entirely appropriate that the couple was caught on a train. Trains in the New South were sites of great contestation, as blacks and whites struggled to reconstruct their social and economic orders in a rapidly changing environment where freedom of movement among blacks aroused white fears of an uncertain world without slavery. The expansion and elaboration of legalized segregation began on the trains, and lynchings in the New South occurred particularly in places of economic and social volatility where "strange blacks" came through town. By the turn of the twentieth century, two people like Susan Percy and John would not be allowed legally to sit next to one another on a train, but a man like John would have understood — like the thirty-three black men lynched for alleged sexual transgressions in Virginia between 1880 and 1930 — that he could very likely "swing" for the crime of "intimacy" with a white woman.[5]

Black women continued to face sexual harassment from white men even in freedom, especially in the fields and the kitchens where southern African American women continued to work well into the twentieth century. On one hand, that white men considered sexual access to black women their prerogative long after slavery suggests that Virginians after emancipation were inconsistent in their ostensible demand that whites and blacks stay apart from one another sexually. But the targeting of black women for sexual assault was inseparable from the larger goal of white men to maintain their racial superiority in the absence of their literal ownership of black bodies. This goal was far more important than any calls for racial purity such as that culminating in the "one-drop rule" of Virginia's Racial Integrity Act of 1924.[6] As historian Jacquelyn Dowd Hall has noted, the lynching of black men and the sexual exploitation of black women in the New South were of a piece. "[R]ape reasserted white dominance and control in the private arena as lynching reasserted hierarchical arrangements in the public transactions of men."[7]

In 1903 W. E. B. DuBois defined the "problem of the Twentieth Century" as "the problem of the color line," and he proved a prophet.[8] The problem demonstrated itself too knotty for Americans in the twentieth century, its solution beyond our grasp. Now, in the early years of the twenty-first century, stories about interracial sex and interracial families are extraordinarily popular in American culture. Memoirs and multigenerational sagas fly off of bookstore shelves. White and black families with pasts that were once shared, almost always denied, and long since diverged meet again on television talk shows. The audience applauds and their eyes mist, as if the embrace across the racial divide they invariably witness on stage salves wounds they feel deep in their own hearts and minds. For many Americans, it seems that the resurrection of truth about this nation's bloodlines provides the collective opportunity to exhale, to see some relief from the exhaustion of racial division and antipathy that returns again and again like an ineradicable national weed. Finally, they seem to feel, we can move on. Tom and Sally were really in love, after all, and slavery was a long time ago.

Yet public recognition of shared biological inheritance is nearly always divorced from any sense of the tragedy revealed every time long-lost white and black cousins reunite on camera. Reunions make for wonderful drama in a sentimental age, but we need to ask at whose expense reconciliation comes. Will we forget our responsibility to bear the burdens of the past so that we can pretend to have solved the social and economic injustices that plague our present? More perhaps than ever before, we want so badly to believe we are one people, but we also face constant reminders that we are not.[9] It is much easier to cultivate the myth of the former than to do anything about the realities of the latter, but they are inseparable pieces of the historical legacy passed down to us from early national and antebellum Virginia. One hopes we can learn from its contradictory past in pursuit of resolving some of the paradoxes of our present. Meaningful reunion must also come with meaningful reckoning.

Notes

INTRODUCTION

1. It is unclear whether Peter Franklin ever actually struck Angela Barnett or, for that matter, what kind of weapon he held. A witness for Barnett testified at trial that Franklin had become violent without provocation, had struck Barnett three times with a small cowhide whip, and had then called to Carpenter to bring him a bludgeon, which Carpenter had concealed in his coat. According to this witness, Franklin advanced toward Barnett with the bludgeon and threatened to kill her, at which point Barnett picked up the adze. Jesse Carpenter, meanwhile, conceded that Franklin warned Barnett that "he would correct her," and that Franklin was advancing, whip in hand, toward Barnett when she struck him. But Carpenter made no mention of a bludgeon, and testified that he never personally saw Franklin strike Barnett. See Henrico County Order Book 5 (1791–94), September 29, 1792, pp. 277–78; and *Commonwealth v. Angela Barnett*, in *Calendar of Virginia State Papers*, 6:337–38 (hereafter *CVSP*).

2. Certificates as to Angelica Barnett, *CVSP*, 6:344–45. Angela Barnett's first name is spelled at least four different ways in the documentary record.

3. Angelia Barnett to the Executive, and Doctors' Certificates as to Angelia Barnett, in *CVSP*, 6:363–64 and 372–73 (quotation on 364); Executive Papers— Letters Received, September–October 1793, box 81, Library of Virginia, Richmond. The case of Angela Barnett and Jacob Valentine is discussed in some detail in Sidbury, *Ploughshares into Swords*, 176–83.

4. Angilla Barnett Reprieved—Jailor's Receipt, Petition to the Governor for the Pardon of Angelica Barnett, and Petition for Angelica Barnett, in *CVSP*, 6:393, 512–13, and 530–31 (quotations on 512 and 531); Executive Papers—Letters Received, September–October 1793, box 81, Library of Virginia, Richmond; Henrico County Will Book 4 (1809–15), 61–62; Henrico County Order Book 15 (1810–11), 279.

5. Angelia Barnett to the Executive, in *CVSP*, 6:363.

6. Ibid., 363–64. It was not unheard-of for women to use pregnancy as a strategic means of avoiding execution. Pleas of pregnancy, for example, were common in British courts from at least the fourteenth century and remained a part of British law until England abolished the death penalty in the twentieth century. I have not been able to document other pregnancy plea cases in Virginia, but it seems highly unlikely that Angela Barnett was the only woman to claim pregnancy, especially given the relative newness of American independence from the British legal system in the 1790s. On pregnancy pleas, see Levin, " 'Murder not then the fruit within my

womb'"; and Oldham, "On Pleading the Belly." Women of color in the South might also use pregnancy achieved through sex across the color line for strategic reasons other than escaping judicial punishment. The example best known to American historians is probably that of Harriet Jacobs, who became pregnant by a white man partially in an effort to protect herself from the sexual harassment of her owner. See Jacobs, *Incidents in the Life of a Slave Girl*, 53–62.

7. Richmond City Hustings Court Order Book 4 (1797–1801), December 11, 1797, p. 67.

8. *Commonwealth v. Valentine* bundles, Richmond City Hustings Court Suit Papers, box 7 (1796–97) and box 8 (1798–99), Library of Virginia, Richmond.

9. In using the word "tolerated" I am building on the definition adopted by Martha Hodes in her work on sex between black men and white women. As Hodes notes, white southerners before the Civil War cannot be said to have been "tolerant" of interracial sex in the sense that they possessed "a liberal spirit toward those of a different mind." But they did "tolerate" such sexual behavior, disapproving but viewing it with "a measure of forbearance." Hodes, *White Women, Black Men*, 3.

10. Johnson and Roark, *Black Masters*; McLaurin, *Celia*; Leslie, *Woman of Color, Daughter of Privilege*; Alexander, *Ambiguous Lives*; and Madden, *We Were Always Free*.

11. Many of these works focus particularly on the relationships between gender and class hierarchies in the nineteenth-century South, which often came into sharpest relief when race and sex were in the mix as well. See, for example, Bynum, *Unruly Women*; Sommerville, "Rape Myth Reconsidered"; Sommerville, "Rape Myth in the Old South"; and especially Hodes, *White Women, Black Men*.

12. As Martha Hodes writes, making an argument that can be extended to the children of white men and free women of color and to children of free people of color with mixed ancestry, "[b]ecause Southern statutes stipulated that a child's legal status as slave or free followed the mother, the children of white women and black men were of partial African ancestry but also free, thereby violating the equation of blackness and slavery." Such children "exposed the potential difficulties of sustaining racial boundaries in a society predicated upon just such distinctions." Hodes, *White Women, Black Men*, 96.

This study does not systematically address the question of how Native Americans fit into the racial calculus of Virginians before the Civil War. As the issues arise in the course of other considerations, I do discuss the presence of Native Americans in Virginia, their importance to matters of racial definition, and the relevance of their sexual intermixture with the rest of Virginia's population, especially with the African American population. By the early nineteenth century, however, when white Virginians worried about racial "amalgamation," they worried primarily about sex between people of European and African descent. Although they never disappeared, questions centered on the racial status of Native Americans in Virginia were far more pressing and conspicuous in the seventeenth and eighteenth centuries than they would ever be again, as the Native American population in Virginia declined or vanished into a binary world, and as Native American slavery was mostly phased out of state law. Certainly by the second or third decade of the nineteenth century, and perhaps even earlier, most Virginians generally thought they lived in a biracial rather than a triracial society.

13. As Kenneth Stampp noted more than forty years ago, "to measure the extent of miscegenation with precision is impossible, because statistical indexes are crude and public and private records fragmentary. But the evidence nevertheless suggests that human behavior in the Old South was very human indeed, that sexual contacts between the races were not the rare aberrations of a small group of depraved whites but a frequent occurrence involving whites of all social and cultural levels." Stampp, *Peculiar Institution*, 350–51.

14. Clinton, *Plantation Mistress*, 221.

INTERLUDE: STORIES TOLD ABOUT MONTICELLO

1. Henry S. Randall to James Parton, June 1, 1868, reprinted in Gordon-Reed, *Thomas Jefferson and Sally Hemings*, 254–57 (quotations on 254 and 255).

2. Ibid., quotation on 256.

3. Journal of John Hartwell Cocke, January 26, 1853, in John Hartwell Cocke Papers, box 188, Alderman Library, University of Virginia.

4. Foster et al., "Jefferson Fathered Slave's Last Child." With a few exceptions, variations on the notion that Thomas Jefferson would never have had sexual relations with an enslaved woman and acceptance of the alternative paternity of one of the Carr brothers dominated American historiography in the 130 years following Henry Randall's letter to James Parton. The results of a DNA study published in November 1998, however, have radically shifted the burden of proof onto those who continue to cling to the theoretical genetic possibility that some other Jefferson fathered Sally Hemings's children. DNA evidence hardly answers every question we might have about the children of Sally Hemings. It will probably always remain possible for those wanting to cast doubt on and disbelieve the reality of her sexual relationship with Thomas Jefferson to do so. But the evidentiary case for the paternity of other male Jeffersons is extremely tendentious and extraordinarily weak, not to mention novel given the utter lack of public suspicion of other Jeffersons until 1998. Important secondary works published in the past thirty years that dismiss the Jefferson-Hemings story include Ellis, *American Sphinx*, 303–7; Wilson, "Thomas Jefferson and the Character Issue"; Virginius Dabney, *The Jefferson Scandals*; Miller, *The Wolf by the Ears*, 148–76; Malone and Hochman, "A Note on Evidence"; Douglass Adair, "The Jefferson Scandals," in Colburn, *Fame and the Founding Fathers*, 160–91; and Malone, *Jefferson and His Time*, 4:494–98. Exceptions to the characterizations of these authors published before the end of 1998 include Gordon-Reed, *Thomas Jefferson and Sally Hemings*; Brodie, *Thomas Jefferson*; and Winthrop Jordan, *White over Black*, 429–81. Also important are Brodie's articles "The Great Jefferson Taboo" and "Thomas Jefferson's Unknown Grandchildren." In the wake of the DNA study, the Thomas Jefferson Memorial Foundation (now known as the Thomas Jefferson Foundation), which owns and operates Monticello, formed a committee to evaluate the scientific and historical evidence relating to Thomas Jefferson and Sally Hemings. In the words of foundation president Dan-

iel P. Jordan, the committee concluded that "the best evidence available suggests the strong likelihood that Thomas Jefferson and Sally Hemings had a relationship over time that led to the birth of one, and perhaps all, of the known children of Sally Hemings." The report of the committee exists in printed form, but it, along with materials assessing the notion that Thomas Jefferson was not in fact the father of Sally Hemings's children, is available online at ⟨http://www.monticello.org/plantation/hemings_resource.html⟩ (quotation from "Statement on the TJMF Research Committee Report on Thomas Jefferson and Sally Hemings"). Efforts to dismiss the case for the paternity of Thomas Jefferson include the Jefferson-Hemings Scholars Commission, "Report on the Jefferson-Hemings Matter," April 12, 2001, available online at ⟨http://www.geocities.com/tjshcommission⟩; and Coates, *The Jefferson-Hemings Myth*. For my own critique of such arguments, see Rothman, " 'Character Defense.' "

CHAPTER ONE

1. Miller, *The Wolf by the Ears*, 154. The best source on Callender's life and career is Michael Durey's biography, *"With the Hammer of Truth."* Also on Callender, see Jellison, "That Scoundrel Callender." On how historians have treated Callender's accusations, see Gordon-Reed, *Thomas Jefferson and Sally Hemings*, ch. 2 (hereafter *TJ and SH*).

2. Malone and Peterson quoted in Virginius Dabney, *The Jefferson Scandals*, 132. Gordon-Reed more fully describes and presents a withering critique of the "character defense" in *TJ and SH*, ch. 4.

3. Scot A. French and Edward L. Ayers discuss some of the divergent and changing readings of the Jefferson-Hemings affair in "The Strange Career of Thomas Jefferson," in Onuf, *Jeffersonian Legacies*, 418–51.

4. Jefferson suggested that Eppes send a slave named Isabel with Mary, but an illness incurred after childbirth prevented Isabel from making the trip. Eppes sent Sally Hemings in her stead. Lucia Stanton, *Free Some Day*, 59.

5. Bear and Stanton, *Jefferson's Memorandum Books*, 1:685 (Sally Hemings inoculated); and "Life among the Lowly, Number I," *Pike County (Ohio) Republican*, March 13, 1873.

6. Peabody, *"There Are No Slaves in France,"* 55.

7. Bear and Stanton, *Jefferson's Memorandum Books*, 1:729, 734 (clothing expenditures for Sally Hemings), 718, 721, 722, and 725 (monthly wages paid Sally Hemings).

8. "Life among the Lowly, Number I."

9. Jefferson, *Notes on the State of Virginia*, 137–43 and 162–63 (quotations on 143, 138).

10. Pierson, *Jefferson at Monticello*, 107.

11. "Life among the Lowly, No. 3," *Pike County (Ohio) Republican*, December 25, 1873, reprinted in *TJ and SH*, 252.

12. Historians have generally accepted that Wayles and Betty Hemings had as many as six children together. Madison Hemings claimed that his grandmother "was taken by the widower Wales as his concubine." Isaac Jefferson, also formerly

enslaved at Monticello, said of Betty Hemings's children that "folks said that these Hemings'es was old Mr. Wayles' children." Thomas Turner, a Virginian who commented on Jefferson's affair with Sally Hemings, reported in 1805 that Sally was "the natural daughter of Mr. Wales, who was the father of the actual Mrs. Jefferson." See "Life among the Lowly, Number I"; Logan, *Memoirs of a Monticello Slave*, 13; and Turner, "Letter."

13. In 1868, when Henry Randall wrote to James Parton of his conversation with Thomas Jefferson Randolph, he noted that even Randolph described Sally Hemings as "decidedly goodlooking." Isaac Jefferson similarly reported that Hemings was "very handsome." See Randall to Parton, June 1, 1868, reprinted in *TJ and SH*, 254; and Logan, *Memoirs of a Monticello Slave*, 13.

14. On sexual abuse of slaves, also see Chapter 4. There is no way to know just how frequently masters and other white men raped female slaves, though some have made attempts at calculation. Robert Fogel and Stanley Engerman suggest that white men fathered only 1 to 2 percent of slave children on plantations. Herbert Gutman and Richard Sutch, challenging Fogel and Engerman, argue that the percentage was closer to 4 percent and perhaps as high as 8 percent by the 1850s. Gutman and Sutch, assuming that white men directed their attentions to enslaved women between the ages of 15 and 30, also note that every slave woman had at least a 5.6 percent chance of being approached sexually by a white man each year and a 58 percent chance of being approached at least once in that fifteen-year span. In Thelma Jennings's study of narratives collected by the Works Progress Administration from formerly enslaved women, she found that over 12 percent of women mentioned interracial sex and that nearly 35 percent of women commenting on the subject indicated either that their fathers were white or that they had given birth to a child or children of a white man. Using evidence from Paul Escott's survey of WPA narratives, Catherine Clinton offers the possibility that "forced sex was a problem on roughly one out of five plantations," while Helene Lecaudey notes that 10.3 percent of female former slaves in South Carolina mentioned interracial sexual liaisons and that 25 percent of female ex-slaves in Virginia did. Regardless of these uncertain indicators, statistics on the threat of sexual abuse ultimately are not wholly relevant. Every slave woman knew that she could and might be sexually assaulted by a white man, and such a fear was constant for all slave women. As Eugene Genovese suggests, "enough violations of black women occurred on the plantations to constitute a scandal and make life hell for a discernible minority of black women and their men." See Fogel and Engerman, *Time on the Cross*, 133; Gutman and Sutch, "Victorians All?," 148–53; Jennings, " 'Us Colored Women Had to Go through a Plenty,' " 66; Clinton, "Caught in the Web," 24; Lecaudey, "Behind the Mask: Ex-Slave Women and Interracial Sexual Relations," in Morton, *Discovering the Women in Slavery*, 264; and Genovese, *Roll, Jordan, Roll*, 415. On white-on-black interracial rape, also see McLaurin, *Celia*; Hine, "Rape and the Inner Lives of Southern Black Women"; Jacqueline Jones, *Labor of Love, Labor of Sorrow*, 25–29 and 37–38; Steven Brown, "Sexuality and the Slave Community"; Johnston, *Race Relations in Virginia*; Blassingame, *Slave Community*, 154–57; Simson, "Afro-American Female"; and Williamson, *New People*, ch. 1.

15. Bardaglio, *Reconstructing the Household*, esp. 48–78; Bardaglio, "Rape and the Law in the Old South"; Painter, "Soul Murder and Slavery"; Getman, "Sexual Control in the Slaveholding South"; Clinton, *Plantation Mistress*, 72–73, 87–91, and 221–22; Catherine Clinton, " 'Southern Dishonor,' " in Bleser, *In Joy and in Sorrow*, 52–68; Stevenson, *Life in Black and White*, 236–40; White, *Ar'n't I a Woman?*, 27–46; Fox-Genovese, *Within the Plantation Household*, 292; Carby, *Reconstructing Womanhood*, 27; Mills, "Miscegenation and the Free Negro," 16; and Angela Davis, *Women, Race, and Class*, 175.

16. According to Madison Hemings, Betty Hemings was the daughter of an African woman and a white ship captain named Hemings. See "Life among the Lowly, Number I."

17. Mrs. Alice Marshall, in Perdue, Barden, and Phillips, *Weevils*, 202.

18. James Smith, *Autobiography*, 4–7.

19. Jefferson to Bentalou, August 25, 1786, in Boyd, *Papers*, 10:296.

20. James Hemings began receiving monthly wages in France from Jefferson in October 1787, shortly after his sister's arrival, and he continued to be paid after returning to the United States. Jefferson put a promise of freedom for James Hemings in writing in 1793, and emancipated him in 1796. This set of circumstances suggests James Hemings made his own arrangement with Jefferson, roughly concurrent with Sally's coming to France, before agreeing to return with his owner. Of course, it is possible that James's beginning to receive wages was of little significance and that Sally Hemings made her deal with Jefferson first, which could have made James Hemings reconsider staying in France alone. See Bear and Stanton, *Jefferson's Memorandum Books*, 1:681, 2:936; Betts, *Thomas Jefferson's Farm Book*, 15–16; and Gordon-Reed, *TJ and SH*, 174. For an alternative explanation of James Hemings's freedom as well as a critique of Jefferson's positions toward slavery, see Paul Finkelman, "Jefferson and Slavery," in Onuf, *Jeffersonian Legacies*, 181–221, esp. 204–5.

21. James Smith, *Autobiography*, 4–7.

22. Randall to Parton, June 1, 1868, in *TJ and SH*, 255.

23. Pierson, *Jefferson at Monticello*, 106–7, quotation on 106.

24. TJR, quoted in Lucia Stanton, " 'Those Who Labor for My Happiness,' " in Onuf, *Jeffersonian Legacies*, 151–52. On the Hemings family more generally, see Stanton, " 'Those Who Labor,' " 147–80; Lucia Stanton, "Monticello to Main Street"; Lucia Stanton, *Slavery at Monticello*; Lucia Stanton, *Free Some Day*, 102–61; Bear, "Hemings Family of Monticello"; and Justus, *Down from the Mountain*.

25. For scholarly considerations of whether sexual relationships between masters and their female slaves could ever be consensual, see Clinton, " 'With a Whip in His Hand' "; Sharon Block, "Lines of Color, Sex, and Service," in Hodes, *Sex, Love, Race*, 141–63; Angela Davis, *Women, Race, and Class*, 25–26; and Stevenson, *Life in Black and White*, 240–41. Cf. Genovese, *Roll, Jordan, Roll*, 415–19. Gordon-Reed considers the issue of consent with particular respect to Jefferson and Hemings in *TJ and SH*, 166–69.

26. Jefferson, *Notes on the State of Virginia*, 139.

27. It is worth noting that when Jefferson returned to Virginia in 1789, he intended on going back to France in the near future. Sally Hemings may or may not

have been aware of Jefferson's long-term considerations, but it is impossible to tell what role, if any, such a proposed return might have played in the mutual calculations of Jefferson and Hemings. The plan never materialized, and explicating all the alternative possibilities of who knew, thought, and told what to whom would not only require an exceedingly long diversion but would also be exceedingly hypothetical. See Boyd, *Papers*, 13:638–39, 14:215, 328–32, and 15:34–35, 364–69, 413–14.

28. Both quoted in Lucia Stanton, " 'Those Who Labor,' " 152 (La Rochefoucauld-Liancourt) and 173 n. 18 (Volney).

29. Foster et al., "Jefferson Fathered Slave's Last Child," 27; and "Life among the Lowly, Number I." Thomas Jefferson, in fact, recorded nothing in his Farm Book pointing to the birth of any child to Sally Hemings around 1790, and it is always possible that no such child ever existed. But it seems unlikely that (presuming Madison Hemings's information originated with his mother) Sally Hemings lied about this aspect of her story when so many other details can be verified, and when James Callender's reports of the story, discussed below, indicate that people in Charlottesville in 1802 believed this first child not only had once but in fact still lived. Thomas Woodson, of course, was a real person, and the oral history shared by many of his descendants certainly suggests he had some kind of connection to Monticello. But barring any new genetic evidence, it seems highly unlikely that he was the son of Thomas Jefferson and Sally Hemings. For a contrary argument, see Byron Woodson, *President in the Family*. For a pre-DNA consideration of the existence of a child named Tom whose parents were Thomas Jefferson and Sally Hemings, see Gordon-Reed, *TJ and SH*, 67–75.

30. On Callender's life and career in Scotland, see Durey, *"With the Hammer of Truth,"* chs. 1–3; quotation on 91.

31. On Callender's role in the Hamilton scandal particularly, see ibid., 97–102; and Jellison, "That Scoundrel Callender," 297–98. Quotation from letter from Callender to Jefferson, September 28, 1797, in Worthington Ford, *Thomas Jefferson and James Thomson Callender*, 8 (hereafter *TJ and JTC*).

32. *Richmond Recorder*, November 3, 1802; Bear and Stanton, *Jefferson's Memorandum Books*, 2:963.

33. For additional payments from Jefferson to Callender, see Bear and Stanton, *Jefferson's Memorandum Books*, 2:971, 975, 976, 979, 980, 984, 986, 1005, 1028, and 1042.

34. Jefferson to Callender, October 6, 1799, in *TJ and JTC*, 19. Also see Jefferson to Callender, September 6, 1799, in *TJ and JTC*, 16–17.

35. As Callender wrote to Jefferson in September 1798, explaining his decision to leave Philadelphia, "I am entirely sick even of the Republicans, for some of them have used me so dishonestly . . . that I have the strongest inclination, as well as the best reason, for wishing to shift the scene." Callender to Jefferson, September 22, 1798, in *TJ and JTC*, 10.

36. Callender to Jefferson, August 10 and September 26, 1799, and March 14 and April 27, 1800, in *TJ and JTC*, 15–16, 17–18, 20–21, and 21–22.

37. See Callender's letters to Jefferson from prison, in *TJ and JTC*, 25–33.

38. Although Jefferson sent Callender $50 in jail, he never wrote to him,

prompting Callender to implore Jefferson for "a few lines, at first or second hand." Ostensibly Callender wanted acknowledgment that Jefferson was receiving political materials he had sent, but, more important, he wanted some sign from Jefferson that he still remembered Callender and valued his support. Callender never got any signal. Michael Durey argues that the Republican political strategy changed around Callender while he remained in jail, and that James Madison suggested to Jefferson that he assume a low profile during the election campaign, advice that Jefferson took. See Bear and Stanton, *Jefferson's Memorandum Books*, 2:1028 n. 53; Callender to Jefferson, October 11, 1800, in *TJ and JTC*, 28–29 (quotation on 28); and Durey, *"With the Hammer of Truth,"* 139–40. On the delay in remitting Callender's fine, his overtures for a patronage position, and his subsequent fury toward Jefferson, see Durey, 143–48, and Gordon-Reed, *TJ and SH*, 59–61 and 74–75.

39. Callender to Jefferson, April 12, 1801, in *TJ and JTC*, 33–34.

40. Callender to Madison, April 27, 1801, in *TJ and JTC*, 35–37 (quotations on 35, 36).

41. Jefferson to Monroe, May 26 and 29, 1801, in *TJ and JTC*, 38–39. Jefferson clearly anticipated that Callender would carry out his threats. In his May 29 letter to Monroe, therefore, he also made a preemptive effort to shape the perception of his prior relationship with Callender, offering the disingenuous explanation that he had long wished Callender would end his activities as a political writer and that any money he had given Callender was strictly charity. Nearly a year later, in another letter to Monroe, Jefferson reiterated a similar and lengthier explanation of his association with Callender (Jefferson to Monroe, June 15, 1802, in *TJ and JTC*, 39–40). Jefferson's transparent strategy of trying to convince his political allies that he had never been a supporter of Callender was prescient. In the wake of the Hemings revelations, Jefferson's defenders claimed the president had never approved of Callender's work, prompting Callender to print the letters Jefferson had sent him indicating otherwise.

42. *Richmond Recorder*, September 1, 1802; and Brodie, *Thomas Jefferson*, 323.

43. *Washington Federalist*, September 14, 1801, cited in Thomas Jefferson Memorial Foundation Research Committee, "Report on Thomas Jefferson and Sally Hemings," appendix F, p. 5.

44. One such poem appeared in July 1802 in the *Port Folio*, a Federalist newspaper in Philadelphia, and Callender reprinted the poem when he publicly revealed the Jefferson-Hemings story in the *Recorder* on September 1, 1802. The verse, written as if authored by one of Jefferson's slaves, included the following:

And why should one hab de white wife,
    And me hab only Quangeroo?
Me no see reason for me life!
    No! Quashee hab de white wife too.
        Huzza, &c.
For make all like, let blackee nab
    De white womans. . . . dat be de track!
Den Quashee de white wife will hab,
    And massa *Jefferson shall hab de black.*

45. Cited in *Richmond Recorder*, September 8, 1802.

46. Callender frequently lambasted members of the Richmond gentry for their interracial sexual affairs, even going so far as to publish the names of white men caught at "dances" where blacks and whites mixed. On the same day that he ran the first Jefferson-Hemings article, in fact, Callender published a story about a man named George Prosser, who supposedly was found dead in the bed of a mulatto woman in Richmond. Callender lamented that "many of our married men go to bed with these Africans, with as much pleasure as a new made bridegroom would his lovely spouse." He hoped that Richmond's white citizens would "take into consideration and prohibit the intercourse betwixt *black* and *white*." *Richmond Recorder*, September 1, 1802. Also see *Richmond Examiner*, April 11, 1800.

47. *Richmond Recorder*, September 1, 15, and 22, and December 15, 1802.

48. *Richmond Recorder*, September 1, 1802; and Brodie, *Thomas Jefferson*, 323.

49. See, for example, *Richmond Examiner*, June 9 and August 11, 1802.

50. *Richmond Recorder*, May 26, 1802.

51. *Aurora*, August 25, 1802; and *Richmond Recorder*, September 1, 1802. Later, Callender explained that he had intended to wait until the election campaign of 1804 to reveal the Hemings story, hoping to cause maximum political damage for Jefferson. When the Republican papers brought his dead wife (she had died in 1798 shortly before Callender left Philadelphia, too poor at the time even to bring his four sons with him) into their personal conflict, though, he decided to run the report early. Writing to Duane at the end of October 1802 in the pages of the *Recorder*, Callender asserted, "if you had not violated the sanctuary of the grave, SALLY, and her son TOM would still, perhaps, have slumbered in the tomb of oblivion. To charge a man as a *thief*, and an *adulterer*, is, of itself, bad enough. But when you charge him with an action that is much more execrable than *an ordinary murder* . . . is the party injured not to repel such baseness, with ten thousand fold vengeance upon the miscreant that invented it?" *Richmond Recorder*, September 22 and October 27, 1802.

52. On the importance of gossip and personal reputation in the politics of the early republic and the political careers of the era's politicians, see Freeman, "Dueling as Politics"; and Freeman, "Slander, Poison, Whispers, and Fame."

53. *Richmond Recorder*, September 1 and 15, 1802.

54. *Richmond Recorder*, September 1, 1802.

55. Durey, *"With the Hammer of Truth,"* 142.

56. *Richmond Recorder*, September 1, 1802.

57. That Sally Hemings had an unnamed daughter in 1799 is indicated by a letter Jefferson wrote to his son-in-law John Wayles Eppes in December 1799 noting that "Maria's maid" had had a child and that both mother and daughter were fine. Jefferson's daughter Mary had already married Eppes in 1797 and left Monticello, but there is no indication anyone other than Sally Hemings had ever served as her maid. Jefferson to Eppes, December 21, 1799, Jefferson Papers, Alderman Library, University of Virginia.

58. "Life among the Lowly, No. 3," 252. Israel Jefferson probably overestimated his "intimacy" with both Thomas Jefferson and Sally Hemings. He claimed in his

interview that he had been Thomas Jefferson's personal attendant for fourteen years, which was not true. Moreover, he was just eight years old when Sally Hemings gave birth to her last child. Nonetheless Israel Jefferson, like other Monticello slaves, believed Jefferson and Hemings had a sexual relationship.

59. *Richmond Recorder*, December 8, 1802.

60. Henry Randall to Hugh Grigsby, February 15, 1856, in Klingberg and Klingberg, *Correspondence*, 30.

61. *Richmond Recorder*, October 20, 1802. The *Richmond Examiner* had pointed out the error in the timing of Sally Hemings's presence in France nearly a month before Callender printed his retraction. Callender, though, certainly trusted his own sources more than Jeffersonian editors, and while the *Examiner* notice may have prompted him to investigate the matter, he probably waited to confirm the error himself before taking any action in print. *Richmond Examiner*, September 25, 1802.

62. *Richmond Recorder*, November 10, 1802.

63. Ibid.; Lucia Stanton, *Free Some Day*, 118–19; and Logan, *Memoirs of a Monticello Slave*, 13.

64. "Life among the Lowly, No. 3," 253.

65. On November 3, for example, Callender refuted a *Lynchburg Gazette* article asserting that Tom had accompanied Sally Hemings to France, arguing that his "correspondent" had seen the boy and denied he could possibly have been as old as the *Gazette* claimed. *Richmond Recorder*, November 3, 1802.

66. As Thomas Jefferson Randolph would later say, Sally Hemings's children "resembled Mr. Jefferson so closely that it was plain that they had his blood in their veins," while Thomas Turner, a Virginian commenting on Jefferson's relationship with Hemings for a Boston paper in 1805, claimed that Beverley Hemings, whom Turner also said was Sally Hemings's "eldest son," was "well known to many" though he was still a child. Randall to Parton, June 1, 1868, reprinted in *TJ and SH*, 254; and Turner, "Letter"; also see Gordon-Reed, *TJ and SH*, 76.

67. Not everyone, obviously, believed the Jefferson-Hemings story, but even several years later, when Vermont schoolteacher Elijah Fletcher passed through Charlottesville and talked to people of varying political persuasions, he reported that "the story of Black Sal is no farce — That [Jefferson] cohabits with her and has a number of children by her is a sacred truth." Elijah Fletcher to Jesse Fletcher, May 24, 1811, quoted in Thomas Jefferson Memorial Foundation Research Committee, "Report on Thomas Jefferson and Sally Hemings," appendix F, p. 5.

68. *Richmond Examiner*, September 25, 1802.

69. See note 20.

70. Ellen Randolph Coolidge to Joseph Coolidge, October 24, 1858, in Ellen Coolidge Letterbook, Coolidge Family Papers, Alderman Library, University of Virginia; and Gordon-Reed, *TJ and SH*, 87–93.

71. Thomas Bell had died in 1800, but he and Mary Hemings had lived together openly even before 1792, and Hemings continued to live in the couple's home even after Bell's death. See Thomas Jefferson to Nicholas Lewis, April 12, 1792,

in Cullen, *Papers of Thomas Jefferson*, 23:408; Lucia Stanton, "Monticello to Main Street," 97–105; and Gordon-Reed, *TJ and SH*, 136.

72. Brodie, *Thomas Jefferson*, 294 and 532 n. 27.

73. Lucia Stanton, "Mountaintop Work Force"; Lucia Stanton, "Sally Hemings"; "Life among the Lowly, Number I"; "Life among the Lowly, No. 3," 252; and Pierson, *Jefferson at Monticello*, 107.

74. *Frederick-town Herald*, printed in *Richmond Recorder*, December 8, 1802. It is highly unlikely that Sally Hemings actually had a bedroom in the main house at Monticello but, as Thomas Jefferson Randolph suggested, she may have lived in one of the three rooms directly underneath the south terrace of the building. Construction of these rooms was completed by 1808. Prior to that year, Hemings probably lived in several different dwellings near the main house. See Randall to Parton, June 1, 1868, in *TJ and SH*, 254; and Lucia Stanton, *Free Some Day*, 112–13.

75. "Life among the Lowly, Number I"; and Pierson, *Jefferson at Monticello*, 107.

76. Betts, *Thomas Jefferson's Farm Book*, 31, 50, 52, and 56.

77. On the significance of the names of Sally Hemings's children, see Gordon-Reed, *TJ and SH*, 196–201. Madison Hemings recalled that Dolley Madison bore responsibility for his name, but he said nothing about the names of his siblings or their origins; see "Life among the Lowly, Number I."

78. "Life among the Lowly, Number I."

79. Ibid.

80. As Civil War diarist Mary Chesnut, whose father-in-law had children with an enslaved woman he owned, wrote in 1861 of plantation life: "Like the patriarchs of old our men live all in one house with their wives and their concubines, and the mulattoes one sees in every family exactly resemble the white children — and every lady tells you who is the father of all the mulatto children in everybody's household, but those in her own she seems to think drop from the clouds, or pretends so to think." White southern women probably did gossip in such a fashion, and few were willing to make in front of others the embarrassing admission that their husbands committed adultery right under their noses. But Chesnut's assessment does not incorporate what such women believed in their own minds. See Woodward, *Mary Chesnut's Civil War*, March 18, 1861, p. 30. In addition to the "blood in their veins" comment, Thomas Jefferson Randolph told other stories suggesting that as the Hemings children, especially the male children, got older, they looked more and more like their father. Randolph, for example, noted that from a distance or under the half light of dusk one of Hemings's sons "might be mistaken for Mr. Jefferson." At least one man having dinner with Jefferson must have had his suspicions confirmed, because Randolph reported he "looked so startled as he raised his eyes . . . to the servant behind him, that his discovery of the resemblance was perfectly obvious to all." Randall to Parton, June 1, 1868, in *TJ and SH*, 254.

81. As Henry Randall wrote to James Parton, "Mr. Jefferson's oldest daughter, Mrs. Gov. Randolph, took the Dusky Sally stories much to heart." Randall to Parton, June 1, 1868, in *TJ and SH*, 255.

82. See Clinton, "Caught in the Web"; and Painter, "Soul Murder and Slavery."

83. Martha Randolph, in fact, tried to cover up what she knew about her father's relationship with Sally Hemings. According to Thomas Jefferson Randolph, she only spoke to any of her children about the Jefferson-Hemings story once, when she sat two of her sons down and told them (mistakenly) that the conception of Sally Hemings's child who most resembled Jefferson occurred at a time when Jefferson and Hemings "were far distant from each other." In this instance, it appears that Martha Randolph lied, not wanting her children ever to think that they shared a direct biological heritage with the Hemingses. Something of the disgust "respectable" white families felt regarding such a situation is reflected in the language of Ellen Coolidge, who in an 1858 letter asked rhetorically if "a man so admirable in his domestic character as Mr. Jefferson, so devoted to his daughters and their children, so fond of their society, so tender, considerate, refined in his intercourse with them, so watchful over them in all respects, would be likely to rear a race of half-breeds under their eyes and carry on his low amours in the circle of his family." Of course, the stories Thomas Jefferson Randolph and his sister told about the Carr brothers did give Thomas Jefferson's grandchildren a blood tie to the Hemingses. But Martha Randolph never said anything to her children about the Carrs. In any event, attributing paternity to the Carrs still allowed Martha Randolph's children to abide by their mother's request that they always "defend the character of their grandfather." Randall to Parton, June 1, 1868, in *TJ and SH*, 255; and Coolidge to Coolidge, October 24, 1858.

84. Betts, *Thomas Jefferson's Farm Book*, 152; Pierson, *Jefferson at Monticello*, 110; "Life among the Lowly, Number I"; *Daily Scioto Gazette*, August 1, 1902; Logan, *Memoirs of a Monticello Slave*, 13; Lucia Stanton, " 'Those Who Labor,' " 166; and Gordon-Reed, *TJ and SH*, 51 and 150–52.

85. Cheek and Cheek, *John Mercer Langston*, 11–20; Langston, *From the Virginia Plantation to the National Capitol*, 11–22. Two of Quarles's brothers, coincidentally, married into the family of Dabney Carr, Jefferson's childhood friend, his brother-in-law, and the father of Peter and Samuel Carr.

86. Henry Ferry, in Perdue, Barden, and Phillips, *Weevils*, 91.

87. Liza McCoy and Mary Wood, in ibid., 201 and 332.

88. Cheek and Cheek, *John Mercer Langston*, 16; Ferry, in Perdue, Barden, and Phillips, *Weevils*, 91; and *A Collection of All Such Acts of the General Assembly of Virginia* (Richmond, 1808), ch. 69, sec. 10, p. 97 (passed January 25, 1806). Ralph Quarles freed Lucy Langston, along with the only child they had together at the time, just one month before the removal bill became law.

89. Annette Gordon-Reed argues persuasively that Beverley and Harriet's departures were very likely coordinated, and that both ended up in Washington (*TJ and SH*, 33).

90. In the 1833 census lists, Eston Hemings was designated as "Negro," while Madison and Sally (who lived in a different parish and were therefore registered by a different census taker) are both listed as "mulatto." Eston and Madison were both employed as carpenters. The census taker indicated that Sally Hemings was living as a free woman and had been recognized as such since 1826. But Hemings apparently was never officially freed. In a will dated 1834, Martha Randolph informally

gave Sally Hemings her "time," something she had probably verbally done much earlier. In the summer of 1830, Madison and Eston Hemings purchased land a few blocks west of downtown, and probably lived there with their mother until her death. Sally Hemings may be buried on this site, currently a Hampton Inn on the corner of 10th and West Main Streets in Charlottesville. See Betts, *Thomas Jefferson's Farm Book*, 130; Will of Thomas Jefferson, in Lipscomb and Bergh, *Writings of Thomas Jefferson*, 17:465–70; "Life among the Lowly, Number I"; Lucia Stanton, "Monticello to Main Street," 107–8 n. 23; United States Census—Virginia, 1830; Ervin Jordan, "'A Just and True Account,'" 129 and 136–37; and Albemarle County Deed Book 29, pp. 276–77.

91. Pierson, *Jefferson at Monticello*, 110.

92. Lipscomb and Bergh, *Writings of Thomas Jefferson*, 17:469–70.

93. Jefferson to Monroe, in Paul Ford, *Writings of Thomas Jefferson*, 8:105.

94. Jefferson to Edward Coles, in ibid., 9:479.

95. Jefferson to William Short, in ibid., 10:362.

96. Peter Onuf draws attention to the links in Jefferson's thought between racial purity and national identity in "'To Declare Them a Free and Independant People.'"

97. Randall to Parton, June 1, 1868, in *TJ and SH*, 254; and Logan, *Memoirs of a Monticello Slave*, 13.

98. For more on the conundrum posed for white Virginians by the existence of such liminal individuals, see Chapter 6.

99. Jefferson to Francis C. Gray, March 4, 1815, in Lipscomb and Bergh, *Writings of Thomas Jefferson*, 14:267–71.

100. Jefferson, *Notes on the State of Virginia*, 162 and 143.

101. Pierson, *Jefferson at Monticello*, 110; Coolidge to Coolidge, October 24, 1858; and *Daily Scioto Gazette*, August 1, 1902.

102. Coolidge to Coolidge, October 24, 1858. Also see Gordon-Reed, *TJ and SH*, 53–56.

103. Robert M. S. McDonald assesses the national impact of Callender's Jefferson-Hemings articles in "Race, Sex, and Reputation." Interest in the Jefferson-Hemings affair was briefly revived in New England in 1805, when Jefferson's political and moral character became part of a debate in the Massachusetts House of Representatives. See Young, *Defence of Young and Minns*.

104. Coolidge to Coolidge, October 24, 1858.

105. *Richmond Recorder*, September 29, 1802.

106. On the ethics of sex across the color line among southern elites, see Wyatt-Brown, *Southern Honor*, ch. 12, esp. 307–10. Wyatt-Brown, who doubted the Jefferson-Hemings story, adds that ethical behavior also demanded that a man's enslaved partner was seen as sexually attractive by other white men, which usually meant that she had light skin, and that a man's sexual practices were not part of a larger pattern of alcoholism or other dissoluteness. Jefferson's relationship with Sally Hemings fit these patterns as well.

107. *Richmond Recorder*, September 1, 1802.

108. *Richmond Recorder*, September 15 and 29, 1802. Historian Jan Lewis has ar-

gued that Callender's publication of the Hemings story coincided with and helped contribute to a rethinking of familial affairs more generally as sacrosanct rather than as acceptable weapons for public political warfare. See Lewis, " 'The Blessings of Domestic Society,' " in Onuf, *Jeffersonian Legacies*, esp. 123–32.

109. The restraint shown by the editors of the *Herald* wore off within a few months. By December they were running stories on Jefferson and Hemings based on information received from their own informants, justifying their change of heart by claiming that "although the subject is indeed a delicate one, we cannot see why we are to affect any great squeamishness against speaking plainly of what we consider as an undoubted matter of fact interesting to the public." *Frederick-town Herald*, quoted in *Richmond Recorder*, September 29 and December 8, 1802.

110. *Richmond Recorder*, January 12, 1803.

INTERLUDE: THE COMMUNITY OF MARY HEMINGS

1. Albemarle County Marriage Registers, 1780–1868; Albemarle County Marriage Bonds; Lucia Stanton, "Monticello to Main Street," 100–102; Rawlings, *Early Charlottesville*, 84; and Orra Langhorne, *Southern Sketches from Virginia*, 81–83. Rawlings noted that longtime Albemarle resident James Alexander recalled Jesse Scott as a "celebrated fiddler — half Indian, half white," while Langhorne described the children of Jesse Scott and Sally Bell as "mulattoes, men of fine manners, good musicians, and generally popular."

2. Albemarle County Will Book 3, pp. 302–3; and Albemarle County Will Book 4, pp. 18–19. James Henry West, "the son [of] Perscilla," was born into slavery. Thomas West sold him his freedom for five shillings in 1785. Nancy West was born a free person in 1782, indicating her mother must have been freed sometime after James's birth. Priscilla, with or without Thomas West, may also have had a third child named Penelope. David Isaacs, Nancy West's husband, left money in his will to Penelope, a free woman of color and the "daughter of old Ciller." Recorded in the West-Isaacs family Bible, meanwhile, is the 1842 death at age sixty-nine of a woman named Penelope Johnson. See Albemarle County Deed Book 9, p. 177; Albemarle County Will Book 12, p. 367; and West-Isaacs family Bible records, privately held. Thomas West's land in Amherst County, to which James Henry West moved sometime shortly before 1800, currently lies within the borders of Nelson County along the Rockfish River.

3. Thomas Bell and Mary Hemings also had a son together, Robert Washington Bell. Duke, quoted in Lucia Stanton, "Monticello to Main Street," 100 n. 8.

CHAPTER TWO

1. Marcus, *United States Jewry*, 1:149–50; Berman, *Richmond's Jewry*, 2–3 and 7–9; Ezekiel and Lichtenstein, *History of the Jews of Richmond*, 13–16 and 240; Ely, Hantman, and Leffler, *To Seek the Peace of the City*, 2; Albemarle County Deed Book 20, p. 436; and Albemarle County Will Book 4, pp. 18–19. Cohen and Isaacs dissolved their partnership in 1792. Isaiah Isaacs first appears on the personal property tax lists in Albemarle County in 1792, and David Isaacs appears first in 1793; see Albemarle County Personal Property Tax Books, 1792, 1793.

2. United States Census—Virginia, 1850. In fact, this made her one of the richest free women of color in the entire Upper South. According to Loren Schweninger, in 1850 just four free women of color in the Upper South owned $5,000 or more in real estate ("Property-Owning Free African-American Women," 34).

3. Virginia's colonial legislature explicitly forbade interracial marriage for the first time in 1691. In 1662, the body addressed the question of interracial fornication specifically, imposing a double fine on extramarital sex involving black and white partners. The law in place by the late eighteenth century levied no such additional penalty. See Hening, *The Statutes at Large*, 2:170 (1662, Act 12) and 3:86–88 (1691, Act 16); *A Collection of All Such Acts of the General Assembly of Virginia*, ch. 138, sec. 6, p. 287; and *Revised Code of the Laws of Virginia* (1819), ch. 141, sec. 6, pp. 555–56. Also see Higginbotham and Kopytoff, "Racial Purity and Interracial Sex"; and Peter W. Bardaglio, "'Shamefull Matches,'" in Hodes, *Sex, Love, Race*, 113–21).

4. For an equally fascinating story of another interracial Virginia family, but one where somewhat different familial, racial, class, and communal dynamics obtained, see Buckley, "Unfixing Race."

5. Albemarle County Law Order Book, 1822–31, October 11, 1822, p. 51.

6. It is unclear whether West and Isaacs even made an effort to deny the charges against them, but it would have been both futile and perjurious to do so. The Albemarle County Court indicted Nancy West's nephew, Nathaniel West, for perjury the same day the court sent his aunt's case to Richmond. Found not guilty many years later, the timing of Nathaniel West's legal trouble suggests that he may have lied in an effort to protect family members from prosecution. Albemarle County Law Order Book, 1822–31, May 13, 1824, pp. 129 and 131; and Albemarle County Law Order Book, 1831–37, October 11, 1832, p. 87.

7. *Commonwealth v. David Isaacs and Nancy West*, 5 Rand. 634 (Va. 1826).

8. Albemarle County Law Order Book, 1822–31, May 8, 1827, p. 246.

9. Unlike the 1810 census taker, those who performed that task for the county in future years failed to separate out the population of Charlottesville from their totaling for the county, making it difficult to chart the town's growth with specificity. The population of Albemarle County as a whole, however, grew slowly between 1810 and 1850, from just 18,268 people in 1810 to 19,750 in 1820, 22,618 in 1830, 22,924 in 1840, and 25,800 in 1850. Even allowing for a generous population increase in the town, by 1822 Charlottesville seems unlikely to have comprised more than 300 to 400 people. In 1810 there were 25 free people of color living in Charlottesville. United States Census—Virginia, 1810; other census figures cited in Moore, *Albemarle*, 115–16.

10. Albemarle County Law Order Book, 1809–21, May 15, 1812, and May 12, 1818, pp. 137 and 328; Albemarle County Will Book 1, pp. 25–29.

11. Rawlings, *Early Charlottesville*, 20–21, 30–31, and 34 (quotation about John Kelly on 34); and Woods, *Albemarle County in Virginia*, 239–40 (quotation about John Jones on 239), 242–43, 341, and 346–47.

12. Albemarle County Will Book 12, p. 370.

13. Woods, *Albemarle County in Virginia*, 201–3 and 243–44; Bear and Stanton,

Jefferson's Memorandum Books, 2:947 n. 71; and Rawlings, *Early Charlottesville*, 11, 12, 35 n. 11 (quotation about Opie Norris on 35), 49 n. 5, and 65.

14. Jefferson was also at least an acquaintance of Nancy West's father, Thomas. David Isaacs sent Jefferson unsolicited books on Judaism, and thought enough of the former president to be one of the earliest contributors to the proposed University of Virginia. See Ely, Hantman, and Leffler, *To Seek the Peace of the City*, 3–4; Albemarle County Will Book 1, pp. 25–29; Marcus, *United States Jewry*, 1:361; and Bear and Stanton, *Jefferson's Memorandum Books* (see the index for mentions of Thomas West, as well as for dozens of notations of payments made to David Isaacs and other Charlottesville merchants).

15. Rosenswaike, "Jewish Population of the United States," 2:2, 8–9, and 19C; Ely, Hantman, and Leffler, *To Seek the Peace of the City*, 3; and Willner, "Brief History of the Jewish Community," 2–3.

16. Marcus, *United States Jewry*, 1: chs. 14–15, quotation on 553. Also see Jaher, *Scapegoat in the New Wilderness*, esp. ch. 4; and Rabinowitz, "Nativism, Bigotry, and Anti-Semitism in the South." That typical contemporary forms of anti-Semitic prejudice also pervaded Charlottesville in this era is suggested by an 1820 editorial reprinted in the *Central Gazette* (Charlottesville) that, while not hostile toward Jews, stereotyped British Jews as "great bankers" whose value to the United States should they immigrate would primarily lie in their talents with money. A particularly anti-Jewish advertisement that ran around the same time in the *Gazette* offered a religious work promising a discussion of "Christian particulars," including "12. A touch of some Jewish and vain Genealogies which hinder truth, and against which the Apostle warneth"; see *Central Gazette* (Charlottesville), February 4 and March 4, 1820.

17. In the late antebellum period, the racial status of Jews was a matter of some inconclusive debate as the language of "racial science" became the primary conceptual framework within which Americans understood racial difference by the 1850s. Before midcentury, Americans discussed the racial position of Jews very little and generally accepted Jews as whites, albeit a distinct category of whites. Most important for David Isaacs's story, as historian Leonard Rogoff has recently written, "the Jewish racial question was not a social or political issue in the antebellum South: whatever anti-Semitism Southern Jews encountered was primarily economic or religious" ("Is the Jew White?," 201). On evolving ideas about the racial position and status of Jews in the United States, also see Jacobson, *Whiteness of a Different Color*, ch. 5; Gilman, *Jew's Body*, ch. 7; Brodkin, *How Jews Became White Folks*; and Jaher, *Scapegoat in the New Wilderness*, ch. 5.

18. Woods, *Albemarle County in Virginia*, 143, 147, 239–40, 243, and 346–47.

19. While there is no direct evidence to implicate him, John R. Jones seems an especially likely candidate to have brought Isaacs and West to the attention of the Albemarle criminal justice system. Not only did he run his mercantile business on property directly across the street from David Isaacs and, as discussed below, act extraordinarily antagonistically toward him in lawsuits beginning in the mid-1820s, but he also served as a member of the grand jury that presented Isaacs and West in 1822. Albemarle County Order Book, 1822–31, October 7, 1822, p. 31.

20. Albemarle County Deed Book 1, p. 162. Nancy West paid taxes on this land in 1800, but did not in 1801, 1802, or 1803, suggesting that someone else — someone other than Thomas Bell, who paid James West for the land, but who died in 1800 — probably took legal responsibility for the land and its taxes. In addition, Nancy West exchanged a small piece of the property in 1803 to have some fences built, further indicating that she probably lived on the property, if at all, only sometimes before that year. Albemarle County Land Tax Books, 1800–1804; and Albemarle County Deed Book 14, pp. 263–64.

21. Albemarle County Deed Book 1, pp. 158–59; and Mutual Assurance Society of Virginia Declaration 619, April 1802, Alderman Library, University of Virginia.

22. United States Census — Virginia, 1810; Rawlings, *Early Charlottesville*, 74 and 79; and Albemarle County Will Book 12, p. 368.

23. Albemarle County Deed Book 22, pp. 46–47.

24. Ibid., pp. 177–78. In 1828, for example, the land was occupied by one Mr. Schroff, a tinner (Rawlings, *Early Charlottesville*, 72).

25. United States Census — Virginia, 1820.

26. Until 1832, while most of the town of Charlottesville lay in Fredericksville Parish, the southern outskirts of town, including the plot on which Nancy West originally lived, were part of neighboring St. Anne's Parish. Albemarle County Land Tax Book, 1833; also see Map 1.

27. Albemarle County Law Order Book, 1822–31, May 13, 1824, p. 131. Two petitions to the General Assembly from Albemarle County in the decade or so before Isaacs and West were presented indicate that Charlottesville residents also had broader concerns beyond interracial sex about immorality and disorder in their midst. In 1815, for example, twenty-five men asked the state legislature to extend the jurisdiction of town trustees one mile beyond Charlottesville's borders, enabling them to suppress "riots" at "some houses of ill fame within a few feet of the town." The legislature refused this entreaty, only to receive another petition in 1818 making a similar request. This time, the thirty-three signatories complained about large Sunday gatherings of blacks at "tipling-shops" just beyond the town's boundaries, activities that were "inimical to sober habits and morals" and "contrary to good policy and our own safety." It is unclear to what extent the changing evangelical culture of early nineteenth-century Virginia might have played a role in these protests. By 1850 Charlottesville had forty-five churches, but no denomination had a church building in town at all until 1826. In addition, prominent among the signatories to both petitions were many members of the merchant community, including David Isaacs, suggesting that concerns about drinking and prostitution may have been economic as much as, if not more than, moral or religious. Legislative Petitions — Albemarle County #6459, December 8, 1815, and #7213, December 14, 1818, Library of Virginia, Richmond; and Moore, *Albemarle*, 77–81 and 155.

28. Census records indicate Joshua Grady and Betsy Ann Farley almost certainly lived together by 1820 and continued to do so until at least the 1830s. The third couple brought before the court in 1822 was Andrew McKee, a white man and a hatter who later was a party to a lawsuit filed against David Isaacs, and Matsy

Cannon, whom I have been unable to locate elsewhere in the public record. Andrew McKee had no free people of color sharing his household in either 1820 or 1830, but a white woman between the ages of twenty-six and forty-five did live with him in 1820. United States Census—Virginia, 1820, 1830; Rawlings, *Early Charlottesville*, 89; Lucia Stanton, "Monticello to Main Street," 97–100 and 109–10; and Ervin Jordan, " 'A Just and True Account,' " 136.

29. Nancy West's original property, lot 46, was valued at just $300, with her house adding an additional $100. By contrast, the land she purchased in 1820, lot 33, was worth $1,000, while the buildings on it were valued at an additional $880. Albemarle County Land Tax Books, 1820–21.

30. *Samuel Anderson v. Commonwealth*, 5 Rand. 627 (Va. 1826).

31. *Commonwealth v. David Isaacs and Nancy West*, 5 Rand. 634 (Va. 1826), quotations at 635.

32. On judicial handling of cases involving interracial sex and interracial marriages in the antebellum South, see Bardaglio, *Reconstructing the Household*, 48–64 and 260 n. 112. On Virginia, see also Wallenstein, "Race, Marriage, and the Law of Freedom," esp. 389–94.

33. *Revised Code of the Laws of Virginia* (1819), ch. 106, secs. 22–23, p. 401.

34. Hening, *The Statutes at Large*, 12:184 (1785, ch. 78).

35. By law, free people of color in antebellum Virginia were required to register with their county court. Nancy West registered as Nancy Isaacs in 1837 and was described as "aged 56 years, 5 feet 1 inch high, light complexion, a scar upon the left cheek, a mole upon the left side of the nose no other scars or marks perceivable." Albemarle County Minute Book, 1836–38, October 2, 1837, p. 263.

36. Albemarle County Marriage Register, 1780–1868, August 29, 1794.

37. Rawlings, *Early Charlottesville*, 73 and 79; and Testimony of Benjamin Wheeler, *Hays v. Hays* [1836?], Albemarle County Ended Chancery Causes (Circuit Superior Court), case #354, Library of Virginia, Richmond. In reminiscing about her conversations with Robert Scott, Orra Langhorne recalled him saying that he too had attended school with white children in Charlottesville. Tucker and Frederick Isaacs were six and nine years younger, respectively, than Robert Scott (born in 1803), suggesting that some children with African ancestry attended school with whites in town for at least a decade, probably during the 1810s and 1820s. Orra Langhorne, *Southern Sketches from Virginia*, 82.

38. On cases involving people of ambiguous race and the process of making racial determinations about them, which points to how racial fixedness was illusory even in law, see Chapter 6. Also see Walter Johnson, "Slave Trader"; Gross, "Litigating Whiteness"; and Hodes, *White Women, Black Men*, ch. 5.

39. *Commonwealth v. David Isaacs and Nancy West*, 5 Rand. 634 (Va. 1826), quotations at 635.

40. *Revised Code of the Laws of Virginia* (1819), ch. 141, sec. 6, pp. 555–56.

41. See Chapter 5 for an assessment of how white community members responded (or, more accurately, usually did not respond overtly) to interracial sexual activity in their midst. Generally, although when whites discussed the matter publicly they said they opposed interracial sex, for practical purposes a sort of white

apathy in Virginia seems to have held even in cases where a white woman became involved with a black man. Nansemond County census totals for 1830, for example, listed at least nine free men of color with white wives, while a divorce case from Campbell County in 1816 involved a free man of color and his white wife who were considered married in their community but not in law. The couple does not appear to have faced any sort of legal persecution. The lack of effort by whites to take action against interracial couples may have pervaded many other parts of the South as well, as suggested by a study of antebellum Alabama pointing to the existence of many stable familial relationships between free men of color and white women. Other studies of antebellum South Carolina and Louisiana point to similar phenomena, although the instances discussed involved enslaved women and it could be argued that whites in these places had somewhat different understandings of racial hierarchy than Virginians. On toleration for sexual intercourse between white women and black men in the South before the Civil War, see Hodes, *White Women, Black Men*, part 1. Also see Johnston, *Race Relations in Virginia*, ch. 10, esp. 265–66; Buckley, "Unfixing Race"; Mills, "Miscegenation and the Free Negro"; Kennedy-Haflett, " 'Moral Marriage' "; Stevenson, *Life in Black and White*, 304–5; and Schafer, *Slavery, the Civil Law, and the Supreme Court of Louisiana*, ch. 7.

42. Isaacs built a one-story wing onto the west side of his home sometime between 1802 and 1806. Tax records suggest he probably made this addition in 1803. A small boost in the rental value of the property between 1815 and 1816 may indicate the second wing was built in one of those years, but insurance records indicate its existence by 1833. Albemarle County Land Tax Books, 1803–4 and 1815–16; and Mutual Assurance Society Declarations 5201 (1806) and 8233 (1833).

43. Albemarle County Law Order Books, 1810–11, pp. 49 and 475; 1811–13, pp. 134–35 and 333; 1813–15, p. 372; and 1821–22, pp. 163 and 363.

44. At the time of his death, Isaiah Isaacs had four children by his wife Hetty Hays, who had also died by 1806 — Fanny, Hays, Patsy, and David. By 1824, only Fanny, who married a man named Abraham Block and moved away from Charlottesville, and Hays, who seems to have moved between Charlottesville and Richmond, still lived. Albemarle County Will Book 1, pp. 25–29; and Albemarle County Deed Book 24, pp. 316–17.

45. Although the Virginia legislature had passed a liberal manumission act in 1782, white Virginians expressed increasing discomfort with the free black population that swelled in its wake. The 1806 removal law marked the beginning of a significant backlash against the presence of free people of color in Virginia. Other restrictive legislation followed over the course of the antebellum period, including waves of laws in the early 1830s and in the late 1840s and early 1850s. Socially, whites generally disliked the very presence of people who were of African descent but were not enslaved and treated them with disdain. Economically, while there were greater opportunities for work in urban areas, most free men of color worked as rural agricultural laborers or as tenant farmers living in a perpetual cycle of debt that prefigured the postbellum status of many freedmen. Free black women most commonly worked where they were allowed to, especially as washerwomen or seam-

stresses, and faced astounding poverty. That some free people of color, including a significant number of women, were able to thrive in Virginia and the South as a whole was the result of great struggle, mutual support forged by communities, families, and institutions, and the occasional ability to form patronage relationships with whites, both sexual and otherwise. The classic study of free blacks remains Berlin, *Slaves without Masters*. Other important general studies include Schweninger, *Black Property Owners in the South*, chs. 1–4; Johnson and Roark, *Black Masters*; Curry, *Free Black in Urban America*; and Genovese, "The Slave States of North America." Studies of free blacks in individual states abound, but those on Virginia in particular include Bogger, *Free Blacks in Norfolk*; Madden, *We Were Always Free*; Higginbotham and Bosworth, " 'Rather Than the Free' "; Stevenson, *Life in Black and White*, ch. 9; Lebsock, *Free Women of Petersburg*, ch. 4; Jackson, *Free Negro Labor and Property Holding*; and Russell, *Free Negro in Virginia*. For a study of one free black family in Albemarle County, see von Daacke, "Slaves without Masters?"

46. West and Isaacs's oldest son, Thomas Isaacs, perhaps could have assisted his mother as well. David Isaacs mentioned Thomas in his will and left him an inheritance, meaning Thomas was still alive as late as 1837, but nothing else is known about him, including his whereabouts.

47. On free women of color and familial concerns, cf. Lebsock, *Free Women of Petersburg*, ch. 4; and Michael P. Johnson and James L. Roark, "Strategies of Survival," in Bleser, *In Joy and in Sorrow*, 88–102. Also see Stevenson, *Life in Black and White*, 307–10; Bynum, *Unruly Women*, 77–82; Whittington Johnson, "Free African-American Women in Savannah"; Alexander, *Ambiguous Lives*; Gould, *Chained to the Rock of Adversity*; and Schweninger, "Property-Owning Free African-American Women."

48. That Isaacs began purchasing the land in 1817, the same year West gave birth to the couple's last child, may suggest that Isaacs and West planned her move closer downtown for a number of years before it actually occurred. Albemarle County Deed Books 20, pp. 436–37 and 449; 21, pp. 380 and 408–9; 22, pp. 177–78; and 23, pp. 255–56.

49. The original deed of sale to Spinner in 1819 conveyed him a specifically measured piece of lot 46, when it fact West should have conveyed the entirety of her remaining interest, which was slightly more than the 1819 deed provided. The consequent legal haggling meant the deed had to be redone in 1829. Until the land exchange was finally completed in 1832, Nancy West technically continued to own and pay annual land taxes on the property, and she received no payment for the land's sale until after the second deed was signed. Albemarle County Deed Books 22, pp. 46–47; and 28, pp. 169–70; and Albemarle County Land Tax Books, 1819–33.

50. Albemarle County Will Book 12, p. 367.

51. Between 1820 and 1824, the estimated annual rent on lot 33 was $100. Albemarle County Land Tax Books, 1820–24.

52. Albemarle County Deed Book 24, pp. 316–17.

53. Albemarle County Deed Books 13, pp. 315–17; 19, pp. 361–62; and 26, p. 379.

54. Albemarle County Will Book 12, pp. 366–70; and Albemarle County Deed Books 39, p. 232; 41, pp. 318–19; and 47, pp. 12–13. Nancy West's purchases from relatives and intimates may also be suggestive of the role race and gender played in economic exchange in Charlottesville. It may simply have been easier to buy land from those one knew or were related to, but the pattern of people from whom West purchased her property might also indicate awareness on her part that others were reluctant to sell land to free blacks or to women (or, in West's case, both). West's economic elevation, then, was not only easier to do through her family, but perhaps she could do it only through her family.

55. As Luther Jackson has suggested about free black property accumulation, for example: "Free Negro ownership of property involved a variety of interests and motives. . . . One of the strongest of these interests was the maintenance and perpetuation of the family. The ownership of property welded the family together and enabled the holder to share his possessions with his family circle" (*Free Negro Labor and Property Holding*, 164).

56. If a trust in equity was established for a married woman, it was often undertaken by a father for his daughter as a means for her security and/or as insurance against a careless or exploitive husband, or sometimes by a husband wishing to protect property from loss. Whatever the motivation, a trust was an option generally available only to relatively wealthy women. On the legal rights of married women in the antebellum era generally, see Warbasse, *Changing Legal Rights of Married Women*. On legal rights of married women in Virginia up to and through the passage of the Married Women's Property Law in 1877, see Gundersen and Gampel, "Married Women's Legal Status"; Lebsock, "Radical Reconstruction and the Property Rights of Southern Women"; Ketchum, "Married Women's Property Law"; and Gianakos, "Virginia and the Married Women's Property Acts." On equity, the multiple motivations that lay behind an estate's establishment, and the complications and restrictions that accompanied equity, see Lebsock, *Free Women of Petersburg*, ch. 3; and Bynum, *Unruly Women*, 64–68.

57. In some ways West and Isaacs's relationship prefigured the effects of the Married Women's Property Law of 1877. For women, as one author writes, that law's "main purpose was to protect the wife's property from being lost to her husband's creditors. . . . A married woman in Virginia could now own, manage, and dispose of her separate property as if a *femme sole*." In the same vein, historian Suzanne Lebsock argues that laws protecting married women's property offered protection to men as well, because "a man who was about to lose his own holdings could rest in the knowledge that in the future his wife's property would be secure." Just so with David Isaacs and Nancy West. See Gianakos, "Virginia and the Married Women's Property Acts," 37; and Lebsock, "Radical Reconstruction and the Property Rights of Southern Women," 203.

58. *Bramham & Bibb v. Isaacs*, Albemarle County Ended Chancery Causes (Circuit Superior Court), Case 58, Library of Virginia, Richmond; *Yancey v. Isaacs*, Albemarle County Ended Chancery Causes (Circuit Superior Court), Case 46, Library of Virginia, Richmond; and Albemarle County Chancery Order Book, 1831–42, May 16, 1834, pp. 97–99. The third case was *John R. Jones v. Isaacs*,

Case 55. The papers for both Yancey's and Jones's lawsuits are archived together in folders under Yancey's name.

59. Albemarle County Chancery Order Book, 1831–42, pp. 21, 32, 45, 50, 96, and 97. The other plaintiffs were Samuel Leitch, Andrew McKee, James Saunders, Fountain Wells, and George Toole. McKee was a hatter, Saunders a lawyer, and Toole a tailor who lived and worked in a house owned by Wells.

60. Statement filed by Rice Wood on behalf of John Jones, June 28, 1826, *Yancey v. Isaacs.*

61. Reply of David Isaacs, March 20, 1827, *Yancey v. Isaacs.* Hays Isaacs's release, dated a few months after his twenty-first birthday, relieved David Isaacs of responsibility for "all and every claim and demand of whatever character or description which . . . I possibbly may have against him . . . it being doubtful upon a full and fair settlement, which of us may be debtor to the other. . . ." Release of Hays Isaacs, June 22, 1824, *Bramham & Bibb v. Isaacs.*

62. Testimony of V. W. Southall, Isaac Raphael, and Daniel Keith, November 1827, *Yancey v. Isaacs.*

63. Testimony of Opie Norris, Isaac Raphael, and Daniel Keith, November 1827, *Yancey v. Isaacs.* Hays put the slaves he had inherited from his father in trust in December 1824 to be sold in the event he could not pay off debts he had to Jane Isaacs, Nancy West, and Fountain Wells. It is not clear whether Jane Isaacs or Nancy West ever actually owned any of these slaves outright — although some of their neighbors believed they did — or even if the sale was necessary. In any event, under a provision of his father's will, eventually Hays Isaacs was legally obligated to free all the slaves that he had inherited. On his death, Isaiah Isaacs, "being of the opinion that all men are by Nature equally free," manumitted a number of slaves outright in addition to devising a plan to free others. According to property tax records, Nancy West, Jane Isaacs, and David Isaacs (who, like many merchants, probably had customers who sometimes settled their debts with slaves rather than in cash) all periodically owned slaves, but never more than a few at once and apparently not for very long at a time. Neither Nancy West nor David Isaacs owned any upon their deaths in 1837 and 1856, respectively. Jane Isaacs died after the Civil War. She owned seven slaves at the war's outbreak. It is unclear if, when, or how either Nancy West or David Isaacs used, sold, or manumitted slaves when they did own them. Thousands of African Americans purchased slaves throughout the South before the Civil War, sometimes for purposes of economic exploitation and sometimes to keep families together. Because Virginia's removal law of 1806 forced emancipated slaves to leave the state, many slave-owning people of color in Virginia actually possessed relatives who would have had to move away if manumitted. Given the intertwined nature of enslaved, free black, Native American, and white ancestries in the extended West-Isaacs-Hemings families, it seems probable that at least some slave ownership by Nancy West and David Isaacs involved protecting family members. Jesse Scott's purchase of three members of the Fossett family, discussed earlier, indicates for certain that members of West and Isaacs's extended family acted from such a motive. See Deed of Trust between Hays Isaacs, Daniel Keith, Nancy West, Jane Isaacs, and Fountain Wells, in *Yancey v. Isaacs* (a copy also appears

in Albemarle County Deed Book 25, pp. 75–77); Albemarle County Will Book 1, pp. 25–29; Albemarle County Personal Property Tax Books, 1815–36; United States Census—Virginia, Slave Schedule, 1860; Lucia Stanton, "Monticello to Main Street," esp. 101–2; and Rawlings, *Early Charlottesville*, 74. On free black slave ownership, see Johnson and Roark, "Strategies of Survival"; Koger, *Black Slave-owners*; Schwarz, "Emancipators, Protectors, and Anomalies"; Wallenstein, *From Slave South to New South*, 92–95; Jackson, *Free Negro Labor and Property Holding*, ch. 7; Carter Woodson, "Free Negro Owners of Slaves"; and Russell, "Colored Freemen as Slave Owners in Virginia."

64. If David Isaacs ever engaged in some creative accounting or exploited his position as his brother's executor, John Jones himself undoubtedly tried to exercise some shady prerogatives of his own. Jones had been a commissioner appointed by the Albemarle County Court in 1823 to help settle David Isaacs's accounts as Isaiah's executor. According to Jones, once Hays Isaacs owed him money, he could no longer act objectively and he excused himself in 1825. He objected to all previous work he had done as a commissioner, which effectively suspended any settlement of accounts. David Isaacs never appealed to the court for new commissioners, which Jones used to accuse him of concealing malfeasance. Jones neglected to mention, however, that after he excused himself he arranged for Hays to sell him all his real estate, which included land in Richmond, two hundred acres in Louisa County, and another seventy-two acres in Henrico County in addition to the land in Charlottesville, if he could not pay a debt of just $254.94. This exchange, of course, was illegal, since Hays had already sold his land in Charlottesville to Nancy West a year earlier, which Jones must have known, having been a commissioner at the time of the sale (Hays had also sold the interest in his inheritance to a man from Lynchburg in exchange for "a valuable consideration" two weeks before he made his deal with Jones. Hays Isaacs thus sold lot 19 in Charlottesville three different times, indicating that he was either very stupid, very criminal, or both). As David Isaacs pointed out in his defense, Jones's dealings also pointed directly to his own efforts to cheat Hays Isaacs and to his own abuse of inside knowledge of Hays's affairs, because Jones knew that the cumulative value of Hays's land far exceeded any debts Hays owed to Jones. In addition, David Isaacs pointed out that it was somewhat illogical and astoundingly duplicitous for Jones to assert that Hays Isaacs was incompetent to make financial decisions while Jones was so obviously willing to take the young man's land at a fraction of its value. Statement filed by Rice Wood on behalf of John Jones, June 28, 1826; Reply of David Isaacs, March 20, 1827; Deed in trust from Hays Isaacs to Rice Wood for John Jones, May 21, 1825; Release of Hays Isaacs to Timothy Fletcher, May 5, 1825, all in *Yancey v. Isaacs*; and Albemarle County Deed Book 25, pp. 223–24 and 231.

65. Reply of David Isaacs, February 5, 1831, *Bramham & Bibb v. Isaacs*.

66. Albemarle County Chancery Order Book, 1831–42, pp. 97–99; and opinion of the court, May 16, 1834, *Yancey and others v. Isaacs*. The court also found that John Jones had not acted at all improperly in his dealings with Hays Isaacs.

67. Bond between David Isaacs et al. and John R. Jones et al., June 27, 1834, *Yancey v. Isaacs*; and Albemarle County Marriage Register, March 27, 1832.

68. Bill of exceptions filed by *Jones and others v. Isaacs et al.*, June 27, 1834, *Yancey v. Isaacs.*

69. Nathaniel West paid personal property taxes in 1834 on just four slaves and three horses. Jane West paid no taxes of her own, and there is no record of a separate estate created for her before her marriage. When Nathaniel West died later in 1834, his estate was valued at just over $1,200. Slightly more than half that sum came from two slaves and a carriage, with the remainder mostly tied up in household goods. In 1835 Jane West paid taxes on one slave, and she paid no land taxes at all until 1838. See Albemarle County Personal Property Tax Books, 1834, 1835; Albemarle County Land Tax Books, 1834–38; and Inventory and Appraisement of the Estate of Nathaniel H. West, Albemarle County Will Book 12, pp. 31–32.

70. Albemarle County Will Book 12, pp. 366–70 and 396–401. Ironically, as county magistrates, Nimrod Bramham and Andrew McKee were among those who appraised David Isaacs's estate in 1837.

71. A complete settlement of David Isaacs's estate was not made until 1850. See Albemarle County Will Books 13, pp. 172–73; 14, pp. 85–86; 15, pp. 210–13; 17, pp. 67–69; 18, pp. 477–82; and 20, pp. 291 and 293; and Albemarle County Deed Book 41, p. 238.

72. Albemarle County Deed Book 35, p. 340. Jane and Nathaniel West and Eston and Julia Ann Hemings probably lived in houses next door to one another on lot 33 from as early as 1832, when both couples married. In 1837 Nancy West sold a portion of the lot on which the Hemingses' home sat to Thomas Grady and Anderson Shiflett. Grady and Shiflett agreed also to buy out Julia Ann's dower claim, even though it was not entirely clear that she had one because, as the deed recorded, the property was "given, but never conveyed" to her and Eston by Nancy West. Jane West's home sat on the portion of the land given to her by her mother in 1836, and she held it until 1850, when she moved to a part of lot 36. See Albemarle County Deed Books 35, pp. 264–67; and 48, pp. 16–17 and 429–30; Albemarle County Marriage Register, March 27 and June 14, 1832; and Mutual Assurance Society Declaration 8597 (1837).

73. Albemarle County Deed Book 35, pp. 205–8. An insurance policy for the property indicates that Nancy West did not live in the house in 1840 (Mutual Assurance Society Declaration 11186 [1840]).

74. Albemarle County Deed Books 39, p. 232; and 41, pp. 267 and 319.

75. Albemarle County Land Tax Book, 1844. West had already sold lot 25 and her share of lot 19 in a series of deals between 1829 and 1837 (see Albemarle County Deed Books 28, pp. 48–49; 33, pp. 383–86; and 35, p. 438).

76. Albemarle County Deed Book 47, pp. 12–13. Also in 1846, and also with Nancy West's consent, Watson sold lot 26, the only other piece of property Isaacs's estate still owned, in an effort to raise money to fulfill the Court of Appeals decree. But this lot was in a swampy and low-lying area and brought in just a few hundred dollars. Albemarle County Deed Book 44, pp. 145–46.

77. Nancy West also indicated she believed Hays had first been in New Orleans before appearing in Arkansas, and she may have been correct on both counts.

Hays's sister Fanny and her husband Abraham Block lived in Arkansas in the 1840s and at least through 1855, when Hays formally released any claim he had left in his sister's half of lot 19. Abraham Block was instrumental in founding a synagogue in New Orleans in 1827. In the 1980s, archaeologists excavated a trash pit behind the Block house in Washington, Arkansas. See Albemarle County Deed Book 54, p. 37; and Stewart-Abernathy and Ruff, "A Good Man in Israel."

78. There is no record of the exact terms of the settlement, but presumably Watson agreed to pay Hays Isaacs's debt to Nancy West rather than deal with the hassles of yet another lawsuit involving David Isaacs's estate. *West v. Isaacs*, Albemarle County Ended Chancery Causes (Circuit Superior Court), case 370, Library of Virginia, Richmond; and Albemarle County Chancery Order Book, 1849–54, p. 78.

79. It is not clear precisely when Nancy West moved to Ohio, although it was probably sometime in 1851 or 1852. She was still in Virginia in December 1850 and bought land from Eston Hemings in Ohio in 1852. By 1854, when she finally sold the last piece of property she held in Virginia, she is referred to in Albemarle County records as Nancy West of Chillicothe, Ohio. See Albemarle County Deed Books 48, pp. 428–29; 49, pp. 197–98; and 53, p. 260; Albemarle County Will Book 25, pp. 156–59; Albemarle County Minute Book, 1850–54, p. 6; and Justus, *Down from the Mountain*, 111.

80. Nothing is known about the *Charlottesville Chronicle*, which was published only in 1832 and 1833 from a site on lot 33, other than James Alexander's recollection that it was a "*quasi* democratic sheet." See Rawlings, *Early Charlottesville*, 72–73; Norfleet, "Newspapers in Charlottesville and Albemarle County," 75–76; *Acts of the General Assembly of Virginia, 1832–1833*, ch. 23; and Higginbotham and Bosworth, "'Rather Than the Free,'" 31.

81. Albemarle County Personal Property Tax Book, 1850; Albemarle County Minute Book, 1850–54, p. 6; *Acts of the General Assembly of Virginia, 1847–1848*, ch. 10, secs. 34–37, pp. 118–19; ch. 13, p. 126; and ch. 26, pp. 162–64; *Acts of the General Assembly of Virginia, 1849–1850*, ch. 6, pp. 7–8; and *Revised Code of the Laws of Virginia* (1849), ch. 107, pp. 465–68; ch. 198, secs. 22–23, pp. 745–48; and ch. 212, pp. 786–89. Ira Berlin documents the increasingly hostile legislation directed toward free people of color in Virginia and across the South in the 1850s, in *Slaves without Masters*, ch. 11. Tommy Bogger documents the hostile social environment for Norfolk's free people of color in the 1850s in *Free Blacks in Norfolk*, ch. 7.

82. Lucia Stanton, "Monticello to Main Street," esp. 111–20; Albemarle oCounty Deed Books 35, pp. 388–89; and 42, pp. 282–83; Albemarle County Minute Book, 1850–54, p. 13; Albemarle County Marriage Register, October 20, 1836; and Albemarle County Will Book 25, pp. 156–59. Peculiarly, the Albemarle county clerk noted in the 1850 minute book that after her emancipation Elizabeth Ann Fossett Isaacs had not been granted permission to remain in Virginia, but the clerk nevertheless entered her registration with the county and did not explicitly note that she had been ordered to leave. In addition to the uncertainty surrounding his wife's status, Tucker Isaacs had some legal troubles of his own that may have played an important role in the couple's decision to remove to Ohio. Before perma-

nently leaving Virginia, Tucker Isaacs had earned a reputation in Charlottesville as a painter and builder. He may also have picked up the skills of a forger, perhaps from his brother Frederick, who was known for his talent of perfectly replicating the signatures of every signer of the Declaration of Independence. In 1850 Tucker Isaacs was tried for forging a free pass for his still-enslaved brother-in-law Peter Fossett, who at the time belonged to none other than John R. Jones. Perhaps Jones's underhanded dealings with his parents gave Tucker Isaacs some extra motivation to free his wife's brother. Then again, Peter Fossett had his own grievances against Jones and may very well have forged his own free papers, having previously done so for his sister Isabella. Jones had purchased Peter Fossett at the 1827 Monticello dispersal sale with the understanding that he would sell Fossett to his father, but Jones then reneged on the deal. Whoever actually forged Peter Fossett's free papers, Tucker Isaacs successfully pleaded not guilty to the charge. See Rawlings, *Early Charlottesville*, 79–80; Albemarle County Minute Book, 1848–50, February 5 and 6, 1850, pp. 308–10; and Lucia Stanton, *Free Some Day*, 150–52.

83. According to the 1860 census, Jane West held personal and real property worth more than $14,000. United States Census — Virginia, 1860; Justus, *Down from the Mountain*, 108 and 111; Lucia Stanton, "Monticello to Main Street," 119–20; West-Isaacs family Bible records, privately held; Albemarle County Will Book 28, p. 207; and Albemarle County Deed Books 34, pp. 510–12; and 35, pp. 47–49 and 51–52.

INTERLUDE: THE FUNERAL OF DAVID ISAACS

1. Berman, *Richmond's Jewry*, 2–3 and 7–9; Ezekiel and Lichtenstein, *History of the Jews of Richmond*, 13–16 and 240; and Will of David Isaacs, Albemarle County Will Book 12, p. 367.

2. Congregation Beth Shalome did not have an ordained rabbi during its existence. Instead, a number of lay community leaders served as "ministers" or "readers." They were often given the title "Reverend" and led the congregation in prayer services.

3. Will of Isaac Judah, Richmond City Hustings Court Will Book 4, pp. 313–18, quotations on 315. Benjamin Wythe's free black registration in Richmond in 1831 as "Benjamin Wythe Judah" provides additional evidence of Judah's parental connection to the two boys. Virginia jurist and Richmond resident (and Jefferson's mentor) George Wythe had close ties to Richmond's Jewish community, and Judah may have added "Wythe" to his son's names as a sign of respect, appreciation, and friendship (Berman, *Richmond's Jewry*, 373 n. 80). For a consideration of the rumor that Wythe himself engaged in an interracial sexual liaison, see Philip D. Morgan, "Interracial Sex in the Chesapeake," in Lewis and Onuf, *Sally Hemings and Thomas Jefferson*, 56–60.

4. Berman, *Richmond's Jewry*, 64–69 and 125–29; and Ezekiel and Lichtenstein, *History of the Jews of Richmond*, 60–62 and 241–42.

5. Guzman-Stokes, "A Flag and a Family," 53–54; and Cohen, *Records of the Myers, Hays and Mordecai Families*. Richard Gustavus Forrester and Narcissa Wilson Forrester returned to Richmond in the mid-1840s, lived with Catharine Hays and her

servant Excey Gill, and inherited their home at the corner of College and Marshall Streets after Gill's death in 1855. The continuing story of the Forrester family is a fascinating one in its own right and is explored at some depth in Guzman-Stokes, "A Flag and a Family," 56–63.

6. The integral and mutually reinforcing economic and familial ties for both whites and blacks between city and countryside in antebellum Richmond are best explored by Gregg Kimball, who also examines Richmond's cultural and economic flourishing in the 1850s and its relationship to other American cities in *American City, Southern Place*, esp. parts 1 and 2. Also on the relationship between Richmond and the Virginia countryside, especially during the 1850s, see Goldfield, *Urban Growth in the Age of Sectionalism*; and Goldfield, "Urban-Rural Relations."

CHAPTER THREE

1. On Richmond's tobacco industry generally, see Robert, *Tobacco Kingdom*. On flour milling, see Thomas Berry, "Rise of Flour Milling in Richmond." On the iron industry, see Bruce, *Virginia Iron Manufacturing*; and Dew, *Ironmaker to the Confederacy*. On Richmond's role in the slave trade, see Bancroft, *Slave-Trading in the Old South*, 88–120; and Tadman, *Speculators and Slaves*, 57–64. Contemporary travel literature and slave narratives are littered with references to Richmond's slave market. See, for example, Bremer, *Homes of the New World*, 2:533–35; Charles Weld, *A Vacation Tour*, 298–304; Chambers, *Things as They Are in America*, 273–85; Hughes, *Thirty Years a Slave*, 6–11; and Veney, *Narrative of Bethany Veney*, 29–30.

2. The literature on urban free blacks and working whites generally is voluminous. On Virginia and Richmond particularly, see Berlin and Gutman, "Natives and Immigrants, Free Men and Slaves"; Schechter, "Free and Slave Labor in the Old South"; Jackson, *Free Negro Labor and Property Holding*; Lebsock, *Free Women of Petersburg*, 87–111; Bogger, *Free Blacks in Norfolk*; McLeod, "Free Labor in a Slave Society"; Rachleff, *Black Labor in the South*, ch. 1; Brown and Kimball, "Mapping the Terrain"; Tyler-McGraw, "Richmond Free Blacks and African Colonization"; and Kimball, "African-Virginians and the Vernacular Building Tradition."

3. On slavery in cities generally, see Wade, *Slavery in the Cities*; Starobin, *Industrial Slavery in the Old South*; and Goldin, *Urban Slavery in the American South*. Some of the works discussing slavery in Richmond also have extended discussions of free blacks and working whites, as well as of the tobacco and iron industries, and are cited above. Also see Takagi, *"Rearing Wolves to Our Own Destruction"*; Weis, "Negotiating Freedom"; Kimball, *American City, Southern Place*, ch. 4; Sidbury, *Ploughshares into Swords*, ch. 6; O'Brien, "Factory, Church, and Community"; Tyler-McGraw and Kimball, *In Bondage and Freedom*; Ethridge, "Jordan Hatcher Affair"; Green, "Urban Industry, Black Resistance, and Racial Restriction"; and Schnittman, "Slavery in Virginia's Urban Tobacco Industry." For evidence of Richmond as a hub for runaways looking to join family members in the city or on their way to the North, see Richmond Police Guard Day Book, 1834–43, Alderman Library, University of Virginia.

4. Residential patterns and the organization of living space in antebellum Richmond were extraordinarily complicated. Whites and blacks, even in wealthy neigh-

borhoods, often lived in direct proximity to one another if not next door. Business and residential areas could be indistinguishable and "respectable" residents might peer out their windows at night and find a grog shop where African Americans gathered or a house of interracial prostitution across the way or in the next alley. Neighborhoods that appeared to be primarily white in fact were shared spaces because of large numbers of slaves who lived in back buildings. Whites and free blacks also shared households and boarding spaces, and individuals of either race might head these households. Frequently, these living arrangements reflected workplace circumstances, but sometimes they reflected more personal attachments. Although people tended to cluster in neighborhoods — many free blacks and slaves in the antebellum period, for example, lived in the northwest section of Richmond that later became Jackson Ward, and wealthy whites frequently sought out large homes in Court End — thinking of Richmond's residential patterns in terms of segregated or integrated neighborhoods is ultimately of limited utility. As Elsa Barkley Brown and Gregg Kimball suggest, it is more useful to look at how individuals and communities used urban spaces to shape their own worlds. The constant movement of people in and through Richmond at all times of day and night suggests that public and private spaces were far more fluid categories than indicated by maps and streets. As Brown and Kimball argue, "the city, its spaces, its forbidden and inviting areas, its pleasures and dangers, even its boundaries existed in people's minds as much as on street maps. . . . It is, therefore, necessary for historians to pay close attention to the actual spaces in which black and white residents carried out their daily lives, seeing the possible simultaneity of relationships of hierarchy and relationships of camaraderie" ("Mapping the Terrain," 337).

5. On early Richmond and its commercial, mercantile, and political growth, see Scott, *Old Richmond Neighborhoods*, 63–119; Virginius Dabney, *Richmond*, chs. 4, 6, and 7; and Mordecai, *Richmond in By-Gone Days*, chs. 4–6. For travelers' accounts of Richmond in the late eighteenth century, see Schoepf, *Travels in the Confederation*, 2:49–64; Duc de La Rochefoucauld-Liancourt, *Travels through the United States*, 2:30–53; and Isaac Weld, *Travels through the States of North America*, 140–44.

6. The best discussion of the development of Richmond's waterfront and its interracial culture is Sidbury, *Ploughshares into Swords*, ch. 5.

7. Both grand jury quotations in Sheldon, "Black-White Relations in Richmond," 36. Running a "disorderly house" could mean a range of things, from holding dances and parties where loud music, foul language, and people engaged in fisticuffs poured out the doors and windows to owning a brothel. That commercial sex was at least part of Richmond's illicit milieu in this early period is indicated by the language of specific grand jury presentments, such as that against Mary Gray, a free woman of color arrested in 1803 for allowing in her house "for her own lucre and gain" women and men of "evil . . . fame and . . . dishonest conversation" who involved themselves in "drinking, tipling whoring quarreling and fighting" (Sidbury, *Ploughshares into Swords*, 248).

8. On Gabriel's Rebellion, see Sidbury, *Ploughshares into Swords*, part 1, and

Egerton, *Gabriel's Rebellion*. On laws passed subsequent to the conspiracies, see Egerton, 163–67.

9. *Richmond Recorder*, October 20, 1802. The third tier as an important site for the commercial sex trade had been customary in America, as well as in England, since at least the middle of the eighteenth century. It is unclear whether prostitutes were in the house on the night of the fire. Structurally, though, the exterior stair-case leading to the gallery in the Richmond theater was similar to those used for prostitutes, whose presence theater owners liked because they brought large crowds, but who owners also tried to hide for fear of offending the sensibilities of elites not wishing to mingle with blacks and prostitutes in the lobby. The third tier existed in theaters in most important American cities in the first third of the nineteenth century, including New York, Boston, Philadelphia, Chicago, St. Louis, Cincinnati, Mobile, and New Orleans. On the Richmond theater fire, see *Calamity at Richmond*; and Murrell, " 'Calamity at Richmond!' " On theater crowds, the third tier, and prostitution, see Claudia Johnson, "That Guilty Third Tier"; Hill, *Their Sisters' Keepers*, 199–206; and Click, *Spirit of the Times*, 35–45.

10. *A Sermon, Delivered in the Presbyterian Meeting-House in Winchester*, 7.

11. *Particular Account of the Dreadful Fire*, quotations on 33, 34, 35, and 35–36.

12. *Calamity at Richmond*, 29–32; and Murrell, " 'Calamity at Richmond!' " Murrell writes of a new theater in Richmond opening in 1819, but Samuel Mordecai recalled that a new theater opened in Richmond almost simultaneous with the opening of the Monumental Church in 1814 (*Richmond in By-Gone Days*, 149).

13. Saunders, "Crime and Punishment"; and Mordecai, *Richmond in By-Gone Days*, 217–22. Although slowing from the nearly 70 percent growth between 1800 and 1810, Richmond's population still grew by roughly 25 percent between 1810 and 1820, from approximately 10,000 to slightly more than 12,000 people. For the latter number, see Wade, *Slavery in the Cities*, 327.

14. Richmond City Hustings Court Order Books 8 (1808–10), p. 377; 10 (1812–13), p. 325; 11 (1813–15), p. 411; and 12 (1815–17), pp. 3–4.

15. Sheldon, "Black-White Relations in Richmond," 38. On crime in Richmond in this era more broadly, see Saunders, "Crime and Punishment."

16. *Virginia Argus*, August 27, 1812. My thanks to Amy Murrell for bringing this letter to my attention.

17. Mordecai, *Richmond in By-Gone Days*, 222–27; and Goldfield, *Urban Growth in the Age of Sectionalism*, ch. 1.

18. Wade, *Slavery in the Cities*, 327.

19. *Ordinances of the Corporation of the City of Richmond*, May 9, 1830, pp. 113–20.

20. In 1836, for example, a white man named Christian Freyfoyle complained to the mayor that Betsey, a slave hired to a man named James Supples, used "abusive and provoking language" toward him in the streets as he walked with his adopted daughter by calling the little girl "a bastard." Betsey received ten lashes for the slur. Richmond Mayor's Court, Private Docket, 1836–39, May 19, 1836, p. 9, Valentine Museum, Richmond (hereafter MCPD).

21. MCPD, July 5 and 9, 1838, pp. 288 and 291 (quotations on 288). Attacks on

a woman's sexuality did not have to impugn her chastity per se to have their desired effect. In late July 1838, for example, a young woman named Mary Ann Ferris and her mother Catherine Clarke brought charges against Mary Smith for slander, claiming that she told many men and women that Ferris was hermaphroditic. Both Ferris and Smith worked at the Richmond Cotton Factory, and Ferris also reported that one day Smith and three other factory girls threw her on her back in the bathroom and inspected her genitalia. Mayor Tate reported that he had no jurisdiction over cases of slander but advised Clarke and Ferris to ignore the talk. He also noted to himself that "the language and behaviour of these girls would lead one to rather an unfavourable conclusion as to the moral condition of the 'factory girls' notwithstanding the vigilant attention of the managers of these establishments." Having young, frequently poor, women from the countryside looking for economic opportunity work in factories was a relatively new labor practice for Richmond in the 1830s. Wages barely kept the young women at subsistence level, and some turned to the sex trade for survival. The path from factory work to prostitution, especially common among women in the sewing trades, was already familiar to early reformers in northern cities, though it does not appear to have been worthy of attention in Richmond until the 1850s. See MCPD, July 31, 1838, p. 299. On prostitution and the sewing trades, see Rosen, *Lost Sisterhood*, 2–4; Stansell, *City of Women*, 176; and Hill, *Their Sisters' Keepers*, 81–87.

22. MCPD, May 20, 1836, p. 9.

23. MCPD, June 8 and 14, 1837, pp. 155 and 158 (quotation on 155).

24. MCPD, October 20, 1837, p. 202.

25. MCPD, June 2 and 5, 1838, pp. 275 and 277. For discussions of cases of sexual slander involving accusations against white women of having sex across the color line, see Kirsten Fischer, " 'False, Feigned, and Scandalous Words,' " in Clinton and Gillespie, *The Devil's Lane*, 139–53; Bynum, *Unruly Women*, 41–45; and Hodes, *White Women, Black Men*, 27, 53, and 81.

26. Peter was dismissed, given that Mull had already beaten him. The mayor did not consider punishing Mull for his actions despite his belief that Peter's character was well established. Daniel Loney received twenty lashes for his comment. MCPD, January 19 and 23, 1838, pp. 232, 233, and 234 (quotations on 232 and 233).

27. John Sacra chose not to appear in court, and the case against Thomas Kennedy (Canady) was dismissed. MCPD, June 7 and 10, 1836, pp. 17 and 18 (quotations on 17).

28. A great deal of research on prostitution in nineteenth-century American cities, especially in New York City, has followed the publication of Judith R. Walkowitz's study of prostitution in Victorian England, *Prostitution and Victorian Society*. Among those most useful for the antebellum period are Carlisle, "Disorderly City, Disorderly Women"; Gilfoyle, "Urban Geography of Commercial Sex"; Gilfoyle, "Strumpets and Misogynists"; Lockley, "Crossing the Race Divide"; Hill, *Their Sisters' Keepers*; Hobson, *Uneasy Virtue*; and Stansell, *City of Women*, esp. 172–92. A fascinating article, showing how in some antebellum cities prostitution was integral to politics as well as to the economy, is Tansey, "Prostitution and Politics." Also

of value for the antebellum period, but extending their analyses well into the late nineteenth and early twentieth centuries, are Barnhart, *Fair but Frail*; Gilfoyle, *City of Eros*; Goldman, *Gold Diggers and Silver Miners*; Humphrey, "Prostitution in Texas"; James Jones, "Municipal Vice"; Riegel, "Changing American Attitudes toward Prostitution"; Rose, "Prostitution and the Sporting Life"; and Rosen, *Lost Sisterhood*.

29. MCPD, July 13, 1836, p. 31.

30. MCPD, May 26 and August 16, 1836, July 17 and August 19, 1837, and September 9, 1838, pp. 13, 46, 170, 181, and 319.

31. MCPD, May 19, 1836, p. 8.

32. MCPD, June 12 and 13, 1836, p. 19.

33. MCPD, August 13 and 14, 1837, p. 180.

34. MCPD, July 16, 1838, October 12, 1837, and March 17 and 18, 1839, pp. 293, 200, and 391.

35. Similarly, in her study of antebellum New York City, Christine Stansell notes that the "bawdy houses" of New York served a wide variety of purposes: "At one end of the spectrum, bawdy houses shaded into groceries, retreats where people stopped to relax and gossip; at the other, into brothel-like establishments that rented rooms for illicit sex. Here, too, black women could earn money, since bawdy houses often catered to an interracial clientele" (*City of Women*, 15).

36. MCPD, July 12, 13, 15, and 18, 1836, pp. 31, 32, 33, and 35.

37. MCPD, August 1 and 2, September 20 and 23, 1836, May 14, June 14 and 19, August 7, and September 5, 1837, June 26, 1838, and March 26, 1839, pp. 39, 61, 62, 141, 158, 160, 177, 187, 284, and 393 (quotation on 187).

38. In August 1836 a white man named Samuel Cosby charged Betsey Horton with "entertaining his slave Joshua Roper, without his consent," while in June 1837 a man was severely beaten at her house, to which two white men present served as witnesses. Also resident in Betsey Horton's house was a white woman named Elizabeth Williams, whom Mayor Tate heard had slept with a slave when she was still a servant girl living with a family in Chesterfield County. A footnote in the mayor's docket indicates that Betsey Horton herself died in August 1838. MCPD, August 30, September 3 and 5, 1836, May 20 and June 6, 1837, pp. 50, 53, 143, and 153 (quotation on 50).

39. MCPD, May 23, 25, and 27, and October 20, 1836, pp. 11, 12, 13, and 73 (quotation on 11).

40. Indicative of the racial ambiguity consequent to Richmond's sexual milieu, Mayor Tate listed Cynthia Conway as a free "mulatto" in 1836 only to make a notation that she was white in 1837. MCPD, June 10, 1836, and March 30, 1837, pp. 18 and 128.

41. MCPD, June 27 and 28, and July 11, 1837, and April 16, 1838, pp. 163, 168, and 254.

42. MCPD, August 28, and November 7 and 9, 1836, and October 11 and 21, 1838, pp. 49, 82, 83, 337, and 342 (quotations on 49, 337, and 342).

43. As Victoria Bynum notes in her study of antebellum North Carolina, most

women who became prostitutes and brothel owners "lacked extensive kinship networks in their communities"; moreover, nearly always, "ostracism from respectable society preceded involvement in prostitution" (*Unruly Women*, 94).

44. On the varied reasons why women entered the sex trade, on their alternative career options, and on their relationships with employers and with other women, see Rosen, *Lost Sisterhood*, 2–4; Hill, *Their Sisters' Keepers*, 81–94, and ch. 9; Stansell, *City of Women*, ch. 9; and Gilfoyle, "Strumpets and Misogynists," 60.

45. MCPD, October 3, 1836, and July 5, 1838, pp. 68 and 288.

46. MCPD, September 13 and 14, and April 9 and 11, 1838, pp. 321, 322, 252, and 253.

47. MCPD, February 24, 26, and 27, 1837, March 14 and 16, 1838, and May 30 and 31, 1836, pp. 116, 117, 244, 245, 14, and 15 (quotations on 116 and 14).

48. As Marcia Carlisle notes in her study of prostitution in Philadelphia, prostitution per se was not made a specific crime in most American cities until early in the twentieth century ("Disorderly City, Disorderly Women," 563).

49. As Dennis Rousey argues, until the middle of the nineteenth century, there were military-style professional police organizations, complete with uniforms and weapons, only in some southern cities, such as New Orleans, Mobile, Savannah, Charleston, and Richmond, primarily established to control large local slave populations. Northern cities, such as New York, Boston, and Philadelphia, did not undertake significant police reforms until the 1840s and 1850s. Rousey, *Policing the Southern City*.

50. Prostitutes, for example, needed fancy clothing and toilet items as well as food and medical care, which all helped retail business. Prostitution was woven into the economies of all major American cities. In New Orleans in the 1850s the sex trade was even central to larger political battles, as new urban elites sought to replace the city's riverside economy with growth from railroads. Shifting the economic foundation of the city required cracking down on riverside vice, including the many houses of prostitution. Landlords and shopkeepers alike mobilized behind the prostitutes, who fought their own battle to remain in place. See Tansey, "Prostitution and Politics."

51. MCPD, April 10, 1837, p. 133. Nancy Tucker spent nearly six months in jail for this arrest, while her sister remained in prison for more than seven.

52. Hobson, *Uneasy Virtue*, 33–34. Similarly, Suzanne Lebsock notes that public authorities in antebellum Petersburg, Virginia, "made next to no effort to regulate sexual behavior" (*Free Women of Petersburg*, 204). Early reform movements were already under way in some cities by the 1830s, most notably the Female Moral Reform Societies middle-class women formed in response to Magdalene Society leader Reverend John McDowall's report on prostitution in New York City. Only in the 1840s and 1850s, though, did large numbers of Americans begin to change their attitudes toward sex and sexual behavior, a change that slowly began to be reflected in urban policies. See Rosen, *Lost Sisterhood*, 8; Hill, *Their Sisters' Keepers*, ch. 1; Stansell, *City of Women*, 171–72; and Ryan, *Cradle of the Middle Class*, 117–21.

53. Wade, *Slavery in the Cities*, 327.

54. Kimball, *American City, Southern Place*, chs. 1–2; Goldfield, *Urban Growth in the*

Age of Sectionalism, chs. 1–5; Goldfield, "Urban-Rural Relations"; Scott, *Old Richmond Neighborhoods*; and McLeod, "Free Labor in a Slave Society," chs. 1 and 3.

55. *Richmond Daily Dispatch*, April 13, 1852.

56. Olmsted, *Journey in the Seaboard Slave States*, 22 and 51 (quotation on 51); and Chambers, *Things as They Are in America*, 271–72.

57. *Richmond Daily Dispatch*, December 2, 1856.

58. *Richmond Daily Dispatch*, March 3 and 6, 1855, and May 6, 1857 (quotation in May 6 issue).

59. *Richmond Daily Dispatch*, March 2, 1859.

60. *Richmond Daily Dispatch*, March 4, 1859.

61. *Richmond Daily Dispatch*, March 19, 1855. At trial in April, Thornton was found guilty of manslaughter and sentenced to seven years in prison (*Richmond Daily Dispatch*, April 26, 1855).

62. *Richmond Daily Dispatch*, March 31, April 1 and 16, June 23, and November 7, 1857 (quotations in June 23 and April 1 issues). Joseph Elam remained in jail for three months awaiting his trial, and in July 1857 he escaped from prison. Reubenetta Dandridge was born into slavery in 1825 and was freed in 1849. While still enslaved, she had a husband, who successfully escaped to Canada. The police reported that Dandridge and her husband remained in correspondence. In 1850 Dandridge lived with a four-year-old girl named Jane Dandridge and a forty-eight-year-old woman named Mary Dandridge. All three were African American and likely were Reubenetta's daughter and mother, respectively. *Richmond Daily Dispatch*, June 23 and July 6, 1857, and July 24, 1858; United States Census—Virginia, 1850.

63. *Richmond Daily Dispatch*, April 27 and 28, and September 22, 1853.

64. *Richmond Daily Dispatch*, May 14, 1855, December 9 and 13, 1856, September 24, 1857, and May 25, 1859.

65. Hodes, *White Women, Black Men*, chs. 6 and 7; Sommerville, "Rape Myth in the Old South," 518; Bardaglio, *Reconstructing the Household*, ch. 6; and Williamson, *New People*, 91–92.

66. "'An Ordinance Concerning Negroes': The Richmond Black Code (1859)," in Duke and Jordan, *A Richmond Reader*, 107–13.

67. *Richmond Daily Dispatch*, November 25, 1853, March 30, 1857, and August 2, 1854. Joseph Mayo was most famous for being the wealthy proprietor of the toll bridge connecting Richmond to the city of Manchester, but before becoming mayor, he had also been a commonwealth's attorney, and he frequently used the Hustings Court as a forum for his views on the need to maintain strict control over the black population of the city. In 1852, for example, Mayo called the special attention of the grand jury "to some glaring evils in the present condition of our slave population." He warned of the dangers of slaves having board money, but also of slaves wearing fancy clothes and riding in carriages where they exhibited "the assumptions of equality." The following February, he warned the grand jury about the need to enforce laws for good order — including those regarding tippling houses, gambling, and houses of ill fame — and made special reference to "the public nuisance, and evil resulting" from the crowds of slaves who gathered an-

nually on Main Street during the hiring season between Christmas and the first of February. *Richmond Daily Dispatch*, August 12, 1852, and February 15, 1853.

68. *Richmond Daily Dispatch*, August 20, 1853, January 4, 1854, December 18, 1856, and January 10, 1857.

69. *Richmond Daily Dispatch*, September 12, 1856.

70. *Richmond Daily Dispatch*, April 11, 1856. Also see May 1, 1857.

71. *Richmond Daily Dispatch*, July 31, 1855.

72. *Richmond Daily Dispatch*, August 16, 1854.

73. Bridgewater had previously served six months in the Henrico County jail for being of "evil name and fame; and of being on intimate terms with negroes." Here, the mayor sentenced Harris to lashes, and Bridgewater to one year in jail. *Richmond Daily Dispatch*, August 21, 1854.

74. *Richmond Daily Dispatch*, September 5, 1854.

75. *Richmond Daily Dispatch*, June 7 and March 19, 1856.

76. *Richmond Daily Dispatch*, September 12, 1853. Also see Scott, *Old Richmond Neighborhoods*, 135.

77. *Richmond Daily Dispatch*, September 25, 1852.

78. *Richmond Daily Dispatch*, August 27, 1853.

79. On antiprostitution reform movements, see Hobson, *Uneasy Virtue*, ch. 3; Barnhart, *Fair but Frail*, 7–14; Mintz, *Moralists and Modernizers*, 66–70; and Smith-Rosenberg, "Beauty, the Beast, and the Militant Woman." The literature on personal and social reform in antebellum America is voluminous. Useful surveys include Mintz, *Moralists and Modernizers*; Walters, *American Reformers*; and Tyler, *Freedom's Ferment*.

80. *Richmond Daily Dispatch*, October 2, 1852.

81. *Richmond Daily Dispatch*, January 26, 1854. Also see January 28 and July 28, 1854. Despite the appearance of editorials reflecting the sentiments of contemporary Americans elsewhere toward prostitution and calling on white women to get involved in addressing the problem, white women in Richmond did not establish and were not active in antiprostitution reform organizations like those existing in other antebellum cities. Richmond was the first southern city where reformers founded a Magdalene Society, but they did not do so until 1874. Perhaps the interracialism of prostitution in Richmond made the issue simply too delicate for women's involvement. Barber, " 'Sisters of the Capital,' " 1:173–74. On white women and reform movements in antebellum Virginia, see Lebsock, *Free Women of Petersburg*, ch. 7; and Varon, *We Mean to Be Counted*, chs. 1–2. On other kinds of reform sentiments in 1850s Richmond, see Kimball, *American City, Southern Place*, 44–49.

82. Stearns, *Narrative of Henry Box Brown*; and Stevens, *Anthony Burns*.

83. *Richmond Daily Dispatch*, April 6 and 8, 1857.

84. *Richmond Daily Dispatch*, June 5 and 6, 1856.

85. *Richmond Daily Dispatch*, June 6 and 7, 1856.

86. The neighborhood of Oregon Hill in particular was a likely location for an event such as the one described above. As Mary Wingfield Scott noted, the neigh-

borhood had a few black residents but was mostly "fiercely white" (*Old Richmond Neighborhoods*, 211).

87. *Richmond Daily Dispatch*, June 28, 1856.

88. Berlin, *Slaves without Masters*, ch. 11; and Williamson, *New People*, 61–75.

89. Barber, " 'Sisters of the Capital,' " 1:168–69 and 2:266–75.

90. *Richmond Daily Dispatch*, November 29 and 30, 1854, and August 19, 1856 (quotation in August 19 issue). It is possible, though hard to determine for certain, that John Thornton was the same man who stabbed Robert Custello in a fight over a woman in 1855.

91. *Richmond Daily Dispatch*, September 29, 1858.

92. *Richmond Daily Dispatch*, January 22, 1857. Also see June 2 and 3, 1857. Houston may have been romantically involved with Francis Bridgwater, a man of mixed race who was also frequently before the mayor. On January 26, 1856, the *Dispatch* reported Bridgwater's arrest for breaking and entering a house, but the evidence showed that Houston rented a room in the house, and Bridgwater "had merely gone there to see his adorable Kate to make love and get his pantaloons which she was shortening for him."

93. Wendell P. Dabney, quoted in Brown and Kimball, "Mapping the Terrain," 335. Also see Scott, *Old Richmond Neighborhoods*, 130.

INTERLUDE: THE CONTEXT FOR LAWMAKING

1. Blair, "Random Sketches of Old-Time Richmond."

2. Walter Johnson, *Soul by Soul*, 113. Also see Walter Johnson, "Slave Trader," 16–18.

3. On the sale of "fancy girls" in Virginia, see Stevenson, *Life in Black and White*, 180–81; Tadman, *Speculators and Slaves*, 125–27; Bancroft, *Slave-Trading in the Old South*, 100 n. 28 and 112; and Bremer, *Homes of the New World*, 2:535. For examples of such sales in the accounts of traders, see Silas and R. F. Omohundro, Account Book—Slave Sales, 1857–63, Alderman Library, University of Virginia.

4. On Robert Lumpkin, see his will in Richmond City Hustings Court Will Book 24, pp. 419–22. Also see a description of his jail in Bancroft, *Slave-Trading in the Old South*, 102–3. Reportedly, the two daughters of Robert and Mary Lumpkin who went to school in Massachusetts were so light-skinned that they passed as white. Lumpkin's daughters moved to Pennsylvania after completing their education, where Lumpkin insisted they remain out of fear they might be sold in the event he went into significant debt. Robert and Mary Lumpkin formally married after the Civil War, shortly before his death. See Corey, *History of the Richmond Theological Seminary*, 42–50 and 74–77. Also see the account of Anthony Burns, the fugitive slave, who was kept in Lumpkin's jail after being captured in Boston and returned to Virginia. Burns reported that while he suffered horribly in jail, Mary Lumpkin treated him kindly. He also indicated that Robert Lumpkin had a slave concubine in addition to his enslaved wife. See Stevens, *Anthony Burns*, 187–93.

5. Like Lumpkin, Omohundro seems to have been a man whose personal life stood in jarring contradiction to his livelihood. Omohundro not only had a pen-

chant for buying members of his family expensive gifts, but he also commonly gave them large outlays of cash and provided schoolbooks and private tutors for both his wife and his children. See Omohundro's will, Richmond City Circuit Court Will Book 2, pp. 228–30. For examples of his provisions for his family, see his Expense Journal, Silas Omohundro business and estate records, 1842–82, Library of Virginia, Richmond. For one scholar's effort to understand the paradox of men who sold enslaved women professionally yet whose families simultaneously comprised the commodity in which they dealt, see Troutman, " 'Fancy Girls' and a 'Yellow Wife.' "

6. Bancroft, *Slave-Trading in the Old South*, 99–100.

7. *Richmond Enquirer*, December 2, 1853. Also see *Richmond Daily Dispatch*, February 20 and 22, 1856.

8. For examples of how sex and crime in urban areas directly helped shape local and national politics, see Link, "Jordan Hatcher Case"; and Tansey, "Prostitution and Politics."

CHAPTER FOUR

1. Martineau, *Society in America*, 2:320.

2. Kemble, *Journal*, 14–15.

3. Buckingham, *Slave States of America*, 2:213–14.

4. Also see Olmsted, *Journey in the Seaboard Slave States*, 126–28, 231–32, and 508; and Bayard, *Travels of a Frenchman*, 41.

5. The historical scholarship on the rape of enslaved women and on sex between masters and slaves and its impact on white and black women, black men, white and black families, and local communities is extensive, and is cited at some length in Chapter 1, notes 14, 15, and 25.

6. Throughout this chapter, I refer to marital relationships between slaves as they considered them to be, despite the reality that slave marriages had no legal standing. Whites also often recognized that slaves could be and were married, but the lack of legal recognition nonetheless enabled white interference with the familial and sexual lives of their property when it suited them, factors that contributed significantly both to the hostilities and the sympathies across the color line evident in the cases discussed above.

7. An extraordinarily poignant story of this sort, one with parallels to several of the cases related here, is that of Celia, an enslaved woman in Callaway County, Missouri, who was sexually abused by her owner for five years until she murdered him in 1855 rather than withstand his assaults any longer. Melton McLaurin tells Celia's story (and tangentially that of her pained and frustrated enslaved lover, George) in *Celia*.

8. As McLaurin has suggested, borrowing Charles Sellers's phrase, cases like these brought the "fundamental moral anxiety" of slavery to the fore (*Celia*, xii–xiii). On the law of slavery in the South generally, see Fede, "Legitimized Violent Slave Abuse"; Flanigan, "Criminal Procedure"; Higginbotham, *In the Matter of Color*, chs. 2, 5, and 6; Hindus, "Black Justice under White Law"; Kay and Cary, " 'The Planters Suffer Little or Nothing' "; Nash, "Reason of Slavery"; Nash, "Fair-

ness and Formalism"; Nash, "A More Equitable Past?"; Morris, *Southern Slavery and the Law*; Tushnet, *American Law of Slavery*; Waldrep, *Roots of Disorder*, chs. 2–3; Bardaglio, *Reconstructing the Household*, 69–72; Schafer, *Slavery, the Civil Law, and the Supreme Court of Louisiana*; and Wyatt-Brown, *Southern Honor*, 387–90. On Virginia specifically, see Schwarz, *Slave Laws in Virginia*; Schwarz, *Twice Condemned*; Schwarz, "Forging the Shackles"; Higginbotham and Kopytoff, "Property First, Humanity Second"; and Higginbotham and Jacobs, " 'Law Only as an Enemy.' "

9. Testimony of Moses, Case of Manuel, Executive Papers — Letters Received, box 276 (June 12, 1818), Library of Virginia, Richmond. Also see King George County Minute Book 10 (1817–22), pp. 66–69.

10. Testimony of Cate, Case of Manuel; King George County Land Tax Books, 1817–18.

11. Harry indicated that the "spate" between Manuel and Harrison was "on account of Betsey." It is unclear to whom this "Betsey" referred. William Jones did own a female slave named Betsey, who testified at Manuel's trial. In her testimony, however, this Betsey refers to Manuel's wife as a third person, and the trial record also notes that Manuel's wife belonged to a Doctor Oldham. It is possible that the Betsey over whom Manuel and Harrison previously bickered was in fact Manuel's wife, as Betsey was a common name among slaves. But without knowing Manuel's wife's name for certain, it seems equally possible that the fight regarded William Jones's Betsey, or still a third woman altogether. Testimony of Harry, Betsey, and Doctor Oldham, Case of Manuel.

12. Testimony of Daniel Coakley, Abrella, Harry, Cate, and John Rawlet, Case of Manuel.

13. Testimony of Moses, William Marders, and Mary, Case of Manuel. Personal property tax records from 1817 and 1818 confirm the purchase of an ordinary license by William Coakley. Langford Harrison owned no land of his own, and he probably lived on property owned by Joseph and Burditt Harrison, his father and brother. The Harrison farm lay just a few miles southwest of William Jones's property, near both the land owned by every landholding white witness and that held by the owners of all the enslaved witnesses. Cate's testimony indicates that Langford Harrison worked at "Turner's," but it is not clear what sort of business Turner ran. It is also uncertain just how Elizabeth Coakley was related to William Coakley, but Harrison and Elizabeth Coakley married in 1805, while William Coakley and his brother Reuben married in 1804 and 1810, respectively, making it very unlikely either had a daughter old enough to marry Harrison. Elizabeth, of course, could also have been a cousin or some other relative. King George County Personal Property Tax Books, 1817–18; King George County Land Tax Books, 1817–18; King George County Will Book 2, pp. 135–36; and King George County Marriage Bonds Book 1 (1786–1850).

14. The charges against Manuel accuse him only of using a "certain instrument in the form or shape of a bayonet or three edged dirk," but the fork attached to the end of the club, which was offered as material evidence at the trial, could explain the "three edged" wound Doctor Oldham, who examined the body (and who was probably also Manuel's wife's owner), testified to at the trial. Oldham also found

Harrison's lower jaw broken, and witness Ritchie Alsap saw wounds on Harrison's corpse's legs that appeared to be dog bites. Charges proffered against Manuel, and testimony of William Coakley, Doctor Oldham, and Ritchie Alsap, Case of Manuel.

15. Testimony of Thomas Baber, Ritchie Alsap, William Thomley, and William Coakley, Case of Manuel. Moses, in fact, had testified that on the Saturday before the murder Manuel had tried to contract Harrison's murder with him, claiming he had powder and shot, could get a gun, and would give Moses $2 to commit the crime. Moses said he refused.

16. After 1692 Virginia tried slaves in local courts of oyer and terminer, each called and in existence only for a specific trial. Five local magistrates served as judges. They heard testimony, passed judgment, and announced a sentence. No juries sat at slave trials, and there was no recourse to appeal to a higher court. The General Assembly made the procedure for assembling an oyer and terminer court easier and faster with legislation passed in 1765, and enacted additional legislation regarding these courts in 1786. Compensation was instituted in Virginia in 1705, designed primarily to discourage owners from protecting slave criminals for fear of losing their investments. See Hening, *The Statutes at Large*, 3:102–3 and 269–70, 8:137–39, and 12:345. Also see Schwarz, *Slave Laws in Virginia*, 86; Schwarz, *Twice Condemned*, 17–21, 25–26, and 52–53; Morris, *Southern Slavery and the Law*, 214–15 and 253–54; Flanigan, "Criminal Procedure," 543–44; Higginbotham and Jacobs, " 'Law Only as an Enemy,' " 984–1005; and Kay and Cary, " 'The Planters Suffer Little or Nothing.' "

17. Massie, in Perdue, Barden, and Phillips, *Weevils*, 207.

18. Lockhart, in Drew, *North-Side View*, 49.

19. This is not to suggest any sort of comparison between the degree of exploitation of slave men and slave women by white men. Both experienced violation, humiliation, and powerlessness in the face of white male sexual aggression, but these feelings were qualitatively different and gender specific. Any effort to gauge a scale of suffering for African American men and women under slavery juxtaposes intimately related yet fundamentally dissimilar forms of power relations. See Clinton, *Plantation Mistress*, 201, for a similar point.

20. Sam and Louisa Everett, in Rawick, *American Slave*, 17:127.

21. Williams, in Drew, *North-Side View*, 46 and 57–58, quotation on 58.

22. See White, *Ar'n't I a Woman?*, 145–47.

23. Massie, in Perdue, Barden, and Phillips, *Weevils*, 207.

24. As Jacqueline Jones has suggested, "the sexual violation of black women by white men rivaled the separation of families as the foremost provocation injected into black family life by slaveholders in general. . . . It would be naive to assume that the rape of a black wife by a white man did not adversely affect the woman's relationship with her husband; her innocence in initiating or sustaining a sexual encounter might not have shielded her from her husband's wrath. The fact that in some slave quarters mulatto children were scorned as the master's offspring indicates that the community in general hardly regarded this form of abuse with equanimity" (*Labor of Love, Labor of Sorrow*, 37–38).

25. Ellett, in Perdue, Barden, and Phillips, *Weevils*, 84.

26. Grandy, in ibid., 117.

27. King George County Personal Property Tax Books, 1817–18; and King George County Land Tax Books, 1817–18.

28. Morris, *Southern Slavery and the Law*, 283–84. In cases where multiple slaves were charged with a single murder, Morris notes that one or more of the accused might be acquitted. But in every case that Morris surveyed save one, at least one slave defendant was found guilty and sentenced to death.

29. By 1858, the state legislature discovered that the markets for selling convicted slave criminals had dried up significantly. Consequently, new legislation sentenced slaves who would have been transported to hard labor on public works. The total of 983 transported slaves, reported by Philip Schwarz, includes those sentenced to hard labor. See *Acts of the General Assembly of Virginia, 1800–1801*, ch. 43, p. 24, and *1857–1858*, ch. 29, pp. 39–40; Schwarz, *Twice Condemned*, 27–30; Schwarz, *Slave Laws in Virginia*, 103; and Higginbotham and Jacobs, " 'Law Only as an Enemy,' " 1005–9.

30. Schwarz, *Slave Laws in Virginia*, chs. 3–4.

31. Ibid., 85.

32. Cases of Shadrack, Squire, and Joe, Executive Papers—Letters Received, box 248, August 1818; and Governor's Council Journals, August 5, 1818, Library of Virginia, Richmond.

33. Petitions from Pittsylvania County, all in Executive Papers—Letters Received, box 248, August 1818. Squire and Joe hanged for their crimes on September 25. Governor's Council Journals, September 14 and October 3, 1818.

34. Case of Harry, Executive Papers—Letters Received, December 1827–January 1828.

35. Undated petitions accompanying Case of Harry, ibid.; and Governor's Council Journals, April 29, May 16, June 20, October 31, November 18, and December 30, 1828.

36. Joe Gooding's race is not indicated in the trial record, but in the inquest performed on Gooding's body after his death the coroner recorded that he was a "free negroe man." Chesterfield County Will Book 5, November 10, 1800, p. 328.

37. All evidence from the trial of Ben is cited from the court proceedings included with the letter from Thomas Watkins to the governor of Virginia. "Tryal of Ware's Ben," Executive Papers—Letters Received, box 116, January–March 1801. Also see Chesterfield County Order Book 14 (1800–1802), p. 28.

38. Records of the Auditor of Public Accounts—Condemned Blacks, Executed or Transported, Library of Virginia, Richmond.

39. Case of John, Executive Papers—Letters Received, box 248, August–September 1818. Also see Caroline County Minute Book, 1815–19, pp. 400–401a.

40. Petition included with Case of John; and Governor's Council Journals, September 15 and October 3, 1818. Before the news of John's pardon reached Caroline County, John escaped from prison. On November 25, his owner submitted a petition to the governor asking that he be compensated for the loss of John, despite the pardon. The Executive Council turned down the request. It is unknown what became of John. Notes from jailer in Bowling Green, Caroline County, dated Sep-

tember 6 and October 6, 1818, Executive Papers—Letters Received, boxes 248 and 249, respectively, September and October 1818; and Governor's Council Journals, November 25, 1818.

41. Philip Schwarz found that slaves were transported in sixty-four cases of murdering other slaves or free blacks between 1785 and 1864, while fifty-six were executed (*Slave Laws in Virginia*, 85). For a case similar to those of Ben and John, see Case of Hubard, Executive Papers—Pardon Papers, box 316, May–September 1830.

42. The 1830 census indicates that John Francis owned ten slaves, eight of whom were over age ten. Personal property tax records for 1830 indicate that Francis owned just five slaves over age twelve. United States Census—Virginia, 1830; and New Kent County Personal Property Tax Book, 1830.

43. Case of Peggy, Patrick, and Franky, Executive Papers—Pardon Papers, box 316, May–September 1830.

44. Testimony of John Royster, Case of Peggy, Patrick, and Franky.

45. Testimony of Jesse, Sucky, Henry, and Richard Burnett, Case of Peggy, Patrick, and Franky. Burnett himself owned around twelve slaves. He and Francis may have been engaged in some joint enterprise, because both their individual properties lay adjacent to land owned by the two men together. United States Census—Virginia, 1830; New Kent County Personal Property Tax Book, 1830; and New Kent County Land Tax Book, 1830.

46. Testimony of Jesse and John Royster, Case of Peggy, Patrick, and Franky.

47. Testimony of Hannah, Case of Peggy, Patrick, and Franky.

48. Testimony of Abner Ellyson, Case of Peggy, Patrick, and Franky. Land tax records do not indicate precisely where the land of Abner Ellyson lay relative to that of John Francis, but Francis's land lay fourteen miles northwest of the courthouse while Ellyson's lay fourteen miles west. Ellyson himself testified that he lived "in the neighbourhood." New Kent County Land Tax Book, 1830.

49. Testimony of Nathaniel White, John Royster, and William E. Clopton, Case of Peggy, Patrick, and Franky. Nathaniel White owned no land. Royster lived just a mile from Francis, and Clopton lived next to both Francis and Richard Burnett. Case of Peggy, Patrick, and Franky; and New Kent County Land Tax Book, 1830.

50. Petition for Transportation of Peggy, Patrick, and Franky, Executive Papers—Pardon Papers, box 316, May–September 1830.

51. Veney, *Narrative of Bethany Veney*, 26.

52. Mrs. May Satterfield, in Perdue, Barden, and Phillips, *Weevils*, 245.

53. Sis Shackleford, in ibid., 250.

54. Julia Williams, in Rawick, *American Slave*, 16:O104.

55. M. Fowler, in Rawick, *American Slave*, supp. ser. 1, 1:150. It is impossible to know for certain, but it seems reasonable to assume that a number of slave women who ran away from plantations across the South in the antebellum period did so to escape the sexual predation that the double bond of race and sex affixed on them as slaves.

56. Sharon Block has demonstrated that masters might also try to produce the illusion of consent by purposefully placing enslaved women in circumstances

where their sexual vulnerability was such that submission was practically their only feasible option. As Block argues, "rape in these situations was not just an act of power, it was also the power to define an act. By translating authority over a woman's labor into opportunities for sexual coercion, economic mastery created sexual mastery, allowing masters to manipulate forced sexual encounters into a mimicry of consensual ones. Servants and slaves could not only be forced *to* consent, but this force was refigured *as* consent." Block, "Lines of Color, Sex, and Service," in Hodes, *Sex, Love, Race,* 143.

57. Cf. Kenneth Greenberg, who focuses on the importance of the body and its integrity to white notions of honor, and suggests that the literal and figurative penetration of rape indicates how the act of rape itself was an effort to control both the bodies and minds of slaves (*Honor and Slavery,* 48–49).

58. Mrs. Minnie Folkes, in Perdue, Barden, and Phillips, *Weevils,* 92–93, quotation on 93.

59. Mrs. Fannie Berry, in ibid., 36.

60. Ibid., 48–49. Sukie retained her defiant posture even on the auction block. As Berry heard the story from her owner's coachman, Sukie became infuriated as slave traders poked and prodded her. Finally, as they stuck their fingers in her mouth to examine her teeth, "she pult up her dress an' tole ole nigger traders to look an' see if dey could fin' any teef down dere."

61. On the struggle for internal strength by African American women, see, for example, Hine, "Rape and the Inner Lives of Southern Black Women." For a detailed personal account of the almost constant daily struggle of enslaved women with white men over control of their sexuality, see Jacobs, *Incidents in the Life of a Slave Girl.* For a literary analysis of women's slave narratives, see Fleischner, *Mastering Slavery.*

62. That members of the white community let slave owners treat their slaves as they wished except in the most extreme circumstances is suggested by the rarity of punishments for masters who severely beat or murdered their own slaves. See, for example, Morris, *Southern Slavery and the Law,* chs. 7–8; Schafer, *Slavery, the Civil Law, and the Supreme Court of Louisiana,* ch. 2; Higginbotham and Jacobs, " 'Law Only as an Enemy,' " 1032–37 and 1044–54; Fede, "Legitimized Violent Slave Abuse"; and Wyatt-Brown, *Southern Honor,* 371–77. For an example of an instance where a master was punished for the way he treated his slaves, see the case of John Hoover, a North Carolina slave owner who was executed for sadistically murdering a female slave whom he may have also sexually assaulted. Of course, in that case as well, Hoover acted without interference from the law or his neighbors until it was too late for his enslaved victim. Carolyn J. Powell, "In Remembrance of Mira," in Morton, *Discovering the Women in Slavery,* 47–60; and Morris, *Southern Slavery and the Law,* 177–79.

63. Although incest across the color line was indeed unusual, it certainly was not unheard of. Ex-slave William Thompson, born eighteen miles from Richmond, claimed that he knew a slave owner who had six children by one of his slaves. "Then there was a fuss between him and his wife, and he sold all the children but the oldest slave daughter. Afterward, he had a child by this daughter, and sold mother

and child before the birth. . . . Such things are done frequently in the South." A number of contemporary authors have pointed out the recurring appearance together of incest and miscegenation themes in nineteenth- and twentieth-century fiction, probably most famously in William Faulkner's *Absalom! Absalom!* See Thompson, in Drew, *North-Side View*, 137. For an exploration of the conjunction of incest and miscegenation themes in literature, see Sollors, *Neither Black nor White yet Both*, ch. 10. On southern attitudes toward incest in the nineteenth century, see Peter Bardaglio, " 'An Outrage upon Nature,' " in Bleser, *In Joy and in Sorrow*, 32–51.

64. Genovese, *Roll, Jordan, Roll*, 25–49.

65. Schwarz, *Slave Laws in Virginia*, 95–96. In arguing that sentencing flexibility reflected and ultimately reinforced the hegemonic power of slave owners in the legal system, I am not suggesting that the law could also entirely bury and suppress the real challenges posed to that power by individuals like Manuel, Franky, Peggy, and Patrick. As Laura Edwards has argued, the very fact that the judicial system processed cases where slaves and other legal dependents violently revolted against the rule of the patriarch of their household "reveal[ed] the contingency and contestation that defined authority in the antebellum South, and that contingency and contestation of authority were precisely what the law sought to control, to diffuse, and to hide." Edwards suggests that the legal system's role in incidents like these ought to make historians reassess their considerations of the power relationships among southerners, and between southerners and the law. See Edwards, "Law, Domestic Violence, and the Limits of Patriarchal Authority," 741. Also see Gross, "Pandora's Box."

66. Schwarz, *Twice Condemned*, 116; and White, *Ar'n't I a Woman?*, 78–79.

67. Case of Malinda, Executive Papers—Letters Received, box 361, January–March 1840.

68. Although there were numerous cases in antebellum Virginia where enslaved women did hang for murdering blacks and whites alike, it is also possible that white men felt uncomfortable executing women in general, regardless of their race. To my knowledge, no one has undertaken a study comparing the percentage of either white or black women convicted of capital crimes with that of men, or of the number of convicted women subsequently spared execution with that of reprieved men. Ulrich B. Phillips, however, reported in his study of slave crime that of 1,418 slaves sentenced to death in Virginia between 1705 and 1865, just 91 were women (cited in Higginbotham and Jacobs, " 'Law Only as an Enemy,' " 1061).

69. Governor's Council Journals, September 25, October 16 and 23, 1830. One member of the council, A. L. Botts, dissented, believing the sentence of the court ought to be carried out on all three slaves. Cf. the case of Celia, who hanged for murdering her master (McLaurin, *Celia*).

70. Case of Carter, Executive Papers—Pardon Papers, box 128, May 9, 1803; and Governor's Council Journals, May 21, 1803. A number of scholars have deconstructed the myth that black men accused of raping white women in the antebellum South invariably faced death for their supposed crimes. These historians draw important attention to how hostile class attitudes toward poor white women

could and often did trump white fears of black male sexuality, which to some extent have been projected back in time from the experience of the twentieth century. See Sommerville, "Rape Myth Reconsidered," esp. chs. 1–4; Hodes, *White Women, Black Men*, 57–66; Bynum, *Unruly Women*, 109–10 and 117–18; Getman, "Sexual Control in the Slaveholding South," 134–42; and Johnston, *Race Relations in Virginia*, 257–65. Peter Bardaglio calls attention to the importance of the class status of white women in cases where courts considered accusations that they had been raped, but also stresses the significance of whites' racialized sexual anxieties about black men (*Reconstructing the Household*, 71–78, and "Rape and the Law in the Old South"). Thomas Morris takes an agnostic position on how gender, race, and class shaped cases where enslaved men were accused of sexually assaulting white women but does conclude that "it is misleading to suggest that slaves charged with such offenses were immediately castrated, burned to death, or hanged" (*Southern Slavery and the Law*, ch. 14, quotation on 321).

71. As Martha Hodes writes, "requests for mercy on behalf of slaves convicted of rape could be accomplished in part by invoking the white woman's bad reputation, thereby demonstrating that a poor and transgressing white woman could be worth less to elite whites than the profitable labor of a slave" (*White Women, Black Men*, 61).

72. Case of Carter, Executive Papers — Pardon Papers, box 128, May 9, 1803. These words were struck through before the note was submitted to the governor. But they are clearly legible and indicate that the financial value of slaves played a significant role in how whites thought about the appropriate judicial resolution of slave crimes, especially when the victim of that crime held a marginal status in the white community.

73. On slavery and honor, see Greenberg, *Honor and Slavery*, esp. ch. 2.

74. Petition for Patrick, and Certificate of Turner H. Christian, Executive Papers — Letters Received, box 317, October–November 1830.

75. Petition for Patrick, Executive Papers — Letters Received, box 317, October–November 1830.

76. I have been unable to locate this third petition, but the journals of the Executive Council clearly indicate the receipt of three petitions. It is possible that the petition signed by ninety-three men is the third petition, in which case the second petition remains missing (Governor's Council Journals, October 28, November 13 and 16, 1830). On November 20, the governor received letters from John D. Christian, New Kent County clerk, and from John A. Taylor, one of the judges who convicted and sentenced the three slaves to death at their original trial. Taylor lived nearly twenty miles from John Francis, on the other side of New Kent County, and he claimed not to know any of the slaves involved in this crime. At the time of the trial, Taylor wrote to the governor, he believed the three slaves deserved to hang, and despite the decision of the governor's council he still believed Peggy deserved to die. But, he claimed, he had had two meetings with Patrick since the trial and wrote that, had he been aware of Patrick's mental state at the time of the trial, he would never have sentenced him to hang. Taylor and Christian asked that Patrick be pardoned altogether, which request was rejected by the council. Letters

of Christian and Taylor, Executive Papers—Letters Received, box 317, October–November 1830; Governor's Council Journals, November 20, 1830; and New Kent County Land Tax Book, 1830.

77. Records of the Auditor of Public Accounts, Condemned Blacks Executed or Transported, Library of Virginia, Richmond. I have been unable to locate a receipt from the public auditor compensating William Jones for Manuel's death, but he was not recommended for reprieve by the governor or his council, and there is no evidence to suggest that any other fate befell him.

INTERLUDE: THE FATE OF LUCY BOWMAN

1. Lucy Bowman's last name was also sometimes spelled Boamen, Boaman, Bomer, or Boomer. Legislative Petitions—Lunenburg County #8815, January 18, 1834, Library of Virginia, Richmond; Will of John Winn Snr., Lunenburg County Will Book 8, pp. 170–71; and *Journal of the House of Delegates, 1833–1834*, February 3, 1834, p. 149.

2. Legislative Petitions—Lunenburg County #10585-a, February 6, 1834, Library of Virginia, Richmond.

3. Depositions of James Winn, Charlotte Winn, and Chasteen Winn, Legislative Petitions—Lunenburg County #10585 and #10585-a, February 6, 1834.

4. Note of Richard May, dated February 28, 1834, included with documentation for petition #8815.

5. Affidavits of David Street and Edward Winn, Legislative Petitions—Lunenburg County #10797-a, January 6, 1835.

6. *Journal of the House of Delegates, 1834–1835*, February 24, 1835, p. 186.

7. Legislative Petitions—Lunenburg County #11056, December 23, 1835; and *Journal of the House of Delegates, 1835–1836*, January 16, 1836, p. 82 (the House journal indicates that the Committee of Courts of Justice brought a report on Bowman's petition to the floor, but does not specify the content of that report. No bill was ever drawn on her behalf in 1836 or in any other year, however, suggesting her request for residence was denied).

CHAPTER FIVE

1. Petition of Thomas Culpepper, Legislative Petitions—Norfolk County #10943, December 9, 1835, Library of Virginia, Richmond (hereafter LP-LOV). It is unclear whether Thomas Culpepper meant that Caroline was a prostitute in the sense that she exchanged sex for money. As Martha Hodes has noted, in the antebellum South, any white woman who had sex outside of marriage might also find herself called a "prostitute" (*White Women, Black Men*, 14).

2. Petition of Elizabeth Pannill, King William County #11713, March 5, 1837, LP-LOV. Also see King William County Circuit Superior Court of Law and Chancery proceedings, May 12, 1836, included with Pannill's petition.

3. The number of Virginians petitioning the legislature for divorce escalated during the first two decades of the nineteenth century. In 1827, the General Assembly passed legislation in an effort both to regularize and clarify the procedures for divorce and to slow the stream of incoming petitions to Richmond. The

law authorized superior courts of chancery to grant divorces *a mensa et thoro* for adultery, cruelty, and fear of bodily harm and to grant full divorces in cases of idiocy, bigamy, and impotence at the time of marriage. This act also required that anyone intending to file a petition with the legislature for a divorce include with his or her petition a copy of either a previous bed-and-board decree or a statement of causes filed with the county clerk, a notice to the partner being filed against of the intent to divorce, and a certified copy of the findings of a jury regarding the charges brought in the statement of causes. In keeping with a national trend of increased judicial jurisdiction over divorces in the antebellum era, the assembly enacted laws in 1841 and 1848 granting further control over divorces to the courts, citing in the latter act that divorce petitions were becoming "increasingly frequent," took up too much of the legislature's time, and "involve[d] investigations more properly judicial in their nature." The state constitution of 1851 provided that the General Assembly would no longer pass private acts for divorce for any reason. See Riley, "Legislative Divorce in Virginia," 52–53; *Acts of the General Assembly of Virginia, 1802–1803*, ch. 64, pp. 46–47; *1826–1827*, ch. 23, pp. 21–22; *1840–1841*, ch. 71, pp. 78–79; and *1847–1848*, ch. 122, pp. 165–67. On divorce in the antebellum United States generally, see Phillips, *Putting Asunder*, esp. 439–61; Riley, *Divorce*, 34–84; and Hindus and Withey, "Law of Husband and Wife." On divorce in the antebellum South and in Virginia specifically, see also Buckley, *Great Catastrophe*; Censer, "'Smiling through Her Tears'"; Stevenson, *Life in Black and White*, ch. 5; Bardaglio, *Reconstructing the Household*, 32–34; Wyatt-Brown, *Southern Honor*, 283–91 and 300–306; and Lebsock, *Free Women of Petersburg*, 68–72. Books and articles on divorce in particular states other than Virginia in the colonial and antebellum periods are numerous. They include Cott, "Divorce and the Changing Status of Women"; Goodheart, Hanks, and Johnson, "'An Act for the Relief of Females'"; Basch, *Framing American Divorce*; Merril Smith, *Breaking the Bonds*; and Chused, *Private Acts in Public Places*.

4. In his study of divorce in early national and antebellum Virginia, Thomas E. Buckley found that among all 583 petitions submitted to the legislature, 53 contained accusations of interracial adultery. That there were 53 (rather than 43) total petitions of this nature reflects the reality that some men and women repeated requests for divorce after being turned down. All told, 460 individuals submitted divorce petitions. Using either standard of measurement (total petitions or total petitioners), interracial adultery was a factor in around 9 percent of Virginia divorce petitions. Interestingly, among divorce applications between 1800 and 1835 in neighboring North Carolina, just under 8 percent included mentions of adultery with African Americans. Of the 153 total legislative divorces in Virginia, 129 were complete divorces, while 24 were separation agreements or divorces that were conditional in some other fashion. See Buckley, *Great Catastrophe*, introd., ch. 4, and appendix; and Riley, *Divorce*, 35.

5. Glenda Riley, for example, writes that sexual liaisons involving enslaved men and white wives were "transgression[s] so serious that even opponents of divorce could see that these marriages could not continue." Thomas E. Buckley writes in a similar vein in connection with the divorce case of Evelina Roane in 1824. The

most harmful charge in Roane's divorce petition, Buckley maintains, was that her husband had an affair with a slave and had made the enslaved woman the effective mistress of the house. "The charges of physical brutality and psychological torture were serious but not unusual. The legislators heard such cases virtually every year. It was the race question that struck at the taproot of their society." See Riley, "Legislative Divorce in Virginia," 57; and Buckley, " 'Placed in the Power of Violence,' " 36.

6. Petition of Richard Hall, Orange County #11955, January 29, 1838, LP-LOV.

7. Petition of Isaac Fouch, Loudoun County #5321a, December 22, 1808, LP-LOV.

8. Petition of Dabney Pettus, Fluvanna County #4472, December 13, 1802, LP-LOV.

9. Petition of Isaac Fouch. On "companionate" marriage in Virginia, see Stevenson, *Life in Black and White*, 47–50; and Lebsock, *Free Women of Petersburg*, 28–35. Bertram Wyatt-Brown, who focuses his study on southern elites, sees economic strategies still playing a significant role in antebellum marriages, but does not deny that mutual affection became increasingly important for married couples in the nineteenth century (*Southern Honor*, ch. 8). For a discussion of marital expectations in neighboring Pennsylvania, see Merril Smith, *Breaking the Bonds*, ch. 2.

10. Petition of Lewis Bourn, Louisa County #8218 and #8305, December 16, 1824, and January 20, 1825, LP-LOV. Petition #8218 contains Lewis Bourn's statement to the legislature, while #8305 consists mostly of affidavits and other documents. Unless otherwise noted, all citations are from #8218. Martha Hodes explores the marriage and divorce of Lewis and Dorothea (Dolly) Bourn at length and mentions some of the other divorce cases discussed here in *White Women, Black Men*, ch. 4.

11. Petition of Thomas Cain, Frederick County #13079, January 9, 1841, LP-LOV.

12. Petition of William Pruden, Nansemond County #13024, December 14, 1840, LP-LOV.

13. Petition of Richard Jones, Northampton County #6364, November 2, 1814, LP-LOV.

14. Petition of William Baylis, Fairfax County #9781, December 8, 1831, LP-LOV; and Petition of Joseph Gresham, James City County #10403, December 10, 1833, LP-LOV.

15. Petition of Lewis Bourn.

16. Petition of Bryant Rawls, Nansemond County #13025, December 14, 1840, LP-LOV.

17. Petition of Isaac Fouch.

18. Censer, " 'Smiling through Her Tears,' " 37.

19. Petition of Joseph Gresham.

20. Wyatt-Brown, *Southern Honor*. In *Honor and Slavery*, Kenneth Greenberg places a greater emphasis than Wyatt-Brown on how white male honor depended on the dishonor of slaves. Given the important links between race and gender dependencies and hierarchies in the early national and antebellum South, these arguments need not be mutually exclusive.

21. Petition of Ayres Tatham, Accomac County #4888, December 13, 1805, LP-LOV.

22. Petition of David Parker, Nansemond County #8683, December 8, 1826, LP-LOV.

23. Petition of Joseph Gresham.

24. Petition of Thomas Cain.

25. Petition of Leonard Owen, Patrick County #5424, December 11, 1809, LP-LOV.

26. Bardaglio, *Reconstructing the Household*, 48–64; Higginbotham and Kopytoff, "Racial Purity and Interracial Sex"; and Getman, "Sexual Control in the Slaveholding South."

27. Petition of William Howard, Amherst County #5202, December 23, 1807, LP-LOV.

28. Petition of William Howard, Amherst County #5370, December 6, 1809, LP-LOV. Neither of Howard's approaches worked. He was denied a divorce again.

29. Petition of Bryant Rawls.

30. As Brenda Stevenson argues, for example, "more than any other act, voluntary biracial sex between a white woman and a black man unquestionably alienated the woman from her community. . . . [A]dultery deemed her no longer white or female, but some monstrous other." Similarly, Victoria Bynum writes that "a white woman who willingly entered a miscegenous relationship forfeited the respect of her community and was shunned by respectable women, who feared that contact with her might also taint them." See Stevenson, *Life in Black and White*, 144; and Bynum, *Unruly Women*, 45. For the most part, scholars discussing the attitude of white southerners toward sexual relationships between white women and black men in the early national and antebellum periods reach conclusions similar to those of Stevenson and Bynum. My own reading lies more along the lines suggested by Martha Hodes. Hodes argues that sex between black men and white women was certainly not deemed socially acceptable or even as acceptable as sex between white men and black women, and agrees that "the female transgressors were judged and ostracized." Still, she writes that such women were not necessarily treated any worse than white women "who had transgressed with a white man," and that "white Southerners could respond to sexual liaisons between white women and black men with a measure of toleration." See Hodes, *White Women, Black Men*, 121, 1. Also see Buckley, "Unfixing Race"; and Mills, "Miscegenation and the Free Negro."

31. Petitions of Thomas Cain, Lewis Bourn, and Richard Hall.

32. There were a few instances where such sentiment did appear. Isaac Fouch was the only man who admitted that even after he had caught his wife on multiple occasions in bed with a free man of color named James Watt, he had tried to get his wife to return to his home in the hope "that she might yet be reclaimed." Lewis Bourn indicated that his wife Dorothea continued in her adultery "in spite of the remonstrances and persuasions of your petitioner." While not as overt as Fouch's statement, this assertion may imply that Bourn would have been willing to take his wife back had she ceased her adulterous affair. Elizabeth Meryman testified in the case of Dabney Pettus that she heard him forgive his wife Elizabeth for her adultery

with a slave. But Meryman also stated that she never heard Pettus say that he would ever live with his wife again. William Howard, meanwhile, wrote in his first petition that "(being willing to forgive past offences) [he] repeatedly solicited and prayed" for his wife to come home. But after he discovered Elizabeth in the embrace of a man of color, he wrote in his second petition, "an immediate separation took place" between the Howards. Petition of Isaac Fouch; Petition of Lewis Bourn; affidavit of Elizabeth Meryman, December 2, 1803, in Petition of Dabney Pettus; and Petitions of William Howard.

33. David Garland et al., undated certificate of support, in second petition of William Howard, Amherst County #5370, December 6, 1809.

34. For examples of testimony from midwives, see the deposition of Elizabeth Holstead in petition of Benjamin Butt, Norfolk County #4594, December 7, 1803, LP-LOV, or that of Christenah Heartman, November 11, 1812, in petition of John Cook, Boutetourt County #6014, December 2, 1812, LP-LOV. Jane Campbell gave testimony that she had lived with the Fouch family for five months and, looking through a hole in a house wall, had seen Elizabeth Fouch and James Watt "several times in the very act" (Deposition of Jane Campbell, December 8, 1808, in petition of Isaac Fouch). Two friends of Richard Jones deposed that the daughter born to Jones's wife Peggy was "the offspring of sd. Peggy Jones by a Black Man — that the whole Features of the face the colour of the skin the formation of its Limbs and state of its hair all indicate it to be the issue of a black Man" (Depositions of John Tyson and Thomas Wingate, October 17, 1814, in petition of Richard Jones).

35. Petition of Richard Jones.

36. Deposition of Steurman Kinzer, November 28, 1837, in petition of Richard Hall; and Thomas Anderson et al., certificate of support, January 1824, in petition of Lewis Bourn, Louisa County #8305, January 20, 1825.

37. Aside from the examples of Tabitha Tatham and Jane Parker mentioned earlier, also see the petitions of Abraham Newton of Fauquier County and William Rucker of Allegheny County, both of whose wives left Virginia for Ohio after having children with African American men. Petition of Abraham Newton, Fauquier County #6729, November 16, 1816; and depositions of Matthew Mayse and Thomas Mayse, February 23, 1849, in Petition of William Rucker, Allegheny County #16648, March 5, 1849, both in LP-LOV.

38. Women's voices in the petitions of their husbands rarely appear, although Joseph Gresham's wife Sarah tried unsuccessfully to protest his divorce petition by claiming Joseph was impotent. Dorothea Bourn defended herself by calling into question the financial motives of her husband's brother William, whom she believed had instigated the divorce proceedings. Caroline Culpepper, meanwhile, in a curious gambit, tried to evade being found guilty of adultery by arguing that she and Thomas Culpepper had never been married. She also tried casting a shadow on Thomas's reputation, arguing that he had seduced her "previous to the time of the supposed marriage" and that he was already "living in a state of illicit intercourse with another woman" by the time of the Culpeppers' divorce hearing. In one particularly remarkable instance of a woman responding to her husband's

actions against her, Betsy Mosby, whose husband Hezekiah filed a petition for divorce against her in 1815, marched with her newborn child (borne to an African American lover) up to her husband, who was speaking to a visitor. When the visitor commented on the child's racial background, Betsy replied that she "had not been the first, nor would she be the last guilty of such an act, and that she saw no more harm in a white woman's having a black child than in a white man's having one, though the latter was more frequent." James City County Circuit Superior Court of Law and Chancery proceedings, October 25, 1833, included with petition of Joseph Gresham; undated statement of Doritha Bourn, in petition of Lewis Bourn, Louisa County #8305, January 20, 1825; plea of Caroline Johnson, made in Norfolk County court, November 10, 1835, in petition of Thomas Culpepper; and undated deposition of Thomas Miller, in petition of Hezekiah Mosby, Powhatan County #6428, December 6, 1815, LP-LOV.

39. Petition of Lewis Bourn.

40. Hodes, *White Women, Black Men*, 68. Cf. Stevenson, *Life in Black and White*, 141–43.

41. Petition of William Rucker.

42. Petition of Isaac Fouch.

43. Petition of Bryant Rawls.

44. Petition of Richard Jones.

45. Petition of Lewis Bourn.

46. Petition of William Baylis.

47. Amherst County Circuit Superior Court of Law and Chancery proceedings, September 11, 1834, included with petition of Lucy Watts, Amherst County #10681, December 8, 1834, LP-LOV.

48. Petition of Sopha Dobyns, Bedford County #A1741, December 16, 1817, LP-LOV.

49. Petition of Charlotte Ball, Culpeper County #5018, December 9, 1806, LP-LOV. On property and married women, and on the connection between marriage and financial concerns, see Lebsock, *Free Women of Petersburg*, chs. 2–3.

50. Campbell County Circuit Superior Court of Law and Chancery proceedings, September 1841, included with petition of Sarah Robinson, Campbell County #13237, December 7, 1841, LP-LOV.

51. Petition of Janet Hunter, Petersburg City #8074a, December 15, 1823, LP-LOV.

52. Petition of Elizabeth Harwell, Petersburg City #7546, December 13, 1820, LP-LOV.

53. Petition of Lucy Norman, Henry County #16315, December 20, 1848, LP-LOV.

54. Petition of Janet Hunter.

55. King William County Circuit Superior Court of Law and Chancery proceedings, November 17, 1835, included with petition of Ann Eliza Eubank, King William County #11312, December 9, 1836, LP-LOV.

56. Petition of Sarah Womack, Halifax County #16137, March 1, 1848, LP-LOV.

57. Henrico County Superior Court of Law proceedings, August 16, 1828, included with petition of Mary Alvis, Richmond City #9080, December 4, 1828, LP-LOV.

58. Petitions of Nancy Rowland, Henry County #7507 (first quotation) and #7643 (second quotation), December 7, 1820, and December 7, 1821, LP-LOV.

59. Petition of Mary Terry, Goochland County #17611, February 2, 1851, LP-LOV.

60. Petition of Ellen Dunlap, Augusta County #6300c, October 12, 1814, LP-LOV. Also see affidavits of James and Thomas Shields, Rachel and Peggy Shields, October 1, 1814, and Samuel Torbet, October 4, 1814, included with Dunlap's petition.

61. Amherst court proceedings, in petition of Lucy Watts.

62. On the prevalence of men's violence against their wives in Western cultures, see Phillips, *Putting Asunder*, 323–44.

63. Ibid., 344–54. In a study of divorce in Pennsylvania, Merril Smith discovered that women were actually slightly more successful than men in procuring a divorce based only on the accusation of adultery. But Smith does acknowledge that awareness of the double standard may have meant that "women believed they would be unsuccessful in gaining a divorce on the basis of their husband's infidelity alone" (*Breaking the Bonds*, 85).

64. Petition of Mary Terry.

65. Petition of Janet Hunter.

66. First petition of Nancy Rowland, Henry County #7507, December 7, 1820.

67. Petition of Lucy Norman. Also see undated depositions of Wilmouth Edwards, Catherine Carter, and Elizabeth Murphy, included with Norman's petition.

68. Censer, " 'Smiling through Her Tears,' " 37. Also see Bardaglio, *Reconstructing the Household*, 34.

69. Petition of Charlotte Ball.

70. Petition of Elizabeth Harwell.

71. Petition of Janet Hunter.

72. King William court proceedings, in petition of Ann Eliza Eubank.

73. Petition of Mary Lawry, Culpeper County #13726, January 8, 1843, LP-LOV.

74. Campbell court proceedings, in petition of Sarah Robinson.

75. Petition of Sopha Dobyns, and affidavit of Stephen Terry, August 27, 1817, included with petition of Dobyns.

76. Discussion of the double standard with respect to interracial sex pervades scholarly accounts of such activity. See, for example, Catherine Clinton, " 'Southern Dishonor,' " in Bleser, *In Joy and in Sorrow*, 52–68; Wyatt-Brown, *Southern Honor*, 307–24; and Getman, "Sexual Control in the Slaveholding South."

77. Petition of Evelina Roane, King William County #8122, December 2, 1824, LP-LOV.

78. Petition of Elizabeth Harwell, and affidavit of Wiley Rosser, November 30, 1820, in petition of Harwell.

79. Undated depositions of Elizabeth Murphy and Wilmouth Edwards, included in petition of Lucy Norman.

80. Petition of Elizabeth Pannill.

81. Petition of Lucy Norman.

82. Joseph Almandis et al., undated certificate of support, in first petition of Nancy Rowland, Henry County #7507, December 7, 1820; and James Rea Snr. et al., undated certificate of support, in second petition of Nancy Rowland, Henry County #7643, December 7, 1821.

83. A rare exception appeared in the petition of Charlotte Ball, whose neighbor Ann Moore testified to a pattern of physical abuse on the part of Ball's husband. In the course of her deposition, Moore also noted that "she considered the said Charlotte to be a very discrete honest woman, and a woman who wished to do well for her family." Even in this instance, however, such a statement was incidental to the more significant reason for Moore's testimony—simply to tell what she had witnessed. Deposition of Ann Moore, November 3, 1806, in petition of Charlotte Ball.

84. Nancy Rowland, for example, waited five years after her husband's mistreatment of her began before petitioning the legislature, while Charlotte Ball waited six years, and Janet Hunter waited nine (Petitions of Nancy Rowland, Charlotte Ball, and Janet Hunter).

85. Petition of Janet Hunter.

86. Petition of Elizabeth Harwell.

87. Petition of Evelina Roane. Thomas Buckley's study of this case follows Evelina beyond her divorce, demonstrating that Virginia women who petitioned for divorce were not always or entirely the weak and needy figures they often implied (" 'Placed in the Power of Violence,' " 65–78).

88. *Acts of the General Assembly of Virginia, 1803–1851*; and Buckley, *Great Catastrophe*, ch. 4. In addition, the legislature passed a bill authorizing Hezekiah Mosby to take his case to court and procure a divorce from his wife Betsy (*Acts of the General Assembly of Virginia, 1815–1816*, ch. 135, pp. 246–47).

89. Buckley, *Great Catastrophe*, appendix.

90. See, for example, the committee's recommendation on the petition of John Cook (*Journal of the House of Delegates, 1812–1813*, p. 39) or the act divorcing Daniel Rose from his wife (*Acts of the General Assembly of Virginia, 1806–1807*, ch. 59, p. 26).

91. Michael Grossberg, for example, suggests that "racism successfully and consistently overcame the law's powerful biases toward the promotion of matrimony. In the clash between racism and nuptial freedom, the latter always gave way" (*Governing the Hearth*, 126).

92. Even in cases where interracial adultery was not an issue, lawmakers did not always disclose why they rejected divorce petitions. Sometimes the Committee of Courts of Justice cited the complaints of the petitioner but rejected the petition without explanation. After 1827 the committee sometimes recommended that petitions be rejected because they failed to include jury findings or to conform to some other aspect of the required legal proceedings; see, for example, *Journal of the House of Delegates, 1816–1817*, pp. 31, 33, and 59; *1831–1832*, p. 146; and *1847–1848*, pp. 46–47, 71, and 140. On rare occasions, Richmond newspapers recorded

the concerns of delegates over particular divorce bills. For example, when Nancy Peyton tried to divorce her husband Valentine in 1850, her bill came to a vote, whereupon James B. Dorman of Rockbridge County announced that "the bill in his judgment, contained a principle which was highly offensive both to law and good morals; one which his judgment did not approve." The bill failed by a vote of 7 to 100. *Richmond Whig*, February 5, 1850. Also see debates over two divorce petitions, recorded in the *Richmond Enquirer*, February 21, 1833.

93. *Journal of the House of Delegates, 1815–1816*, p. 82.

94. Ruffin, quoted in Bardaglio, *Reconstructing the Household*, 63.

95. Bynum, *Unruly Women*, 70. On the resistance of state officials to granting divorces in order to keep the white family — and, by extension, the social order — intact, also see Hodes, *White Women, Black Men*, 68, 76, 114–15.

96. Ruffin, quoted in Bardaglio, *Reconstructing the Household*, 63. On the Scroggins and Barden cases, also see Hodes, *White Women, Black Men*, 52, 54, 75–76; Bynum, *Unruly Women*, 69; and Victoria Bynum, "Reshaping the Bonds of Womanhood," in Clinton and Silber, *Divided Houses*, 322–23.

97. The notion that marriage was a contract became prevalent in postrevolutionary America. This idea reflected, in the words of Michael Grossberg, "the broader use of contract as the central metaphor for social and economic relations in early nineteenth-century America" and eroded the colonial-era emphasis on hierarchy in marriage. Southerners seem to have held on to patriarchal ideas of matrimony for longer than northerners, although ideas about marriage as a reciprocal contractual arrangement certainly pervaded the minds of many southerners as well. As Bardaglio writes, white southerners "shared with the broader Victorian culture a growing emphasis on affectionate love between husband and wife. . . . At the same time, however, white southerners clung to traditional notions of patriarchal authority that stressed the importance of harmony, dependency, and hierarchy. . . . Southern whites, in short, found themselves caught between contradictory impulses." See Grossberg, *Governing the Hearth*, 18–24, quotation on 19; and Bardaglio, *Reconstructing the Household*, xiii–xiv.

98. Petition of William Bartlam, Chesterfield County #14152, December 10, 1844, LP-LOV.

99. Petition of Polly Carver, Pittsylvania County #7431, December 16, 1819, LP-LOV.

100. *Journal of the House of Delegates, 1835–1836*, p. 135.

101. *Journal of the House of Delegates, 1838*, p. 298; *Acts of the General Assembly of Virginia, 1838*, ch. 303, p. 220.

INTERLUDE: THE MYSTERIES OF WILLIAM CARLTON

1. Petition of Lewis Bourn, Louisa County #8218, December 16, 1824, Legislative Petitions, Library of Virginia, Richmond (hereafter LP-LOV). Also see affidavits of George Bourn, November 25, 1823; William Kimbrough, November 25, 1823; Wilson Sayne, January 28, 1824; Thomas Pulliam, January 29, 1824; John Richardson, January 18, 1825; Thomas Sayne, January 29, 1824; and Thomas Anderson, January 23, 1824, included with petition of Lewis Bourn, Louisa County

#8305, January 20, 1825, LP-LOV; and Hodes, *White Women, Black Men*, 94–95. "White slaves" also served as staples of abolitionist travel narratives, newspaper propaganda, and fiction. Studies of literature that invoked interracial sex, individuals of mixed race, and the literary themes of "passing" and the "tragic mulatto" are voluminous and constantly growing. A select list of works includes Sollors, *Neither Black nor White yet Both*; Ginsberg, *Passing and the Fictions of Identity*; and Kinney, *Amalgamation!*

2. *Watkins and Wife v. Carlton*, 10 Leigh 560 (Va. 1840); and King and Queen County Order Book, 1831–58, pp. 45, 46, and 51. One can only wonder about the familial dynamics among the Carltons while John Carlton lived, but we can speculate that calling them strained understates the matter significantly. It seems likely that suspicion about Sarah Carlton's sexual behavior played some role in John Carlton's decision to leave his wife and her youngest son out of his will, and perhaps bore some relationship to his insanity as well. Moreover, simply by bringing her lawsuit, Mary Watkins effectively accused her mother of adultery with an African American, and made that accusation a matter of public record. For an analysis of a similar inheritance lawsuit in which determining the racial identity of a child and his parents was a central issue, see Martha Hodes's discussion of the case of Georgia's Franklin Hugly in *White Women, Black Men*, 108–16.

3. *Watkins and Wife v. Carlton*, at 561–65, quotations at 562 and 565.

4. Ibid., at 563–65; and Essex County Order Book 1, October 26, 1837, pp. 145–46 (quotation on 145); and September 28, 1838, pp. 168–71.

5. *Watkins and Wife v. Carlton*, at 566–68, quotation at 567.

6. Ibid., at 568–70.

7. Ibid., at 574–77, quotation at 577.

8. Essex County Order Book 1, April 28, 1841, pp. 224–26.

CHAPTER SIX

1. Richmond Police Guard Day Book, 1834–43, MSS 1481, Alderman Library, University of Virginia. All spellings are transcribed exactly, except for the word "mulatto," which was sometimes written with a single "t." In law, "mulatto" described an imagined biological category, but antebellum Virginians clearly utilized the term to connote a broad color distinction as well as a genetic one.

2. Martha Hodes lists sixteen different color descriptions used in 1862 by slave owners in Washington to describe their slaves, including several terms not mentioned here (*White Women, Black Men*, 97). One can only imagine how lengthy a comprehensive tally of color descriptions might be, particularly when one considers the subregionally specific usages of terms like "griffe" or "mestizo."

3. Hening, *The Statutes at Large*, 3:250–52 (1705, ch. 4). The act also placed in the mulatto category anyone with one Native American parent. Although "mulatto" only entered the legal code in 1705, Leon Higginbotham and Barbara Kopytoff have found the word in print in the minutes of the Virginia Council and General Court as early as 1655, and Thomas Morris notes that the word began to be used in English sometime around 1600. See Higginbotham and Kopytoff, "Racial Purity and Interracial Sex," 1976–77 n. 44; and Morris, *Southern Slavery and the*

Law, 22. Attitudes of southern whites toward people of mixed race varied in place and time. Some whites viewed slaves of mixed race favorably in the belief that they possessed superior intelligence and beauty as a consequence of their "white blood." Additionally, in the Deep South, mixed ancestry seems to have been of significant importance to whites and blacks alike in determining the status of free people of color. Nonetheless, in Virginia, whatever the preferred treatment slaves of mixed race may or may not have received, such treatment was only relative to that of other slaves. The general presumption of whites was that dark skin, whether on an enslaved person or a free person of color, signified inferiority. On attitudes toward people of mixed ancestry, see Toplin, "Between Black and White"; Berlin, *Slaves without Masters*, 109–10, 151–52, 177–81, 195–98, 247–48, and 267–68; and Johnston, *Race Relations in Virginia*, part 3, esp. ch. 12. Joel Williamson draws attention to attitudinal differences between the Upper and Lower South in *New People*, 14–24, as does Berlin in *Slaves without Masters*, ch. 6. Also see Johnson and Roark, *Black Masters*, 59–64; and Mills, *Forgotten People*. Walter Johnson offers a brilliant analysis of how slave owners crafted their own identities by projecting meaning onto the varying skin tones (and more broadly onto the bodies) of the slaves they purchased in *Soul by Soul*, esp. ch. 5. Less studied, but no less significant, are the import and meaning of distinctions of color within the enslaved and free African American communities and how they affected individual and collective black identity before the Civil War. A sustained discussion of such issues is beyond the scope of this chapter. For a number of recent works grappling with these questions, see Gomez, *Exchanging Our Country Marks*, 214–43; and Horton, *Free People of Color*, ch. 6. Also see Berlin, *Slaves without Masters*, 56–58, 177–81, and 269–83; Johnson and Roark, *Black Masters*, esp. ch. 6; and Dominguez, *White by Definition*.

4. In 1849, the General Assembly amended state law such that for all legal purposes the word "negro" entailed "mulatto," codifying what had long been common practice (*Code of Virginia* [1849], p. 458, ch. 103, sec. 3). In contemporary America, the term "mixed blood" is generally associated with individuals of some Native American ancestry. While a desire to define the racial status of those descended from Native Americans may have played some role in why antebellum white Virginians created the category of "mixed blood," the legal definition of the term as constructed in the 1830s made no specific reference to Native Americans (see notes 15 and 16). Moreover, it is clear that in the 1850s the controversy over the term and its significance grew specifically out of white concern about the ability of those with African ancestry to occupy an ambiguous racial position.

5. Hodes, *White Women, Black Men*, 98–99.

6. It has become a standard trope of historical treatments of race that the category itself is a fiction, constructed socially, legally, culturally, economically, and in a multitude of other ways. This chapter contributes to an understanding of the constructive process, mostly at the social and legal levels, as the process of determining the positions of persons of ambiguous race shows white Virginians overtly and repeatedly recreating race. Barbara Fields's famous essays are useful places to begin a historical investigation of the concept of race as a constructed category in

the United States, although a scholarly understanding of race as a fiction goes back at least to the work of W. E. B. DuBois. The debate over the chronological precedence of race or slavery in the American colonies implicitly engages this matter. Works discussing particularly the construction of "whiteness," though mostly not in the antebellum South, have become increasingly numerous of late, in the spirit of "critical race theory," whose foundational premise is the examination of racial construction. See Fields, "Slavery, Race, and Ideology," and "Ideology and Race in American History." Also see Holt, "Marking." On the origins of race and racism in the colonial period, see Winthrop Jordan, *White over Black*; Kathleen Brown, *Good Wives*; Edmund Morgan, *American Slavery, American Freedom*, esp. 295–337; Fredrickson, *Arrogance of Race*, ch. 13; and Vaughan, "The Origins Debate." Some important recent works on the historical construction of whiteness include Walter Johnson, *Soul by Soul*; Bay, *White Image in the Black Mind*; Hale, *Making Whiteness*; Allen, *Invention of the White Race*; Haney Lopez, *White by Law*; Lott, *Love and Theft*; and Roediger, *Wages of Whiteness*.

7. On racial intermixture in the colonial Chesapeake, see Breen and Innes, *"Myne Owne Ground"*; Deal, *Race and Class in Colonial Virginia*; Hodes, *White Women, Black Men*, ch. 2; essays by Diane Miller Sommerville and Paul Finkelman in Clinton and Gillespie, *The Devil's Lane*, 74–89 and 124–35; Philip Morgan, *Slave Counterpoint*, 398–405; Higginbotham and Kopytoff, "Racial Purity and Interracial Sex"; Winthrop Jordan, *White over Black*, esp. chs. 2 and 4; and Kathleen Brown, *Good Wives*.

8. Higginbotham and Kopytoff, "Racial Purity and Interracial Sex," 1981.

9. Wallenstein, "Race, Marriage, and the Law of Freedom," 392 n. 99; and Higginbotham and Kopytoff, "Racial Purity and Interracial Sex," 1978. On the importance of Bacon's Rebellion and the politics of class to the construction of race in colonial Virginia, see Edmund Morgan, *American Slavery, American Freedom*, chs. 15–16. Kathleen Brown sees the rebellion additionally as an important turning point in restoring gender order. See Brown, *Good Wives*, ch. 5.

10. Hening, *The Statutes at Large*, 12:184 (1785, ch. 78).

11. Both Higginbotham and Kopytoff and James Johnston suggest the latter possibility. Higginbotham and Kopytoff suggest that by 1785 "mulatto" technically might have even applied to some "white men of power and position." See Higginbotham and Kopytoff, "Racial Purity and Interracial Sex," 1979; and Johnston, *Race Relations in Virginia*, 193–94.

12. Hening, *The Statutes at Large*, 12:184 (1785, ch. 78). Unlike the 1705 law, the 1785 legislation made no reference to Native American ancestry.

13. *Acts of the General Assembly of Virginia, 1831–1832*, ch. 22.

14. *Journal of the House of Delegates, 1832–1833*, January 29, 1833, p. 131. Also see *Richmond Enquirer*, January 31, 1833.

15. *Journal of the House of Delegates, 1832–1833*, March 6, 1833, p. 259; *Acts of the General Assembly of Virginia, 1832–1833*, ch. 80. Curiously, although John Murdaugh explicitly mentioned Native Americans when proposing his plan to the General Assembly, the final legislation did not.

16. Higginbotham and Kopytoff suggest the 1833 law's only real purpose re-

lated to the status of Native Americans and their descendants and looked to distinguish them from African Americans. Ira Berlin, meanwhile, stresses the desire to allow light-skinned free people of color to escape the harsh new restrictions of the 1830s as a motivation behind the law. The important point here is less the particular purpose of the law, which cannot be known for certain, so much as how the law generally both drew attention to racial ambiguity and, in its failure to be entirely specific as to the meaning of being a "free person of mixed blood," perpetuated it, leading to confusion in the 1850s that the legislature had not anticipated. See Higginbotham and Kopytoff, "Racial Purity and Interracial Sex," 1984–85 n. 78; and Berlin, *Slaves without Masters*, 162.

17. Petition of sundry Inhabitants of the County of Stafford praying that Wm. Horton and others *free white persons* who have acquired title to their freedom since 1806 may be permitted to remain in this Commonwealth, Stafford County #10243, January 14, 1833, Legislative Petitions, Library of Virginia, Richmond (hereafter LP-LOV).

18. Ibid.

19. Cases like these were hardly exclusive to Virginia. In Louisiana in 1857, for example, a woman named Alexina Morrison was sold as a slave but sued for her freedom, claiming that she was born free and to white parents. As Walter Johnson notes, her case "posed a troubling double question: Could slaves become white? And could white people become slaves?" ("Slave Trader," 16).

20. See Gross, "Litigating Whiteness." For the most part, Gross found appellate cases from states across the South involving racial determination and uses the testimony and evidence from the original lawsuits to make her argument. In Virginia, if a case reached the General Court, the court papers from the original suits passed up as well, but all such papers burned in a fire during the Civil War. Only the opinions delivered by the General Court remain on record. They usually included some indication of the kinds of evidence at play, and some of these cases are discussed later in this chapter. Cases dealing with the matter of racial definition also appeared at the local level but can only be found by happenstance or by rooting through the court papers of local county courts. This process is both time-consuming and rarely rewarding, because even on finding such cases the courtroom testimony is infrequently extant. Instead, I have relied mostly on legislative petitions in which racial definition was an issue as a means of discussing communal understandings of the social position of people of mixed race. Gross also draws attention to the importance of gender differences in cases of racial determination, and argues that where men might "perform white manhood" by demonstrating they exercised the rights of white men, women could never make such a demonstration. Instead, their racial definition turned on their beauty and their moral character in addition to their appearance. Although Nancy Wharton was included in the petition from Stafford County, these kinds of issues were not alluded to by the petitioners. On racial determination trials and race as a performance and a matter of self-presentation, also see Walter Johnson, "Slave Trader"; and Hodes, *White Women, Black Men*, 98–108.

21. Petition by Betty Dean and others to stay in state, Amherst County #5818, December 4, 1811, LP-LOV.

22. Dillard Gordon's Petition, Essex County #8468, December 15, 1825, LP-LOV.

23. *Journal of the House of Delegates, 1832–1833*, March 9, 1833, p. 265; *Acts of the General Assembly of Virginia, 1832–1833*, ch. 243.

24. *Chaney v. Saunders*, 3 Munf. 51 (Va. 1811).

25. *Dean v. Commonwealth*, 4 Gratt. 541 (Va. 1847). Quotation at 541.

26. As Martha Hodes concludes in her discussion of cases of racial ambiguity, "what emerges so strikingly in these cases is the ability of white people residing in such close proximity to live with enormous contradictions. Although the law insisted on formal categories of race, white neighbors were willing not only to determine racial status on an ad hoc basis but also to disagree among themselves on such matters" (*White Women, Black Men*, 98). Also see Gross, "Litigating Whiteness," 158–76; and Walter Johnson, "Slave Trader," 20–29.

27. On black laws in Ohio, see Middleton, *Black Laws in the Old Northwest*; Gerber, *Black Ohio and the Color Line*, 3–7; and "Race Hate in Early Ohio."

28. Had Hyden been able to prove successfully that he was free, by law the court would have been required only to make sure he left Virginia within ten days. As it was, the court order of his sale described him as "William a negro man slave" (*Revised Code of the Laws of Virginia* [1819], ch. 111, sec. 64; *Code of Virginia* [1849], ch. 198, secs. 26 and 28; and Prince William County Minute Book, 1833–36, December 2, 1833, p. 79). All material in this section, unless otherwise indicated, is derived from the petition of Basil Brawner and accompanying affidavits of James Fewell and M. B. Finelain, Prince William County #10906, February 20, 1835, LP-LOV.

29. If a runaway slave was sold at auction, after paying jailer's fees, a reward for whoever arrested the runaway, and a 5 percent commission to Brawner as the officer of the court in charge of the sale, whatever money remained was to be turned over to the state treasury. Without any money coming in for William Hyden, Brawner had to pay the state out of his own pocket unless the General Assembly decided to accept his plea.

30. Brawner's petition was forwarded to the Committee for Claims in the House of Delegates and was rejected in March 1835 (*Journal of the House of Delegates, 1834–1835*, February 20 and March 5, 1835, pp. 167 and 214).

31. Walter Johnson, "Slave Trader," 16.

32. *Chaney v. Saunders*, 3 Munf. 51 (Va. 1811). Quotation at 52.

33. Ibid. Quotation at 53.

34. *Dean v. Commonwealth*, 4 Gratt. 541 (Va. 1847). Quotations at 541. Also see Culpeper County Law Order Book 4, pp. 259, 260, 265, 266, and 273.

35. *Dean v. Commonwealth*, 4 Gratt. 541 (Va. 1847). Quotation at 543.

36. Culpeper County Law Order Book 4, pp. 300, 304, and 306.

37. The precise relation of the Wrights to Butterwood Nan is unclear from the opinion of the General Court. They were direct descendants, and witnesses testified that Butterwood Nan was at least sixty years old in 1755. Both she and Hannah

are written of in the past tense, suggesting they were both dead by 1805, but Jacky Wright's mother appeared with her in court that year. While it is possible there was a generation between Hannah and Jacky Wright's mother, it seems most likely that Butterwood Nan was Jacky Wright's great-grandmother and Hannah her grandmother. *Hudgins v. Wrights*, 1 Hen. and M. 134 (Va. 1806), esp. at 134, 137, 142, and 143 (quotations at 134 and 142); and Virginia Supreme Court of Appeals (Richmond City), Order Book 5 (1804–7), pp. 345 and 348.

38. *Hudgins v. Wrights*, at 134. Cases of enslaved Native Americans and their descendants suing for freedom appeared dozens of time before the General Court alone throughout the late eighteenth century, although they seem mostly to have petered out around the end of the second decade of the nineteenth century. They often turned on complex issues of slave law as it related to Native Americans as well as on issues of pedigree and descent. Usually, if racial intermixture was an issue, it was between African Americans and Native Americans. See, for just a few examples, *Robin v. Hardaway*, Jefferson 109 (Va. 1772); *Jenkins v. Tom*, 1 Washington 123 (Va. 1792); *Coleman v. Dick and Pat*, 1 Washington 233 (Va. 1793); *Pegram v. Isabell*, 2 Hen. and M. 194 (Va. 1808); and *Hook v. Nanny Pagee and Her Children*, 2 Munf. 379 (Va. 1811). In one of the last cases of this sort in 1827, the justices made important distinctions about what kinds of evidence regarding pedigree were considered hearsay. See *Gregory v. Baugh*, 4 Randolph 612 (Va. 1827). For a more comprehensive list of cases, see Catterall, *Judicial Cases*, 1:99–166. Also see Peter Wallenstein, "Indian Foremothers," in Clinton and Gillespie, *The Devil's Lane*, 57–73.

39. *Hudgins v. Wrights*, at 142.

40. Ibid., at 136.

41. Ibid., at 141. On the importance of *Hudgins v. Wrights*, see Wallenstein, "Indian Foremothers," 65–69; Gross, "Litigating Whiteness," 129–30; Adrienne Davis, "Identity Notes Part One," 702–17, esp. 702–10; Haney Lopez, "Social Construction of Race," 1–5, 61–62; and Higginbotham and Kopytoff, "Racial Purity and Interracial Sex," 1985–88. On the matter of legal presumption and the servile status of individuals of mixed ancestry throughout the South, see Morris, *Southern Slavery and the Law*, 21–29.

42. *Hudgins v. Wrights*, at 139 and 141.

43. Ibid., at 139.

44. Ibid., at 141.

45. Ibid.

46. On the pressures against free people of color and racial anxieties in the 1850s, see Berlin, *Slaves without Masters*, ch. 11; Williamson, *New People*, 61–75; Johnson and Roark, *Black Masters*, chs. 5 and 7; Bogger, *Free Blacks in Norfolk*, ch. 7; and Fields, *Slavery and Freedom on the Middle Ground*, ch. 4.

47. On the rise of racial "science" in the United States, see Horsman, *Race and Manifest Destiny*, esp. chs. 6–8; Fredrickson, *Black Image in the White Mind*, esp. ch. 3; and William Stanton, *Leopard's Spots*. Also see Gross, who discusses the increasing importance of "scientific" evidence in cases of racial determination in the 1850s in "Litigating Whiteness," 151–56. On scientific ideas about racial difference in the

late eighteenth and early nineteenth centuries, see Winthrop Jordan, *White over Black*, esp. chs. 13–14.

48. *Richmond Daily Dispatch*, September 1, 1853.

49. Similarly, Gross finds that legal cases of racial determination increased dramatically throughout the South between 1845 and 1860. Also in keeping with the trend of hostility seen toward people of mixed race in Virginia, Gross finds that the chances of winning a lawsuit of this nature decreased significantly during this period ("Litigating Whiteness," 120 and 152–53 nn. 177–78).

50. Richmond City Hustings Court Minute Book 19, February 10, 1852, p. 504; and *Richmond Daily Dispatch*, February 11 and 12, 1852 (quotation in February 11 issue). Ira Berlin suggests the "mixed-blood law" allowed "hundreds of fair-skinned persons of African ancestry" in Virginia to escape legal disabilities before the 1850s, and one letter writer to the *Richmond Enquirer* did suggest in 1854 that the law had "been in force for many years, and the Courts have been constantly acting under it." Even Berlin, however, concedes that "until a survey of county court records is made, precisely how many free Negroes used the Virginia law to pass into the white caste will be a moot question." Berlin, *Slaves without Masters*, 365 and 162 n. 40; and *Richmond Enquirer*, February 24, 1854.

51. *Richmond Enquirer*, October 18, 1853.

52. *Richmond Daily Dispatch*, September 14, 1853.

53. Ibid.

54. Richmond City Hustings Court Minute Book 20, October 14, 1853, p. 501.

55. *Richmond Daily Dispatch*, September 14, 1853.

56. *Richmond Enquirer*, October 18, 1853.

57. *Richmond Enquirer*, November 29, 1853; and *Richmond Daily Dispatch*, November 28 and 29, 1853.

58. *Journal of the House of Delegates, 1853–1854*, December 8, 1853, p. 51.

59. Ibid., January 5, 1854, p. 137; and *Code of Virginia* (1849), ch. 107, sec. 17.

60. *Richmond Enquirer*, February 24, 1854.

61. To modern scholars, the most familiar instance of this type of escape strategy is probably William and Ellen Craft's flight from Georgia, recounted in William Craft's *Running a Thousand Miles for Freedom*. But Virginia slave owners acknowledged the phenomenon at least as early as 1788, when a B. Middleton advertised in the *Virginia Independent Chronicle* that an enslaved woman named Rachel had run away from his farm and would probably pass for a free woman, "from being uncommonly white" (*Independent Chronicle*, July 9, 1788, printed in Windley, *Runaway Slave Advertisements*, 1:396–97).

62. It could be argued that people like the Whartons "passed" in antebellum Virginia, but they made no secret of their ancestry. As Ira Berlin has argued, secretive forms of "passing" were probably more common in the Lower South. Georgia, in fact, recognized this reality with 1840 legislation allowing whites to take their neighbors to court for a racial trial if they suspected them to be of more than one-eighth "negro blood" but were exercising the rights of whites. Berlin, *Slaves without Masters*, 161–65.

63. *Richmond Whig,* January 13, 1854; and *Journal of the House of Delegates, 1853–1854,* January 10, 1854, p. 155.

64. *Journal of the House of Delegates, 1853–1854,* January 19, 1854, p. 188; and Rough Bills — House of Delegates, box 103, December 5, 1853–March 4, 1854, Bill #177, Library of Virginia, Richmond.

65. *Journal of the House of Delegates, 1853–1854,* January 30 and February 16, 1854, pp. 243 and 337.

66. *Richmond Daily Dispatch,* August 25, 1858.

67. *Richmond Daily Dispatch,* August 26, 1858.

68. William Ferguson was tried by the Hustings Court, found guilty, and sentenced to a $20 fine. Agnes Cosby was arraigned for beating Andrew Cosby, but a Hustings Court grand jury dismissed the indictment and discharged her. *Richmond Daily Dispatch,* September 1, 2, and 16, November 9, and December 16, 1858.

69. Unless otherwise noted, all quotations regarding this case are from the Petition of Samuel Gresham and others praying the release of the commonwealth's right to certain lands in the county of Lancaster in favor of the children of James Corsey, Lancaster County #19708, February 25, 1858, LP-LOV. My thanks to Jim Watkinson for calling this document to my attention.

70. The Lancaster petition was referred to the Committee of Courts of Justice on February 25, 1858. It never emerged from the committee and when the legislative session ended, it effectively died. *Journal of the House of Delegates, 1857–1858,* February 25, 1858, p. 350.

INTERLUDE: TOWARD A NEW RACIAL ORDER

1. *Richmond Enquirer,* December 31, 1853.

2. All quotations from the letter of "A Lawyer" appear in *Richmond Enquirer,* January 3, 1854.

EPILOGUE

1. *Richmond Daily Dispatch,* November 17, 1857.

2. *Richmond Daily Dispatch,* November 18 and 30, 1857.

3. *Richmond Daily Dispatch,* November 17, 1857; and Mecklenburg County Order Book 6, 1853–58, December 21, 1857, and February 20, 1858, pp. 483 and 501. Percy's case does not appear in the Mecklenburg County order books through 1865.

4. Eugene Genovese, " 'Our Family, White and Black,' " in Bleser, *In Joy and in Sorrow,* 69–87.

5. Ayers, *Promise of the New South,* ch. 6; and Brundage, *Lynching in the New South,* 281–83. Also on lynching, segregation, and fears of black male sexuality in the post–Civil War South, see Williamson, *Crucible;* Hall, *Revolt against Chivalry;* Wriggins, "Rape, Racism, and the Law"; Rabinowitz, *Race Relations in the Urban South;* Woodward, *Strange Career of Jim Crow;* Fredrickson, *Black Image in the White Mind,* chs. 7–9; Hodes, *White Women, Black Men,* chs. 7–8; and Hale, *Making Whiteness,* esp. ch. 5.

6. On the Racial Integrity Act, see J. Douglas Smith, "Campaign for Racial

Purity"; Sherman, " 'The Last Stand' "; and Lombardo, "Miscegenation, Eugenics, and Racism."

7. Hall, " 'Mind That Burns in Each Body,' " 333. Also see Hine, "Rape and the Inner Lives of Black Women in the Middle West"; Hannah Rosen, " 'Not That Sort of Women,' " in Hodes, *Sex, Love, Race*, 267–93; Clinton, "Reconstructing Freedwomen," in Clinton and Silber, *Divided Houses*, 306–19; and Edwards, "Sexual Violence."

8. DuBois, *Souls of Black Folk*, 209.

9. Indeed, as of the writing of this book, the Monticello Association, which comprises descendants of Thomas Jefferson, continues to refuse admission to the descendants of Sally Hemings, claiming that Jefferson's paternity remains unproven to its satisfaction.

Bibliography

MANUSCRIPTS

Charlottesville, Virginia
    Albemarle County Courthouse
        Administrator of Accounts Books
        Chancery Order Books
        Deed Books
        Law Order Books
        Marriage Bonds
        Marriage Registers
        Minute Books
        Order Books
        Will Books
    Alderman Library, University of Virginia
        Albemarle County Land Tax Books
        Albemarle County Personal Property Tax Books
        Cocke Family Papers, Journals of John Hartwell Cocke
        Coolidge Family Papers
        Jefferson Papers
        Mutual Assurance Society Declarations
        Richmond Police Guard, Day Book, 1834–43
        Silas and R. H. Omohundro Account Book — Slave Sales, 1857–63
Richmond, Virginia
    Library of Virginia
        Albemarle County, Ended Chancery Causes (Circuit Superior Court)
        Auditor of Public Accounts, Public Claims. Condemned Blacks Executed or
            Transported, 1783–1865
        Caroline County Minute Books
        Chesterfield County Land Tax Books
        Chesterfield County Order Books
        Chesterfield County Personal Property Tax Books
        Chesterfield County Will Books
        Culpeper County Law Order Books
        Essex County Order Books
        Executive Papers: Letters Received, Pardon Papers
        Governor's Council Journals
        Henrico County Order Books

Henrico County Will Books
King and Queen County Order Books
King George County Land Tax Books
King George County Marriage Bonds
King George County Minute Books
King George County Personal Property Tax Books
King George County Will Books
Legislative Petitions
Lunenburg County Will Books
Mecklenburg County Order Books
New Kent County Land Tax Books
New Kent County Personal Property Tax Books
Norfolk County Will Books
Petersburg City Order Books
Prince William County Minute Books
Richmond City Hustings Court Minute Books
Richmond City Hustings Court Order Books
Richmond City Hustings Court Suit Papers
Richmond City Will Books (Hustings and Circuit Courts)
Rough Bills — House of Delegates
Silas Omohundro business and estate records, 1842–82
Virginia Supreme Court of Appeals, Order Book 5 (1804–7)
Valentine Museum
Richmond Mayor's Court, Private Docket, 1836–39
Richmond Police Records, 1861–67
Vertical Files: Richmond, Va. — History — 1820–61

NEWSPAPERS

Central Gazette (Charlottesville)
Jeffersonian Republican (Charlottesville)
Richmond Daily Dispatch
Richmond Enquirer
Richmond Examiner
Richmond Recorder
Richmond Whig
Virginia Advocate (Charlottesville)
Virginia Argus (Richmond)

PUBLISHED PRIMARY SOURCES

Travel Narratives and Contemporary Slavery Works
Bayard, Ferdinand M. *Travels of a Frenchman in Maryland and Virginia with a Description of Philadelphia and Baltimore in 1791.* Ann Arbor: Edwards Brothers, 1950. Originally published in French, 1797.

Bremer, Fredrika. *The Homes of the New World; Impressions of America.* 2 vols. New York, 1854.

Buckingham, J. S. *The Slave States of America.* 2 vols. London, 1842.

Chambers, William. *Things as They Are in America.* London and Edinburgh, 1854.

Chastellux, Marquis de. *Travels in North America in the Years 1780, 1781, and 1782.* 2 vols. Chapel Hill: University of North Carolina Press, 1963. Originally published in French, 1785.

Dickens, Charles. *American Notes for General Circulation.* Boston, 1867. Originally published 1842.

Kemble, Frances Anne. *Journal of a Residence on a Georgia Plantation in 1838–1839.* New York, 1863.

La Rochefoucauld-Liancourt, Duc de. *Travels through the United States of North America, the Country of the Iroquois, and Upper Canada, in the Years 1795, 1796, and 1797.* 2 vols. London, 1799.

Martineau, Harriet. *Society in America.* 3 vols. London, 1837.

Olmsted, Frederick Law. *The Cotton Kingdom: A Traveller's Observations on Cotton and Slavery in the American Slave States.* New York, 1861.

———. *A Journey in the Seaboard Slave States, with Remarks on Their Economy.* New York, 1856.

Schoepf, Johann David. *Travels in the Confederation, 1783–1784.* 2 vols. Philadelphia, 1911. Originally published in German, 1788.

Trollope, Frances. *Domestic Manners of the Americans.* 2 vols. London, 1832.

Tower, Philo. *Slavery Unmasked: Being a Truthful Narrative of a Three Years' Residence and Journeying in Eleven Southern States: To Which Is Added the Invasion of Kansas, Including the Last Chapter of Her Wrongs.* Rochester, 1856.

Weld, Charles R. *A Vacation Tour in the United States and Canada.* London, 1855.

Weld, Isaac, Jr. *Travels through the States of North America, and the Provinces of Upper and Lower Canada, during the Years 1795, 1796, and 1797.* London, 1800. Originally published 1798.

Slave Narratives

Bayley, Solomon. *A Narrative of Some Remarkable Incidents in the Life of Solomon Bayley, Formerly a Slave, in the State of Delaware, North America.* London, 1825.

Boney, F. W., ed. *Slave Life in Georgia: A Narrative of the Life, Sufferings, and Escape of John Brown, a Fugitive Slave.* Savannah: Beehive Press, 1991. Originally published 1855.

Bratton, Mary J., ed. "Fields's Observations: The Slave Narrative of a Nineteenth-Century Virginian." *Virginia Magazine of History and Biography* 88 (January 1980): 75–93.

Craft, William. *Running a Thousand Miles for Freedom; or, The Escape of William and Ellen Craft from Slavery.* London, 1860.

Drew, Benjamin. *A North-Side View of Slavery.* New York: Negro Universities Press, 1968. Originally published Boston, 1856.

Eliot, William G. *The Story of Archer Alexander, from Slavery to Freedom.* Boston, 1885.

Grimes, William. *Life of William Grimes, the Runaway Slave.* New York, 1825.

Hayden, William. *Narrative of William Hayden*. Cincinnati, 1846.

Hughes, Louis. *Thirty Years a Slave: From Bondage to Freedom*. Milwaukee, 1897.

Jacobs, Harriet. *Incidents in the Life of a Slave Girl*. Edited by Jean Fagan Yellin. Cambridge, Mass.: Harvard University Press, 1987.

Langston, John Mercer. *From the Virginia Plantation to the National Capitol, or The First and Only Negro Representative in Congress from the Old Dominion*. Hartford, 1894.

"Life among the Lowly, Number I." *Pike County (Ohio) Republican*, March 13, 1873.

Logan, Rayford W., ed. *Memoirs of a Monticello Slave, as Dictated to Charles Campbell in the 1840s by Isaac, One of Thomas Jefferson's Slaves*. Charlottesville: University Press of Virginia, 1951.

Offley, G. W. *A Narrative of the Life and Labors of the Rev. G. W. Offley*. Hartford, 1860.

Perdue, Charles L., Thomas E. Barden, and Robert K. Phillips, eds. *Weevils in the Wheat: Interviews with Virginia Ex-Slaves*. Charlottesville: University Press of Virginia, 1976.

Rawick, George P., ed. *The American Slave*. 17 vols.; supp. 1, 12 vols.; supp. 2, 10 vols. Westport, Conn.: Greenwood Press, 1972.

Smith, James L. *Autobiography of James L. Smith*. New York: Negro Universities Press, 1969. Originally published 1881.

Stearns, Charles. *Narrative of Henry Box Brown, Who Escaped from Slavery Enclosed in a Box 3 Feet Long and 2 Wide*. Boston, 1849.

Stevens, Charles Emery. *Anthony Burns: A History*. Boston, 1856.

Veney, Bethany. *The Narrative of Bethany Veney, a Slave Woman*. Worcester, Mass., 1890.

Government and Legal Sources

Acts of Assembly Relating to the City of Richmond, and Ordinances of the Common Council, Subsequent to January, 1831. Richmond, 1839.

Acts Passed at a General Assembly of the Commonwealth of Virginia. Richmond, 1802–61.

Calendar of Virginia State Papers and Other Manuscripts. Richmond, 1866.

Catterall, Helen Tunnicliff, ed. *Judicial Cases Concerning American Slavery and the Negro*. 5 vols. Washington, D.C., 1926–37.

Charters and Ordinances of the City of Richmond, with the Declaration of Rights, and Constitution of Virginia. Richmond, 1859.

Code of Virginia. Richmond, 1849, 1860.

A Collection of All Such Acts of the General Assembly of Virginia. Richmond, 1794, 1803, 1808.

Guild, Jane Purcell. *Black Laws of Virginia: A Summary of the Legislative Acts of Virginia Concerning Negroes from Earliest Times to the Present*. New York: Negro Universities Press, 1969. Originally published 1936.

Hening, William Waller, ed. *The Statutes at Large, Being a Collection of All the Laws of Virginia from the First Session of the Legislature in 1619*. 13 vols. New York, Richmond, and Philadelphia, 1809–23.

Index to Enrolled Bills of the General Assembly of Virginia, 1776–1910. Richmond, 1911.

Journal of the House of Delegates of the Commonwealth of Virginia. Richmond, 1803–61.

Ordinances of the City of Richmond, Revised and Passed by the Council between May 1851, and January, 1852. Richmond, 1852.

Ordinances of the Corporation of the City of Richmond, and the Acts of Assembly Relating Thereto. Richmond, 1831.

Ordinances Passed by the Council of the City of Richmond, since the Year 1839. Richmond, 1847.

Revised Code of the Laws of Virginia. Richmond, 1819.

Revised Code of the Laws of Virginia. Richmond, 1849.

United States Manuscript Census Returns — Virginia, 1790, 1810–60 (and Slave Schedule, 1860). Library of Virginia, Richmond. Microfilm.

Virginia Reports, Annotated: Reports of Cases Argued and Determined in the Court of Appeals of Virginia, Jefferson-33 Grattan, 1730–1880. Charlottesville, 1900–1904.

Other Published Primary Materials

Bear, James A., Jr., and Lucia C. Stanton, eds. *Jefferson's Memorandum Books: Accounts, with Legal Records and Miscellany, 1767–1826.* 2 vols. Princeton: Princeton University Press, 1997.

Betts, Edwin Morris, ed. *Thomas Jefferson's Farm Book.* Princeton: Princeton University Press, 1953.

Blair, Lewis H. "Random Sketches of Old-Time Richmond." *Richmond Times-Dispatch,* July 2, 1916.

Boyd, Julian, ed. *Papers of Thomas Jefferson.* 20 vols. Princeton: Princeton University Press, 1950–82.

Brown, William Wells. *Clotel; or, the President's Daughter: A Narrative of Slave Life in the United States.* London, 1853.

Calamity at Richmond, Being a Narrative of the Affecting Circumstances Attending the Awful Conflagration of the Theatre, in the City of Richmond, on the Night of Thursday, the 26th of December, 1811. Philadelphia, 1812.

Cohen, Caroline. *Records of the Myers, Hays and Mordecai Families from 1707 to 1913.* Washington, D.C., 1913.

Corey, Charles H. *A History of the Richmond Theological Seminary, with Reminiscences of Thirty Years' Work among the Colored People of the South.* Richmond, 1895.

Cullen, Charles T., ed. *Papers of Thomas Jefferson.* 7 vols. to date. Princeton: Princeton University Press, 1982–. (Continuing Boyd, *Papers of Thomas Jefferson,* beginning with vol. 21.)

Duke, Maurice P., and Daniel P. Jordan, eds. *A Richmond Reader, 1733–1983.* Chapel Hill: University of North Carolina Press, 1983.

Ellyson's Richmond Directory, and Business Reference Book. Carefully Arranged for 1845 to 1846. Richmond, 1845.

Ford, Paul Leicester, ed. *The Writings of Thomas Jefferson.* 12 vols. New York, 1897.

Ford, Worthington C., ed. *Thomas Jefferson and James Thomson Callender, 1798–1802.* Brooklyn, 1897.

Jefferson, Thomas. *Notes on the State of Virginia.* Edited by William Peden. New York: W. W. Norton, 1972. Originally published in France, 1785.

Klingberg, Frank I., and Frank W. Klingberg, eds. *Correspondence between Henry Stephens Randall and Hugh Blair Grigsby, 1856–1861*. Berkeley: University of California Press, 1952.

Langhorne, Orra. *Southern Sketches from Virginia, 1881–1901*. Edited by Charles E. Wynes. Charlottesville: University Press of Virginia, 1964.

Lipscomb, Andrew A., and Albery Ellery Bergh, eds. *The Writings of Thomas Jefferson*. 20 vols. Washington, D.C., 1904.

Mayo, Bernard, ed. *Thomas Jefferson and His Unknown Brother Randolph*. Charlottesville: Tracy W. McGregor Library, University of Virginia, 1942.

Miscegenation: The Theory of the Blending of the Races, Applied to the American White Man and Negro. New York, 1864.

Mordecai, Samuel. *Richmond in By-Gone Days: Being the Reminiscences of an Old Citizen*. Richmond, 1856.

Page, Thomas Nelson. *Social Life in Old Virginia before the War*. New York, 1897.

Particular Account of the Dreadful Fire at Richmond, Virginia, December 26, 1811. Baltimore, 1812.

Paxton, J. D. *Letters on Slavery; Addressed to the Cumberland Congregation, Virginia*. Lexington, Ky., 1833.

Pierson, Hamilton W., ed. *Jefferson at Monticello: The Private Life of Thomas Jefferson*. New York, 1862.

Rawlings, Mary, ed. *Early Charlottesville: Recollections of James Alexander, 1828–1874*. Charlottesville, 1942.

Richmond Directory, Register and Almanac, for the Year 1819. Richmond, 1819.

A Sermon, Delivered in the Presbyterian Meeting-House in Winchester, on Thursday the 23D Jan. 1812; Being a Day of Fasting and Humiliation, Appointed by the Citizens of Winchester on Account of the Late Calamitous Fire at the Richmond Theatre. Winchester, Va., 1812.

Turner, Thomas. "Letter." *Boston Repertory*, May 31, 1805.

Windley, Lathan A., ed. *Runaway Slave Advertisements: A Documentary History from the 1730s to 1790*. Vol. 1: *Virginia and North Carolina*. Westport, Conn.: Greenwood Press, 1983.

Woodward, C. Vann, ed. *Mary Chesnut's Civil War*. New Haven: Yale University Press, 1981.

Young, Alexander. *The Defence of Young and Minns, Printers to the State, before the Committee of the House of Representatives; with an Appendix, Containing the Debate, &c*. Boston, 1805.

SECONDARY SOURCES

Alexander, Adele Logan. *Ambiguous Lives: Free Women of Color in Rural Georgia, 1789–1879*. Fayetteville: University of Arkansas Press, 1991.

Allen, Theodore W. *The Invention of the White Race*. Vol. 2: *The Origin of Racial Oppression in Anglo-America*. New York: Verso, 1997.

Applebaum, Harvey M. "Miscegenation Statutes: A Constitutional and Social Problem." *Georgetown Law Journal* 53 (1964): 49–91.

Aptheker, Herbert. *American Negro Slave Revolts*. New York, 1943.

Avins, Alfred. "Anti-Miscegenation Laws and the Fourteenth Amendment: The Original Intent." *Virginia Law Review* 52 (1966): 1224–55.

Ayers, Edward L. *The Promise of the New South: Life after Reconstruction*. New York: Oxford University Press, 1992.

Bancroft, Frederic. *Slave-Trading in the Old South*. Baltimore, 1931.

Barber, Edna Susan. " 'Sisters of the Capital': White Women in Richmond, Virginia, 1860–1880." 2 vols. Ph.D. diss., University of Maryland, 1997.

Bardaglio, Peter. "Rape and the Law in the Old South: 'Calculated to excite indignation in every heart.' " *Journal of Southern History* 60 (November 1994): 749–72.

———. *Reconstructing the Household: Families, Sex, and the Law in the Nineteenth-Century South*. Chapel Hill: University of North Carolina Press, 1995.

Barnhart, Jacqueline Baker. *The Fair but Frail: Prostitution in San Francisco, 1849–1900*. Reno: University of Nevada Press, 1986.

Basch, Norma. *Framing American Divorce: From the Revolutionary Generation to the Victorians*. Berkeley: University of California Press, 1999.

Bay, Mia. *The White Image in the Black Mind: African-American Ideas about White People, 1830–1925*. New York: Oxford University Press, 1999.

Bear, James A. "The Hemings Family of Monticello." *Virginia Cavalcade* 29 (Autumn 1979): 78–87.

Bell, Landon C. *The Old Free State: A Contribution to the History of Lunenburg County and Southside Virginia*. 2 vols. Richmond: William Byrd Press, 1927.

Berlin, Ira. *Slaves without Masters: The Free Negro in the Antebellum South*. New York: Vintage Books, 1976.

Berlin, Ira, and Herbert G. Gutman. "Natives and Immigrants, Free Men and Slaves: Urban Workingmen in the Antebellum South." *American Historical Review* 88 (December 1983): 1175–1200.

Berman, Myron. *Richmond's Jewry, 1769–1976: Shabbat in Shockoe*. Charlottesville: University Press of Virginia, 1979.

Berry, Mary Frances. "Judging Morality: Sexual Behavior and Legal Consequences in the Late Nineteenth-Century South." *Journal of American History* 78 (December 1991): 835–56.

Berry, Thomas S. "The Rise of Flour Milling in Richmond." *Virginia Magazine of History and Biography* 78 (October 1970): 387–408.

Blassingame, John W. *The Slave Community: Plantation Life in the Antebellum South*. Rev. and enl. ed. New York: Oxford University Press, 1979.

Bleser, Carol. *Secret and Sacred: The Diaries of James Henry Hammond, a Southern Slaveholder*. New York: Oxford University Press, 1988.

———, ed. *In Joy and in Sorrow: Women, Family, and Marriage in the Victorian South, 1830–1900*. New York: Oxford University Press, 1991.

Bogger, Tommy L. *Free Blacks in Norfolk, Virginia, 1790–1860: The Darker Side of Freedom*. Charlottesville: University Press of Virginia, 1997.

Breen, T. H., and Stephen Innes. *"Myne Owne Ground": Race and Freedom on Virginia's Eastern Shore, 1640–1676*. New York: Oxford University Press, 1980.

Brodie, Fawn M. "The Great Jefferson Taboo." *American Heritage* 33 (Autumn 1979): 48–57, 97–100.

——. *Thomas Jefferson: An Intimate History.* New York: W. W. Norton, 1974.

——. "Thomas Jefferson's Unknown Grandchildren: A Study in Historical Silence." *American Heritage* 27 (October 1976): 28–33, 94–99.

Brodkin, Karen. *How Jews Became White Folks and What That Says about Race in America.* New Brunswick, N.J.: Rutgers University Press, 1998.

Brown, Elsa Barkley, and Gregg D. Kimball. "Mapping the Terrain of Black Richmond." *Journal of Urban History* 21 (March 1995): 296–346.

Brown, Kathleen M. *Good Wives, Nasty Wenches, and Anxious Patriarchs: Gender, Race, and Power in Colonial Virginia.* Chapel Hill: University of North Carolina Press, 1996.

Brown, Phil. "Black-White Interracial Marriages: A Historical Analysis." *Journal of Intergroup Relations* 16 (Fall–Winter 1989–90): 26–36.

Brown, Steven E. "Sexuality and the Slave Community." *Phylon* 42 (Spring 1981): 1–10.

Brown, Thomas. "The Miscegenation of Richard Mentor Johnson as an Issue in the National Election Campaign of 1835–1836." *Civil War History* 39 (1993): 5–30.

Bruce, Kathleen. *Virginia Iron Manufacturing in the Slave Era.* New York, 1931.

Brundage, W. Fitzhugh. *Lynching in the New South: Georgia and Virginia, 1880–1930.* Urbana: University of Illinois Press, 1993.

Buckley, Thomas E., S.J. *The Great Catastrophe of My Life: Divorce in the Old Dominion.* Chapel Hill: University of North Carolina Press, 2002.

——. " 'Placed in the Power of Violence': The Divorce Petition of Evelina Gregory Roane." *Virginia Magazine of History and Biography* 100 (January 1992): 29–78.

——. "Unfixing Race: Class, Power, and Identity in an Interracial Family." *Virginia Magazine of History and Biography* 102 (July 1994): 349–80.

Burg, B. R. "The Rhetoric of Miscegenation: Thomas Jefferson, Sally Hemings, and Their Historians." *Phylon* 47 (June 1986): 128–38.

Burstein, Andrew. "The Seductions of Thomas Jefferson." *Journal of the Early Republic* 19 (Fall 1999): 499–509.

Bynum, Victoria. *Unruly Women: The Politics of Social and Sexual Control in the Old South.* Chapel Hill: University of North Carolina Press, 1992.

——. " 'White Negroes' in Segregated Mississippi: Miscegenation, Racial Identity, and the Law." *Journal of Southern History* 64 (May 1998): 247–76.

Carby, Hazel V. *Reconstructing Womanhood: The Emergence of the Afro-American Woman Novelist.* New York: Oxford University Press, 1987.

Carlisle, Marcia. "Disorderly City, Disorderly Women: Prostitution in Ante-Bellum Philadelphia." *Pennsylvania Magazine of History and Biography* 110 (October 1986): 549–68.

Censer, Jane Turner. *North Carolina Planters and Their Children, 1800–1860.* Baton Rouge: Louisiana State University Press, 1984.

———. " 'Smiling through Her Tears': Ante-Bellum Southern Women and Divorce." *American Journal of Legal History* 25 (January 1981): 24–47.

Chase-Riboud, Barbara. *Sally Hemings: A Novel.* New York: Viking Press, 1979.

Cheek, William, and Aimee Lee Cheek. *John Mercer Langston and the Fight for Black Freedom, 1829–1865.* Urbana: University of Illinois Press, 1989.

Chused, Richard H. *Private Acts in Public Places: A Social History of Divorce in the Formative Era of American Family Law.* Philadelphia: University of Pennsylvania Press, 1994.

Clarke, Peyton Neale. *Old King William Homes and Families.* Louisville, 1897.

Click, Patricia C. *The Spirit of the Times: Amusements in Nineteenth-Century Baltimore, Norfolk, and Richmond.* Charlottesville: University Press of Virginia, 1989.

Clinton, Catherine. "Caught in the Web of the Big House: Women and Slavery." In *The Web of Southern Social Relations: Women, Family, and Education*, edited by Walter J. Fraser Jr., R. Frank Saunders Jr., and Jon L. Wakelyn, 19–34. Athens: University of Georgia Press, 1985.

———. *The Plantation Mistress: Women's World in the Old South.* New York: Pantheon Books, 1982.

———. " 'With a Whip in His Hand': Rape, Memory, and African-American Women." In *History and Memory in African-American Culture*, edited by Genevieve Fabre and Robert O'Meally, 205–18. New York: Oxford University Press, 1994.

Clinton, Catherine, and Michelle Gillespie, eds. *The Devil's Lane: Sex and Race in the Early South.* New York: Oxford University Press, 1997.

Clinton, Catherine, and Nina Silber, eds. *Divided Houses: Gender and the Civil War.* New York: Oxford University Press, 1992.

Coates, Eyler Robert, Sr., ed. *The Jefferson-Hemings Myth: An American Travesty.* Charlottesville: Jefferson Editions, 2001.

Colburn, Trevor, ed. *Fame and the Founding Fathers.* New York: W. W. Norton, 1974.

Cott, Nancy F. "Divorce and the Changing Status of Women in Eighteenth-Century Massachusetts." *William and Mary Quarterly* 33 (October 1976): 586–614.

Curry, Leonard P. *The Free Black in Urban America, 1800–1850: The Shadow of the Dream.* Chicago: University of Chicago Press, 1981.

Dabney, Virginius. *The Jefferson Scandals: A Rebuttal.* New York: Dodd, Mead, 1981.

———. *Richmond: The Story of a City.* Rev. and exp. ed. Charlottesville: University Press of Virginia, 1990. Originally published 1976.

Dabney, Virginius, and Jon Kukla. "The Monticello Scandals: History and Fiction." *Virginia Cavalcade* 29 (Autumn 1979): 52–61.

Dabney, William Minor. "Jefferson's Albemarle: History of Albemarle County, Virginia, 1727–1819." Ph.D. diss., University of Virginia, 1951.

Davis, Adrienne D. "Identity Notes Part One: Playing in the Light." *American University Law Review* 45 (February 1996): 695–720.

———. "The Private Law of Race and Sex: An Antebellum Perspective." *Stanford Law Review* 51 (January 1999): 221–88.

Davis, Angela Y. *Women, Race, and Class*. New York: Random House, 1981.

Day, Caroline Bond. *A Study of Some Negro-White Families in the United States*. Cambridge, Mass., 1932.

Deal, J. Douglas. *Race and Class in Colonial Virginia: Indians, Englishmen, and Africans on the Eastern Shore during the Seventeenth Century*. New York: Garland, 1993.

D'Emilio, John, and Estelle B. Freedman. *Intimate Matters: A History of Sexuality in America*. New York: Harper and Row, 1988.

Dew, Charles B. *Ironmaker to the Confederacy: Joseph R. Anderson and the Tredegar Iron Works*. New Haven: Yale University Press, 1966.

Dominguez, Virginia R. *White by Definition: Social Classification in Creole Louisiana*. New Brunswick, N.J.: Rutgers University Press, 1986.

DuBois, W. E. B. *The Souls of Black Folk*. 1903. Reprinted in *Three Negro Classics*. New York: Avon Books, 1965.

Durey, Michael. *"With the Hammer of Truth": James Thomson Callender and America's Early National Heroes*. Charlottesville: University Press of Virginia, 1990.

Edwards, Laura F. "Law, Domestic Violence, and the Limits of Patriarchal Authority in the Antebellum South." *Journal of Southern History* 65 (November 1999): 733–70.

———. "Sexual Violence, Gender, Reconstruction, and the Extension of Patriarchy in Granville County, North Carolina." *North Carolina Historical Review* 68 (July 1991): 237–60.

Egerton, Douglas R. *Gabriel's Rebellion: The Virginia Slave Conspiracies of 1800 and 1802*. Chapel Hill: University of North Carolina Press, 1993.

Ellis, Joseph J. *American Sphinx: The Character of Thomas Jefferson*. New York: Alfred A. Knopf, 1997.

Ely, Carol, Jeffrey Hantman, and Phyllis Leffler. *To Seek the Peace of the City: Jewish Life in Charlottesville*. Charlottesville: Hillel Jewish Center, 1994.

Ethridge, Harrison. "The Jordan Hatcher Affair of 1852: Cold Justice and Warm Compassion." *Virginia Magazine of History and Biography* 84 (October 1976): 446–63.

Ezekiel, Herbert T., and Gaston Lichtenstein. *The History of the Jews of Richmond from 1796 to 1917*. Richmond: H. T. Ezekiel, 1917.

Faust, Drew Gilpin. *James Henry Hammond and the Old South: A Design for Mastery*. Baton Rouge: Louisiana State University Press, 1982.

Fede, Andrew. "Legitimized Violent Slave Abuse in the American South, 1619–1865: A Case Study of Law and Social Change in Six Southern States." *American Journal of Legal History* 29 (April 1985): 93–150.

Fields, Barbara J. "Ideology and Race in American History." In *Region, Race, and Reconstruction: Essays in Honor of C. Vann Woodward*, edited by J. Morgan Kousser and James M. McPherson, 143–77. New York: Oxford University Press, 1982.

———. *Slavery and Freedom on the Middle Ground: Maryland during the Nineteenth Century*. New Haven: Yale University Press, 1985.

———. "Slavery, Race, and Ideology in the United States of America." *New Left Review* 181 (May–June 1990): 95–118.

Finkelman, Paul. "The Crime of Color." *Tulane Law Review* 67 (June 1993): 2063–2112.

Flanigan, Daniel J. "Criminal Procedure in Slave Trials in the Antebellum South." *Journal of Southern History* 40 (November 1974): 537–64.

Fleischner, Jennifer. *Mastering Slavery: Memory, Family, and Identity in Women's Slave Narratives*. New York: New York University Press, 1996.

Fogel, Robert William, and Stanley L. Engerman. *Time on the Cross: The Economics of American Negro Slavery*. Boston: Little, Brown, 1974.

Forbes, Jack D. "The Evolution of the Term Mulatto: A Chapter in Black–Native American Relations." *Journal of Ethnic Studies* 10 (1982): 45–66.

Formwalt, Lee W. "A Case of Interracial Marriage during Reconstruction." *Alabama Review* 45 (July 1992): 216–24.

Foster, Eugene A., et al. "Jefferson Fathered Slave's Last Child." *Nature* 396 (November 5, 1998): 27–28.

Fowler, David H. "Northern Attitudes towards Interracial Marriage: A Study of Legislation and Public Opinion in the Middle Atlantic States and the States of the Old Northwest." Ph.D. diss., Yale University, 1963.

Fox-Genovese, Elizabeth. *Within the Plantation Household: Black and White Women of the Old South*. Chapel Hill: University of North Carolina Press, 1988.

Fredrickson, George. *The Arrogance of Race: Historical Perspectives on Slavery, Racism, and Social Inequality*. Middletown, Conn.: Wesleyan University Press, 1988.

———. *The Black Image in the White Mind: The Debate on Afro-American Character and Destiny, 1817–1914*. Middletown, Conn.: Wesleyan University Press, 1971.

———. *White Supremacy: A Comparative Study in American and South African History*. New York: Oxford University Press, 1981.

Freeman, Joanne B. "Dueling as Politics: Reinterpreting the Burr-Hamilton Duel." *William and Mary Quarterly* 53 (April 1996): 289–318.

———. "Slander, Poison, Whispers, and Fame: Jefferson's 'Anas' and Political Gossip in the Early Republic." *Journal of the Early Republic* 15 (Spring 1995): 25–57.

Genovese, Eugene. *Roll, Jordan, Roll: The World the Slaves Made*. New York: Random House, 1974.

———. "The Slave States of North America." In *Neither Slave nor Free: The Freedmen of African Descent in the Slave Societies of the New World*, edited by David W. Cohen and Jack P. Greene, 258–77. Baltimore: Johns Hopkins University Press, 1972.

Gerber, David A. *Black Ohio and the Color Line, 1860–1915*. Urbana: University of Illinois Press, 1976.

Getman, Karen A. "Sexual Control in the Slaveholding South: The Implementation and Maintenance of a Racial Caste System." *Harvard Women's Law Journal* 7 (1984): 115–52.

Gianakos, Cynthia. "Virginia and the Married Women's Property Acts." M.A. thesis, University of Virginia, 1982.

Gilfoyle, Timothy J. *City of Eros: New York City, Prostitution, and the Commercialization of Sex, 1790–1920*. New York: W. W. Norton, 1992.

———. "Strumpets and Misogynists: Brothel 'Riots' and the Transformation of

Prostitution in Antebellum New York City." *New York History* 68 (January 1987): 44–65.

———. "The Urban Geography of Commercial Sex: Prostitution in New York City, 1790–1860." *Journal of Urban History* 13 (August 1987): 371–93.

Gilman, Sander. *The Jew's Body*. New York: Routledge, 1991.

Ginsberg, Elaine K., ed. *Passing and the Fictions of Identity*. Durham: Duke University Press, 1996.

Goldfield, David R. *Cotton Fields and Skyscrapers: Southern City and Region, 1607–1980*. Baton Rouge: Louisiana State University Press, 1982.

———. *Urban Growth in the Age of Sectionalism: Virginia, 1847–1861*. Baton Rouge: Louisiana State University Press, 1977.

———. "Urban-Rural Relations in the Old South: The Example of Virginia." *Journal of Urban History* 2 (February 1976): 146–68.

———. "The Urban South: A Regional Framework." *American Historical Review* 86 (December 1981): 1009–34.

Goldin, Claudia Dale. *Urban Slavery in the American South, 1820–1860: A Quantitative History*. Chicago: University of Chicago Press, 1976.

Goldman, Marion S. *Gold Diggers and Silver Miners: Prostitution and Social Life on the Comstock Lode*. Ann Arbor: University of Michigan Press, 1981.

Gomez, Michael. *Exchanging Our Country Marks: The Transformation of African Identities in the Colonial and Antebellum South*. Chapel Hill: University of North Carolina Press, 1998.

Goodheart, Lawrence B., Neil Hanks, and Elizabeth Johnson. " 'An Act for the Relief of Females . . .': Divorce and the Changing Legal Status of Women in Tennessee, 1796–1860." *Tennessee Historical Quarterly* 44 (Fall–Winter 1985): 318–39, 402–16.

Gordon-Reed, Annette. *Thomas Jefferson and Sally Hemings: An American Controversy*. Charlottesville: University Press of Virginia, 1997.

Gould, Virginia Meacham, ed. *Chained to the Rock of Adversity: To Be Free, Black and Female in the Old South*. Athens: University of Georgia Press, 1998.

Green, Rodney Dale. "Urban Industry, Black Resistance, and Racial Restriction in the Antebellum South: A General Model and a Case Study in Urban Virginia." Ph.D. diss., American University, 1980.

Greenberg, Kenneth. *Honor and Slavery: Lies, Duels, Masks, Dressing as a Woman, Gifts, Strangers, Humanitarianism, Death, Slave Rebellions, the Proslavery Argument, Baseball, Hunting, and Gambling in the Old South*. Princeton: Princeton University Press, 1996.

Gross, Ariela J. "Litigating Whiteness: Trials of Racial Determination in the Nineteenth Century South." *Yale Law Journal* 108 (October 1998): 109–88.

———. "Pandora's Box: Slave Character on Trial in the Antebellum Deep South." *Yale Journal of Law and the Humanities* 7 (Summer 1995): 267–316.

Grossberg, Michael. *Governing the Hearth: Law and the Family in Nineteenth-Century America*. Chapel Hill: University of North Carolina Press, 1985.

Gundersen, Joan R., and Gwen Victor Gampel. "Married Women's Legal Status in

Eighteenth-Century New York and Virginia." *William and Mary Quarterly* 39 (January 1982): 114–34.

Gutman, Herbert, and Richard Sutch. "Victorians All?: The Sexual Mores and Conduct of Slaves and Their Masters." In *Reckoning with Slavery: A Critical Study in the Quantitative History of American Negro Slavery*, by Paul A. David et al., 134–62. New York: Oxford University Press, 1976.

Guzman-Stokes, Theresa M. "A Flag and a Family: Richard Gill Forrester, 1847–1906." *Virginia Cavalcade* 47 (Spring 1998): 52–63.

Hale, Grace Elizabeth. *Making Whiteness: The Culture of Segregation in the South, 1890–1940*. New York: Pantheon Books, 1998.

Hall, Jacquelyn Dowd. " 'The Mind That Burns in Each Body': Women, Rape, and Racial Violence." In *Powers of Desire: The Politics of Sexuality*, edited by Ann Snitow, Christine Stansell, and Sharon Thompson, 328–49. New York: Monthly Review Press, 1983.

———. *Revolt against Chivalry: Jessie Daniel Ames and the Women's Campaign against Lynching*. New York: Columbia University Press, 1974.

Haney Lopez, Ian F. "The Social Construction of Race: Some Observations on Illusion, Fabrication, and Choice." *Harvard Civil Rights–Civil Liberties Law Review* 29 (Winter 1994): 1–62.

———. *White by Law: The Legal Construction of Race*. New York: New York University Press, 1996.

Harris, Cheryl I. "Whiteness as Property." *Harvard Law Review* 106 (1993): 1707–91.

Harris, Malcolm Hart. *Old New Kent County*. 2 vols. West Point, Va., 1977.

Harrison, Susan. "Black Women in the Nineteenth-Century South." *Mississippi Quarterly* 46 (Spring 1993): 284–90.

Higginbotham, A. Leon, Jr. *In the Matter of Color: Race and the American Legal Process*. New York: Oxford University Press, 1978.

Higginbotham, A. Leon, Jr., and Greer C. Bosworth. " 'Rather Than the Free': Free Blacks in Colonial and Antebellum Virginia." *Harvard Civil Rights–Civil Liberties Law Review* 26 (Winter 1991): 17–66.

Higginbotham, A. Leon, Jr., and Anne F. Jacobs. "The 'Law Only as an Enemy': The Legitimization of Racial Powerlessness through the Colonial and Antebellum Criminal Laws of Virginia." *North Carolina Law Review* 70 (April 1992): 969–1070.

Higginbotham, A. Leon, Jr., and Barbara K. Kopytoff. "Property First, Humanity Second: The Recognition of the Slave's Human Nature in Virginia Civil Law." *Ohio State Law Journal* 50 (1989): 511–40.

———. "Racial Purity and Interracial Sex in the Law of Colonial and Antebellum Virginia." *Georgetown Law Journal* 77 (1989): 1967–2029.

Hill, Marilynn Wood. *Their Sisters' Keepers: Prostitution in New York City, 1830–1870*. Berkeley: University of California Press, 1993.

Hindus, Michael S. "Black Justice under White Law: Criminal Prosecutions of Blacks in Antebellum South Carolina." *Journal of American History* 63 (December 1976): 575–99.

Hindus, Michael S., and Lynne E. Withey. "The Law of Husband and Wife in Nineteenth-Century America: Changing Views of Divorce." In *Women and the Law: A Social Historical Perspective*, edited by D. Kelly Weisberg, 2:133–54. Cambridge, Mass.: Schenkman, 1982.

Hine, Darlene Clark. "Rape and the Inner Lives of Black Women in the Middle West: Preliminary Thoughts on the Culture of Dissemblance." *Signs* 14 (Summer 1989): 912–20.

———. "Rape and the Inner Lives of Southern Black Women: Thoughts on the Culture of Dissemblance." In *Southern Women: Histories and Identities*, edited by Virginia Bernhard, Betty Brandon, Elizabeth Fox-Genovese, and Theda Perdue, 177–89. Columbia: University of Missouri Press, 1992.

History of the Upper Ohio Valley, with Family History and Biographical Sketches: A Statement of Its Resources, Industrial Growth and Commercial Advantages. 2 vols. Madison, Wisc., 1890.

Hobson, Barbara Meil. *Uneasy Virtue: The Politics of Prostitution and the American Reform Tradition.* New York: Basic Books, 1987.

Hodes, Martha. *White Women, Black Men: Illicit Sex in the Nineteenth-Century South.* New Haven: Yale University Press, 1997.

———, ed. *Sex, Love, Race: Crossing Boundaries in North American History.* New York: New York University Press, 1999.

Holt, Thomas C. "Marking: Race, Race-Making, and the Writing of History." *American Historical Review* 100 (February 1995): 1–20.

Horsman, Reginald. *Race and Manifest Destiny: The Origins of American Racial Anglo-Saxonism.* Cambridge, Mass.: Harvard University Press, 1981.

Horton, James Oliver. "Freedom's Yoke: Gender Conventions among Antebellum Free Blacks." *Feminist Studies* 12 (Spring 1986): 51–76.

———. *Free People of Color: Inside the African American Community.* Washington, D.C.: Smithsonian Institution Press, 1993.

Hudson, Janet. "From Constitution to Constitution, 1868–1895: South Carolina's Unique Stance on Divorce." *South Carolina Historical Magazine* 98 (January 1997): 75–96.

Humphrey, David. "Prostitution in Texas: From the 1830s to the 1960s." *East Texas Historical Journal* 33 (1995): 27–43.

Ireland, Robert M. "Frenzied and Fallen Females: Women and Sexual Dishonor in the Nineteenth-Century United States." *Journal of Women's History* 3 (Winter 1992): 95–117.

———. "The Libertine Must Die: Sexual Dishonor and the Unwritten Law in the Nineteenth-Century United States." *Journal of Social History* 23 (Fall 1989): 27–44.

Jabour, Anya. " 'It Will Never Do for Me to Be Married': The Life of Laura Wirt Randall, 1803–1833." *Journal of the Early Republic* 17 (Summer 1997): 193–236.

Jackson, Luther. *Free Negro Labor and Property Holding in Virginia, 1830–1860.* New York, 1942.

Jacobson, Matthew Frye. *Whiteness of a Different Color: European Immigrants and the Alchemy of Race.* Cambridge, Mass.: Harvard University Press, 1998.

Jaher, Frederic Cople. *A Scapegoat in the New Wilderness: The Origins and Rise of Anti-Semitism in America.* Cambridge, Mass.: Harvard University Press, 1994.

Jefferson-Hemings Scholars Commission. "Report on the Jefferson-Hemings Matter." April 12, 2001. Available online at ⟨http://www.geocities.com/tjshcommission⟩.

Jellison, Charles A. "James Thomson Callender: 'Human nature in a hideous form.'" *Virginia Cavalcade* 29 (Autumn 1979): 62–69.

———. "That Scoundrel Callender." *Virginia Magazine of History and Biography* 67 (July 1959): 295–306.

Jennings, Thelma. " 'Us Colored Women Had to Go through a Plenty': Sexual Exploitation of African-American Slave Women." *Journal of Women's History* 1 (Winter 1990): 45–74.

Johnson, Claudia. "That Guilty Third Tier: Prostitution in Nineteenth-Century American Theaters." *American Quarterly* 27 (December 1975): 575–84.

Johnson, Michael P. "Smothered Slave Infants: Were Slave Mothers at Fault?" *Journal of Southern History* 47 (November 1981): 493–520.

Johnson, Michael P., and James L. Roark. *Black Masters: A Free Family of Color in the Old South.* New York: W. W. Norton, 1984.

Johnson, Walter. "The Slave Trader, the White Slave, and the Politics of Racial Determination in the 1850s." *Journal of American History* 87 (June 2000): 13–38.

———. *Soul by Soul: Life Inside the Antebellum Slave Market.* Cambridge, Mass.: Harvard University Press, 1999.

Johnson, Whittington B. "Free African-American Women in Savannah, 1800–1860: Affluence and Autonomy amid Adversity." *Georgia Historical Quarterly* 76 (Summer 1992): 260–83.

Johnston, James Hugo. *Race Relations in Virginia and Miscegenation in the South, 1776–1860.* Amherst: University of Massachusetts Press, 1970.

Jones, Jacqueline. *Labor of Love, Labor of Sorrow: Black Women, Work, and the Family, from Slavery to the Present.* New York: Basic Books, 1985.

Jones, James B., Jr. "Municipal Vice: The Management of Prostitution in Tennessee's Urban Experience. Part I: The Experience of Nashville and Memphis, 1854–1917," and "Part II: The Examples of Chattanooga and Knoxville, 1838–1917." *Tennessee Historical Quarterly* 50 (Spring–Summer 1991): 33–41, 110–22.

Jones, Newton Bond. "Charlottesville and Albemarle County, Virginia, 1819–1860." Ph.D. diss., University of Virginia, 1950.

Jordan, Ervin L., Jr. " 'A Just and True Account': Two Parish Censuses of Albemarle County Free Blacks." *Magazine of Albemarle County History* 53 (1995): 114–39.

Jordan, Winthrop. *White over Black: American Attitudes toward the Negro, 1550–1812.* Chapel Hill: University of North Carolina Press, 1968.

Justus, Judith P. *Down from the Mountain: The Oral History of the Hemings Family*. Perrysburg, Ohio: Jeskurtara, 1990.

Kay, Marvin L. Michael, and Lorin Lee Cary. " 'The Planters Suffer Little or Nothing': North Carolina Compensations for Executed Slaves, 1748–1772." *Science and Society* 40 (Fall 1976): 288–306.

Kennedy-Haflett, Cynthia. " 'Moral Marriage': A Mixed-Race Relationship in Nineteenth-Century Charleston, South Carolina." *South Carolina Historical Magazine* 97 (July 1996): 206–26.

Ketchum, Sara Frances. "Married Women's Property Law in Nineteenth-Century Virginia." M.A. thesis, University of Virginia, 1985.

Kimball, Gregg D. "African-Virginians and the Vernacular Building Tradition in Richmond City, 1790–1860." In *Perspectives in Vernacular Architecture IV*, edited by Thomas Carter and Bernard L. Herman, 121–29. Columbia: University of Missouri Press for the Vernacular Architecture Forum, 1991.

———. *American City, Southern Place: A Cultural History of Antebellum Richmond*. Athens: University of Georgia Press, 2000.

———. "Place and Perception: Richmond in Late Antebellum America." Ph.D. diss., University of Virginia, 1997.

Kinney, James. *Amalgamation! Race, Sex, and Rhetoric in the Nineteenth-Century American Novel*. Westport, Conn.: Greenwood Press, 1985.

Klineberg, Otto, ed. *Characteristics of the American Negro*. New York, 1944.

Koger, Larry. *Black Slaveowners: Free Black Slave Masters in South Carolina, 1790–1860*. Jefferson, N.C.: McFarland, 1985.

Lander, Eric S., and Joseph J. Ellis. "Founding Father." *Nature* 396 (November 5, 1998): 13–14.

Landers, Jane, ed. *Against the Odds: Free Blacks in the Slave Societies of the Americas*. London: Frank Cass, 1996.

Langhorne, Elizabeth. "A Black Family at Monticello." *Magazine of Albemarle County History* 43 (1985): 1–16.

Lebsock, Suzanne. *The Free Women of Petersburg: Status and Culture in a Southern Town, 1784–1860*. New York: W. W. Norton, 1984.

———. "Radical Reconstruction and the Property Rights of Southern Women." *Journal of Southern History* 43 (May 1977): 195–216.

Lee, Deborah A., and Warren R. Hofstra. "Race, Memory, and the Death of Robert Berkeley: 'A murder . . . of . . . horrible and savage barbarity.' " *Journal of Southern History* 65 (February 1999): 41–76.

Leslie, Kent Anderson. *Woman of Color, Daughter of Privilege: Amanda America Dickson, 1849–1893*. Athens: University of Georgia Press, 1995.

Levin, Carole. " 'Murder not then the fruit within my womb': Shakespeare's Joan, Foxe's Guernsey Martyr, and Women Pleading Pregnancy in Early Modern English History and Culture." Paper presented at the University of Alabama, September 25, 2000.

Lewis, Jan. *The Pursuits of Happiness: Family and Values in Jefferson's Virginia*. Cambridge: Cambridge University Press, 1983.

Lewis, Jan, et al. "*Forum*: Thomas Jefferson and Sally Hemings Redux." *William and Mary Quarterly* 57 (January 2000): 121–210.

Lewis, Jan, and Peter S. Onuf, eds. *Sally Hemings and Thomas Jefferson: History, Memory, and Civic Culture*. Charlottesville: University Press of Virginia, 1999.

Link, William A. "The Jordan Hatcher Case: Politics and 'A Spirit of Insubordination' in Antebellum Richmond." *Journal of Southern History* 64 (November 1998): 615–48.

Lockley, Timothy J. "Crossing the Race Divide: Interracial Sex in Antebellum Savannah." *Slavery and Abolition* 18 (December 1997): 159–73.

Lombardo, Paul A. "Miscegenation, Eugenics, and Racism: Historical Footnotes to *Loving v. Virginia*." *University of California, Davis, Law Review* 21 (Winter 1988): 421–52.

Lott, Eric. *Love and Theft: Black Minstrelsy and the American Working Class*. New York: Oxford University Press, 1993.

Madden, T. O., Jr., with Ann L. Miller. *We Were Always Free: The Maddens of Culpeper County, Virginia, a 200-Year Family History*. New York: W. W. Norton, 1992.

Malone, Dumas. *Jefferson and His Time*. 6 vols. Boston: Little, Brown, 1948–81.

Malone, Dumas, and Stephen H. Hochman. "A Note on Evidence: The Personal History of Madison Hemings." *Journal of Southern History* 41 (November 1975): 523–28.

Marcus, Jacob Rader. *United States Jewry, 1776–1985*. 2 vols. Detroit: Wayne State University Press, 1989.

Martin, Byron Curti. "Racism in the United States: A History of the Anti-Miscegenation Legislation and Litigation." 3 vols. Ph.D. diss., University of Southern California, 1979.

Mathews, Jean. "Race, Sex, and the Dimensions of Liberty in Antebellum America." *Journal of the Early Republic* 6 (Fall 1986): 275–92.

McCray, Carrie Allen. *Freedom's Child: The Life of a Confederate General's Black Daughter*. Chapel Hill, N.C.: Algonquin Books, 1998.

McDonald, Robert M. S. "Race, Sex, and Reputation: Thomas Jefferson and the Sally Hemings Story." *Southern Cultures* 4 (Summer 1998): 46–64.

McFerson, Hazel M. " 'Racial Tradition' and Comparative Political Analysis: Notes toward a Theoretical Framework." *Ethnic and Racial Studies* 2 (October 1979): 477–97.

McKinney, Richard I. "Keeping the Faith: A History of the First Baptist Church, West Main and Seventh Streets, Charlottesville, Virginia, 1863–1980." *Magazine of Albemarle County History* 39 (1981): 13–92.

McLaurin, Melton. *Celia, a Slave*. Athens: University of Georgia Press, 1991.

McLeod, Norman C., Jr. "Free Labor in a Slave Society: Richmond, Virginia, 1820–1860." Ph.D. diss., Howard University, 1991.

Merrill, Boynton, Jr. *Jefferson's Nephews: A Frontier Tragedy*. Princeton: Princeton University Press, 1976.

Middleton, Stephen. *The Black Laws in the Old Northwest: A Documentary History*. Westport, Conn.: Greenwood Press, 1993.

Miller, John Chester. *The Wolf by the Ears: Thomas Jefferson and Slavery*. New York: Free Press, 1977.

Mills, Gary B. *The Forgotten People: Cane River's Creoles of Color*. Baton Rouge: Louisiana State University Press, 1977.

———. "Miscegenation and the Free Negro in Antebellum 'Anglo' Alabama: A Reexamination of Southern Race Relations." *Journal of American History* 68 (June 1981): 16–34.

———. "Tracing Free People of Color in the Antebellum South: Methods, Sources, and Perspectives." *National Genealogical Society Quarterly* 78 (1990): 262–78.

Mintz, Steven. *Moralists and Modernizers: America's Pre–Civil War Reformers*. Baltimore: Johns Hopkins University Press, 1995.

Moore, John Hammond. *Albemarle: Jefferson's County, 1727–1976*. Charlottesville: University Press of Virginia, 1976.

Moran, Rachel F. *Interracial Intimacy: The Regulation of Race and Romance*. Chicago: University of Chicago Press, 2001.

Morgan, Edmund. *American Slavery, American Freedom: The Ordeal of Colonial Virginia*. New York: W. W. Norton, 1975.

Morgan, Kathryn L. *Children of Strangers: The Stories of a Black Family*. Philadelphia: Temple University Press, 1980.

Morgan, Philip D. *Slave Counterpoint: Black Culture in the Eighteenth-Century Chesapeake and Lowcountry*. Chapel Hill: University of North Carolina Press, 1998.

———, ed. *"Don't Grieve after Me": The Black Experience in Virginia, 1619–1986*. Hampton, Va.: Hampton University, 1986.

Morris, Thomas D. *Southern Slavery and the Law, 1619–1860*. Chapel Hill: University of North Carolina Press, 1996.

Morrison, Toni. *Beloved*. New York: Alfred A. Knopf, 1987.

Morton, Patricia, ed. *Discovering the Women in Slavery: Emancipating Perspectives on the American Past*. Athens: University of Georgia Press, 1996.

Moss, Sidney P., and Carolyn Moss. "The Jefferson Miscegenation Legend in British Travel Books." *Journal of the Early Republic* 7 (Fall 1987): 253–74.

Murray, Pauli. *Proud Shoes: The Story of an American Family*. New York: Harper and Row, 1956.

Murrell, Amy E. " 'Calamity at Richmond!': Fire and Faith in a Young Virginia City." Unpublished seminar paper, University of Virginia, December 1995.

Nash, A. E. Keir. "Fairness and Formalism in the Trials of Blacks in the State Supreme Courts of the Old South." *Virginia Law Review* 56 (1970): 64–100.

———. "A More Equitable Past?: Southern Supreme Courts and the Protection of the Antebellum Negro." *North Carolina Law Review* 48 (1970): 197–241.

———. "Reason of Slavery: Understanding the Judicial Role in the Peculiar Institution." *Vanderbilt Law Review* 32 (1979): 7–218.

Norfleet, Elizabeth Copeland. "Newspapers in Charlottesville and Albemarle County." *Magazine of Albemarle County History* 50 (1992): 66–93.

O'Brien, John T. "Factory, Church, and Community: Blacks in Antebellum Richmond." *Journal of Southern History* 44 (November 1978): 509–36.

Oldham, James. "On Pleading the Belly: A History of the Jury of Matrons." *Criminal Justice History* 6 (1985): 1–64.

Onuf, Peter S. " 'To Declare Them a Free and Independant People': Race, Slavery, and National Identity in Jefferson's Thought." *Journal of the Early Republic* 18 (Spring 1998): 1–46.

———, ed. *Jeffersonian Legacies*. Charlottesville: University Press of Virginia, 1993.

Painter, Nell Irvin. "Of *Lily*, Linda Brent, and Freud: A Non-Exceptionalist Approach to Race, Class, and Gender in the Slave South." *Georgia Historical Quarterly* 76 (Summer 1992): 241–59.

———. "Soul Murder and Slavery: Toward a Fully Loaded Cost Accounting." In *U.S. History as Women's History: New Feminist Essays*, edited by Linda K. Kerber, Alice Kessler-Harris, and Kathryn Kish Sklar, 125–46. Chapel Hill: University of North Carolina Press, 1995.

Pascoe, Peggy. "Miscegenation Law, Court Cases, and Ideologies of 'Race' in Twentieth-Century America." *Journal of American History* 83 (June 1996): 44–69.

———. "Race, Gender, and Intercultural Relations: The Case of Interracial Marriage." *Frontiers: A Journal of Women Studies* 12 (1991): 5–18.

Peabody, Sue. *"There Are No Slaves in France": The Political Culture of Race and Slavery in the Ancien Régime*. New York: Oxford University Press, 1996.

Peterson, Merrill D. *The Jeffersonian Image in the American Mind*. New York: Oxford University Press, 1960.

Phillips, Roderick. *Putting Asunder: A History of Divorce in Western Society*. Cambridge: Cambridge University Press, 1988.

Rabinowitz, Howard N. "Nativism, Bigotry, and Anti-Semitism in the South." *American Jewish History* 77 (March 1988): 437–51.

———. *Race Relations in the Urban South, 1865–1920*. Urbana: University of Illinois Press, 1980.

"Race Hate in Early Ohio." *Negro History Bulletin* 10 (1946–47): 203–10.

Rachleff, Peter J. *Black Labor in the South: Richmond, Virginia, 1865–1890*. Philadelphia: Temple University Press, 1984.

Riegel, Robert E. "Changing American Attitudes toward Prostitution (1800–1920)." *Journal of the History of Ideas* 29 (July–September 1968): 437–52.

Riley, Glenda. *Divorce: An American Tradition*. New York: Oxford University Press, 1991.

———. "Legislative Divorce in Virginia, 1803–1850." *Journal of the Early Republic* 11 (Spring 1991): 51–67.

Robert, Joseph C. *Tobacco Kingdom: Plantation, Market, and Factory in Virginia and North Carolina, 1800–1860*. Durham: Duke University Press, 1938.

Roediger, David R. *The Wages of Whiteness: Race and the Making of the American Working Class*. London: Verso, 1991.

Rogoff, Leonard. "Is the Jew White?: The Racial Place of the Southern Jew." *American Jewish History* 85 (September 1997): 195–235.

Rose, David W. "Prostitution and the Sporting Life: Aspects of Working Class Culture and Sexuality in Nineteenth Century Wheeling." *Upper Ohio Valley Historical Review* 16 (1987): 7–31.

Rosen, Ruth. *The Lost Sisterhood: Prostitution in America, 1900–1918*. Baltimore: Johns Hopkins University Press, 1982.

Rosenswaike, Ira. "An Estimate and Analysis of the Jewish Population of the United States in 1790." In *The Jewish Experience in America: Selected Studies from the Publications of the American Jewish Historical Society*, edited with an introduction by Abraham J. Karp, 1:391–403. Waltham, Mass.: American Jewish Historical Society, 1969.

———. "The Jewish Population of the United States as Estimated from the Census of 1820." In *The Jewish Experience in America: Selected Studies from the Publications of the American Jewish Historical Society*, edited with an introduction by Abraham J. Karp, 2:1–19D. Waltham, Mass.: American Jewish Historical Society, 1969.

Rothman, Joshua D. "Can the 'Character Defense' Survive?: Measuring Polar Positions in the Jefferson-Hemings Controversy by the Standards of History." *National Genealogical Society Quarterly* 89 (September 2001): 219–33.

Rousey, Dennis C. "Aliens in the WASP Nest: Ethnocultural Diversity in the Antebellum Upper South." *Journal of American History* 79 (June 1992): 152–64.

———. *Policing the Southern City: New Orleans, 1805–1889*. Baton Rouge: Louisiana State University Press, 1996.

Russell, John H. "Colored Freemen as Slave Owners in Virginia." *Journal of Negro History* 1 (July 1916): 233–42.

———. *The Free Negro in Virginia, 1619–1865*. Johns Hopkins University Studies in Historical and Political Science, vol. 31, no. 3. Baltimore, 1913.

Ryan, Mary P. *Cradle of the Middle Class: The Family in Oneida County, New York, 1790–1865*. Cambridge: Cambridge University Press, 1981.

Saks, Eva. "Representing Miscegenation Law." *Raritan* 8 (Fall 1988): 39–69.

Saunders, Robert M. "Crime and Punishment in Early National America: Richmond, Virginia, 1784–1820." *Virginia Magazine of History and Biography* 86 (January 1978): 33–44.

Savitt, Todd L. *Medicine and Slavery: The Diseases and Health Care of Blacks in Antebellum Virginia*. Urbana: University of Illinois Press, 1978.

Schafer, Judith Kelleher. "The Long Arm of the Law: Slave Criminals and the Supreme Court in Antebellum Louisiana." *Tulane Law Review* 60 (1986): 1247–68.

———. *Slavery, the Civil Law, and the Supreme Court of Louisiana*. Baton Rouge: Louisiana State University Press, 1994.

Schechter, Patricia A. "Free and Slave Labor in the Old South: The Tredegar Ironworkers' Strike of 1847." *Labor History* 35 (Spring 1994): 165–86.

Schnittman, Suzanne Gehring. "Slavery in Virginia's Urban Tobacco Industry, 1840–1860." Ph.D. diss., University of Rochester, 1987.

Schwarz, Philip J. "Emancipators, Protectors, and Anomalies: Free Black Slaveowners in Virginia." *Virginia Magazine of History and Biography* 95 (July 1987): 317–38.

———. "Forging the Shackles: The Development of Virginia's Criminal Code for Slaves." In *Ambivalent Legacy: A Legal History of the South*, edited by David J.

Bodenhamer and James W. Ely, 125–46. Jackson: University Press of Mississippi, 1984.

———. *Slave Laws in Virginia*. Athens: University of Georgia Press, 1996.

———. *Twice Condemned: Slaves and the Criminal Laws of Virginia, 1705–1865*. Baton Rouge: Louisiana State University Press, 1988.

Schweninger, Loren. *Black Property Owners in the South, 1790–1915*. Urbana: University of Illinois Press, 1990.

———. "Property-Owning Free African-American Women in the South, 1800–1870." *Journal of Women's History* 1 (Winter 1990): 13–44.

Scott, Mary Wingfield. *Old Richmond Neighborhoods*. Richmond: Whittet and Shepperson, 1950.

Sheldon, Marianne Buroff. "Black-White Relations in Richmond, Virginia, 1782–1820." *Journal of Southern History* 45 (February 1979): 27–44.

Sherman, Richard B. " 'The Last Stand': The Fight for Racial Integrity in Virginia in the 1920s." *Journal of Southern History* 54 (February 1988): 69–92.

Sidbury, James. *Ploughshares into Swords: Race, Rebellion, and Identity in Gabriel's Virginia, 1783–1810*. Cambridge: Cambridge University Press, 1997.

Simson, Rennie. "The Afro-American Female: The Historical Context of the Construction of Sexual Identity." In *Powers of Desire: The Politics of Sexuality*, edited by Ann Snitow, Christine Stansell, and Sharon Thompson, 229–35. New York: Monthly Press, 1983.

Small, Stephen. "Racial Group Boundaries and Identities: People of 'Mixed-Race' in Slavery across the Americas." *Slavery and Abolition* 15 (December 1994): 17–37.

Smith, Glenn Curtis. "Newspapers of Albemarle County, Virginia." *Papers of the Albemarle County Historical Society* 1 (1940–41): 36–37.

Smith, J. Douglas. "The Campaign for Racial Purity and the Erosion of Paternalism in Virginia, 1922–1930: 'Nominally White, Biologically Mixed, and Legally Negro.' " *Journal of Southern History* 68 (February 2002): 65–106.

Smith, Merril D. *Breaking the Bonds: Marital Discord in Pennsylvania, 1730–1830*. New York: New York University Press, 1991.

Smith, Valerie. "Split Affinities: The Case of Interracial Rape." In *Conflicts in Feminism*, edited by Marianne Hirsch and Evelyn Fox Keller, 271–87. New York: Routledge, 1990.

Smith-Rosenberg, Carroll. "Beauty, the Beast, and the Militant Woman: A Case Study in Sex Roles and Social Stress in Jacksonian America." *American Quarterly* 23 (October 1971): 562–84.

Sollors, Werner. *Neither Black nor White yet Both: Thematic Explorations of Interracial Literature*. New York: Oxford University Press, 1997.

Sommerville, Diane Miller. "The Rape Myth in the Old South Reconsidered." *Journal of Southern History* 61 (August 1995): 481–518.

———. "The Rape Myth Reconsidered: The Intersection of Race, Class, and Gender in the American South, 1800–1877." Ph.D. diss., Rutgers University, 1995.

Stampp, Kenneth M. *The Peculiar Institution: Slavery in the Ante-Bellum South*. New York: Alfred A. Knopf, 1956.

Stansell, Christine. *City of Women: Sex and Class in New York, 1789–1860*. New York: Alfred A. Knopf, 1986.

Stanton, Lucia. *Free Some Day: The African-American Families of Monticello*. Charlottesville: Thomas Jefferson Foundation, 2000.

——. "Monticello to Main Street: The Hemings Family and Charlottesville." *Magazine of Albemarle County History* 55 (1997): 95–126.

——. "The Mountaintop Work Force, 1794–1796." Monticello Research Department, Charlottesville, Va., November 1990.

——. "Sally Hemings (1773–1835)." Monticello Research Department, Charlottesville, Va., rev. ed., October 1994.

——. *Slavery at Monticello*. Charlottesville: Thomas Jefferson Memorial Foundation, 1996.

Stanton, William. *The Leopard's Spots: Scientific Attitudes toward Race in America, 1815–1859*. Chicago: University of Chicago Press, 1960.

Starobin, Robert S. *Industrial Slavery in the Old South*. London: Oxford University Press, 1970.

Steckel, Richard H. "Miscegenation and the American Slave Schedules." *Journal of Interdisciplinary History* 11 (Autumn 1980): 251–63.

Sterling, Dorothy, ed. *We Are Your Sisters: Black Women in the Nineteenth Century*. New York: W. W. Norton, 1984.

Stevenson, Brenda E. *Life in Black and White: Family and Community in the Slave South*. New York: Oxford University Press, 1996.

Stewart-Abernathy, Leslie C., and Barbara L. Ruff. "A Good Man in Israel: Zooarchaeology and Assimilation in Antebellum Washington, Arkansas." *Historical Archaeology* 23 (1989): 96–110.

Tadman, Michael. *Speculators and Slaves: Masters, Traders, and Slaves in the Old South*. Madison: University of Wisconsin Press, 1989.

Takagi, Midori. *"Rearing Wolves to Our Own Destruction": Slavery in Richmond, Virginia, 1782–1865*. Charlottesville: University Press of Virginia, 1999.

Tansey, Richard. "Prostitution and Politics in Antebellum New Orleans." *Southern Studies* 18 (Winter 1979): 449–79.

Thomas Jefferson Memorial Foundation Research Committee. "Report on Thomas Jefferson and Sally Hemings." Charlottesville: Thomas Jefferson Memorial Foundation, January 2000. Also available online at ⟨http://www.monticello.org/plantation/hemings_resource.html⟩.

Toplin, Robert Brent. "Between Black and White: Attitudes toward Southern Mulattoes, 1830–1861." *Journal of Southern History* 45 (May 1979): 185–200.

Towler, Sam. "The West Family." *Central Virginia Heritage* 10 (Summer 1993): 55.

Troutman, Phillip D. " 'Fancy Girls' and a 'Yellow Wife': Sex and Domesticity in the Domestic Slave Trade." Paper presented to the Southern Historical Association, New Orleans, November 10, 2000.

Tushnet, Mark V. *The American Law of Slavery, 1810–1860: Considerations of Humanity and Justice*. Princeton: Princeton University Press, 1981.

Tyler, Alice Felt. *Freedom's Ferment: Phases of American Social History from the Colonial*

Period to the Outbreak of the Civil War. Minneapolis: University of Minnesota Press, 1944.

Tyler-McGraw, Marie. "Richmond Free Blacks and African Colonization, 1816–1832." *Journal of American Studies* 21 (August 1987): 207–24.

Tyler-McGraw, Marie, and Gregg D. Kimball. *In Bondage and Freedom: Antebellum Black Life in Richmond, Virginia*. Richmond: Valentine Museum, 1988.

Varon, Elizabeth R. *We Mean to Be Counted: White Women and Politics in Antebellum Virginia*. Chapel Hill: University of North Carolina Press, 1998.

Vaughan, Alden T. "The Origins Debate: Slavery and Racism in Seventeenth-Century Virginia." *Virginia Magazine of History and Biography* 97 (July 1989): 311–54.

von Daacke, Kirt. "Slaves without Masters?: The Butler Family of Albemarle County, 1780–1860." *Magazine of Albemarle County History* 55 (1997): 38–59.

Wade, Richard C. *Slavery in the Cities: The South, 1820–1860*. New York: Oxford University Press, 1964.

Wadlington, Walter. "The *Loving* Case: Virginia's Anti-Miscegenation Statute in Historical Perspective." *Virginia Law Review* 52 (November 1966): 1189–1223.

Waldrep, Christopher. *Roots of Disorder: Race and Criminal Justice in the American South, 1817–1870*. Urbana: University of Illinois Press, 1998.

Walkowitz, Judith R. *Prostitution and Victorian Society: Women, Class, and the State*. Cambridge: Cambridge University Press, 1980.

Wallenstein, Peter. *From Slave South to New South: Public Policy in Nineteenth-Century Georgia*. Chapel Hill: University of North Carolina Press, 1987.

———. "Race, Marriage, and the Law of Freedom: Alabama and Virginia, 1860s–1960s." *Chicago-Kent Law Review* 70 (1994): 371–437.

Walters, Ronald G. *American Reformers, 1815–1860*. New York: Hill and Wang, 1978.

———. "The Erotic South: Civilization and Sexuality in American Abolitionism." *American Quarterly* 25 (May 1973): 177–201.

Warbasse, Elizabeth Bowles. *The Changing Legal Rights of Married Women, 1800–1861*. New York: Garland, 1987.

Weis, Tracey M. "Negotiating Freedom: Domestic Service and the Landscape of Labor and Household Relations in Richmond, Virginia, 1850–1880." Ph.D. diss., Rutgers University, 1994.

Weisenburger, Steven. *Modern Medea: A Family Story of Slavery and Child-Murder from the Old South*. New York: Hill and Wang, 1998.

White, Deborah Gray. *Ar'n't I a Woman?: Female Slaves in the Plantation South*. New York: W. W. Norton, 1985.

———. "Mining the Forgotten: Manuscript Sources for Black Women's History." *Journal of American History* 74 (June 1987): 237–42.

Wiencek, Henry. *The Hairstons: An American Family in Black and White*. New York: St. Martin's Press, 1999.

Williamson, Joel. *The Crucible of Race: Black-White Relations in the American South since Emancipation*. New York: Oxford University Press, 1984.

————. *New People: Miscegenation and Mulattoes in the United States*. New York: Free Press, 1980.

Willner, Nancy E. "A Brief History of the Jewish Community in Charlottesville and Albemarle." With a preface by Rabbi Sheldon Ezring. *Magazine of Albemarle County History* 40 (1982): 1–24.

Wilson, Douglas. "Thomas Jefferson and the Character Issue." *Atlantic Monthly* 270 (November 1992): 57–74.

Woods, Edgar. *Albemarle County in Virginia*. Berryville, Va.: Virginia Book Company, 1978. Originally published 1901.

Woodson, Byron, Sr. *A President in the Family: Thomas Jefferson, Sally Hemings, and Thomas Woodson*. Westport, Conn.: Praeger Books, 2001.

Woodson, Carter G. "The Beginnings of the Miscegenation of the Whites and Blacks." *Journal of Negro History* 3 (October 1918): 335–53.

————. "Free Negro Owners of Slaves in the United States in 1830." *Journal of Negro History* 9 (January 1924): 41–85.

Woodward, C. Vann. *The Strange Career of Jim Crow*. New York: Oxford University Press, 1955.

Wriggins, Jennifer. "Rape, Racism, and the Law." *Harvard Women's Law Journal* 6 (Spring 1983): 103–41.

Wyatt-Brown, Bertram. *Southern Honor: Ethics and Behavior in the Old South*. New York: Oxford University Press, 1982.

Index

and black women, 3, 12–13, 14, 15, 18, 19–20, 38, 43, 50, 53, 56, 68, 117–18, 127–28, 129, 133–34, 136, 138–40, 165, 166, 167, 169–70, 171, 185–86, 187, 188–89, 190–91; and blurring of idealized racial boundaries, 4, 9, 50, 202–3, 206, 218, 240; considered degrading for white participants, 4, 18, 46, 49, 50, 174, 188; ethics of, 22–23, 44, 46, 50–51, 257 (n. 106); as foundation of large social networks, 89, 90–91; incest and, 151–52, 285 (n. 63); responses to by public authorities, 5–6, 66–68, 94–95, 96, 110–13, 115, 118–20, 127–28, 129, 131–32, 167–68, 177, 193–96, 241; responses to by white communities, 4–5, 56, 58, 60, 63, 64–65, 67, 69–70, 121–22, 124, 127–28, 133–35, 156–57, 178, 180, 189, 191, 195, 233–34, 240, 262 (n. 41); romantic love and, 24–25, 44; and sexual double standard, 171, 172, 189–90, 292 (n. 38). *See also* Adultery; Gossip; Laws: against interracial marriage, inability of to control sex across the color line; Rape; Richmond: anxiety about interracial sex in, interracial nighttime leisure scene in

Sexual assault. *See* Rape

Sexuality: and insults, 100–104; public space and, 119–20, 122–23; and slave trade, 130–31; in theaters, 96–97; and white ideas about black female, 19. *See also* Violence: and sexuality

Shadrack (slave), 142, 143–44

Short, William, 46

Skin color: descriptive terms for, 204; significance of to slavery and racial identity, 47, 48, 69, 199, 200, 205, 207, 208, 210, 213, 214, 217, 218, 221, 222–25, 230. *See also* Carlton,

William; Hemings, Beverley; Hemings, Eston; Hemings, Sally; "Mixed bloods"; Race, ambiguities of; West, James Henry; West, Nancy; Whiteness; "White slaves"

Slave crime: approach of white communities to, 135, 141–45, 146–49, 156–58; extenuating circumstances and, 142, 143, 145, 147, 148, 151–52, 156, 157, 162–63; provoked by sexual assault, 9, 134, 136, 145–48, 149–52; in Richmond, 96, 100, 103, 105, 107, 108, 110, 117, 120–22; white fears of, 135, 144–45, 157. *See also* Transportation

Slave criminals: compensation for owners of executed, 138, 142, 157, 282 (n. 16); flexibility in sentencing and punishment of, 141–45, 147, 158–60, 162–63; pardons of, 147, 148; significance of gender of, 149, 159–62, 163, 286 (n. 68); white petitions on behalf of convicted, 142–43, 144, 146–47, 148, 152, 156, 158, 161, 162–63. *See also* Ben (slave); Carter (slave); Franky (slave); Harry (slave, Powhatan County); John (slave, Caroline County); Malinda (slave); Manuel (slave); Patrick (slave); Peggy (slave)

Slave insurrections: fear of, among whites, 135, 157, 208, 209; possible plan to instigate, 3. *See also* Gabriel's Rebellion; Nat Turner's Rebellion

Slave runaways, 22, 44, 93, 96, 126–27, 139–40, 204, 213, 216, 218, 230, 239, 284 (n. 55), 301 (n. 29)

Slavery: and racial hierarchy, 4, 9, 47–48, 50, 102–3, 121, 128, 135–36, 148–49, 156, 162, 171, 190, 208, 220, 221, 222–23, 225, 240. *See also* Laws: regarding slavery and

"white slaves" at; Race, ambiguities of; Wharton family

Wilson, Ellen, 90

Wilson, Narcissa, 90

Winn, John (Albemarle County), 60, 62

Winn, John, Sr. (Lunenburg County), 164, 165, 166, 167

Winn, Susanna, 164, 165, 166, 167

Winn family (Lunenburg County), 164–67

Wolfe, Nathaniel, 61

Womack, Sarah, 185

Women, black: efforts to conceal sexual assault from husbands, 140; and exchange of sex for favored treatment, 20–21, 24, 153–54; punished for refusal to consent to sex, 117–18, 151, 154–55; and relationships with white women, 41, 101–3, 129, 165–66, 190–91; and resistance to sexual abuse, 149–51, 154, 155, 159–60; sense of powerlessness among, 152–53; sexual vulnerability of, 2, 3, 19, 38, 133, 134, 138–39, 152, 159–60, 163, 240, 241–42. *See also* Free people of color; Rape; Richmond: multiracial

workforce of; Sex across the color line: between white men and black women

Women, white: deemed in need of protection from black men, 119–20, 122–23; idealized view of, 175, 177, 186, 188, 191, 192, 195; and knowledge of husbands' sex across the color line, 40–41, 43, 44, 134, 185–86, 187, 188, 189, 190–91; marital expectations of, 182–84, 186, 193, 196–97, 198; poor, as rape victims, 161; and relationships with black women, 41, 101–3, 129, 165–66, 190–91; as victims of domestic violence, 172, 184–85, 186, 187, 188, 189–90. *See also* Adultery; Divorce; Property: married women and; Sex across the color line: between black men and white women

Wooding, Thomas, 143

Woodson, Thomas, 26, 251 (n. 29)

Wright, Jane, 123–24, 127, 129

Wythe, George, 221, 222, 223, 270 (n. 3)

Yancey, Joel, 76

ML   5/03